JAPAN'S DECISION FOR WAR
Records of the 1941 Policy Conferences

JAPAN'S DECISION FOR WAR

RECORDS OF THE 1941 POLICY CONFERENCES

Translated, edited, and with an Introduction by

NOBUTAKA IKE

STANFORD UNIVERSITY PRESS

STANFORD, CALIFORNIA

1967

Stanford University Press
Stanford, California
© 1967 by the Board of Trustees of the
Leland Stanford Junior University
Printed in the United States of America
L.C. 67-13659

To Tai, Linda, and Brian

PREFACE

When the translation of these documents was begun in the spring of 1964, I did not anticipate their publication. The initial reason for translating the Liaison and Imperial Conference notes was my wish to analyze them by means of the General Inquirer, a method of automated content analysis extensively used by the Studies in International Conflict and Integration in the Institute of Political Studies at Stanford University. This phase of the work will take place in the near future.

Many persons who saw the first drafts of the translations told me the documents contained much information that was of interest to them. It occurred to me that there might be others—political scientists concerned with decision making, specialists on diplomatic history, and students of military affairs, for example—who would also find them interesting or useful. I was encouraged to publish the documents by several of my colleagues, especially Professors Richard Brody, Robert North, and Ole Holsti, all associated with the Studies in International Conflict and Integration, and by Mr. Leon Seltzer, Director, and Mr. J. G. Bell, Editor, of Stanford University Press. I am indebted to all these friends for their encouragement.

In preparing the documents for publication, I had the assistance of many people, and I wish to thank them. Mr. Takeshi Naito and Mrs. Yoko Murai, both of Tokyo, undertook to make first draft translations of many documents. Others who served as translators were Mr. Henry H. Hoshino, Mr. Yasuo Murata, and Mr. Takashi Wakiyama. The final product is a composite of the work of these translators and my extensive revisions. I should add that I am solely responsible for any shortcomings in the translation.

Mrs. Jean Heflin, my research assistant, spent many hours digging up background material for the Notes, reading proofs, and preparing the Index; Mrs. Helen Grace went beyond the call of duty in taking care of administrative chores; Miss Virginia Martino and Mrs. Cheryl Malone typed the manuscript with great efficiency; and Mr. Tamotsu Takase of the Japanese Collections in the Hoover Institution assisted me in numerous ways.

While in Tokyo, I received cordial cooperation and assistance from several Japanese scholars. In particular, I wish to thank Dr. Nobushige Ukai, President of the International Christian University, the faculty of the Social Science Division of that university, and Miss Tane Takahashi, Chief Librarian, and her staff. Dr. Jun Tsunoda of the National Diet Library and Professor Chihiro Hosoya of Hitotsubashi University were most generous with their hospitality and help.

The editorial staff of Stanford University Press was very helpful; my special thanks go to Mr. James R. Trosper, whose meticulous editorial work greatly improved the translations. I must thank my wife, Tai Ike, for reading the manuscript and helping me with the proofs.

This book, like many others, could not have been completed without financial assistance from several sources. The initial translation was made possible by Contract No. N60540-9838, entered into between Stanford University, with myself as principal investigator, and Project Michelson of the Behavioral Sciences Group of the United States Naval Ordnance Test Station at China Lake, California. Dr. Thomas W. Milburn and Lt. William Parker of the Behavioral Sciences Group were very kind to me. The Rockefeller Foundation awarded me a fellowship, which enabled me, together with my family, to spend my sabbatical year in Japan; and the East Asian Studies Committee at Stanford provided additional funds to take care of costs incurred in connection with travel and research. I wish to thank all these individuals and organizations. It goes without saying that they are responsible neither for the opinions I have expressed nor for the errors I have committed.

N. I.

CONTENTS

The adjustment of diplomatic relations with the United States. The Japanese-Soviet Neutrality Pact. Negotiations with the Netherlands East Indies. Recognition of the Nanking Government. Fireside Chats. The possibility of a German-Soviet war. "Acceleration of the Policy Concerning the South." "Outline of National Policies in View of the Changing Situation." Message to Germany concerning Japan's new policy.

Ratification of "Outline of National Policies in View of the Changing Situation."

PART TWO: PREPARE FOR WAR NOW, BUT CONTINUE TO NEGOTIATE

The adjustment of diplomatic relations with the United States. Japanese reaction to the reply from Secretary Hull dated June 21. The first meeting of the Third Konoye Cabinet. The occupation of southern Indochina. Exchange of general information. "Essence of Diplomatic Negotiations with the Soviet Union." "Measures the Empire Should Take Regarding the Present Situation between Japan and the Soviet Union." Diplomacy toward Britain. Security measures. Prime Minister Konoye's reply to President Roosevelt and Secretary Hull. Talks with the German, Italian, and British Ambassadors. "The Essentials for Carrying Out the Empire's Policies."

DOCUMENTS INCLUDED IN THE TEXT

U. S. S. R.
KAMCHATKA
Irkutsk
L. Baikal
SEA OF OKHOTSK
MONGOLIA
SAKHALIN
MARITIME
PROVINCES
MANCHUKUO
Vladivostok
Peking
KOREA
Taiyuan
SEA OF JAPAN
Yenan
KWANTUNG
Tokyo
Huang Ho
YELLOW
SEA
Chungking
Hankow
Nanking
Shanghai
INDIA
Yangtze
Foochow
Wenchow
Kunming
Amoy
Canton
Swatow
TAIWAN
BURMA
Hong Kong (Br.)
HAINAN I.
EAST ASIA
THAILAND
INDOCHINA
SOUTH
Manila
PHILIPPINES (U.S.)
GUAM (U.S.)
Mekong R.
Saigon
CHINA
SEA
MALAYA (Br.)
BRUNEI
(Br. Prot.)
N. BORNEO (Br.)
SARAWAK
(Br. Prot.)
Singapore (Br.)
SUMATRA
BORNEO
CELEBES
MOLUCCAS
NETHERLANDS
NEW GUINEA
PAPUA
Batavia
JAVA
TIMOR
(Port.)
(Neth.)

0   100
50   500 MILES

Territory controlled by
Japan, March 1, 1941

Extent of Japanese Control
in China, March 1, 1941

Area ceded by Indochina to Thailand
after Japanese arbitration in 1940

Introduction

I

This book is part of a larger study of decision making and foreign policy, particularly as they relate to the outbreak of war between the United States and Japan in 1941. A current theory about preventing war is the theory of deterrence, whose proponents argue that the best way for the United States to avoid war is to be strong militarily: according to this theory, other countries, especially dictatorships, will not attack us if they judge that they are likely to be defeated and destroyed in the process. One way to test such a theory is to take a concrete case and see how political leaders actually arrived at a decision involving the great issues of war and peace.

It is often difficult for an investigator to get reliable information that throws light on the decision-making process. Such information, if recorded at the time of the decision, usually belongs in the top-secret category and is not made public, even many years after the event; in this sense, the documents here translated are probably unique. I was eventually persuaded that there would be merit in making them available to those who could not read them in their original form.

The documents were found in the Military History Archives (Senshi-shitsu) of the Japanese Defense Agency by a committee of scholars working under the chairmanship of Dr. Tsunoda Jun, of the National Diet Library. This committee, organized by the Japan International Politics Association, was also allowed to see a large body of unpublished material held by the families of Japan's wartime leaders, and committee members interviewed many leaders who are still alive. Its findings were subsequently published by the Asahi Newspaper Publishing Company in a seven-volume work, *Taiheiyo Senso e no Michi* (*The Road to the Pacific War*). The work begins with the invasion of Manchuria, and ends with the attack on Pearl Harbor. A large supplementary volume (*Bekkan Shiryo-hen*) contains the full texts of many documents—including those relating to the Liaison and Imperial Conferences of 1940 and 1941, the proceedings of which form the substance of this book.

As the reader will note, the proceedings as translated here are not minutes of meetings in the conventional American sense; rather, they are detailed notes, taken for subsequent use by the Army high command, on what was said and decided at high-level meetings. Apparently no official set of minutes exists. According to Dr. Tsunoda (in personal conversation), notes were also kept by representatives of the Government and of the Navy, but these appear to have been destroyed, and are not, to his knowledge, available today; thus the set translated here is the only surviving one. It is clear from internal evidence that the notes were recorded by someone representing the Army Chief of Staff; hence they no doubt reflect a certain amount of bias, and the reader should be aware of this.

Any doubts about the authenticity of the notes should be dispelled by the scholarly standing of the sponsoring organization, the Japan International Politics Association, and by the reputation and integrity of Dr. Tsunoda and his committee. Moreover, the documents agree with material on some of the Conferences published as part of the documentation submitted to the International Military Tribunal for the Far East, and with the frequent references to the Conferences found in Hattori Takushiro's *Dai To-A Senso Zenshi* (*History of the War in Eastern Asia*). Hattori, who was Chief of the Operations Section in the Army General Staff, quotes frequently from documentary sources in describing what went on in these Conferences. The quotations in Hattori's book were quite clearly taken from the documents translated here.

In making the translations, I have included the notes on Liaison Conferences 19 through 75, covering the period April 18 to December 4, 1941. The first eighteen Conferences, although available in the Japanese volume, were not translated because they were concerned largely with matters pertaining to Southeast Asia rather than with American-Japanese relations, which are the chief concern of this book. Similarly, Japanese texts for four more Liaison Conferences after December 4 are available, but were not translated because they do not pertain directly to the decision for war. Notes on several Liaison Conferences were not included in the Japanese version; I presume that they were destroyed or lost, and hence were not available to the com-

mittee that compiled the supplementary volume. Finally, notes on
five Imperial Conferences are translated and included in this book.

No two persons will translate a document in precisely the same way.
My own philosophy of translation, if it can be called that, is to try to
keep the translation as close as possible to the Japanese text and yet
reasonably readable in English. The notes of the Liaison Conferences,
as well as all the important policy documents approved by the decision makers, have been translated in their entirety. In the case of
the Imperial Conferences, I have taken the liberty of rearranging the
order of presentation. The usual order in the Japanese text is to give
the transcript of the discussion first, followed by the text of the statements made by the Prime Minister and other participants, and then by
policy documents adopted by the conference. I felt that it would be
easier for American readers to follow the proceedings if the order of
presentation were reversed.

The Army transcriber of these notes contented himself with providing a summary of the Conference discussion, occasionally para-
phrasing the remarks of the speakers in the form of direct quotations.
His references are often cryptic, he omits mention of many things
that would already be known to the Army High Command, and he is
often unclear about who is speaking. Wherever possible, I have tried
to explain puzzling remarks and indicate lacunae in the record, but
many can only be guessed at.

To assist the reader in following the proceedings, the remarks or
summaries of the transcriber have been enclosed in double brackets
[ ] to distinguish them from his transcriptions and paraphrases of
the remarks of others. Ordinary brackets [ ] indicate my own insertions or comments in the translation. All the footnotes are mine.

II

As already indicated, the documents translated here are detailed notes
of two kinds of meetings, Liaison Conferences and Imperial Conferences. The Liaison Conferences, which were held every few days,
brought together representatives of the Cabinet—the Prime Minister,
the Foreign Minister, the War Minister, the Navy Minister, and sometimes other ministers of state like the Finance Minister or the Director
of the Planning Board—and the Army and Navy Chiefs and Vice
Chiefs of Staff, representing the Supreme Command. The Chief Secretary of the Cabinet, the Chief of the Military Affairs Bureau of the
War Ministry, and the Chief of the Naval Affairs Bureau of the Navy

Ministry acted as secretaries, taking care of such matters as setting up the agenda.

The following description of the Liaison Conferences was given by one of the secretaries, Muto Akira, Chief of the Military Affairs Bureau of the War Ministry:

Liaison Conferences were held in a smaller conference room, and around the conference room were armchairs. Somewhat in the center along the farther end of the room sat the Prime Minister, and a circle was formed around him. And the three secretaries sat together near the entrance of the conference room.

Liaison Conferences were held between the representatives of the Government and of the High Command for the purpose of bringing about a meeting of minds between the two on various issues; therefore there was no presiding officer, and every member spoke freely. And therefore at times two men would start talking at the same time, or one member would be whispering to another while another one was speaking. Secretaries were constantly leaving and entering the room to make telephone calls, to call in subordinates who could provide detailed information, or to bring in documents.[1]

These Conferences were established by Cabinet order in late 1937 in order to provide "liaison" between the Government and the military. For a time the Liaison Conferences were discontinued and replaced by the Four- and Five-Minister Conferences, which were attended by the Prime Minister, the Foreign Minister, the War Minister, the Navy Minister, and sometimes the Finance Minister. The absence of the Chiefs of Staff at these meetings made coordination between the Government and the military difficult, and as a result the Liaison Conferences were revived in November 1940 and continued until 1944.[2]

Whenever a major policy decision was reached, it was necessary to have it ratified, so to speak, at an Imperial Conference. The custom of holding Imperial Conferences originated in the late nineteenth century; in the early days they were real decision-making meetings, and not ceremonial occasions for approving decisions arrived at elsewhere. In 1941, an Imperial Conference included the members of the Liaison Conference plus the President of the Privy Council. The Conference met in the presence of the Emperor, who sat in front of a gold

---

[1] As quoted in Yale Candee Maxon, *Control of Japanese Foreign Policy* (Berkeley, Calif., 1957), p. 153, with minor stylistic alterations.

[2] See *ibid.*, pp. 127–28, 153 ff.

screen "mounted on a dais at the superior end of the chamber," while the "others would sit down at two long, brocade-covered tables, which faced each other and were at right angles to the Emperor's throne-like sanctuary."[3]

Typically, certain policy documents embodying the decision were on the agenda. As a rule these documents had a complicated history: they had probably been drawn up by an ad hoc committee of middle grade officers in the Army or Navy General Staffs, circulated to the War, Navy, and Foreign Ministries for comments and revisions, discussed and amended in numerous Liaison Conferences, and finally approved by the top leaders.

At the Imperial Conference the Prime Minister made the opening statement setting forth the purpose of the meeting. He was followed by the Foreign Minister, the Army and Navy Ministers, the other members of the Cabinet, and the Chiefs of Staff, all of whom read previously prepared statements. After this part of the ceremony, the President of the Privy Council directed questions at the representatives of the Government and the Supreme Command. The ostensible purpose of these proceedings was to inform the Emperor—who would normally sit quietly and not utter a single word—about the situation, so that after the Conference he could give his "sanction," thereby making the decision legal. The practical significance of the Imperial Conference was to make the decision binding on all, and very difficult to change at a later date.

In this volume, notes on five Imperial Conferences are included. The first one, held on September 19, 1940, confirmed Japan's decision to sign the Tripartite Pact with Germany and Italy. Although this decision does not relate in particular to American-Japanese relations, I include it because it later proved to be a major stumbling block in the negotiations between Washington and Tokyo. The other Imperial Conferences specifically concern negotiations with the United States.

A brief discussion of the military's role in the political system may help explain the need for the Liaison and Imperial Conferences. After the Meiji Restoration in 1868, the feudal warrior class (the samurai), and later their successors, the professional military class, played an important role in the modernization of Japan. At first this was because Japanese modernization was seen to some extent as "defensive mod-

[3] Robert J. C. Butow, *Tojo and the Coming of the War* (Princeton, N.J., 1961), p. 172.

ernization"—that is, a reaction to what was viewed as a military threat from the more advanced Western nations. Later there came the possibility that the government might ultimately be controlled by political parties, and this was something that the professional soldiers disapproved of and feared. In 1878 the General Staff Office, which was responsible for national defense and strategy, was removed from the control of the War Minister and placed directly under the Emperor. A few years later the same arrangement was made for the Navy.[4]

The practical effect of this change was to divide the military into two parts. The War and Navy Ministers were members of the Cabinet and hence part of the Government; they reported to the Emperor either through the Prime Minister or directly. The prime responsibility of these service ministers, who had to be professional officers with the rank of lieutenant general or vice admiral or higher, was military administration: that is, personnel and related matters. Strategy, planning, and operations, on the other hand, were the responsibility of the Supreme Command, made up of the Army and Navy Chiefs of Staff, who reported directly to the Emperor. There was a further division, in practice, between the Army and Navy. These two branches were often jealous of each other, indulging in a good deal of guessing about each other's intentions and plans, as well as jockeying for appropriations and power.

In theory, the Emperor coordinated the work of the Government and the Supreme Command; in practice, he never made personal decisions, but always followed advice given him by his ministers and military leaders. To be sure, the Emperor sometimes raised embarrassing questions, or even scolded the Chiefs of Staff when they came to report the latest developments in military and naval matters, but he would never go so far as to tell the Chiefs of Staff what to do or what not to do. The result was that the Chiefs of Staff were responsible to no one but themselves. They enjoyed the "independence of the Supreme Command" and guarded it with great tenacity.

In the 1930's, when most foreign policy issues directly or indirectly involved the armed forces, it was impossible to carry out foreign policy —or even formulate it—without some idea of the thinking of the Chiefs of Staff. It was for the purpose of bringing together the Government and the Chiefs of Staff that the Liaison Conference came into being. It was not long before the Liaison Conference became the

---

[4] Maxon, *Japanese Foreign Policy*, pp. 22ff.

principal decision-making body in the field of foreign policy, over-shadowing the Cabinet, which concentrated on domestic affairs.

III

Although the Liaison Conferences of 1941 dealt with many prob-lems, the most difficult and significant ones involved relations with the United States. In the nineteenth century, America had been a friend and supporter of Japan as the island country sought to trans-form itself into a modern nation-state. However, with each successive Japanese war of expansion, and with the emergence of the United States as a power with Asian colonial interests in the Philippines, the earlier friendship gradually gave way to rivalry and hostility. By the 1920's, commentators on both sides of the ocean were openly specu-lating about a war between the two nations.

The main reason for Japan's drive to modernize was her ambition to become a great power in the world community. One mark of great-power status was the possession of colonies; Japan secured Formosa and Korea fairly early, and later sought, by degrees, to control China. In 1931 Japan seized Manchuria, and starting in 1937 she undertook a large-scale invasion of China proper. The Japanese, who badly un-derestimated the strength of Chinese nationalism, had counted on a quick campaign; but they were soon bogged down, unable to force Chiang Kai-shek to capitulate and unwilling to withdraw.

Meanwhile, Hitler launched his war to take over the whole of Europe. The German conquest of France and the Netherlands left the colonial possessions of these two countries unprotected. French Indochina and the Netherlands East Indies, rich in oil and other resources, were a great prize from the Japanese point of view. Access to these raw materials would help Japan become self-sufficient, free from economic dependence on the Western powers. The Japanese began to talk of a "Greater East Asia Co-prosperity Sphere," a self-contained empire extending from Manchuria in the north to the Dutch East Indies in the south. There was much talk in Japanese circles of a "never-to-be-repeated" opportunity to build a great empire. In 1940 Japan signed the Tripartite Pact with Germany and Italy in the hope of making the most of this opportunity.

One obstacle to the realization of the Japanese dream was the United States. The Open Door Policy, which stipulated that no one nation should get political control of China and that the Chinese mar-ket should remain open to all nations, was the keystone of American policy in the Far East. When China was invaded by Japan in 1937, the United States naturally gave moral, military, and economic support to Chiang's government. The Japanese believed that this aid was what kept Chiang from capitulating, and resented it. Moreover, the United States clearly opposed the possible takeover of European colonies by Japan. The two nations, therefore, were on a collision course, given Japanese ambitions and American determination to prevent Japanese expansion.

An informal American effort to prevent a collision was made in the fall of 1940. Two Maryknoll priests, Bishop James E. Walsh and Father James M. Drought, arrived in Tokyo with letters of introduction from Lewis L. Strauss, then connected with the Wall Street firm of Kuhn, Loeb and Company, to several Japanese, including Ikawa (sometimes romanized Wikawa) Tadao, formerly an official in the Ministry of Finance and in 1940 associated with a semiofficial bank. Since Kuhn, Loeb had helped the Japanese government float a loan during a critical period in the Russo-Japanese War, it was well known in Japan. Many Japanese, including persons of a conservative persuasion, believed that Wall Street exerted great influence on American politics, and so it was assumed that the two Catholic priests were acting in some kind of semiofficial capacity. Ikawa, who was an acquaintance of Prince Konoye Fumimaro, then Prime Minister, informed Konoye of his conversations with the priests. In addition, Bishop Walsh and Father Drought saw Matsuoka Yosuke, the Foreign Minister; Muto Akira, Chief of the Military Affairs Bureau of the War Ministry; and Colonel Iwakuro Hideo, who was later sent to Washington.[5]

Father Drought gave Ikawa a long memorandum in three parts, which he had written from the point of view of a Japanese.[6] The first part called for a Japanese "Far Eastern Monroe Doctrine": "In exercising what will really be political hegemony over this area [China, Indochina, Thailand, Malaya, the Dutch East Indies], we must recognize that we cannot afford to permit, in any considerable or important section, such political or economic weakness as would entice European powers to a resumption of extracontinental imperialism, or as would dispose any section toward Communism, which is not a politi-

[5] I have drawn heavily on John H. Boyle, "The Drought-Walsh Mission," *Pacific Historical Review*, vol. 34, no. 2 (May 1965), pp. 141–61.

[6] This document is reprinted in *Bekkan Shiryo-hen* (Tokyo, 1963), the documentary appendix volume of *Taiheiyo Senso e no Michi* (*The Road to the Pacific War*).

cal form of government but a corroding social disease that becomes epidemic." The second part discussed Japan's bargaining position vis-à-vis the United States, including Japan's military and political position in China and her adherence to the Tripartite Pact. The third part called for a high-level Japanese-American conference to be held in Tokyo, or possibly in Honolulu. The Japanese who read the document were naturally pleased, since it contained everything their country wanted.

The two priests returned to the United States in December 1940, and obtained access to President Roosevelt through the good offices of Postmaster General Frank Walker. Bishop Walsh presented a memorandum, which was quite different in tenor from the Drought memorandum given to the Japanese. The Walsh statement intimated that Japan was willing to alter her commitment to the Axis, and that she was weary of war in China and would accept American cooperation in a settlement there. It suggested a "Far Eastern Monroe Doctrine," based on a Japanese-American guarantee of the status quo in the Philippines, Hong Kong, Singapore, and Malaya and on the "establishment of autonomous governments in Indochina and the Dutch East Indies." The argument was that this would enable the moderates in Japan to hold down the militarists. Secretary of State Cordell Hull advised the President to be extremely wary of the suggestions being offered, but the priests were encouraged to keep up their contacts with the Japanese.

Late in January 1941 the priests wired Ikawa, "As a result of meeting with the President, hopeful of progress, awaiting developments."[7] In response Ikawa, presumably with the support of the Prime Minister, came to New York, where he conferred with Bishop Walsh, Father Drought, and Postmaster General Walker. The end product of a series of meetings was a long document entitled "Preliminary Draft of Agreement in Principle," the joint work of Bishop Walsh and Ikawa. At this point Colonel Iwakuro Hideo, who had been sent by the Army as an adviser to Ambassador Nomura Kichisaburo, arrived on the scene, and proceeded to make a number of changes in the "Preliminary Draft." For example, where the Walsh-Ikawa draft called for the evacuation of Japanese troops from China, the Iwakuro draft made any evacuation contingent on an agreement to be reached between Japan and China. After Iwakuro's revisions the document

[7] Boyle, "Drought-Walsh Mission," p. 153.

favored the Japanese position, and hence was less acceptable to the American side. The Iwakuro draft, which is frequently referred to in the 1941 Conferences as the "Draft Understanding," is reproduced in Appendix A.

Meanwhile, Admiral Nomura, who had become Japanese Ambassador to the United States in January 1941, carried on informal talks with Secretary Hull in the hope of improving relations between the two countries. Early in April 1941 the Draft Understanding—which, as we have seen, was not the product of negotiations between the Department of State and the Foreign Ministry carried on by accredited representatives—was brought into the picture. Secretary Hull knew of it through the Postmaster General, and Nomura through Iwakuro and Ikawa. Secretary Hull realized in advance that it was not acceptable to the United States, but was willing to discuss it and use it as a starting point for further negotiations. When he met with Ambassador Nomura on April 14, Secretary Hull asked the Ambassador whether the Japanese Government wished to present the Draft Understanding as the first step in negotiations, with the understanding that both sides would want to propose changes. Two days later, Hull saw Nomura again and sought assurance in advance that Japan was prepared to go forward with a plan for settlement. By way of indicating the American position, Hull gave the Ambassador a paper containing four principles:[8] (1) respect for the territorial integrity and sovereignty of all nations; (2) support of the principle of noninterference in the internal affairs of other countries; (3) support of the principle of equality, including equality of commercial opportunity; (4) nondisturbance of the status quo in the Pacific, except as the status quo may be altered by peaceful means. Hull's "Four Principles" were obviously incompatible with the Draft Understanding in many respects. After this meeting, Ambassador Nomura cabled the text of the Draft Understanding to the Foreign Office, but it appears highly unlikely that he sent the Four Principles along with it.

When the text of the Draft Understanding arrived in Tokyo on April 17, Matsuoka Yosuke, the Foreign Minister, was absent on a trip to Germany, Italy, and the Soviet Union. Although Prime Minister Konoye knew something about its background, thanks to reports from Ikawa, neither the Foreign Minister nor his staff had been informed about it. Konoye feared that the impulsive Matsuoka would be en-

[8] Herbert Feis, *The Road to Pearl Harbor* (New York, 1963), pp. 176–78.

raged when he learned that negotiations were about to begin on the basis of a proposal originating outside regular diplomatic channels. Accordingly, he went to the airport to meet Matsuoka's plane, with the intention of explaining the situation to his Foreign Minister as they were driven into Tokyo. For Matsuoka, this was something of a triumphal return. He was at the crest of his prestige and popularity, thanks to his visit with Hitler and his signing of a neutrality pact with Stalin; there was even talk that he would be the next Prime Minister. As it happened, he made up his mind to go directly from the airport to the Imperial Palace to pay his respects to the Emperor. He expected to be greeted by a large crowd in front of the Palace. Since the Prime Minister was by temperament a retiring individual who did not relish contact with hordes of people, he decided not to get into the same car, and instead the Vice Foreign Minister rode in with Matsuoka.

Just as Konoye had feared, Matsuoka reacted violently when he learned of the Draft Understanding. When he first heard that a message had come from the United States, he thought that it must be in response to an overture he had made to President Roosevelt through Laurence Steinhardt, the American Ambassador in Moscow. Now that he had gone to Berlin and Moscow, he had visions of going to Washington and personally negotiating with President Roosevelt. It is not hard to understand, therefore, why he was put out when he learned that the communication from the United States was not a reply to the message he had sent through Steinhardt.

The deliberations of the Japanese decision makers in response to the Draft Understanding can be followed in the notes of the Liaison and Imperial Conferences. The deliberations eventually led to a Japanese counterproposal, which in turn produced an American response, and so on. With each exchange, the range of alternatives seemed to narrow rather than broaden; and in the end, as the sense of crisis heightened, there appeared to be no alternative to war.

IV

Three general observations may be made about the material presented in this volume. First, the decision makers all had the same basic values. All the leaders, civilian and military, favored the "Greater East Asia Co-prosperity Sphere," and believed that this would contribute to world peace. All saw the American position as threatening to Japan's deepest interests. Their disagreements were exclusively over methods and timing. They realized that Japanese expansion would arouse the antagonism and resistance of other nations, which meant that risks were involved. Some leaders, of course, were more willing than others to take risks.

Second, as Japan and the United States negotiated, neither side was willing to make any significant concessions. Each side held pretty much to its position, and was unwilling or unable to see the other side's point of view. By the fall of 1941, the Japanese leaders, rightly or wrongly, had come to believe that they were being pushed into a corner by the United States and her allies. To make matters worse, time was running out for them: As the notes of these Conferences demonstrate, the status quo seemed intolerable to them. The consequences of this sense of crisis were, perhaps, inevitable—no course but war seemed possible to the Japanese.

Third, there is the matter of willingness to take risks. If two nations are on unfriendly terms, how can one prevent the other from attacking it? One answer is the theory of deterrence, which holds that a weaker nation will not attack a stronger one for fear of suffering defeat and destruction. No doubt the fear of defeat has deterred leaders from starting wars, but the Japanese example in 1941 shows that there can be exceptions.

Indeed, the notes of the Liaison and Imperial Conferences contain almost no discussion of the probable consequences of defeat. One side in a war is usually the loser; yet to openly admit the possibility of defeat before or during a war smacks of treason. For this reason, there is an understandable reluctance to bring the issue out into the open.[9] Of course, Japanese leaders may well have thought about defeat, or even discussed it privately with their trusted colleagues. But anything like the following conversation, supposed to have taken place between two peasants, could hardly occur in a Liaison or Imperial Conference:

We might just as well have a Japanese-American war very soon while we are at it.

I agree. . . . But, you know, you can't fight a war on an empty stomach.

---

[9] Emotions run high on this point in all countries. In 1958, when Paul Kecskemeti published *Strategic Surrender,* a theoretical study undertaken by the RAND Corporation with Air Force funds, American newspapers described the book as an officially sponsored inquiry into the conditions under which the United States might surrender in a future nuclear war. As the author observes in a note to the second printing, this caused nationwide excitement, culminating in a Senate debate in August 1958—even though the book's discussion was entirely hypothetical, and the United States was not mentioned by name.

Yes, that's true. But so what if we lose? We should go after them, win or lose. If we win, that's fine: we'll just grab their money. And if we lose, I doubt that the United States would treat us so terribly. Who knows, if we became a dependency of the United States, life might be easier.[10]

But if the possibility of defeat was not openly discussed, neither was it altogether ignored. One might say that it was indirectly considered, since the chances of a Japanese victory were assessed in detail. A good deal of statistical information on shipbuilding capacity, oil supply, and the like was brought before the Liaison Conferences. It turned out that many of the projections were far too optimistic; but even so the picture that emerged was not too reassuring. No one was confident enough to say flatly that Japan could win the war. The Navy's position, for instance, was that it could put up a good fight for two years, but no more. Moreover, there was no thought of landing invasion forces in the United States to compel her to surrender: the most that Japan could expect was a negotiated peace. The big hope was that the Americans, confronted by a German victory in Europe and weary of war in the Pacific, would agree to a negotiated peace in which Japan would be recognized as the dominant power in Eastern Asia. The peace negotiations, of course, would be greatly facilitated if a third party were to act as a mediator. There is some evidence that Japan counted on one of the Latin American countries, Switzerland, Portugal, or the Vatican to act in such a role.

As can be seen, there were many imponderables in the picture. Americans might not get war-weary, Germany might not win in Europe, no third party might be willing to act as a mediator. Nevertheless, the Japanese leaders were not deterred from going to war because of these uncertainties; they were willing to assume great risks.

To round out the picture, two other factors might be mentioned in connection with Japan's gamble. The first of these is memory. The memory of the Russo-Japanese War of 1905 was very much present among the decision makers in 1941. Even though Russia had been a giant compared to Japan, Japan had enjoyed early success in the fighting. As the war progressed, there were increasing signs of national exhaustion as a result of the war effort; but fortunately for Japan, before the tide turned President Theodore Roosevelt stepped in and arranged a peace between the two antagonists. One suspects that

---

[10] Quoted in Kamishima Jiro, *Gendai Nihon no Seishin Kozo* (*The Contemporary Japanese Mentality*) (Tokyo, 1961), p. 39.

either consciously or unconsciously the Japanese leaders in 1941 were hoping for a more or less similar sequence of events.

The second factor is fatalism. It is easier to make decisions in the face of uncertainty if one is a fatalist. If a decision maker believes, for example, that human affairs are ultimately controlled by superhuman forces, then he is not really a free agent, and so is ultimately not responsible for his actions. Fatalism of this kind was common among Japanese high officials. It has been reported, for example, that when Admiral Yamamoto Isoroku, who developed the idea of a surprise attack on Pearl Harbor, found the Navy Chief of Staff hesitant to accept the great risks involved, he remarked: "The only question that remains is the blessing of Heaven. If we have Heaven's blessing, there will be no doubt of success."[11]

What lessons, if any, may be drawn from the Liaison and Imperial Conference notes? One lesson is that there are definite limits to the effectiveness of threats used by one nation to deter another nation from pursuing a certain course of action—in this case, choosing the alternative of war. Against those who are willing to take great risks, deterrence may not be effective. If nothing else, the Japanese data for 1941 cast serious doubt on the validity of the deterrence theory, which has dominated American military policy since the end of 1945.

[11] Quoted in Fujiwara Akira, *Nihon Gendai-shi Taikei: Gunji-shi* (*An Outline of Contemporary Japanese History: Military History*) (Tokyo, 1961), p. 246.

IMPORTANT PERSONS IN THE TEXT

Prince Fushimi—An Imperial Prince, he was Navy Chief of Staff until April 9, 1941.

Hara Yoshimichi—President of the Privy Council, a group of distinguished leaders who collectively advised the Emperor. He often asked questions in the Imperial Conferences on behalf of the Emperor. He did not favor war with the United States.

Hiranuma Kiichiro—A former Prime Minister, he served as Minister for Home Affairs in the second and third Konoye Cabinets. Although a long-standing leader of the Right, he was shot by an ultranationalist in August 1941 because of his failure to resign after Matsuoka's ouster.

Emperor Hirohito—He was opposed to war with the United States because of the high risks involved. He tried to use his personal influence to avoid war, but in the end was unsuccessful.

Hoshino Naoki—He had worked with General Tojo in Manchuria, and Tojo appointed him Chief Secretary of the Cabinet in October 1941. He had previously served as President of the Planning Board.

Ikawa Tadao—Formerly an official in the Ministry of Finance, he served as an unofficial negotiator in the early stages of the negotiations between the United States and Japan.

Ito Seiichi—Appointed as Navy Vice Chief of Staff on September 1, 1941, he supported what the lower echelons of the Navy had been saying: that a decision for war or peace could not be delayed.

Iwakura Hideo—A colonel in the Japanese Army, he was sent to Washington to advise Ambassador Nomura Kichisaburo. He was one of the principal authors of the document known as the "Draft Understanding."

Prince Kan'in—An Imperial Prince, and Army Chief of Staff until October 3, 1940.

Kawada Isao—Finance Minister during the second Konoye Cabinet, he had a long career in the government service and had previously been Chief Secretary of the Cabinet.

Kaya Okinori—He accepted the post of Finance Minister in Tojo's Cabinet only after being assured that efforts to achieve a settlement with the United States would be continued. He had been a civil servant in the Finance Ministry.

Kondo Nobutake—Navy Vice Chief of Staff from October 1939 to September 1941.

Konoye Fumimaro—Prince Konoye was a member of the Fujiwara Clan and distantly related to the Emperor. He served in the House of Peers and Privy Council, and was Prime Minister on three occasions in the late 1930's and 1940–41. He felt that war with the United States was inadvisable, but he was not forceful enough to stop the trend toward war.

Kurusu Saburo—A career diplomat, he was sent to Washington in November 1941 to assist Ambassador Nomura. Official Washington did not like him, perhaps because of his part in the signing of the Tripartite Pact.

Matsuoka Yosuke—Matsuoka was a fiery, sometimes imprudent, and often intransigent advocate of an aggressive, expansionist Japan. He had received his college education in the United States, and had served as president of the South Manchuria Railroad. He favored a close alliance with Germany.

Muto Akira—Lt. General Muto was Chief of the Military Affairs Bureau of the War Ministry, which was in charge of political affairs involving the army. As head of this important bureau, he exercised considerable influence behind the scenes.

Nagano Osami—Admiral Nagano was Navy Chief of Staff from early 1941 until February 1944. Although he opposed war with the United States at first, he later became a strong advocate of immediate action in order to prevent a further decline in Japanese strength.

Nomura Kichisaburo—Admiral Nomura was appointed Ambassador to the United States in December 1940, in part because he was personally acquainted with President Roosevelt. He was accepted by most of Washington as a diplomat genuinely striving for an agreement between the two nations. His difficulties with the English language, his unprofessional methods, and his attitude toward diplomacy often tangled official communications between the two governments.

Ogura Masatsune—Finance Minister in the third Konoye Cabinet.

Oikawa Koshiro—Admiral Oikawa was Navy Minister from September 1940 to October 1941. During the October debates he continued to hold reservations about war with the United States but would not take a strong stand against war.

Oka Takasumi—As Chief of the Naval Affairs Bureau of the Navy Ministry, he was Muto's naval counterpart.

Sawada Shigeru—Sawada was Army Vice Chief of Staff from October 1939 to November 5, 1940.

Shimada Shigetaro—Before becoming Navy Minister in Tojo's Cabinet, he had served as Navy Vice Chief of Staff and as Commander-in-Chief of the China Fleet.

Sugiyama Gen—General Sugiyama became Army Chief of Staff in 1940. After the United States froze Japanese funds in July 1941, he took the position that further negotiation was useless. His attitude may be inferred from his statement: "If you are strong, the other side will back down."

Suzuki Teiichi—A professional Army officer, he once headed the Asia Development Board. At Konoye's invitation, he became head of the Planning Board in April 1941. He later complained that his work was hampered by his inability to get vital information from the armed forces.

Tanabe Moritake—He succeeded Tsukada as Army Vice Chief of Staff on November 6, 1941.

Togo Shigenori—A career diplomat, Togo had been Ambassador to Berlin but was sent to Moscow because he opposed the Tripartite Pact. Dismissed while Matsuoka was in power, he remained inactive until he was made Foreign Minister by General Tojo. He took office believing that the major cause of the deadlock between the United States and Japan was the question of stationing troops in China, and that if Japan would make concessions, peace might be possible.

Tojo Hideki—General Tojo established a reputation in the Army as an able administrator, and became War Minister in 1940. As War Minister he often advocated strong policies; but as Prime Minister he was more cautious, partly because of an increased sense of responsibility, and partly because of the personal influence of the Emperor.

Toyoda Teijiro—Admiral Toyoda held the post of Minister of Commerce, Industry, Overseas Affairs in the second Konoye Cabinet, and that of Foreign Minister in the third Konoye Cabinet. He believed that Japan should not become too closely tied to Germany and instead should seek to improve relations with the United States.

Tsukada Ko—He was appointed Army Vice Chief of Staff in November 1940, and reflected the views of a clique of younger officers who favored a war policy.

Yoshida Zengo—He was forced to resign his post as Navy Minister in September 1940 because of an illness presumably brought on by his opposition to the Tripartite Pact.

PROLOGUE

The Tripartite Pact

The Tripartite Pact

Germany, Italy, and Japan signed the Tripartite Pact on September 27, 1940. Since the Pact was in fact directed against the United States, it is not surprising that it subsequently proved to be one of the greatest obstacles to an accord between Japan and the United States. Indeed, the fear of antagonizing the United States had been one of the influences restraining a decision in favor of the Pact; but in the end pro-Axis pressures prevailed. A brief account of the pressures and counterpressures will provide a background for understanding the document reproduced below.

In the late 1930's pro-German sentiment in Japan was particularly strong in the Army General Staff, and in certain right-wing organizations. The announcement of the Nazi-Soviet treaty in August 1939 came as a shock to the pro-German groups, whose influence was temporarily curtailed, only to rise to new heights when German armies rapidly overran Western Europe in the late spring and summer of 1940. With the fall of France and the Low Countries, the Japanese began to wonder about the disposition of French and Dutch colonial possessions in Asia. They feared that Germany might seek political control of French Indochina and the Netherlands East Indies, territories that the Japanese would have liked to bring into their Greater East Asia Co-prosperity Sphere. In July 1940 the Foreign Office, the Army, and the Navy came to an agreement to seek Japanese control of Southeast Asia in return for aid to Germany in the form of pressure on the British in the Far East. Japan, however, was not to enter the war on the German side.

A few days later a change in the Cabinet occurred. Prince Konoye Fumimaro was named Prime Minister, and he brought in General Tojo Hideki as War Minister and Matsuoka Yosuke as Foreign Minister. Matsuoka, a strong-willed person, rejected the proposal agreement as too weak; instead, he advocated strengthening political ties with the Axis and a commitment to cooperate militarily with Germany

*and Italy against Britain if the Axis powers sought such aid. Matsuoka
had the support of the Prime Minister and the Army. The Navy Minister, Admiral Yoshida Zengo, and a number of senior naval officers
were reluctant to go along because they feared that such an alliance
would antagonize the United States. However, some of the lower-
ranking naval officers who headed the various bureaus and divisions
within the Navy Ministry and the Navy General Staff favored Matsuoka's position. Admiral Yoshida, caught in these cross pressures,
became ill; he was succeeded on September 5, 1940, by Admiral
Oikawa Koshiro.*

*Meanwhile, Foreign Minister Matsuoka and his subordinates were
working up another proposal, which enlarged the aims of the proposed alliance to include the United States, as well as Britain, as a
target. Many senior officers in the Navy continued to be less than enthusiastic about an alliance with the Axis powers because they felt
that the Navy was not ready to fight the United States; but the new
Navy Minister was much less adamant than his predecessor and finally agreed to the Tripartite Pact. After the detailed provisions of the
Pact were hammered out in personal negotiations between Foreign
Minister Matsuoka and the German Minister, Heinrich Stahmer, who
arrived in Tokyo early in September 1940, the matter was brought
before an Imperial Conference.*

*The notes of the Conference, which were apparently made by
Army Vice Chief of Staff Sawada, reveal that the Foreign Minister
used the same argument the Germans had used on him, namely that
the Pact would prevent the United States from entering the war. This
position was questioned by Hara Yoshimichi, President of the Privy
Council. The notes also show that the Navy wished to avoid war with
the United States.*

[Participants: Prime Minister Konoye Fumimaro, Foreign Minister
Matsuoka Yosuke, War Minister Tojo Hideki, Navy Minister Oikawa
Koshiro, Finance Minister Kawada Isao, Director of the Planning
Board Hoshino Naoki, Army Chief of Staff Prince Kan'in, Army Vice
Chief of Staff Sawada Shigeru, Navy Chief of Staff Prince Fushimi,
Navy Vice Chief of Staff Kondo Nobutake, President of the Privy
Council Hara Yoshimichi.]

ARMY CHIEF OF STAFF PRINCE KAN'IN: What effect would closer cooperation between Japan, Germany, and Italy have on the settlement
of the China Incident?

FOREIGN MINISTER MATSUOKA: In order to strengthen and improve Japan's position in negotiating this Pact, we have informed Germany that Japan would settle the China Incident through her own efforts. However, we hope to receive help from Germany after the conclusion of the Pact: for example, we hope to persuade her to cooperate with us in direct negotiations with China, which the military are now conducting. I believe we can anticipate considerable results.

NAVY CHIEF OF STAFF PRINCE FUSHIMI: To what extent will the conclusion of this alliance contribute to improving diplomatic relations between Japan and the Soviet Union?

MATSUOKA: I want Germany to serve as a mediator in improving diplomatic relations between Japan and the Soviet Union. Since better Japanese-Soviet relations will benefit Germany, she wants to act as a mediator. Minister Stahmer says that Germany has never discussed this matter with the Soviet Union. Last year, when the German-Soviet Neutrality Pact was signed, Foreign Minister Ribbentrop asked Stalin what he intended to do about Japanese-Soviet relations. At that time Stalin said that if Japan wanted peace, he would also want peace; and if Japan wanted war, he would also want war. So one can conclude that the Soviets are quite interested in improving relations between our two countries. Germany believes that better relations can be brought about without any trouble. Since Minister Stahmer could hardly have passed through the Soviet Union without the Russians knowing about it, I suspect he might have had talks in Moscow with the Soviet authorities. At any rate, I think we can reasonably expect that Germany will act as a mediator in improving Japanese-Soviet relations.

FUSHIMI: I foresee that as a result of this alliance our trade with Great Britain and the United States will undergo a change; and that if worst come to worst, it will become increasingly difficult to import vital materials. Moreover, it is quite likely that a Japanese-American war will be a protracted one. What are the prospects for maintaining our national strength in view of the present situation, which finds our national resources depleted because of the China Incident? And what measures are contemplated?

PRIME MINISTER KONOYE: We can anticipate that trade relations with Britain and the United States will deteriorate even more. If worst comes to worst, it may become impossible to obtain any imported goods. At the present time our country depends to a large extent on Britain and the United States for her principal war materials. Accordingly, we cannot help but experience considerable difficulties.

We have been aware of this problem, and we have increased our domestic production and added to our stockpiles. Hence, if we tighten controls over consumption by the military, the Government, and the people, and if we limit consumption to the most critical areas, we should be able to meet military needs for an extended period; and in the event of a war with the United States, we should be able to supply the military and thus withstand a rather prolonged war.

DIRECTOR OF THE PLANNING BOARD HOSHINO: Since scrap iron is the principal raw material for steel, our steel production will suffer if the United States bans the export of scrap iron. But as the Prime Minister has explained, we should be able to produce a considerable amount of steel because we have expanded our steel-producing capacity, and because we can use production methods that do not call for scrap iron. Our planning estimates for this year call for a steel production of 5.4 million tons. However, if the United States bans the export of scrap iron, production will drop to 4 million tons for the first year of the plan; and because of the decrease in our stockpiles it will remain at that figure for the second year, even though our production capacity is expanded. If we resort to emergency measures, we should be able to maintain current levels. At present, direct and indirect consumption by the Army and Navy amounts to 1.4 million tons, and civilian consumption is 4 million tons. Even if total production shrinks to 4 million tons, the continuation of the war in China should not be difficult if we cut down on civilian consumption. If, in addition, we revise our planning and increase our steel capacity (including those facilities that are almost completed or will be completed in the near future), steel production in Japan proper and in Manchuria should amount to 8 million tons of pig iron and 5.4 to 5.5 million tons of steel. Our present steel capacity is 4 million tons because we are rapidly expanding other production facilities, and because of the deterioration in the quality of coal. If in the future we concentrate our major efforts in this area, and if we fully utilize our facilities, we should be able to increase production by 1.2 to 1.3 million tons. Consequently, we should be able to meet our present military needs indefinitely, to say nothing of the steel used in the China war.

As for nonferrous metals (copper and zinc), our planning estimates call for about 200,000 tons of copper this year. In the event of an embargo, copper production will decline to 180,000 tons the first year and 130,000 to 140,000 tons the second year; after that it will gradually increase. Since civilian demand for copper this year will be 200,000 tons, and the Army and Navy demand, both direct and indirect, will be 110,000 tons, we should be able to meet the military demand, although with some difficulty. However, the copper shortage will be more serious than the steel shortage. We must look into the use of substitutes and investigate all possible ways of obtaining copper. We are making a great effort to obtain copper, and we recently purchased a considerable amount of it from the United States; this has already arrived, is in transit, or is ready to be shipped.

Since the domestic production of petroleum is low, oil presents even more difficulties than steel and nonferrous metals. We must meet the needs of the Army and Navy from the stockpiles set aside for them. We will, of course, be in difficulty if the war is prolonged. However, since our stockpiles are fairly large, they should be all right. Aviation gasoline, which has been a major weakness until recently, is now in a rather advantageous position compared to other petroleum products because we have obtained a considerable amount of it by our two accelerated imports, and by our special imports.[1] Since it is of course impossible to meet Army, Navy, Government, and civilian needs from production within the yen bloc and by drawing on our stockpiles, it will ultimately be necessary to work out a way of obtaining oil from northern Sakhalin, the Netherlands East Indies, and other places.

FUSHIMI: If we ever get into a war with the United States, the Navy will be fighting on the front line. In that event, even though we have stockpiles of war materials and prospects of turning to northern Sakhalin and the Netherlands East Indies for additional supplies, the Navy cannot carry on a protracted war on the basis of its own stockpiles. I would like to know how we will get the additional oil necessary for a long war.

HOSHINO: The oil situation is as I have already explained. If there should be a fairly prolonged war, it will be necessary to get oil from northern Sakhalin and the Netherlands East Indies. Also it will be necessary to get additional supplies from the Soviet Union and Europe through the good offices of Germany. In short, it will be essential to acquire a large amount of oil any way we can. The Netherlands East Indies and northern Sakhalin are the places one thinks of first; once we have made up our minds, we will have to get oil

---

[1] Japanese imports of aviation gasoline were as follows: 440,000 bbl. in 1939; 1,447,000 bbl. in 1940; and 1,529,000 bbl. in 1941. These are the figures given by the Nihon Gaiko Gakkai (Japan Foreign Affairs Association) in *Taiheyo Senso Genin Ron* (*On the Origins of the Pacific War*) (Tokyo, 1953), p. 658.

from these places. Actually, we are now buying a considerable amount of oil in the South Seas, China, and other areas. We should also pay a great deal of attention to domestic production. We are producing 400,000 tons of natural oil; the production of synthetic petroleum has progressed considerably in recent years, and it is anticipated that we will be able to produce 300,000 tons next year. Domestic production of oil should reach a substantial figure, if facilities planned and under construction are included. We have to plan for an increase in supplies from abroad and added domestic production on the one hand, and a reduction in domestic consumption on the other.

FUSHIMI: May I interpret this to mean that there is, in general, no assurance that additional oil can be obtained? I will add that we cannot count on supplies from the Soviet Union. In the end, we will need to get oil from the Netherlands East Indies. There are two ways of getting it—by peaceful means, and by the use of force. The Navy very much prefers peaceful means.

MATSUOKA: In negotiating the Pact, we paid most attention to the question of procuring oil. Even though British and American capital is involved, since it is under Dutch control we asked Ott[2] and Stahmer what Germany, which controls the Netherlands, could do to help us obtain oil from the Netherlands East Indies, and develop Japanese enterprises there in the future. They said that Germany could do a good deal. Also, according to Stahmer, the amount of oil that Germany obtained from France is greater than the amount she used from last September to the present time. Moreover, the Soviet Union has been faithfully carrying out her economic agreements with Germany, and British propaganda to the contrary, a considerable amount of oil is being shipped to Germany from the Soviet Union. It is also said that Germany is getting a considerable amount of oil from Rumania, and so Germany has no need to worry about oil. Hence I asked the Germans to share half their oil with Japan, since we would be in a most difficult position should the United States impose an embargo as a result of the Pact; they said that they would cooperate as much as possible. I have also asked the Germans to use their influence with the Soviet Union to get the Soviets to sell us all or part of the oil in northern Sakhalin and avoid interfering with Japanese enterprises there. They stated that this problem could be solved easily after the adjustment of Japanese-Soviet relations.

FUSHIMI: Oil in the Netherlands East Indies is controlled by Amer-

[2] Eugen Ott, German Ambassador to Japan. Stahmer was Minister to Japan, and ranked below Ott.

ican and British capital. Since the Dutch government has fled to Great Britain, can Germany freely dispose of the Netherlands East Indies oil simply because she controls the mother country? What is the Foreign Minister's opinion on this point?

MATSUOKA: It would be difficult. Although the Dutch Shell shares belong to the British, the company is Dutch, so the British and Americans cannot complain on the basis of their stock holdings. The Standard Oil Company has even tried to sell us the Standard Oil Company in the Netherlands East Indies because it feared losses from war. If possible, we should buy it.

FUSHIMI: Even if we should find that we must enter the war because of American participation in the war in Europe, it will be necessary for us to determine independently when we should commence hostilities. What has been done about this?

MATSUOKA: It is clear that Japan will automatically be under an obligation to participate in the war; but the question of whether or not the United States has really entered the war will be decided by consultation among the three Pact countries. There is also a joint Military and Naval Affairs Commission, which will study the problem of how to meet the situation at any given moment and advise the respective governments. Since our Government will make the final decision, it will be made independently.

PRESIDENT OF THE PRIVY COUNCIL HARA: Although what I was going to ask has been covered in the questions put by the Navy Chief of Staff, I should like to add that this Pact is a treaty of alliance with the United States as its target. Germany and Italy hope to prevent American entry into the European war by making this Pact public. Recently the United States has been acting as a watchdog in Eastern Asia in place of Great Britain. She has applied pressure to Japan, but she has probably been restraining herself in order to prevent Japan from joining Germany and Italy. But when Japan's position becomes clear with the announcement of this Pact, she will greatly increase her pressure on us, she will greatly step up her aid to Chiang, and she will obstruct Japan's war effort. I assume that the United States, which has not declared war on Germany and Italy, will put economic pressure on Japan without declaring war on us. She will probably ban the export of oil and iron, and will refuse to purchase goods from us. She will attempt to weaken us over the long term so that we will not be able to endure war. The Director of the Planning Board has said that all available steps will be taken to obtain iron and oil, but the results are uncertain. Also, the Foreign Minister's statement shows that we cannot obtain iron and oil right away, and that in any case the amount will be restricted. You cannot carry on a war without oil. The capital in Netherlands East Indies oil is British and American, and the Dutch Government has fled to England; so I think it will be impossible to obtain oil from the Netherlands East Indies by peaceful means. I would like to hear the Government's views on this.

MATSUOKA: What the President of the Privy Council says is quite true. But Germany, which is now in control of the Netherlands, could also put great pressure on the Netherlands East Indies. Furthermore, in international relations one can quite often work behind the scenes, and for this purpose Germans and Italians can be used to advantage. When an embargo was declared against Italy, and again when Japan withdrew from the League of Nations some years ago, so many people wanted to sell us munitions that one had difficulty turning them down.

If Japan would abandon all, or at least half, of China, it might be possible for the time being to shake hands with the United States; but [American] pressure on Japan will certainly not come to an end in the future. The Presidential election that is coming up very shortly is especially dangerous. Roosevelt, who has high ambitions, will stop at nothing to achieve them if he believes that he is in danger. He might well undertake a war against Japan, or enter the war in Europe. Both of the Presidential candidates can build up their popularity by condemning Japan. Minor military clashes between Japan and the United States in China could easily lead to war. At present, American sentiment against Japan has become stronger, and this cannot be remedied by a few conciliatory gestures. Only a firm stand on our part will prevent a war. Of course, we should firmly suppress any useless anti-British and anti-American activities. Hitler's idea is to avoid war with the United States if he possibly can; in fact, he would like to establish friendly relations with the United States once the war with Britain is over. There are 23 million Americans of German descent in the United States, and they will play an important role. Japan seeks the same thing from the United States. We, too, should strive to improve Japanese-American relations when an opportunity presents itself. We might make use of American citizens of German and Italian extraction.

HOSHINO: What I said earlier assumed the worst possible situation that could develop. So long as war does not break out between Japan and the United States, we will never reach a point where it will be impossible to continue the war in China simply because of economic pressure from the United States. We can obtain a considerable amount of materials from countries other than the United States. The only exception is aviation gasoline. American aviation gasoline is the best, and we cannot yet produce high-grade aviation gasoline. However, since we have recently obtained a large amount of it, we are in a good position. As for other petroleum products, although there are some problems of price and quality, we can obtain them elsewhere. We cannot believe that other countries will impose an embargo at the same time as the United States. To begin with, American economic action against Japan is aimed at certain crucial points, where it hurts Japan the most and the United States the least. Even if there is maximum economic pressure in the future, there will not be additional suffering for us, since the most painful measures have already been taken. As I explained earlier, we are even now buying a considerable amount of oil from the United States. Also the amount of oil imported from northern Sakhalin is by no means small. Although it is less than 100,000 tons at the present time, this is because of Soviet interference. With existing facilities we should be able to obtain several hundred thousand tons more. If the 400,000 tons that the Soviet Union is taking were to be added, the total would be 700,000 to 800,000 tons, which is not an insignificant figure.

WAR MINISTER TOJO: The Army, like the Navy, considers oil important. I think this question, in the end, comes down to the matter of the Netherlands East Indies. The matter was decided by the Liaison Conference between the Government and Imperial Headquarters held shortly after the formation of the present Cabinet, when the policy statement "Outline of Policy on the Settlement of the Situation" was adopted.[3] It was agreed that we should settle the China Incident quickly and at the same time cope with the Southern Question, taking advantage of favorable opportunities. As for the Netherlands East Indies, it was decided that we would try to obtain vital materials by diplomatic means, and that we might use force, depending on the circumstances. We are most certainly not moving forward without a policy. The Government has a policy: it desires to obtain materials peacefully from the Netherlands East Indies, but depending on the circumstances, it could use force.

HARA: I am glad to be informed about policy by the Foreign Minister, and to learn from the War Minister that policy with respect to

[3] Approved in a Liaison Conference on July 27, 1940.

the South has already been decided. At present, the Netherlands East Indies are our only source of [additional] oil. There would be no problem if oil could be obtained peacefully; but what arrangements have been made with Germany and Italy in case we have to use force?

MATSUOKA: We have begun discussions. The use of force would provoke a war with Great Britain. Also, we would be making a one-sided demand on Germany and Italy. Furthermore, there is the problem of face on both sides, and the problem of security. Germany might also demand some compensation. So I would like to continue discussions on this matter in the future.

HARA: It is necessary now to get Germany and Italy to acknowledge Japan's freedom of action in the Netherlands East Indies. I want to refer to the Foreign Minister's statement on the interpretation of a covert attack. I would like to ask if, supposing that the United States should lease bases in New Zealand, Australia, etc. and encircle Japan, we have decided whether such an act should be interpreted as an American attack on Japan.

MATSUOKA: The object of this Pact is to prevent the United States from encircling us in that way. The only thing that can prevent an American encirclement policy is a firm stand on our part at this time. As to whether an encirclement—should such a thing take place —is to be regarded as an attack, no doubt the Supreme Command and the War and Navy Ministers have views on the subject. I am inclined to think that it should be decided on the basis of the situation at that time.

TOJO: One can only decide on the basis of the situation at that time.

HARA: The United States is a self-confident nation. Accordingly, I wonder if our taking a firm stand might not have a result quite contrary to the one we expect.

MATSUOKA: I see your point; but Japan is not Spain. We are a great power with a strong navy in Far Eastern waters. To be sure, the United States may adopt a stern attitude for a while; but I think that she will dispassionately take her interests into consideration and arrive at a reasonable attitude. As to whether she will stiffen her attitude and bring about a critical situation, or will levelheadedly reconsider, I would say that the odds are fifty-fifty.

KONOYE: I believe that all of you have now finished giving your opinions. Will you please give your concluding remarks.

KAN'IN: On the basis of our studies to date, the Army section of Imperial Headquarters agrees with the Government's proposal for a stronger Axis Pact with Germany and Italy. Furthermore, since the improvement of relations with the Soviet Union is extremely important both for the settlement of the China Incident and for future defense policies, we would strongly urge that the Government redouble its efforts in this area.

FUSHIMI: The Navy section of Imperial Headquarters agrees with the Government's proposal that we conclude a military alliance with Germany and Italy. However, on this occasion we present the following desiderata: (1) that even though this alliance is concluded, every conceivable measure will be taken to avoid war with the United States; (2) that the southward advance will be attempted as far as possible by peaceful means, and that useless friction with third parties will be avoided; (3) that the guidance and control of speech and the press will be strengthened, that unrestrained discussion of the conclusion of this Pact will not be permitted, and that harmful anti-British and anti-American statements and behavior will be restrained.

Although it is recognized that the Government and the Navy Supreme Command agree on the need to speed up the strengthening of naval power and preparedness, since this matter is of great importance, we would ask the Government on the occasion of this Conference for its full cooperation in this matter.

HARA:[4] I give my approval on the ground that action to this end is essential to carry on the China Incident, and in the light of the changing international situation. We will encounter many difficulties in the future. We cannot be optimistic about the possibility of an American embargo. Even though a Japanese-American clash may be unavoidable in the end, I hope that sufficient care will be exercised to make sure that it will not come in the near future, and that there will be no miscalculations. I give my approval on this basis.

[4] Here the President of the Privy Council appears to be speaking on behalf of the Emperor, as was the custom.

PART ONE

The Decision to Move South

The Decision to Move South

19TH LIAISON CONFERENCE
April 18, 1941

The telegram from Ambassador Nomura containing the text of the Draft Understanding arrived at the Foreign Ministry on the evening of April 17. In an accompanying message Nomura stated that he and his associates had worked behind the scenes on the document, and that to his certain knowledge Secretary Hull had no objections to it. He added that the Draft Understanding did not go against the spirit of the Tripartite Pact. He made no mention of Hull's Four Principles.[1]

Prime Minister Konoye knew something of the document's background through reports from Ikawa Tadao. Nomura, however, had neglected to send word of the Draft Understanding negotiations either to Foreign Minister Matsuoka, who was then out of the country, or to anyone at the Foreign Ministry. Hence Nomura's telegram came as a surprise to Foreign Ministry officials.

Army Chief of Staff Sugiyama Gen took a cautious position at this Conference. As many students of Japanese politics have pointed out, in this period the actual power to formulate policy within the armed forces usually resided in the middle-ranking officers who headed the various bureaus and sections, rather than in the titular leaders.[2] Since neither the War Ministry nor the Army General Staff had had an opportunity to study the Draft Understanding and formulate a policy concerning it, Sugiyama was careful not to commit the General Staff without prior study of the matter by his subordinates.

Agenda: The Adjustment of Diplomatic Relations with the United States.

[The conference started at 8 P.M. at the Prime Minister's official

---

[1] The text of this telegram is in *Taiheiyo Senso e no Michi* (*Road to the Pacific War*) (Tokyo, 1963), VII, 153–54. Hereafter this work will be cited as *TSM*.

[2] Robert Butow, *Tojo and the Coming of the War* (Princeton, 1961); Masao Maruyama, *Thought and Behavior in Modern Japanese Politics* (London, 1963), Chapter III.

residence. The Army Chief of Staff, after consultation with the War
Minister, attended on the condition that the Conference be limited
to explanations, that there be free discussion, and that no decisions
be taken.

[Prime Minister Konoye gave a briefing on Ambassador Nomura's
telegram.]

QUESTION: Why is it that all of a sudden we received this telegram?

PRIME MINISTER KONOYE: Toward the end of last year, two American missionaries came to Japan. I met them, and other leaders also
met them. They returned home after learning something of the atmosphere in our country. Roosevelt, by the way, knows these missionaries well. Ikawa, a former official in the Ministry of Finance,
got in touch with the missionaries in the United States. When Colonel
Iwakuro arrived in San Francisco, Ikawa went there to show him a
draft proposal, which was then sent to me via the S.S. *Tatsuta Maru*;
I received it several days ago. A short while after that we received
this telegram. There are some differences between the letter and the
telegram, but in the main they are the same.

[It is not known to what extent Foreign Minister Matsuoka has
been informed of this matter. It was decided that we should study
it further until the Foreign Minister returns, and then decide what
position to take. It was agreed, therefore, to wire the Foreign Minister, urging him to return as soon as possible.]

[The impressions of Army Chief of Staff Sugiyama:]

1. The United States is thinking of this draft proposal in terms of
its effect on Germany. [After all] isn't the United States about to
step up her aid to Britain?

2. Doesn't this draft proposal conflict with the Tripartite Pact? To
what extent does it actually conflict? What disadvantages would it
bring to Germany, and what advantages would it bring to Britain?

3. Wouldn't peace overtures to China conflict with our past position toward her? Isn't there a conflict here with the Konoye Statement?[3]

4. What effect would the proposal have on the establishment of
the Greater East Asia Co-prosperity Sphere?

[3] Issued on December 22, 1938, by the First Konoye Cabinet, this statement
declared that Japan, Manchukuo, and China would pursue the common aim of
establishing a New Order in East Asia. In effect, this meant that the Cabinet had
decided not to deal with the Chinese Government under Chiang Kai-shek unless
that Government gave in to Japanese terms. Instead, the Japanese set up a puppet
regime under Wang Ching-wei, which eventually came to be called the "National
Government."

5. Should we get started on an amended draft after we have sufficiently studied the present draft proposal, or should we reject the proposal?

6. It is necessary to study the effects on the United States and Britain in case we amend the draft, and also in case we reject it.

7. Sufficient precautions should be taken to maintain secrecy.

8. Consideration should be given to the fact that negotiations are already in progress with Roosevelt and Hull, and to the need to maintain international good faith.

20TH LIAISON CONFERENCE
April 22, 1941

Foreign Minister Matsuoka returned on April 22 from his trip to Europe and Russia, and was told about the Nomura telegram containing the Draft Understanding by Ohashi Chuichi, Vice Foreign Minister.

Meanwhile, different groups in the Army and Navy met every day to study the document. On April 18 a telegram addressed to War Minister Tojo Hideki, Chief of the Military Affairs Bureau of the War Ministry Muto Akira, and Tanaka Shin'ichi of the Army General Staff arrived from Colonel Iwakuro in Washington.[4] The telegram said that the United States was headed for war but wished to avoid a two-front war. Iwakuro believed that this was a good time to press the United States, and urged that an attempt be made to arrive at an overall solution to Japanese-American problems. He touched on his negotiations with Father Drought, Bishop Walsh, and Postmaster General Walker, which had led to the Draft Understanding. He stated that President Roosevelt was in favor of the Draft Understanding. Iwakuro urged its immediate acceptance by Japan without revision.

Tojo was skeptical of the Draft Understanding, and Muto half suspected that Iwakuro had written it. Some thought the United States was willing to compromise because of the Japanese-Soviet Neutrality Pact; others felt that the German successes had forced America to back down on the China issue; and still others saw the document as an American plot. Nevertheless, there was a willingness to negotiate on the basis of the document because the Army was anxious to end the war in China.

---

[4] The text of this telegram is in *TSM, Bekkan*, pp. 392–94.

*On April 21 an agreement on a unified position was reached among
the Bureau and Division Chiefs of the War and Navy Ministries and
the Army and Navy Chiefs of Staff. This is the study referred to in
the text below,*[5] *and its main points were as follows:*

*The United States sought to prevent Japan from moving south-
ward, to step up American aid to Britain, to weaken the Tripartite
Pact, and to attain world hegemony through increased armament.
Japan should take advantage of these preoccupations on the part of
the United States to settle the China Incident, strengthen her military preparedness, and secure a voice in establishing world peace.
There should be no interference with Japan's establishing the Greater
East Asia Co-prosperity Sphere and achieving her goals in China.
Japan must not be asked to violate the Tripartite Pact, and she must
be free to increase her armaments. The basic idea was for Japan and
the United States to cooperate in establishing peace in the Pacific
and restoring peace in Europe.*

Agenda: Foreign Minister Matsuoka's Report upon Returning
Home; the Adjustment of Diplomatic Relations with the United
States.

[Time: from 9:20 P.M. to 12:20 A.M. Participants: Vice Foreign
Minister Ohashi participated by special request.

[Summary: First the Foreign Minister reported on Germany, Italy,
and the Soviet Union. Then, concerning the adjustment of diplomatic
relations with the United States proposed by Ambassador Nomura,
Foreign Minister Matsuoka stated that the proposal differed considerably from what he had in mind, and that he would like to think
about it at his leisure after he had taken care of some business matters during the next few days. Accordingly, he was given a list of
views and amendments resulting from a study made by the Army
and Navy, and was asked to consider them. The Foreign Minister
left the Conference early to go home, saying that he was tired because he hadn't had much sleep since the day before yesterday. After
that, the War and Navy Ministers spoke on the views of the Army
and Navy. A discussion followed, and the conference was adjourned
at 12:30 [sic].

[Regarding Matsuoka's opinion that it might take two weeks to
two months for him to decide what position to take toward the
United States, the great majority of Conference participants felt
that it would be a mistake to take too long in determining policy

[5] The text of the agreement is in *ibid.*, pp. 408–9.

toward either the United States or Germany. Minister of Home Affairs Hiranuma also stated that it was necessary to proceed as quickly as possible because a delay would give rise to doubts within Japan. Foreign Minister Matsuoka looked tired at the beginning, but he gradually overcame his fatigue and looked very vigorous.

[Summary of the Foreign Minister's statement:]

[1. Relations with the United States.] In Moscow I told the American Ambassador to Russia what I had been thinking about for three months, namely, that the American President is quite a gambler, and that the United States has kept the European War and the China Incident going with her aid.[6] I told him that the peace-loving President of the United States should work with Japan, which also loved peace, and that the President should urge Chiang to propose peace. The Ambassador sent a telegram to the President; and I expected to receive a reply in Moscow, but I did not. After returning to Japan, I learned of the proposal sent by Nomura. Since this proposal includes important matters besides the settlement of the China Incident, I will have to consider it carefully for two weeks, or perhaps for one or two months.

[2. Conferences with the German and Italian leaders.] I have not said anything for which we will be held responsible. I stated that the Southern Question is something that Japan herself should decide. Germany often referred to the Southern Question; Italy made no reference to it, and instead said that our common enemy was the Soviet Union. Both Ribbentrop and Mussolini agreed that the Tripartite Pact was aimed at preventing the United States from entering the war.

[3. The background of the Japanese-Soviet Neutrality Pact.] When I left here for Germany I told Stahmer that my stay in Russia might be an extended one, since I was going to Leningrad; and I implied that I might see about a Japanese-Soviet Neutrality Pact on my way back to Japan.

I met with Molotov three times, but because he stuck to his opinions and would make no concessions I thought that the Pact could not be agreed upon. I therefore expressed my ideas to him rather bluntly and gave him a letter in English for future reference. That evening, I received a phone call saying that Stalin could see me any time the

---

[6] A report by Laurence Steinhardt, American Ambassador to the U.S.S.R., to Secretary of State Hull regarding this meeting with Matsuoka is in U.S. State Department, *Papers Relating to the Foreign Relations of the United States: Japan, 1931–1941* (U.S. Government Printing Office, Washington, 1943), Vol. II, pp. 143–44.

following day, so I made an appointment with him for five o'clock the next afternoon.

At five o'clock the following afternoon, I greeted Stalin in his room; and I took this opportunity to speak on Hakko Ichiu.[7] Stalin had on his desk the protocol of the Neutrality Pact and the letter I had handed to Molotov, and was impatiently listening to my talk on Hakko Ichiu. Presently Stalin said, "I trust you, and I trust Konoye," and started talking about the draft of the Pact.

Since there were references to Manchukuo in the Pact, I stated that we should not deal with an independent country in this way, and Stalin agreed with this. Stalin sent for a map, and insisted that we sell southern Sakhalin. I stated that [northern] Sakhalin had belonged to Japan since the sixteenth century, until it was annexed by Russia; and that since then our nation had wanted very much to recover it. Stalin replied that the Soviet Union had the Kamchatka Peninsula to the east and the Maritime Provinces to the west; and that Sakhalin fell between them, which was not a good situation. I replied, pointing to the map, that he should take a larger view of the map: that it would be better for the Soviet Union to move toward India and Iran. I said that in such a case Japan would look the other way. Our conversation became more and more interesting, and at last we agreed to conclude the Pact.[8]

While we cannot tell exactly what the Soviet Union's intention was in concluding the Pact, it is certain that she was in the mood to go through with it.

[4. On German-Soviet relations.] When I asked Ribbentrop whether there was any understanding between Germany and the Soviet Union concerning Finland, Bulgaria, Turkey, and so on, he answered that there was none. Ribbentrop said: "It was because of unavoidable circumstances that Germany concluded a nonaggression pact with the Soviet Union. Germany would somehow or other like to defeat the Soviet Union; at present, we can probably defeat her in three or four months. I think the Soviet Union would disintegrate if she were defeated. If Japan were to attempt a conquest of Singapore, she would no longer need to worry about the North. Although the surrender of Greece is certain, Britain is extending her activities into the Balkans. Since Stalin is a cautious man, I don't think he will act in a reckless manner."

[7] Literally "eight corners of the world under one roof," a concept of universal brotherhood that came to mean Japanese domination of Asia.

[8] The Japanese-Soviet Pact was announced on April 14.

When I asked Ribbentrop if Germany would attack the British Isles before or after attacking the Balkans, he refused to answer, saying he could not state one way or the other. I said that we had proposed a Japanese-Soviet Neutrality Pact as early as July of last year, and that because the situation had changed in the meantime, we would like to simply go ahead with it. I told him that if the Soviet Union was anxious to conclude a Pact, my intention was to do so. Ribbentrop said "I understand," but I think he did not believe that a Pact would be concluded. He was probably surprised when he learned of its signing the other day.

[5. The situation in Italy.] Italy is under Germany's control. She should be able to get along by depending on Germany. Since this was the domestic situation in Italy, she was apparently very much impressed by the visit of a Foreign Minister from an allied country. Britain is trying hard to get Italy to come over to her side, but Italy will not move. Although the Italian people are not dependable, Mussolini is a very fine person; and he is on very close terms with Hitler. Ciano [Italian Foreign Minister] says Mussolini is the sort of person who does what he says he will, so one can depend on Italy.

[Conversations with the American Ambassador to the Soviet Union in Moscow (omitted). Meeting with the British Ambassador to the Soviet Union at a theater.][9]

[Summary of the discussion after Foreign Minister Matsuoka left the Conference:

[Despite Foreign Minister Matsuoka's opinion that we should move slowly and carefully because of the importance of the matter, the majority felt that negotiations should be resumed as soon as possible, since it was necessary to work on the American psychology. Minister of Home Affairs Hiranuma also urged haste because of the domestic political situation.

[Vice Foreign Minister Ohashi said that Matsuoka had told him in the car coming in from Tachikawa airfield that it would be necessary to secure the full agreement of Germany. Ohashi had told Matsuoka that an agreement was not necessary, and that notification would be sufficient; but the Foreign Minister held firmly to his view. In response to this, Navy Minister Oikawa said: "You may talk about getting [Germany's] agreement, but what if we can't? The purpose of the draft proposal is to end the China Incident, isn't it? I think it

---

[9] The person who took these notes apparently did not feel that the content of these two conversations was important enough to warrant a detailed summary.

is important, in considering the proposal, to distinguish what is important from what is not."

[At the Conference, the War Minister reported the general opinion of the Army and Navy, while the Navy Minister stated a somewhat different view.]

21ST LIAISON CONFERENCE
May 3, 1941

Three items were discussed at this meeting. First, Japan had not yet responded to the Draft Understanding, and most of her leaders felt that it was important to send an immediate reply to Washington. Matsuoka, however, was not in a mood to cooperate. He pressed instead for an attempt to conclude a neutrality pact with the United States; and although many at the Conference opposed this plan, the matter seems to have been left up to him. Second, the problem of consulting Japan's Axis partners about the Draft Understanding was raised; but no group decision seems to have been reached. Third, Matsuoka urged the Japanese conquest of Singapore. We cannot be sure whether he meant this seriously, or whether, knowing that the Army was not likely to try to seize Singapore, he raised the question to embarrass the Army, which, to his annoyance, had a powerful voice in matters of foreign policy.

Agenda: The Adjustment of Diplomatic Relations with the United States.

[The Conference took place at the Prime Minister's official residence from 1 P.M. to 4:30 P.M. First, Foreign Minister Matsuoka gave his views on the pending problem of the adjustment of relations with the United States as follows:]

I would like to offer the United States a neutrality pact like our pact with Russia (excluding nonaggression articles) and see how she reacts to the proposal. What do you think? The United States would probably refuse, since she traditionally avoids this sort of thing; but I think it might be worth trying in view of the present world crisis.

At the same time that we make the above proposal, I would suggest that we also ask the United States to agree to guarantee eventual Philippine independence and nondiscriminatory treatment of Japanese residents in the Philippines. Also, we should tell the United States what Germany and Italy are thinking: namely, that they are certain of victory; that they will not make peace with Great Britain, except possibly an unconditional peace; that American entry into the war might prolong it, but would not end it; and that since American participation in the war would lead world civilization to its destruction, the United States should exercise great care, etc. We should also add that Japan will not do anything that might go against her obligations under the Tripartite Pact.

[There was a discussion of the foregoing remarks by the Foreign Minister. Almost all the members expressed their disagreement.]

FOREIGN MINISTER MATSUOKA: All we will do is suggest the idea. If the United States goes along with us, that's fine; if not, that's all right, too. If she agrees with us, we are that much ahead.

SOMEONE: It is necessary to keep in mind that the United States might get a strong impression from this proposal, especially since it would follow last night's radio broadcast regarding the convening of a Liaison Conference. Moreover, the conclusion of a Neutrality Pact with Stalin was achieved by Foreign Minister Matsuoka's brain and eloquence; things probably won't go so well when you work through Nomura.

MATSUOKA: I myself will write out a detailed message and have Nomura read it.

[The majority clearly opposed the pact, and there was silence for a while.]

PRIME MINISTER KONOYE: Since everyone is opposed to a neutrality pact, how about withdrawing your proposal?

MATSUOKA: Let me think about it. One thing we might do would be to treat it lightly, by proposing it to them as if Nomura had just happened to think of it. Anyway, let me think about it.

[At this point discussion on the neutrality pact was suspended. Next, the revised draft by the Foreign Ministry in reply to the Draft Understanding sent by Ambassador Nomura was discussed, taking into account opinions regarding revision put forward by the Army and Navy, and the revised draft appended here was adopted.[10] All agreed with the Foreign Minister's proposal that the essence of the revised draft be communicated to the United States, Germany, and Italy. It was decided that we would go forward with the negotiations, with proper regard for any comments that Germany and Italy might make. (Note: It was not clear whether these steps would be taken after the neutrality pact was proposed, since the matter of diplomatic

[10] This document was not included in the published version from which these translations were made.

negotiations was not discussed. It appeared that everything had been left up to the Foreign Minister, but this was not certain.)

[Next, in addition to the adjustment of diplomatic relations with the United States, the problem of the conquest of Singapore was discussed.]

MATSUOKA: Regarding the conquest of Singapore, I made no commitments to Germany, nor did Germany demand any.

Germany says that she will let Japan take care of Greater East Asia. Germany says that when she seriously thinks about the problem of Greater East Asia from Japan's point of view, she is convinced that Japan should undertake the conquest of Singapore now. She is not thinking of her own interests. Whether we go ahead or not is our decision, and I have not made any promises. I personally think that it would be better to go ahead now. Ribbentrop says that if the Soviet Union starts a war, Germany will fight her. However, he is not asking Japan to attack Singapore in order to cooperate with Germany.

[In response to this, the War Minister stated that in order to carry out operations in Malaya, Thailand and French Indochina would be needed as bases. The Army Chief of Staff elaborated on this point. The Foreign Minister asked if Saigon could be used as a base for military operations. In response, the Army Chief of Staff said that Saigon was inadequate. He further stated that in order not to excite third parties, we might simply send in supervisors or employ civilians; and that it would be necessary to somehow build airfields and stockpile materials by these means. This was the reason, he said, that he had advocated the early conclusion of a military agreement at the time the "Summary of Measures to be Taken against French Indochina and Thailand"[11] was adopted.]

MATSUOKA: Since the Japan-Indochina Economic Agreement has been concluded, we should try to get at this other matter as soon as possible.

ARMY CHIEF OF STAFF SUGIYAMA: Although Germany and Italy have built many bases in northern France for the invasion of the British Isles, they have not yet attempted an invasion. Operations in Malaya would not be easy.

MATSUOKA: Germany says she can beat Russia in two months. Singapore should not be difficult.

[11] This document was approved on January 30, 1941. Its chief recommendations were: (1) to put pressure on French Indochina and Thailand, using force if necessary, in order to establish Japanese leadership in these two countries; (2) to set up air and naval bases in selected areas in French Indochina.

[Foreign Minister Matsuoka emphasized the following point at this Conference (it is recorded here especially).]

This is top secret. Hitler intends to strengthen France and make her work with Germany in attacking Britain. Under these circumstances, Germany probably will not take a definite position vis-à-vis French Indochina.

[The Foreign Minister stated his observations regarding Chiang Kai-shek. When asked his opinion regarding peace with Chiang Kai-shek, the Foreign Minister replied as follows:]

Although Chiang wants peace, he probably can't do anything unless he gets the approval of the United States.

[At this Conference, Foreign Minister Matsuoka emphasized that we should regard the following as the minimum conditions for the adjustment of diplomatic relations with the United States: (1) any agreement must contribute to the settlement of the China Incident; (2) it must not conflict with the Tripartite Pact; (3) Japan must not betray international good faith. We should pay particular attention to these points.][12]

22D LIAISON CONFERENCE
May 8, 1941

On May 3 Foreign Minister Matsuoka sent Ambassador Nomura an unofficial interim reply to the Draft Understanding for transmittal to Hull, together with instructions that Nomura try out the idea of a neutrality pact, which had found no support in the previous Liaison Conference. In the reply, which he described as an "Oral Statement," Matsuoka said that the German and Italian leaders considered the war as good as won, that American intervention would only prolong it and cause untold misery and human suffering, that the President of the United States held the key to whether this would occur, and that Japan could not and would not do anything to jeopardize the Tripartite Pact.[13] No doubt Nomura felt that it would be unwise to present such an inflammatory statement. He read parts of it to Hull, skipping over the passages he considered most provocative. According to Hull's account, Nomura said that the paper contained many

---

[12] These conditions later came to be known as "Matsuoka's Three Principles." By "international good faith" Matsuoka meant Japan's promise to Germany to try to keep the United States from entering the European war.

[13] The text of the "Oral Statement" is in State Department, *Documents on German Foreign Policy, 1918–1945*, XII, 713–14.

things "that were wrong," but offered to hand it to Hull.[14] Hull declined—presumably because he had already seen it, thanks to the
breaking of the Japanese code. Nomura also suggested the neutrality
pact idea, and Hull's response was to brush it aside.[15]

Meanwhile, Matsuoka had been in touch with the German Government through Eugen Ott, the German Ambassador in Tokyo. The
Germans and Italians were told about the Draft Understanding, but
were not given a copy of the text. Matsuoka, however, did give Ott
a copy of the "Oral Statement." Matsuoka promised not to do anything in the negotiations with the United States that would jeopardize
the Tripartite Pact. Ott pressed Matsuoka not to respond to the Draft
Understanding officially until Japan had obtained the reaction of
the other Axis powers.

Agenda: Recent Progress in the Adjustment of Diplomatic Relations with the United States, and an Exchange of Views on the
Subject.

[Foreign Minister Matsuoka spoke as follows:]

Since there had been no reply from Ambassador Nomura, I sent
a wire requesting one. I also wanted to talk with him over the international telephone service last night, the 7th, but I could not reach
him until nine o'clock this morning. I was not able to talk with him
to my satisfaction because the connection was poor, and because of
time limitations. Nomura said he had read my Oral Statement to Secretary of State Hull. Nomura's opinion was that it would be difficult
to conclude a neutrality pact, especially since he [Nomura] was not
empowered to negotiate such a pact.

As for Germany and Italy, I had Bureau Chief Sakamoto inform
the German and Italian Ambassadors in Tokyo on Sunday.[16] On the
morning of the 6th, German Ambassador Ott asked for a meeting
with me and said that he thought Ribbentrop would be very grate-
ful for receiving information on such an important matter.

I told Ott that we have been working on this since last November
or December; that we are trying to prevent the United States from
entering the war and trying to get her to withdraw from China;
that I had talked with the American Ambassador regarding this

[14] State Department, Papers Relating to the Foreign Relations of the United
States: Japan, 1931–41, II, 411–12.
[15] Ibid.
[16] Sakamoto Mizuo, Chief of the European Bureau, Ministry of Foreign Affairs.

matter on my way to and from Europe; that Howard had asked me if I would not go to the United States aboard a ship from Lisbon, but I had turned him down.[17]

I told Ott definitely that if the United States entered the war, Japan would also have to get into the war. I also told him that Roosevelt's intention, as I see it, is to keep peace in the Pacific and aid Britain, but that Japan would never do anything to violate the Tripartite Pact in any way, and that if Germany had any views on this they should let us know about it as soon as possible. Accordingly, I think we will get some opinions from Germany. I also think it possible that we will get a telegram in reply from the United States.

Depending on the results of the foregoing communications, I would like to hold another Liaison Conference and discuss whether we should go ahead with the revised draft, which we have already agreed upon, or make further revisions.

WAR MINISTER TOJO: Have you informed Ambassador Oshima of this matter?[18] Also, have you told Ambassador Nomura about the revised draft? Wouldn't it facilitate their work if we let them know about it?

MATSUOKA: Even if we inform them, we will have to make revisions if we get an answer from Ribbentrop. This might lead to trouble later on. I also think that informing them is not a good idea from the point of view of maintaining secrecy. It was my decision not to inform them. On this occasion, the Vice Foreign Minister [Ohashi Chuichi] also advised me to inform them; but I told him to keep quiet when it came to diplomatic tactics.

It appears that word of the draft has leaked out to some non-Government people. In the Foreign Ministry I am the only one who knows anything about important matters of this kind. [He thus seemed to be warning that secrets were leaking out from departments other than the Foreign Ministry.]

America's actions to date are certainly tantamount to participation in the war. I think that Japan, as a great power, should protest them; we know what is happening, but are pretending to be unaware of it. So far Hitler has put up with it, but he might unexpectedly go to war with the United States. I think it might be argued that if this happens, Japan, as a treaty partner, should also go to war. However,

---

[17] Roy Howard, of the Scripps-Howard newspaper chain.

[18] General Oshima Hiroshi, Japanese Ambassador to Germany, known for his strongly pro-German views.

from the diplomatic standpoint it's not so easy to do that. It is my intention to prevent the United States from entering the war, and to make her withdraw from China. So please don't rush me.

Even if we secure an understanding with the United States, we might not be able to prevent war. If [American] patrolling [in the Atlantic] were stepped up, this sort of understanding would go flying out the window.[19] In that event, Japan will probably have to go to war.

NAVY MINISTER OIKAWA: The Foreign Minister keeps talking about American participation in the war, but does the United States have anything to gain from participation? I think she has much to lose. She has taken as much as she can from Britain. Any further aid to Britain would only be a loss. Although Roosevelt, because of circumstances, is acting as if he were going to jump into the war, I think that now is the most likely time for the United States to make a major change in her national policy.

MATSUOKA: Roosevelt is ready to start a war; he is, after all, a big gambler. I am considering sending a private message to him one of these days.

I would guess that the United States would not enter the war if Britain surrendered one hour before her entry; but she would continue fighting if Britain surrendered one hour after the United States entered the war. I think the second situation is more likely to occur. The United States has recently made up her mind to engage in patrolling, so the situation has changed since Ribbentrop said that there was a 70 per cent probability that the United States would not enter the war. I think the probability that the United States will not enter the war is now about 60 per cent.

If the United States participates in the war, it will last a long time, and world civilization will be destroyed. If the war lasts ten years, Germany will fight the Soviet Union to secure war materials and food, and will then advance into Asia. What do you think would be the proper position for Japan to take at that time?

[No one at the Conference answered this question. However, one person said that although the Foreign Minister talked repeatedly about the possibilities of new wars, the settlement of the China Incident was most urgent; and that therefore we should continue our

---

[19] In April 1941 the United States Navy began a "neutrality patrol" in the western Atlantic, escorting convoys, patrolling the waters, and reporting the movements of German ships to the British.

efforts to adjust relations with the United States. Thus it was decided that we would deal with the matter after receiving an answer from Ambassador Nomura and opinions from Germany.]

23D LIAISON CONFERENCE
May 13, 1941

Bowing to German pressure, Matsuoka had promised Ott that he would wait until noon of May 12 to cable instructions to Nomura, so that the Axis powers would have time to respond to the proposed negotiations between Japan and the United States. As the notes of this Conference indicate, the German response was delayed, so instructions were sent to Nomura to begin negotiations on the basis of the revised draft that had been approved by the Liaison Conference of May 3. The text of the revised draft, together with an "Oral Explanation" of the various changes, was presented by the Ambassador to Secretary Hull on May 12 (Washington time).

In this draft the United States was asked to recognize the Tripartite Pact as defensive, and, obviously in reference to the Atlantic war, to affirm that she would take "no such aggressive measures as to assist any one nation against another." Japan proposed that the United States act as a go-between in peace negotiations between Japan and China. The terms of the peace, however, were to be based on the "Konoye Principles" of "neighborly friendship," "joint defense against Communism," and "economic cooperation." Japan also sought a secret assurance that the United States would cut off its aid if Chiang should refuse to negotiate. To the dismay of Americans, the wording of the draft had been changed to eliminate Japan's pledge to refrain from force in the Southwest Pacific; it merely stated that the peaceful policy of the Japanese Government had been made clear on many occasions.

During the conference, Matsuoka alluded several times to President Roosevelt's speech of May 14. Reports from Nomura, Colonel Iwakuro, and the Japanese Naval Attaché in Washington expressed the fear that Roosevelt might order American convoying of merchant ships in the Atlantic, and indicated that this would be a major step toward American entry into the war. Reports from Washington also suggested that the President might announce a policy of convoying in the May 14 speech; the Japanese military therefore put considerable pressure on Matsuoka to send the Japanese reply before the 14th, in the hope that such action would deter Roosevelt from making

*the announcement. Actually, the speech was postponed until May 27,
and the President did not mention convoying. The Axis nations seem
to have interpreted the omission as a sign that the President had
backed down in the face of Japanese and German pressure.*

Agenda: Latest Developments in the Adjustment of Diplomatic
Relations with the United States.

[The Conference lasted from 5:00 P.M. to 7:00 P.M. Foreign Minister Matsuoka gave a briefing on the latest developments in the adjustment of diplomatic relations with the United States. Its essence
was as follows:]

It was necessary to wait for answers from Germany and Italy
before we could cable Ambassador Nomura the amended proposal
approved by the Liaison Conference. Therefore, we delayed cabling
instructions to begin formal negotiations with the United States all
through Sunday (11th); but we received no answer from Germany
and Italy. We waited until noon on the 12th, but Germany's answer
still did not arrive. We therefore instructed Ambassador Nomura by
wire at a little past noon to begin negotiations with Hull. Of course,
we had previously wired the amended proposal to Ambassador Nomura, stipulating that instructions regarding the time to begin negotiations would be sent later, so the cable finally sent to Ambassador
Nomura contained only two lines in all. Therefore, we expect the
cable to reach Ambassador Nomura prior to the President's speech
on the 14th. At 4 P.M. today, just before coming to this Liaison
Conference, I left instructions to telephone Ambassador Nomura and
tell him that the revised proposal of the Imperial Government could
not be amended any further.

Ott told us that although a cable had arrived from his Government, it was interrupted in the course of transmission, and he wanted
us to wait. However, he did not show up this morning, or at noon.
Therefore, the steps already mentioned were taken.

Our diplomatic efforts are concentrated on keeping the United
States out of the war and preventing her from convoying. Our efforts will be in vain if the convoying should lead to participation in
the war. Of course, as we indicated in the "Oral Statement," we
have told the United States that we will not do anything in the present negotiations that might go against the Tripartite Pact.

We have not yet received an answer from Hitler. But we told Germany that she should act with great caution, since grave consequences would ensue from German actions toward convoying by the

United States. We added also that the Japanese Foreign Minister had personally prayed at the Ise Grand Shrine that the United States would not participate in the war, and that no war between Germany and the United States would occur.[20]

That's the situation. But if the United States engages in convoying, and this leads to war between Germany and the United States, I think that the war will be long and will develop into a big world war.

First of all, an alliance requires the exchange of views between allies in advance; it is only when one country intends to break off friendly relations that she undertakes diplomatic action without first seeking the views of the other party in the alliance. This time I thought it necessary to proceed carefully by getting a German answer beforehand. However, we waited in vain, and were compelled to cable Ambassador Nomura without obtaining a German reply. On Sunday morning Ott came to see me and told me that the main points in the information coming from Berlin and the United States were materially different from those he had heard from me; he asked me to show him the telegram from the United States. I repeated that Japan maintains three principles—nonparticipation of the United States in the war, American withdrawal from China, and no alteration in the Tripartite Pact—and I refused to show him the American telegram, saying that not only would it be improper in view of diplomacy but also it might lead to diplomatic confusion.

Italy wishes to have herself represented by Ott, and so we shall have dealt with Italy when we have dealt with Germany.

The most likely German reply, in my opinion, is that Germany will not agree with us completely; but even if she disagrees in part, I am confident that I can persuade her to come around to our position.

As for the United States, I anticipate that Roosevelt's speech on the 14th will take our proposal into account to a certain extent, since Ambassador Nomura is expected to approach the United States Government today [today's cable is expected to reach the Ambassador in the early morning of the 12th, as there is a 14-hour time difference between Tokyo and Washington]. I have hopes that we will be able to assess the American sentiment from that speech. If our proposal is not taken into account in that speech, we will know

[20] This shrine is dedicated to the Sun Goddess, from whom the Emperors were said to have descended. Emperors and statesmen went there to pay their respects and to report important political developments.

the American reaction in a week's time, and we will reconsider the matter at that time.

24TH LIAISON CONFERENCE
May 15, 1941

The Germans were worried about a possible Japanese-American agreement; such an agreement would have destroyed the usefulness of the Tripartite Pact, which had been signed with the hope of deterring the United States from entering the European war. As the notes of this Liaison Conference show, Ribbentrop put pressure on Japan not to sign an agreement with the United States unless the latter agreed to abandon her hostile policies toward Germany.

Matsuoka was sympathetic to the German overtures, and adopted a threatening attitude toward the United States. He reported to the Conference his attempt to convey his views to Hull through Nomura. The telegram he mentions here was sent on May 13;[21] on the same day, Nomura wired back, saying that to present this kind of a document then "would make the negotiations very difficult and obstruct our reaching an understanding." He virtually refused to present the telegram to Secretary Hull. On May 15, Matsuoka sent another cable instructing Nomura to give the document to Hull, but there is no evidence that the Ambassador actually did so.[22] On May 14, to make sure that his message was delivered, Matsuoka talked to Joseph Grew, the American Ambassador in Tokyo. What he said, according to Grew, was "bellicose both in tone and substance." Matsuoka said he was afraid that the United States might convoy its ships to Britain. He suggested that Hitler's patience and restraint could not go on indefinitely; and that if Hitler's submarines sank American ships, and the United States in turn attacked German submarines, Japan would regard this as American aggression. All this, he said, would lead to war between Japan and the United States.[23]

Agenda: The Latest Developments in the Adjustment of Diplomatic Relations with the United States.

[21] The text is in *TSM*, VII, 181.

[22] Matsuoka's cable is quoted in *ibid*. Nomura's account of the negotiations in his *Beikoku ni Tsukaishite* (*My Mission to the United States*), does not mention this episode.

[23] Grew's account of his meeting with Matsuoka is in State Department, *Papers Relating to the Foreign Relations of the United States: Japan, 1931–41*, II, 146–48.

[Foreign Minister Matsuoka gave a briefing on the latest developments as follows:]

A reply from Ribbentrop was interrupted during reception, and the full text was unavailable; but the German and Italian Ambassadors came to see me on the night of the 12th with the full text of that cable. The Italian Ambassador said that what the German Ambassador was going to tell me was precisely the opinion of the Italian Government also.

The gist of the Ribbentrop reply was as follows [the Foreign Minister did not disclose the full text]:[24]

"We think Japan is well aware that the American proposal is going to hinder her efforts to build the Greater East Asia Co-prosperity Sphere. With this proposal, the United States will obtain security in the Pacific, mitigate the antiwar sentiment among her people, and be able to turn in any direction she chooses. If the United States enters the war, so will Japan. Therefore, the United States wants to manipulate the situation so as to prevent war between the United States and Japan, so that she can play an active part in the Atlantic theater. The United States is also expected to aggravate the situation and provoke Germany to take reprisals against her—thus shifting the responsibility for initiating war onto the Axis countries—and then enter the war herself. Accordingly, Germany hopes that Japan will make it clear that she is prepared to consider the American proposal only if the United States agrees to refrain from these activities. We ask that Japan inform both Germany and Italy before sending a final answer to the United States, since this proposal greatly affects the Tripartite Pact."

[In the Foreign Minister's view, there were no discrepancies between Japan's three principles on this matter and the views held by Germany and Italy. So the Foreign Minister handed the drafts of Japan's revised proposal to the German and Italian Ambassadors; and asked the German Ambassador to convey to Ribbentrop the following points: (a) Japan is not ignoring Germany's wishes; (b) Japan is not ignoring the Tripartite Pact; (c) Japan wishes it understood that she had no alternative but to instruct Ambassador Nomura before getting replies from Germany and Italy.]

Since I wanted to have these feelings clearly conveyed to Hull, I sent Ambassador Nomura a cable in English, the main points of

[24] The full text of the Ribbentrop cable is in State Department, *Documents on German Foreign Policy, 1918–1945*, XII, 777–80.

which were as follows: "Although I [Matsuoka] myself deem it unnecessary, I would like to get the following points on the record so
that there will be no room whatever for misunderstanding. As I
have often repeated formally and informally, and I believe Hull is
aware of it, my determination to instruct Nomura to talk with and
enter into negotiations with Hull has been based on the following
assumptions: (a) the United States will not enter the European war;
(b) the United States will advise Chiang Kai-shek to enter into direct negotiations with Japan in order to bring about peace between
Japan and China at the earliest possible opportunity. I would like
to have it understood, therefore, that negotiations not based on the
above assumptions could not lead to an understanding."

To the above cable, Nomura replied that because he had often
stated the above points, and because he did not see the need to repeat them at this time, he would like to refrain from so doing. But
I told Nomura to convey the above to Hull immediately, since I had
my own convictions. The fact that I had instructed Nomura to make
the above representation was also conveyed to Germany and Italy.

Since Japan negotiated with the United States at her own discretion, without waiting for answers from Germany and Italy, it is conceivable that Germany may conclude a unilateral peace treaty with
Britain or attack the Soviet Union. But I don't think that Germany
will do these things, because I told both countries [i.e., Germany and
Italy] that there were no discrepancies between the German representation and Japan's amended proposal.

The Foreign Ministry has said nothing on this matter to our Ambassadors in Germany and Italy; so I request that the Military Attachés not be informed of it either.

25TH LIAISON CONFERENCE
May 22, 1941

*Following the abrogation of the Japanese-American Commercial
Treaty in July 1939, the United States reduced the flow of some vital
war materials to Japan, and threatened to reduce or completely stop
the flow of others. Japan, therefore, was anxious to develop alternative sources of supply, and the Netherlands East Indies and
French Indochina were obvious choices: these areas were rich in resources, and their home countries had been overrun by the Nazis.
The Japanese put increasing pressure on the Dutch administrators
in control of the East Indies, asking for large quantities of oil, tin,*

and other essential materials. These administrators, in a polite but firm way, refused to make sweeping concessions. The Japanese government sent several missions—the last one headed by a veteran diplomat, Yoshizawa Kenkichi—to persuade the Dutch in the East Indies to give in to Japanese demands. As the notes of this Liaison Conference reveal, Yoshizawa was unable to make headway and became increasingly despondent about the chances of success.[25] *Accordingly, there was talk of using force; but as Army Chief of Staff Sugiyama argued at this Conference, to seize the Netherlands East Indies it was first necessary to obtain bases in Thailand and Indochina.*

The second topic on the agenda was the recognition of the Nanking puppet government nominally led by Wang Ching-wei, who had recently defected from Chiang's government. It was decided to delay action, pending developments in the negotiations with the United States.

Finally, Matsuoka reported on a telegram from Ambassador Oshima in Berlin. It is not altogether clear why Matsuoka referred to this telegram. One possible interpretation is that Oshima's advice paralleled Matsuoka's: Japan should compel the United States to pledge neutrality, and Japan must stick to the Tripartite Pact. Matsuoka noted a telegram from Nomura reporting progress in the negotiations in Washington, but he himself remained skeptical about the probabilities of ultimate success.

Agenda: Negotiations with the Netherlands East Indies; the Recognition of the National [Nanking] Government; and Latest Developments in the Adjustment of Diplomatic Relations with the United States.

[The Conference lasted from 11:30 A.M. to 1:30 P.M. On the negotiations with the Netherlands East Indies, Foreign Minister Matsuoka reported as follows:]

The Netherlands East Indies seemed to yield to us when the Neutrality Pact between Japan and the Soviet Union was concluded. However, recently conditions there have reached the state noted in a separate paper [not reproduced].

At this rate, it now seems inevitable that we must begin an economic war with Britain and the United States. It was agreed at the

---

[25] For details of the negotiations, see Hubertus J. Van Mook, *The Netherlands Indies and Japan: Battle on Paper, 1940–1941* (New York, 1944).

time Mr. Arita was Foreign Minister that although fourteen items would be embargoed, 20,000 tons of tin and 3,000 tons of rubber would be exported to Japan; but the Netherlands East Indies now refuse to export more than part of this amount. Furthermore, they say that if Japan procures tin and rubber from such areas as Malaya and French Indochina, their own exports to Japan will be reduced by the amount thus secured. These recent developments suggest that they may eventually embargo even tin and rubber. It seems that they are taking advantage of Japan's plight and treating us as a minor power. We would endure it if they would give us half the amount of tin and rubber; but we can no longer put up with it under the present circumstances.

Yoshizawa requested that he be recalled when I was in Europe, but I persuaded him to stay on with his assignment. However, the situation being what it is, I think it will be necessary to have Yoshizawa return to Japan, and to take other measures. Today I talked to the Netherlands Minister [General J. C. Pabst] and asked him to think the matter over again. At two o'clock this afternoon I am going to summon the British Ambassador [Sir Robert Craigie] and ask him to tell his Government that the Imperial Government will be forced to resort to armed measures in the South if the present situation continues. If these statements should fail to make them reconsider, I think we will have to recall Yoshizawa, tell the world what the Imperial Government's attitude is, and then take such steps as we may think fit.

I want to have the above-mentioned measures studied by all of the Ministries. Today I am going to urge the British Ambassador to settle the matter amicably, and warn him that serious consequences may ensue, depending upon the British Government's attitude. I think that we have put up with it long enough, and that the time for action has come. If the Netherlands East Indies persist in their present attitude, many of our people will feel a righteous indignation; and I, as Foreign Minister, will sympathize with them.

[There was much discussion of the report by the Foreign Minister. The main arguments were as follows:]

MATSUOKA: I would like to discontinue negotiations with the Netherlands East Indies and recall Yoshizawa. I would also like to have the timing left up to me.

SOMEONE: I can well understand that the present attitude of the Netherlands East Indies compels Japan to recall Yoshizawa; but it is British and American support that allows the East Indies to take such an attitude. If we take this final step against the East Indies, it will eventually be necessary to expand our military operations to the Philippines and Malaya. This is of life-and-death importance to the nation, and the timing and means should be considered with utmost care.

MATSUOKA: If we do not make up our minds, won't Germany, Britain, the United States, and the Soviet Union be united in the end and bring pressure to bear on Japan? It is possible that Germany and the Soviet Union may form an alliance and turn against Japan, and also possible that the United States may begin a war with Japan. I would like to know how the Army and Navy Chiefs of Staff intend to deal with such an eventuality.

ARMY CHIEF OF STAFF SUGIYAMA: This is a serious matter. For the Malayan part of this decision alone, it will be necessary to lay the groundwork in Thailand and French Indochina for operations to be carried out from there. I fully explained this point at one of the previous Liaison Conferences. The Foreign Minister has not yet taken these measures, and I would like to be told the reason why.

MATSUOKA: Before we proceed to take action against Thailand and French Indochina, we must decide what to do about Britain and the United States. We cannot enter into negotiations without having our minds made up on this point. We will go ahead when we make up our minds.

[The Navy said very little throughout the above discussion.]

NAVY MINISTER OIKAWA: Is Matsuoka sane?

[As can be seen above, no conclusion was reached.]

[On the recognition of the National [Nanking] Government, the Foreign Minister reported as follows:]

Concerning the problem of having Germany and Italy recognize the National Government, when I recently visited Europe, I asked Germany and Italy to defer to Japan's opinion on the timing of recognition. I intend to decide on the timing after I have heard Ambassador Honda's[26] views; I have, in fact, kept Germany and Italy waiting. I have explained these developments to Honda. At this point I think it is desirable to let Germany and Italy recognize the National Government: to make our attitude toward that Government clear, foster that Government, and manipulate the other Axis countries so that they will recognize it also. I also think we had better make this attitude clear in discussing our dealings with the

---

[26] Honda Kumataro, Ambassador to the Nanking Government.

Chungking regime. Under the present circumstances, it is 97 per cent
unlikely that we will succeed in dealing with the Chungking regime.

WAR MINISTER TOJO: I think we had better delay having Germany,
Italy, and other Axis countries recognize the National Government.
We would be seeking two irreconcilable aims at the same time, in
view of our request to the United States, during the Japanese-American negotiations, to advise China to cease hostilities against Japan.

SOMEONE: We should carefully consider whether Germany is prepared to give Japan a free hand in the Far East, even on economic
matters. We must be cautious about having Germany recognize the
National Government immediately.

MATSUOKA: Politics and economics are inseparable.

OIKAWA: Since Wang Ching-wei is soon coming to Japan, why not
give it [the German recognition of the National Government] to him
as our gift?

CHIEF OF THE NAVAL AFFAIRS BUREAU OKA: Since Japanese-American negotiations are now in progress, should we not be very cautious
about having the National Government recognized too soon, provided we intend to reach an effective understanding in the negotiations?

[On the latest developments in the Japanese-American talks, the
Foreign Minister first gave the gist of a telegram he had received
from Ambassador Oshima. Although the Foreign Minister did not
agree to make the cable available to the Army, the Chief of the Military Affairs Bureau was able to see it. The gist of the cable from
Ambassador Oshima:]

On May 3, I had my first meeting with Ribbentrop. Ribbentrop
revealed to me the salient points of the information he had received,
saying that he had been asked by Matsuoka not to tell me anything.
Perhaps Ribbentrop told me because of the importance of this Ambassador [Oshima], who has a special relationship with Germany.
I myself did not have this information at that time. It seems that
it was conveyed from Ott to Ribbentrop, then from Ribbentrop to
me. I did not disclose my opinion at all, because I regarded the matter as being very important.

Our second meeting was on May 9. Ribbentrop disclosed to me
in detail the contents of the cable from Ott, and said: "We have a
great deal of information revealing that this proposal was initiated
by the Japanese side. We understand that Foreign Minister Matsuoka unwillingly consented to negotiate on the basis of this proposal
because of pressure from other people, and also that he has now

given up the idea of capturing Singapore. In my view this means that Japan will hold hands with the United States and stay out of the fighting when the United States enters the war. As to the inquiry from Japan regarding the negotiations, Germany has two replies ready. The first is to tell Japan not to negotiate; the second is to sanction the negotiations under certain conditions. I myself would like to take the first course."

In answer to the above I said: "I am not familiar with the nature of the negotiations, since I have not yet received any instructions from my Government. If the supposed Japanese proposal should materialize, however, I do not think that it would adversely affect Germany's attack on Britain. On the other hand, if it does not materialize, we will at least have sounded out President Roosevelt's feelings and given the pro-American groups among the Japanese people the impression that reconciliation between Japan and the United States is impossible after all. So I prefer the second course." Ribbentrop did not agree to the second course. He recommended the first course to Hitler as his own opinion. But Hitler decided to adopt the second course.

While on a trip to Italy, I had my third meeting with Ribbentrop. He began: "Ott has reported that Japan started negotiations with the United States without waiting for the answer from Germany. I was most displeased to hear of it. I am most displeased that Japan did not wait, although the German reply was due to arrive in a few hours." He added: "Although I had several meetings with Matsuoka in Berlin, he did not say anything to me about this matter. Now I feel that I have been betrayed. According to the talks between Matsuoka and Ott, Matsuoka reportedly said that Japan would attack the Soviet Union should Germany and the Soviet Union go to war. But this differs from Matsuoka's statement in Berlin. It seems that in Berlin he did not grasp the nature of German-Russian relations."

I said: "I think that administrative reasons must have made it unavoidable that Japan proceed in the talks with the United States without waiting for Germany's answer. As for Matsuoka's statement reportedly made to Ott regarding the Japanese attitude in case of a war between Germany and the Soviet Union, I daresay the attitude of the Imperial Government cannot be easily decided. It is up to the Emperor to decide. If, therefore, Matsuoka has in fact stated the position of Japan, it cannot be more than his personal opinion."

My own [Oshima's] opinion on this proposal is as follows: According to the German interpretation of the Japanese proposal, Germany has been betrayed by Japan. Germany thinks that Japan intends, by this proposal, to avoid entering the war in case of American participation in the war. I, as Ambassador, am aware of the "aims" of Japan; but I think it unwise to make Germany doubt Japan's sincerity, since Germany will certainly gain a great victory in a few months. I also suspect that this proposal might be a plot by Roosevelt. If Japan accepts this proposal, she will be internationally isolated after the war. If it becomes clear that Japan will not send forces to the South, she will invite the contempt of Germany and Italy. If the United States gets involved in the South Pacific, Germany and Italy will also get involved shortly thereafter. If it is imperative that Japan carry out this proposal, the following two points should be kept in mind:

1. In the course of the present negotiations Japan should require the United States to keep strictly neutral. Japan should make it clear that she will carry out her responsibilities under the Tripartite Pact should the United States enter the war.

2. Japan should undertake to exchange frank views with Germany and Italy. In particular, she should try to correct their mistaken idea that she intends to avoid getting into the war.

[The Foreign Minister then gave a briefing on the latest developments in the negotiations held in the United States:]

On the night of May 11, after they had talked for about forty minutes, Nomura handed the amended Japanese proposal to Hull.[27] Hull said that although he would try his best, it would take quite a long time to consider this proposal. On the night of May 13, Nomura again met with Hull, and told him that the main points of the Imperial Government's aims, as given by the Foreign Minister, were that the United States should not enter the war and that the United States should advise China to negotiate peace with Japan. On May 14 another meeting was held. Hull said that the United States must talk with China and Britain before advising China to negotiate peace, that Germany will inevitably move into South America if she conquers Europe, and that the United States must fight to defend democracy. We received a telegram from Nomura on the 19th. He said

[27] Matsuoka appears to be confused about the dates. Actually Nomura met with Hull on May 11, when he presented the Japanese reply to the Draft Understanding. Then he saw Hull again on the 12th, and handed him another document, which was a slightly revised version of the one presented on the 11th. This seems to have been the official document. The next meeting between the two took place on May 14.

that the Japanese-American negotiations were proceeding amicably. [According to the Foreign Minister's view, the chances that the negotiations will end in an agreement are only three out of ten. He said he would like to report informally to the Emperor on the basis of the above cables from Ambassadors Oshima and Nomura.]

26TH LIAISON CONFERENCE
May 29, 1941

Following the presentation of the amended Draft Understanding by Nomura on May 12, informal discussions between Secretary Hull and the Ambassador took place at frequent intervals. These discussions, however, did not lead to a written American counterproposal until May 31. The American effort in these talks was aimed at persuading the Japanese to agree to certain things: (1) to agree that the United States was acting only in self-defense in aiding Britain, and therefore to pledge not to enter the war on the German side if the United States went to war with the Nazis; (2) to agree to withdraw troops from China; (3) to agree not to use force in Southeast Asia. The American position was the exact reverse of what Matsuoka wanted to hear. He had hoped to use the threat implicit in the Tripartite Pact to coerce the United States into stopping its aid to Britain and China. Moreover, he appears to have believed that a substantial portion of the American public was opposed to supporting Britain and China, but that they were being persuaded to do so by the President, who in Matsuoka's view was a warmonger.

Agenda: Negotiations with the Netherlands East Indies; Fireside Chats; the Adjustment of Diplomatic Relations with the United States.

[The Foreign Minister reported on the above subjects as follows. On the negotiations with the Netherlands East Indies:]

The other day I summoned the British Ambassador and the Netherlands Minister and talked with them, but they have not replied since. Both Ambassadors have called commercial attachés assigned to Tokyo into meetings, and they are now assessing the actual amount of materials needed by Japan. They invited the Foreign Minister to participate in these meetings, but we refused to do so and have had the Chief of the South Seas Bureau attend as a matter of formality.

It seems that the Netherlands East Indies, following the suggestion of Great Britain, intend to prevent rubber, among the goods ex-

ported to Japan, from being shipped to Germany. They are not
especially concerned with tin. The British Ambassador has repeatedly
inquired into the amount [of materials] needed by Japan, but we
have replied that we see no reason to answer such questions. I have
told him that it would be impertinent for the Netherlands East Indies
to adjust the amount exported to Japan in accordance with the
amount Japan gets from French Indochina and Thailand, and that
it would also be impertinent for a small country like the Netherlands
to demand that Japan guarantee not to re-export to Germany. The
British Ambassador said that this procedure is inevitable from the
viewpoint of "business," to which I replied that even in "business"
we can't allow this sort of thing.

The British Ambassador wanted to know if Japan would actually
take as much as 40,000 tons [of rubber] from French Indochina, as
rumored. I said that Japan would take only 15,000 tons; and that as
far as Germany was concerned it was none of our business, since
the Germans had already cleared their demands with the Vichy regime. The British Ambassador said that this was the first time he
had heard of it.

This, then, is where we stand in our negotiations with the Netherlands East Indies, and I think I shall have to recall Yoshizawa in the
near future.

[On the Fireside Chats and the Adjustment of Diplomatic Relations with the United States:]

We have not yet received an official report from Nomura. It is
irritating that the United States should emphasize that she will fight
to defend democracy and will aid Britain and China, but I do not
intend to make an issue of it at this time. I have not yet used strong
language.

Sometimes it seems that the United States is in difficulties. The
American people must be disappointed; the President may hit back
after seeing the public reaction. It is not correct, therefore, to think
that the American attitude has softened simply because of what the
President said in his Fireside Chat.[28]

As to the amended proposal of the Imperial Government, it is
likely that the United States has consulted Britain, since she said

[28] In this speech President Roosevelt declared an "unlimited national emergency" and stated that America had "doubled and redoubled our vast production,
increasing month by month our material supply of tools of war for ourselves and
Britain and China—and eventually for all the democracies." He pledged to deliver goods to Britain, but did not announce a policy of convoying merchant
ships. He did not specifically name Japan.

that she would sound out the opinions of the British and Chinese Governments. Judging from Craigie's statement that the British Government thinks that a peaceful settlement between Japan and China would enable Japan to move southward, I would say that when Britain sees the amended Japanese proposal she will regard it as a trick.

[With this the briefing given by the Foreign Minister came to an end, and free discussion followed:]

WAR MINISTER TOJO: It is necessary to control the expression of opinions that criticize Government actions or confuse the people. It is also necessary for each Government department to maintain strict control of security. I hope the Minister of Home Affairs will give special consideration to this matter.

MATSUOKA: I quite agree. Yesterday the newspaper *Hochi* printed a statement by Muto Teiichi[29] saying that the United States should enter the war in alliance with Japan. I do not think such remarks are appropriate.

[It was suggested that now was the time for the Government to make its attitude clear; but it was agreed that we had better wait for a while, since America's views would be coming in soon.]

MINISTER OF HOME AFFAIRS HIRANUMA: As for the control of speech, a certain person of fairly high status visited my house and remarked, "It is outrageous that Wang Ching-wei should be coming to Japan in June," a statement contrary to the view of the Government. It is not appropriate to express opinions that run counter to measures taken by the Government.

SOMEONE: Then who sowed the seeds of the present Japanese-American negotiations?

MATSUOKA: It was Nomura's own idea to start talks with Hull to the extent that he did. However, I don't know how far he has gone. It was not because I appealed to the United States from Moscow that Nomura started the talks. He had already begun some time before that. Before Nomura left Japan I gave him a written memo, and that memo suggested the exact opposite of what he is doing now. I apologize for this failure to control Nomura's diplomatic efforts. I cannot resign immediately, but I will hold myself responsible to the Emperor some time in the future.

NAVY MINISTER OIKAWA: Didn't you get an American priest to start things off?

---

29 At this time Muto was Editor-in-Chief of the *Hochi*.

MATSUOKA: No.

SOMEONE: Did someone give money to Ikawa?[30]

MATSUOKA: I didn't. I know who did, but please do not press me now to tell you who it was.

27TH LIAISON CONFERENCE

[The notes on this conference are not available.]

28TH LIAISON CONFERENCE
June 7, 1941

In May and June the Japanese had been moving in two directions: they continued informal discussions in Washington in search of concessions from the United States, and they simultaneously prepared for a push southward to establish Japanese hegemony in the South. Early in June Japan received information that predicted a great change in the international situation. On June 5 General Oshima, the Japanese Ambassador in Berlin, reported on several conversations he had had with Hitler and Ribbentrop. The Nazi leaders had told him that Germany would very likely declare war on the Soviet Union at a time as yet unspecified. They were certain of victory in two or three months, and they proposed to dismember Soviet Russia once her armies were decimated. Oshima asked what effect a war with Russia would have on German plans to invade Britain. The German response was that victory over Russia would facilitate an attack on Britain, and that if things went well a landing on the British Isles might take place in autumn. Hitler told Oshima that by crushing the Soviet Union he would realize his ambition of destroying Communism. The defeat of Russia, Hitler added, would greatly enhance Japan's position in East Asia. Japan, of course, was free to do what she liked; but Germany would welcome Japanese cooperation against Russia if Japan was not quite ready to move southward. Oshima got the impression that Hitler very much wanted Japanese cooperation.[31]

Despite this news, Foreign Minister Matsuoka remained unconvinced that a war would break out between Germany and Russia.

---

[30] According to one source, Col. Iwakuro arranged financing for Ikawa's trip. See *TSM*, VII, 137.

[31] The text of these telegrams is in *TSM, Bekkan*, pp. 423–26.

He asked the Army and Navy Chiefs of Staff how they proposed to respond to such a war if it came. As usual in such cases, they were unable to answer without first consulting with their subordinates.

Agenda: The Recognition of Croatia and Croatia's Joining the Tripartite Pact; The Beginning of a German-Soviet War.

[Army Chief of Staff Sugiyama was absent; Vice Chief Tsukada attended in his place. Foreign Minister Matsuoka proposed the recognition of Croatia and her admission to the Tripartite Pact, and the Supreme Command agreed.[32] In regard to the outbreak of a German-Soviet war, the Foreign Minister gave a briefing on the Foreign Ministry telegrams numbered 636, 638, and 639, which concern the meetings on June 3 and 4 between Ambassador Oshima, Hitler, and Ribbentrop. After the briefing the Foreign Minister gave his impressions as follows:]

Although I do not intend to contradict Oshima, I wonder whether Hitler's intention to wage a war [against Russia] is actually based on his reported intention to smash Communism. I wonder if instead he does not intend to attack [Russia] because the war is going to last for twenty or thirty years.[33] (I think that we should be alert for a possible reconciliation between Britain and Germany.) Since Germany will need a pretext when she declares war on the Soviet Union, she is expected to impose conditions first and then go to war.

[In connection with the above opinion, the Foreign Minister inquired about the attitudes of the Army and Navy Chiefs of Staff. Both replied that careful consideration should be given to this matter, but that they did not regard it as urgent. They left the clarification of their attitudes for another occasion.]

29TH LIAISON CONFERENCE
June 11, 1941

Negotiations with the Netherlands East Indies continued to make little progress, so the Japanese mission was recalled and left for Ja-

[32] Croatia, a part of Yugoslavia, was made an autonomous puppet state by Hitler in April 1941.
[33] My interpretation of this statement is as follows: that in order to be able to withstand a long war against the U.S. and Britain, Hitler would find it necessary to smash Russia so that he would no longer need to worry about the threat from the East.

pan on June 17. Relations were maintained, however, in the hope that talks might be resumed at a later date.

The issue of French Indochina and Thailand was now approaching a critical stage. Japanese pressure in Southeast Asia had been building up since 1940, when Thailand had signed nonaggression pacts with Britain, France, and Japan, and Vichy France had been compelled to allow the Japanese occupation of Haiphong and the establishment of air bases in Tonkin. Early in 1941 Japan had acted as a mediator in a territorial dispute between Thailand and Indochina. Finally, in May 1941, Japan had signed an economic agreement with Indochina.

Now the armed forces wanted to establish air and naval bases in various parts of Indochina and subject the southern part of the country to military occupation. This could hopefully be achieved through diplomatic negotiations; but if the French or Indochinese officials refused to comply, Japan would use force. The general attitude of the military was that if they were strong, the other side would back down. Foreign Minister Matsuoka, on the other hand, had a somewhat inconsistent policy. He often spoke in favor of attacking Singapore, but temporized when it came down to getting footholds in Thailand and Indochina, which the military felt were necessary for large-scale action in Southeast Asia.

When news that a war between Germany and Russia was likely began to come in, the Navy became especially anxious to push south. It feared that the Army General Staff, whose personnel favored an attack on Russia in the event of a German-Soviet war, would commit the country to going northward.

One deterrent to an aggressive policy in Southeast Asia at this time was the probable reaction of the United States and Great Britain. Matsuoka argued that Japanese action in Indochina would provoke the United States. Sugiyama, the Army Chief of Staff, disagreed. Nagano, the Navy Chief of Staff, was particularly forceful, and said that Japan should attack anyone who tried to stop her—apparently including even Britain and the United States. Sugiyama was reportedly made uneasy by Nagano's unusually strong position, and so did not support him.[34] As a result, this Conference ended without a decision.

[34] Tanemura Sako, Dai Hon'ei Kimitsu Nisshi (The Secret Diary of Imperial Headquarters) (Tokyo, 1952), p. 61.

Agenda: Negotiations with the Netherlands East Indies.

[The Chief of the Commerce Bureau of the Foreign Ministry [Mizuno Itaro] was present by special invitation. At the outset he explained the background of the negotiations between Japan and the Netherlands East Indies. The Foreign Minister said that this morning he had received a cable from Yoshizawa saying there was some room for further negotiations, but that he [Yoshizawa] did not have much to say in detail. After discussion, it was decided that the following actions should be taken: (1) Representative Yoshizawa should be instructed to return home; (2) the signing of an agreement should not take place because it would not produce a worthwhile result; (3) we should avoid making it appear that negotiations have been cut off; we should tell them politely than an agreement has not been reached, and leave room for further negotiations; (4) we should let the [Japanese] Consul General [in Batavia] undertake the negotiations if the Netherlands East Indies wish to go ahead with them; (5) if the Netherlands East Indies indicate that they have something to offer, we should let Yoshizawa proceed with the talks to some extent; but we should not expect much from them; (6) when Yoshizawa returns home, the entire mission should also be recalled. We will send the necessary staff again if circumstances call for it.

[The Chief of the South Seas Bureau [Saito Otoji] asked what Japan would do in case the East Indies refused to give us rubber. It was agreed that we could do nothing but watch developments. There was much discussion of whether or not we should sign an agreement. The Foreign Minister at first seemed to favor signing. The military argued against signing on the grounds that the Netherlands East Indies had behaved badly, that the amount they had agreed to export to Japan was insufficient, and that the signing not only would incur the disapproval of the Japanese people but also give Indochina, Thailand, etc., the impression that the Imperial Government had weakened. Eventually, it was decided not to sign. On the other hand, it was deemed undesirable to cause public opinion to flare up. Therefore this problem was left for further study.]

[There was some debate about policy toward French Indochina. The gist was as follows:]

FOREIGN MINISTER MATSUOKA: Judging from developments to date, I would say the Netherlands East Indies have insulted the Imperial Government. Therefore, it seems necessary for Japan to take a stronger attitude in putting an end to the negotiations. In this connection

we must take our national strength into account. In particular, I
would like to know the attitudes of the Army and Navy Chiefs of
Staff.

ARMY CHIEF OF STAFF SUGIYAMA: The views of Army and Navy
Chiefs of Staff on the policy toward the South have already been indicated. If we confronted the Netherlands East Indies alone, no serious problems would arise. But since Britain and the United States
support the Netherlands East Indies, we will have problems if we
take a strong attitude toward the East Indies. Since we are now
faced with problems relating to Germany, the Soviet Union, and the
United States, we should carefully consider whether we ought to
undertake military operations immediately.

For the time being, we had better put an end to the talks and be
satisfied with the amount [of material] that can be obtained at present. It is desirable that we do not give up the matter completely,
but leave room to resume the negotiations later. The Supreme Command expects the Foreign Minister to take steps to carry out our
policies not only toward the Netherlands East Indies but also, in line
with our many appeals, toward French Indochina, so that we can
send troops into Indochina.

MATSUOKA: If we sent in troops, it is apparent that our action
would provoke Britain and the United States, and that British forces
would move into Thailand.

SUGIYAMA: That is not the way I interpret the situation.

MATSUOKA: You ask me to negotiate with French Indochina, but
I think it preferable to make Germany negotiate with the Vichy regime.

SUGIYAMA: We leave the method to the discretion of the Foreign
Minister.

MATSUOKA: If we are to send troops in, we shall have to do so not
only in Indochina but also in Thailand. The deployment of our forces
in Indochina and Thailand would necessarily affect Burma and Malaya, and Britain would inevitably get involved.

SUGIYAMA: If we are strong, I believe the other side will refrain
from action.

MATSUOKA: From the point of view of diplomacy, I would like to
go on a sudden rampage, but I won't because the Supreme Command
tells me not to.

NAVY CHIEF OF STAFF NAGANO: We must build bases in French Indochina and Thailand in order to launch military operations. We must

resolutely attack anyone who tries to stop us. We must resort to force if we have to.

[As is evident from the foregoing, the Foreign Minister did not promise to carry out our policies toward French Indochina and Thailand. He also suggested the inadvisability of using armed force. Thus today's discussion centered on the Netherlands East Indies. It was decided to meet again at 11 o'clock tomorrow, the 12th, to continue our discussion of policy toward French Indochina.]

30TH LIAISON CONFERENCE
June 12, 1941

At this meeting a policy document entitled "Acceleration of the Policy Concerning the South" was presented for formal approval. The goals outlined in the document had been discussed in the previous day's Conference; now the armed forces, especially the Navy, sought to overcome the resistance shown by the Foreign Minister. The main points in the document may be summarized as follows:

1. A military union would be established with French Indochina, and troops would be sent into southern Indochina.

2. Diplomatic negotiations for this purpose would be begun, and at the same time preparations would be made to send in troops. If Indochina refused to accede to Japanese demands, force would be used.

3. If Britain, the United States, and the Netherlands tried to obstruct Japan, and if it was necessary for her survival, she would "not refuse to risk a war with Britain and the United States."

Agenda: "Acceleration of the Policy Concerning the South."

[The Navy Chief of Staff gave a briefing on the "Acceleration of the Policy Concerning the South." In this briefing the Navy Chief of Staff strongly recommended using force in case French Indochina did not agree with us, and also in case Great Britain, the United States, and the Netherlands hindered us. The discussion went as follows:]

FOREIGN MINISTER MATSUOKA: Since the term "sending in troops" has newly come up, I cannot give a definite opinion now. However, my thoughts on Navy Chief of Staff Nagano's briefing are these. Sending in troops should be regarded as a military occupation. What effect would this occupation have on French Indochina? Japan declared that she would respect the integrity of Indochina when she recently acted as a mediator in the conflict between Indochina and Thailand.

I doubt that Indochina will really agree with us, especially on sending in our troops. Even though we do not regard this as a military occupation, Great Britain and the United States, who are hostile to us, will regard it as such. Won't this action hasten a clash with Great Britain? Taking these points into consideration, I think we will have no success in the negotiations if we add the entry of troops to items being negotiated. Therefore, how about negotiating to build bases for the Air Force and the Navy as the first step? I think it will be difficult to reach an agreement if we bring up the sending in of troops from the beginning. Why not talk about that at the second stage?

ARMY CHIEF OF STAFF SUGIYAMA: As has already been explained by the Navy Chief of Staff, we do not intend to establish a military occupation from the beginning. We will do it only if the negotiations are not successful. We need not hesitate to send troops, even if Great Britain and the United States regard the move as a military occupation. To negotiate for bases for the Air Force and the Navy is merely to do what was decided on half a year ago. The situation today is different: there is no need to take moderate measures.

MATSUOKA: What do we seek to achieve by sending in troops?

SUGIYAMA: This action will assure the integrity of French Indochina, and it will also allow us to exert pressure against China and in the Southwest Pacific region.

MATSUOKA: The other party will not agree with us if we say such a thing at the outset.

CHIEF OF THE BUREAU OF MILITARY AFFAIRS MUTO: Air bases cannot be built without military force. Airfields can be constructed quickly if we send in troops.

MATSUOKA: How about limiting the troops to the number necessary for that purpose and negotiating on the other forces later?

SUGIYAMA: We cannot do that. It was difficult to send in forces afterward in the case of northern French Indochina. The entrance of troops this time is not for building airfields.

[Thus views were exchanged. The Foreign Minister said that he wanted to think it over.]

SOMEONE: Do you agree to using military force? Or do you disagree?

MATSUOKA: I do not disagree. But it will be difficult to succeed in the negotiations if we make bringing in troops a key issue. I would like to delete Clause 1 [including the part about sending in troops], although I agree with it in principle. I would also like to delete Clauses 2 and 3, which I would like to change to "understanding" clauses. There is a very serious problem in maintaining secrecy when it comes to sending in troops.

SOMEONE: It is not proper to change them to understanding clauses if you do not disagree. How about the following arrangement? Keep everything secret, adopt the present draft, and add the following three clauses as understanding clauses: (1) We will carry out the present draft in the end. (2) It is permissible to negotiate on matters in two separate stages, since it will take considerable time to prepare for troop movements. (3) When negotiations at the first stage are completed, second-stage negotiations will be started without delay.

[All agreed, and the above understanding clauses were added to the draft. Everyone signed the text. Although one copy was left with the Cabinet, all the rest were collected for the sake of maintaining secrecy.]

MATSUOKA: By what time do you want the negotiations completed?

SUGIYAMA: We would like them completed as soon as possible. We will not set a deadline.

MATSUOKA: Let us consider later the wording of the final draft to be brought to the negotiations.

[Today neither the War Minister nor the Navy Minister said a word. The Navy Chief of Staff spoke sharply for the Navy, while the Navy Minister, who usually talks a great deal, was silent.]

31ST LIAISON CONFERENCE
June 16, 1941

Although "Acceleration of the Policy Concerning the South" was approved on June 12, the continued opposition of Foreign Minister Matsuoka forced a reconsideration of the question of moving into French Indochina. Part of his opposition appears to have stemmed from his concern over the possible reaction of the Emperor to this policy. Legally, the movement of troops outside the country required the formal assent of the Emperor, and Matsuoka might have feared that he would get a scolding when he sought Imperial approval.[35] Matsuoka was also concerned about the effects of the German-Soviet war that would break out soon, according to Oshima in Berlin.

[35] Tanemura, *Dai Hon'ei Kimitsu Nisshi,* pp. 62–63.

Agenda: "Acceleration of the Policy Concerning the South."

[Gist of the remarks by the Foreign Minister:]

I urge that we give further thought to something that would prove to be most injurious to the Empire in the event of our military occupation of French Indochina. Oshima was instructed to ask Germany to persuade Vichy; but Oshima sent a reply asking what the Empire's attitude would be if Vichy should refuse to agree to the Japanese occupation. I have discussed this matter at previous Liaison Conferences, and I thought about it until 3 A.M. last night. My feeling is that the occupation will unavoidably discredit us internationally. We must remember that Japan has been said to lack integrity in international relations. Another reason the occupation needs to be reconsidered is that Russo-German relations are strained at present. I would like to study this matter until such time as I can say, as Foreign Minister, that the occupation is not in bad faith. I urge all of you to think about this, too.

[Nothing was decided at this meeting, and the meeting was adjourned. Gist of the questions and answers:]

MATSUOKA: If we undertake an occupation, the Arsène-Henry–Matsuoka agreement of August 31 of last year would become null and void.[36] Accordingly, stationing troops in northern Indochina would become illegal. When it comes to an occupation—to say nothing of establishing military bases—France will not consent to letting troops come into her territory unless Germany intervenes on our behalf. So far as the French are concerned, since the occupation will be military, it is about 95 per cent certain that they will not agree to it. Because of this, too, the recently signed mediation agreement and the economic collaboration agreement, etc. will also become void. The effects will be felt in the Netherlands East Indies and Thailand. We will probably lose the 20,000 tons of rubber, the 3,000 tons of tin, and all our rice supply from the Netherlands East Indies. I have just described what would be the worst possible development. I don't expect that things will be all that bad, but we must consider all possibilities.

According to Oshima's telegram, war between Germany and Soviet Russia will break out next week. This will mean a world war. Soviet Russia and Britain will become allies. The United States will enter the war on the side of Britain. We must give careful considera-

[36] The agreement, signed in Tokyo, provided for the movement of Japanese troops through French Indochina and Japanese use of airfields there.

tion to these developments. Principally, by occupying [southern Indochina] the Empire is acting in bad faith. Perhaps it might be said that this is essential to the survival of our country, but in any case it is a great act of bad faith.

NAVY MINISTER OIKAWA: What have been our recent attitudes toward French Indochina and Thailand?

ARMY CHIEF OF STAFF SUGIYAMA: There has been no change. They ought to agree to our demands if we can make them understand that the occupation will protect Indochina from American and British oppression.

MATSUOKA: Yes. However, if Vichy does not agree to the occupation, it would be bad faith to force it on her. The previously signed treaty has not yet been ratified. Occupation by force is an act of bad faith. Japan is internationally said to lack integrity. I will fight for our international reputation, even if I have to fight all by myself. How can we say that a forceful occupation is not an occupation? Frankly, as Foreign Minister, I must tell the Emperor that this is an act of bad faith.

How long will it take to prepare for the occupation? How many days do you need to build the military bases? By what time do you need the military bases?

SUGIYAMA: Preparations will take about twenty days. Two to three months are needed for the airfields. The airfields there now are for commercial use, and they have to be paved for the heavy bombers and expanded for large squadrons. We must finish the occupation by the end of July. August, September, and October will be needed for equipping the airfields. For the occupation we must transfer troops from China. Ships must be assembled, too. That area is entering the rainy season soon, so we must act fast.

MATSUOKA: War is going to break out between Germany and Russia. Don't you think we should study this?

SUGIYAMA: Even if there is a war between Germany and Russia, we must go this far.

OIKAWA: An alliance between Britain and Soviet Russia is something I have just heard about for the first time. If this is so, I might reconsider. However, it is not good to alter what was decided the other day.

MATSUOKA: I'm not very intelligent, and when I thought about it later . . .

SOMEONE: Can't you change your mind?

MATSUOKA: No, I can't.

WAR MINISTER TOJO: If we don't finish the job before the end of the year, we will have to abandon our policy of establishing the Greater East Asia Co-prosperity Sphere. After the preparations are completed, what we need is a decision.

MATSUOKA: Is it necessary to report to His Majesty about the preparations?

SUGIYAMA: We can't make preparations when there are no objectives. Of course we can proceed with education and training. But we are restricted in the movement, transfer, mobilization, and organization of troops unless we obtain His Majesty's permission.

[The War Minister supported the foregoing point.]

NAVY CHIEF OF STAFF NAGANO: How about making all preparations and then obtaining His Majesty's approval?

MATSUOKA: The Army cannot do that. At the time of the first Shanghai Incident the divisional commander, Uyeda, had to wait four or five days after he reached Shanghai.[37] I can see that it takes a lot of time for the Army.

[The War Minister elaborated on the foregoing point.]

SUGIYAMA: I would like to see blitzkrieg diplomacy as soon as the army is assembled on Hainan Island. From this point of view, we cannot do as the Navy Chief of Staff has suggested.

MATSUOKA: In either case, let me think about it for two or three days. You say the occupation isn't an act of bad faith, but I think it is. I must clarify this point for His Majesty. So long as I am not clear on this point, I cannot report to His Majesty. All this has happened because you didn't take Singapore last year as I suggested. When are we going to report the matter to His Majesty? I would like to have you give some thought to how we report to His Majesty.

[Thus the meeting was adjourned, so that the matter could be studied for two or three days.]

32D LIAISON CONFERENCE
June 25, 1941

The revised version of "Acceleration of the Policy Concerning the South" was adopted at this Liaison Conference. The major change

[37] The Ninth Division, under General Uyeda Kenkichi, landed in Shanghai on February 15, 1932. Uyeda had been ordered by Tokyo to negotiate with the Chinese authorities and get them to withdraw their troops from the area. The negotiations failed, and the division launched an attack on February 20. See *TSM*, II, 130–32. The issue here appears to be that it might take time to get Imperial sanction.

*was the deletion of the clause asserting that Japan would be willing
to risk a war with Great Britain and the United States. The Cabinet
was then convened to give formal approval to the document. This
sequence clearly shows that the Liaison Conference had become the
prime policy-making body in foreign affairs.*

*On June 22, the expected German-Soviet war had broken out. As
Matsuoka admitted, he had not anticipated this possibility when he
signed the Tripartite Pact; the question now was what position Japan should take in response to this new development. The position
of the Army and Navy in the altered international situation was expressed in a policy document, "Outline of National Policies in View
of the Changing Situation," which was brought before this Liaison
Conference for the first time. In the discussion, the Navy Minister opposed military action against the Soviets, while the Foreign Minister
began to urge a move northward.*

*On June 21 Secretary Hull gave Ambassador Nomura the Ameri-
can reply to the Japanese proposal of May 12, together with an "Oral
Statement" that was to arouse Matsuoka's anger. At the moment, however, the decision makers in Tokyo were absorbed in wrangling over
the proposed military occupation of French Indochina and what to
do about the German-Soviet war; as a result, the American note was
put aside for the time being.*

Agenda: "Acceleration of the Policy Concerning the South" and
"Outline of National Policies in View of the Changing Situation."

[Those present: The two Vice Chiefs of the Supreme Command
were specially invited.[38] First the Army Chief of Staff gave a briefing
on the "Acceleration of the Policy Concerning the South." This was
adopted. Accordingly, starting at 3 P.M. an extraordinary Cabinet
meeting was called. The Prime Minister read from the prepared paper (military matters excluded) and answered questions from the
Cabinet members, and the document was approved. It was decided
that at 4 P.M. the Prime Minister and the two Chiefs of Staff would
report to the Emperor. Gist of the [Conference] deliberations:]

FOREIGN MINISTER MATSUOKA: The Background Document[39] is fine,
but the way it is written tends to imply that nothing has been done

---

[38] Army Vice Chief of Staff Tsukada Ko; Navy Vice Chief of Staff Kondo
Nobutake.
[39] This was a document prepared for the Emperor and signed by the Prime
Minister and the two Chiefs of Staff. It reviewed the reasons for sending troops
into southern Indochina. The text is in *TSM, Bekkan,* pp. 447–48.

previously. It's a matter of wording, but I would like to have it stated that we have been doing something all along. I have been negotiating about military bases and harbors. We asked Germany to put pressure on Vichy to grant us military bases, but Ribbentrop said, in effect, that he could not do so. So I told Oshima that Japan would do it alone.

[It was decided to convene the extraordinary Cabinet meeting at 3 P.M., after the Foreign Minister said: "It would be better to make haste on this matter. Now that a decision has been made, it is better to put it into effect immediately. Convening an extraordinary Cabinet meeting might cause a stir, but it is unavoidable under the circumstances."]

MATSUOKA: In carrying out this policy, I would like to maintain effective liaison with the Supreme Command, and carefully coordinate diplomacy and military affairs. I would like to have liaison with the Supreme Command so that it will be possible to execute blitzkrieg diplomacy once the troops have been assembled.

ARMY CHIEF OF STAFF SUGIYAMA: It will take twenty days, from the time we receive His Majesty's approval, to complete the troop concentration.

MATSUOKA: I understand that.

[The Army Vice Chief of Staff felt that so far as this matter was concerned, the Foreign Minister was eager to go ahead with it. Next the Foreign Minister revealed the content of his conversations with the German, Italian, and Soviet Ambassadors regarding the relationship between the Tripartite Pact and the [Japanese-Soviet] Neutrality Pact. The gist was as follows:]

The Tripartite Pact will not be affected or influenced by the signing of the Neutrality Pact. This interpretation was announced after my return to Japan. Moreover, there has been no response from the Soviet Union. As a matter of fact, I concluded a Neutrality Pact because I thought that Germany and Soviet Russia would not go to war. If I had known that they would go to war, I would have preferred to take a more friendly position toward Germany, and I would not have concluded the Neutrality Pact. I told Ott we would stick to the alliance regardless of the wording in the treaty [Japanese-Soviet Pact], and that when we were about to do something, I would speak to him as the need arose. I spoke to the Soviet Ambassador along the lines I have just discussed.

SOMEONE: What impression do you think the Soviet Ambassador got from your statement?

MATSUOKA: "Japan is calm, but nothing seems to be very clear," was what he said, so I suppose he felt that way.

SOMEONE: I wonder if he didn't think that Japan was being faithful to the Tripartite Pact and unfaithful to the Neutrality Pact?

MATSUOKA: I don't think it had that much of an effect. Of course, I didn't speak to him about breaking the Neutrality Pact.

[On the basis of the Foreign Minister's statement, the Army Vice Chief of Staff judged that the Soviet Ambassador had received the impression that the Neutrality Pact was void.]

MATSUOKA: I have not said anything official to Ott. I would like to have an early decision on our national policy. Ott keeps talking about the movement of the Soviet Far Eastern troops to the West.

WAR MINISTER TOJO: The dispatch of the Far Eastern troops to the West no doubt affects the Germans greatly, but it is natural that Japan should not feel strongly about it. We shouldn't put our complete faith in Germany.

NAVY MINISTER OIKAWA: On behalf of the Navy I want to say something about diplomacy in the future. I'm not questioning the past. Given the delicate international situation at the present time, you shouldn't talk about the distant future without consulting the Supreme Command. The Navy is confident about a war against the United States and Britain, but not confident about a war against the United States, Britain, and the Soviet Union. Suppose the Soviets and the Americans get together, and the United States builds naval bases, air bases, radar stations, etc. on Soviet soil. Suppose the submarines stationed at Vladivostok are transferred to the United States. This would make it very difficult for naval operations. In order to avoid a situation of this kind, don't tell us to strike at Soviet Russia and also tell us to go south. The Navy doesn't want the Soviet Union stirred up.

MATSUOKA: You say you are not afraid of a war with the United States and Britain, so why is it that you do not wish to see the Soviets enter the war?

OIKAWA: If the Soviets come in, it means fighting an additional country, doesn't it? At any rate, don't talk too much about the future.

MATSUOKA: Have I ever talked that way? This is why I say we should hurry up and make a decision on the basic principles of our national policy.

[The above conversation prompted a discussion of the basic principles of our national policy. The Army Chief of Staff orally explained the main points of the Army-Navy draft.[40] The Foreign Minister

---

[40] This was the draft of the "Outline of National Policies in View of the Changing Situation." The final version of this document was adopted by the Imperial Conference of July 2, 1941.

urged an aggressive policy, but the Army and Navy had not yet completed their preparations for war. Their position was that the decision would depend on conditions in China, in the North, and in the South: for example, the outbreak of an incident in the Far East, the dispatch of Soviet Far Eastern troops to the West, and the collapse of the Soviet regime. We must be cautious about going to war against the Soviet Union prematurely; if we do so, the United States will enter the war.]

MATSUOKA: When Germany wins and disposes of the Soviet Union, we can't take the fruits of victory without having done something. We have to either shed blood or engage in diplomacy. It's best to shed blood. The question is what Japan would want when the Soviet Union is disposed of. Germany is probably wondering what Japan is going to do. Aren't we going to war when the enemy forces in Siberia have gone westward? Shouldn't we at least make a diversionary move?

WAR AND NAVY MINISTERS: There are a variety of diversionary moves. The fact that our Empire stands firm is in itself a diversionary move, isn't it? Aren't we going to respond in this way?

MATSUOKA: At any rate, please hurry up and decide what we are going to do.

SOMEONE: Whatever you do, don't do anything prematurely.

[The Foreign Minister was in general agreement with what the Army Chief of Staff had said, but noted that he was not sure about the United States coming in if we attacked the Soviets. It was now time for a Cabinet meeting, so the Conference adjourned with the understanding that it would resume at 10 A.M. the following day.]

33D LIAISON CONFERENCE
June 26, 1941

On the previous day, the decision had been made to seek bases in French Indochina. The problem of what to do about the Soviet Union, now that Germany had attacked her, remained unresolved. Moreover, a consensus was not likely to emerge easily; the Navy opposed a war with Russia, while the Foreign Minister favored it. The Army basically wanted to go northward, but was hesitant because it was bogged down in China. Hence there was a tendency to adopt a wait-and-see policy.

Although Japan was still allied with Germany, the German-Soviet war had reduced the effectiveness of the alliance as a means of end-

ing the war in China and deterring the United States from taking a strong position in the Pacific. Now doubts about it were openly expressed. At this Conference, the Foreign Minister and the Army Vice Chief of Staff debated the question of Japan's obligation to consult Germany before taking military action.

Agenda: "Outline of National Policies in View of the Changing Situation."[41]

[Participants: same as before. The "Outline of National Policies" approved by the Army and Navy was discussed. First, Army Vice Chief of Staff Tsukada read the text, and Army Chief of Staff Sugiyama explained it (it was based on the Background Document).]

FOREIGN MINISTER MATSUOKA: I have no disagreement with Sections 1 and 3 under "Policy." With reference to Section 2, I approve continuing the effort to settle the China Incident, and I approve establishing a "basis for the security and preservation of the nation."[42] But I do not understand the phrase "taking steps to advance to the South" or the word "furthermore" in the phrase "furthermore, a settlement of the Northern Question." Also, I do not understand the phrase "in carrying out the various policies" in Section 3 [should be 4] under "Summary."

ARMY CHIEF OF STAFF SUGIYAMA: What do you want to know? Do you want to know which is more important, the South or the North?

MATSUOKA: That's what I want to know.

SUGIYAMA: There is no difference in importance. We are going to see how the situation develops.

MATSUOKA: Does "taking steps to advance to the South" mean that we will not take action in the South very soon?

[Navy Chief of Staff Nagano was unable to answer and called Vice Chief Kondo. Kondo whispered that the South came first. (Later, he said that this referred to the southern part of French Indochina.)]

MATSUOKA: If that is the case, the Army and Navy differ in their views.

ARMY VICE CHIEF OF STAFF TSUKADA: Well, then, I will state it more clearly. There is no difference in importance between North and

---

[41] For the final text of this document, see the Imperial Conference record of July 2, 1941.

[42] The original text of Section Two reads: "Our Empire will continue its efforts to effect a settlement of the China Incident, and will seek to establish a solid basis for the security and preservation of the nation. This will involve taking steps to advance to the South and, furthermore, a settlement of the Northern Question, depending on changes in the situation."

South. The order and method will depend on the situation. We cannot do both simultaneously. At the present time we cannot decide which it will be, North or South.

MATSUOKA: What is meant by "the rights of a belligerent will be exercised" in Section 1 under "Summary"?

NAVY VICE CHIEF OF STAFF KONDO: It means ordering foreign envoys to evacuate, making bombing attacks, and extending the right of inspection to the high seas.

WAR MINISTER TOJO: There are many things to do: evacuating all foreign nationals, making bombing attacks, etc.

MATSUOKA: I have no objection to this part. The seizure of Foreign Settlements controlled by the enemy will necessitate determination on our part. What does "depending on future developments" mean?

CHIEF OF THE NAVAL AFFAIRS BUREAU OKA: Depending on such things as the commencement of a war against Britain and the United States.

TOJO: There are other things, too.

MATSUOKA: The Nanking Government cannot seize the Foreign Settlements. Japan must undertake the seizure. What is meant by "independently"?[43] Are you going to confer with Germany on military measures?

[The following were mostly questions and answers between the Foreign Minister and the Army Vice Chief of Staff.]

TSUKADA: Matters pertaining to political policies are one thing, but on matters pertaining purely to the Supreme Command we will not consult Germany. But this sort of situation will not arise. If we confer, there will be delays, so we are going to make decisions independently in order to avoid being delayed.

MATSUOKA: Do you mean to say that you will not confer, even though you have an alliance? Participation in the war and resorting to armed force cannot be separated. If you are not going to confer, then a joint committee is unnecessary, isn't it?

TSUKADA: I don't know about political policies, but [on matters pertaining to the Supreme Command] hasn't Germany done what she wanted to do without consulting anyone? There is no need to consult her. We can't confer because we have to transmit the secret military orders of the Supreme Command as swiftly as possible.

TOJO: To date Germany has not consulted us.

---

[43] The document said that Japan would decide "independently" whether or not to go to war with the Soviet Union.

SUGIYAMA: Germany, as a matter of fact, has not consulted us on appropriate occasions.

MATSUOKA: Regardless of whether Germany does or does not consult us, we must do things sincerely. We need to exercise our influence over Germany with our sincerity.

TSUKADA: It is all right to consult Germany on matters of political policy, but military force is a question of defeat or victory. We can confer on matters of high political policy, but not on those pertaining to the Supreme Command.

MATSUOKA: What happens if the situation does not change so as to be extremely advantageous to us?

TSUKADA: We will go ahead if we perceive that conditions are extremely advantageous, and not go ahead if they are disadvantageous. That is why we wrote "extremely advantageous." Moreover, there are various points of view. Even if Germany perceives conditions to be extremely advantageous, if they are not advantageous for us we will not go ahead; even if Germany perceives conditions to be disadvantageous, if they are advantageous for us we will go ahead.

MATSUOKA: What is meant by "great" in "no great obstacles to the maintenance of our basic posture with respect to the South"?[44]

TSUKADA: "Great" refers to major obstacles; there are bound to be minor obstacles. The Supreme Command does not have as much military capability as it would like to have. What is a great obstacle and what is not cannot be determined until the time comes.

MINISTER OF HOME AFFAIRS HIRANUMA: You can enter a war without using military force. Entering a war is entering a war, even though you don't use force. Although the Foreign Minister has said that a state of belligerency—that is, entering a war—and the use of military force cannot be separated, can't you enter a war without the use of force?

MATSUOKA: I agree. You can have a time difference between entering a war and using military force.

TSUKADA: Isn't that why we can separate out the use of military force and take independent action?

[The questions and answers ended with the foregoing. But Nagano, Navy Chief of Staff, spoke in order to give his impressions.]

NAGANO: Even though we say we will act independently, I think that when we are about to go to war, it will be necessary to consult Germany because of the friendship involved in the alliance. Unless

---

[44] This would appear to be in error, and it should read ". . . with respect to war with Great Britain and the United States."

the declaration of war can be tied in with instantaneous military action, I don't think we will make a declaration.

[The Army Vice Chief of Staff took this as an attempt to soften the strong views he, i.e., the Vice Chief, had expressed.]

MATSUOKA: I have some basic reservations about the Army-Navy draft, but in the main I agree with it.

CHIEF OF THE MILITARY AFFAIRS BUREAU MUTO: If that is the case, please put your agreement in writing.

MATSUOKA: I won't put it in writing.

34TH LIAISON CONFERENCE
June 27, 1941

At this Conference the Foreign Minister elaborated on his view of the world situation in an effort to persuade the armed forces to attack the Soviet Union immediately. It is clear that he made several important assumptions. He expected the Germans to defeat both Britain and Russia before the end of the year. He did not expect the Chinese to give in until it was made clear to them that no more support and aid would be forthcoming; hence he wanted to reach an understanding involving Germany, Russia, the United States, and Japan. Finally, he believed that if Japan struck quickly, the United States, confronted by a fait accompli, would not intervene.

Agenda: "Outline of National Policies in View of the Changing Situation."

[Participants: same as before. Devoted to questions directed at the Army-Navy draft by the Government. The Foreign Minister explained the diplomatic plans based on his personal views, and tried to get Imperial Headquarters to reconsider. In the Foreign Minister's judgment, based on diplomatic considerations, Japan should immediately decide to enter the German-Soviet war, attack first the North, then the South, and meanwhile settle the China Incident. Although the Foreign Minister was generally in agreement with the draft by Imperial Headquarters, he differed on the point about making an immediate decision to enter the war. The details of debate are as follows:]

FOREIGN MINISTER MATSUOKA: I have had several reports from Oshima. Their gist is that the Empire's policy would appear to be rather difficult to carry out, but that the German-Soviet war will end in a short time, and the German-British war will end this fall or within this year. We cannot wait too long to find out what the trend will be.

Earlier I devised a plan for [coordinating] diplomacy and military operations, and since then I have given it much careful thought. Although I had calculated the chances of a German-Soviet war breaking out to be 50 per cent, this war has already broken out. In general I am in agreement with yesterday's draft by Imperial Headquarters, but I have some opinions from the diplomatic point of view. I will tell you what I have been thinking.

There was no hope of direct negotiations with Chungking to achieve an overall peace. Therefore, I decided that it would be necessary to surround Chiang on a large scale: I concluded a Neutrality Pact with the Soviet Union, and although I did not ask the Germans for their help, we clasped hands with them; the only one left was the United States. I sent a personal message to the United States, proposing that she keep out of the war in Europe and stop her aid to Chiang. When I saw the American reply after returning to Tokyo, it was not what I had expected. The reason it turned out to be so odd was that other people intervened.[45]

Another reply came from the United States several days ago, but it is indeed a strange one.[46] Of course, things might go well if we give up the China Incident, but that would not be appropriate. In the end matters have gone awry because of the difficulty of pinning down the United States.

War has now broken out between Germany and Soviet Russia. Even though our Empire may wait and observe the trend for a while, eventually we will have to make an important decision and bring the impasse to an end. If we decide that the German-Soviet war will end quickly we cannot say that we will strike neither north nor south. If we judge that the war will end quickly, we should strike north first. If we start talking about the Soviet problem after the Germans have disposed of the Soviets, we won't get anywhere diplomatically. If we attack the Soviets quickly, the United States won't come in. In actual practice the United States cannot help Soviet Russia; for one thing, she does not like the Soviet Union. On the whole, the United States will not enter the war. There might be some mistakes in my judgment; nevertheless, first strike north, and then go south. If we go south, we will have to fight Britain and the United

---

[45] This obviously refers to the earlier efforts of Iwakuro and Ikawa.
[46] This was the note that Secretary Hull gave Nomura on June 21.

States. If we advance into French Indochina we might have to fight Britain and the United States. But because the Supreme Command has briefed me during the past two weeks I fully understand the necessity of going into Indochina.

I am not speaking from desperation. If we go to war against Soviet Russia, I am confident that I can hold down the United States by diplomacy for three or four months. If we wait and see how the trend goes, as proposed in the draft by the Supreme Command, we will be surrounded by Britain, the United States, and Russia. We should first strike north, and then strike south. Nothing ventured, nothing gained. We should take decisive action.

[While the Foreign Minister was speaking, the Navy Chief of Staff remarked: "Although it was stated yesterday that the United States would enter the German-Soviet war, I asked you to use diplomacy to prevent the United States from getting into the war, and to prevent a [Japanese] war with three countries at once." The Foreign Minister replied that he agreed with that.]

WAR MINISTER TOJO: What is the relationship [of this problem] to the China Incident?

MATSUOKA: Until the end of last year I thought in terms of the South first and the North next. I thought that if we struck south, the Chinese situation would be solved; but it didn't work out. We ought to proceed north and go as far as Irkutsk. I think that if we got even halfway there, our action might have an effect on Chiang that would lead to an overall peace.

TOJO: Do you think we should strike north even if we have to give up the China Incident?

MATSUOKA: We ought to strike north, even if we give up to a certain extent in China [this was not forcefully said].

TOJO: The China Incident must be continued and settled.

NAVY MINISTER OIKAWA: A world war would be a ten-year matter. In that period the China Incident would be blown to the winds. It would be easy to strike north during that period.[47]

MATSUOKA: I advocate a moral diplomacy. We cannot abandon the Tripartite Pact. We could have avoided concluding the Neutrality Pact from the very beginning. If we are going to talk about dropping out of the Tripartite Pact, then prepare to face an uncertain future. We must strike while the German war situation is still unclear.

---

[47] Presumably what he meant here was: if there were a long-term war, Japan would be able to conquer China; and sometime during the course of this long war Japan could also attack Russia.

MINISTER OF HOME AFFAIRS HIRANUMA: Mr. Matsuoka, think carefully about the problem before us. Do you propose to attack Soviet Russia immediately, to enter the war against the Soviets immediately as a matter of national policy?

MATSUOKA: Yes.

HIRANUMA: Nowadays we have to do things in a hurry; but we must be well prepared. You talk of using military power, but this requires preparation. We must also prepare in order to carry out national policy. In short, won't we need time to get ready?

MATSUOKA: I would like a decision to strike north first, and would like to communicate this intention to Germany.

ARMY CHIEF OF STAFF SUGIYAMA: A moral and honorable diplomacy is fine, but at present we have a large force stationed in China. It's fine to talk about integrity, but we can't actually afford it. The Supreme Command must get ready; we cannot decide now whether or not we will strike. It will take forty to fifty days to get the Kwantung Army ready.[48] It will take additional time to organize our present forces for war and get them ready to take the offensive. The German-Soviet situation should be clarified by then. If conditions are good, we will fight.

MATSUOKA: I don't like the "extreme" in "extreme advantage."[49] I would like a decision to attack the Soviet Union.

SUGIYAMA: No.

NAVY CHIEF OF STAFF NAGANO: Since this is a fairly important question, the Supreme Command will also think about it.

MATSUOKA: In general I have no objections to the previous Supreme Command draft. But are you going to accept my views or aren't you?

SUGIYAMA: Let's mention diplomacy in this draft.

MATSUOKA: Well, then, we can add at the end, "In keeping with this, diplomatic negotiations will be carried out." You tell me to engage in diplomacy, but I don't think our negotiations with the United States will last much longer.

HIRANUMA: I would like to see it added that the Tripartite Pact will guide us where Germany is concerned.

[48] The Kwantung Army, stationed in Manchuria for the protection of Japanese interests (including the South Manchurian Railroad), virtually ruled the puppet state of Manchukuo. It was a crack army, and would have borne the brunt of the fighting in a Japanese-Soviet war.

[49] "In case the German-Soviet war should develop to the extreme advantage of our Empire, we will, by resorting to armed force, settle the Northern Question and assure the security of the northern borders." At Matsuoka's insistence the word "extreme" was later deleted.

35TH LIAISON CONFERENCE
June 28, 1941

*The Foreign Minister continued to advocate his favorite theme, but
could not persuade the armed forces to make a firm commitment to
attack the Soviet Union.*

Agenda: "Outline of National Policies"; Notification to Germany,
etc.

[Participants: same as before. The Foreign Minister's opinions on
amending the Army-Navy draft were the major topic of discussion.
By and large, there was agreement on the Imperial Headquarters
draft.[50]

[Earlier this morning the Chiefs of the Military and Naval Affairs
Bureaus, the Foreign Minister, and the Vice Foreign Minister met
to negotiate. They drafted a proposal that inserted matters pertaining to diplomacy in the Imperial Headquarters draft. The approved
draft merely added "outline of policies toward French Indochina and
Thailand."

[The Foreign Minister said that he interpreted the phrase "will remove all obstacles," in Section 3 under "Policy," to include removing
by diplomatic measures. Also, prefacing his remarks with the comment that he agreed with Section 3 of the Summary that the attitude
toward the German-Soviet war would be based on the Tripartite
Pact, he stated the following desiderata:]

1. Adequate control over the domestic situation should be exercised.

2. To strike south is like playing with fire; and if we strike south,
we will probably go to war against Britain, the United States, and
Soviet Russia. I would like to have this point amended, but because
of its serious nature I will repeat my observations.

3. Ambassador Oshima has expressed his views on the operations
against French Indochina. Are we going through with them as
planned? Ribbentrop might ask us not to resort to military force, so
I would like to have this matter held in abeyance.

NAVY MINISTER OIKAWA: Are there any signs of a request from Ribbentrop of the kind you mention?

FOREIGN MINISTER MATSUOKA: No.

WAR MINISTER TOJO: We will go ahead in Indochina after we have

---

[50] For the text of the document in its final form, see pp. 78–79.

agreed on the nature of the situation; it will be necessary to exercise the utmost care in this matter.

[The Army Vice Chief of Staff got the impression that military action against Indochina must be undertaken with great care.]

[Next there was discussion concerning a message to be sent to Germany:]

MATSUOKA: Eventually we must communicate our decision to enter the war to Germany. I don't believe that now is the best time to enter the war, given the general situation. It will be all right to inform Germany when the time comes. However, it would not be appropriate to give an answer in response to an inquiry from Germany. I think that even if we don't say anything now, it will be necessary to say something in the future. Hence the Empire must make up its mind today to enter the war.

ARMY CHIEF OF STAFF SUGIYAMA: We cannot at present tell Germany [that we will enter the war]. We will go forward if the situation develops in our favor; it would be awkward if we prematurely said that we would enter the war, and then the situation did not work out in our favor.

NAVY CHIEF OF STAFF NAGANO: I agree with the Army Chief of Staff.

[Prior to this, the Navy Chief of Staff had informed the Army Chief of Staff of the Navy's strong opposition to entering the war on the German side. When the Foreign Minister spoke as above, both Army Chief of Staff Sugiyama and Army Vice Chief of Staff Tsukada remained silent. All three of the Navy people, including the Navy Chief of Staff, also said nothing. After a short silence, the Foreign Minister asked the Army Chief of Staff for his opinion; in response to this, the Chief of Staff replied as indicated above, and the Navy Chief of Staff said that he agreed with him. Although the Navy has expressed the view that it is absolutely opposed to entering the war, it will not say so openly. Thus it is difficult to see exactly what the Navy wants.]

MATSUOKA: When on June 22 I sent a telegram[51] to Germany,

---

[51] In this telegram Matsuoka stated that he had gained the impression from Ambassador Oshima that Hitler and Ribbentrop did not expect Japanese participation against the Soviet Union under the Tripartite Pact. He thought, however, that "in the long run Japan could not remain neutral in the conflict"; in the event of American entry into the war as a result of the Russo-German conflict, he personally felt the alliance would become operative for Japan under the terms of the Tripartite Pact. See State Department, *Documents on German Foreign Policy, 1918–1945,* XIII, 1.

through Ott, stating that our Empire would base its actions on the Tripartite Pact, Ribbentrop sent a reply thanking us. Also, Oshima asked whether we would go forward in French Indochina as planned, and I told him that there had been no changes. When Oshima asked Ribbentrop whether Germany would attack Britain, Ribbentrop said that Germany was waiting for the effects of the submarines, and that she would not conclude a peace unless Britain surrendered unconditionally.

I would be pleased if our operations toward French Indochina were suspended. I would like to see them suspended if the situation changes.

[Thus the "Outline of National Policies" was adopted. It was decided that a Liaison Conference would be convened at 5 P.M. on the 30th to discuss the message to be sent to Germany and the communiqué to be issued by the Imperial Government. It was also decided that on the morning of July 1 the "Outline of National Policies" (excluding the sections on the Supreme Command) would be discussed at a Cabinet meeting; and in the afternoon His Majesty's assent would be obtained at an Imperial Conference. It was decided that at the Imperial Conference the President of the Privy Council, the Minister of Finance, and the Director of the Planning Board would be present. It was decided further that until the decision at the Imperial Conference no word on this matter would be transmitted to our diplomatic representatives abroad.]

36TH LIAISON CONFERENCE
June 30, 1941

Foreign Minister Matsuoka kept trying to persuade his colleagues to reverse the decision to occupy French Indochina, and to attack the Soviet Union instead. He spoke of German pressure to enter the German-Soviet war. But as before, he was unsuccessful; and when Prime Minister Konoye sided with the Supreme Command, Matsuoka was left without support.

It was now necessary to get the formal approval of the Cabinet and of the Supreme War Council. (The War Council consisted of Marshals, Fleet Admirals, the War and Navy Ministers, the Army and Navy Chiefs of Staff, and other generals and admirals appointed by the Emperor. Its chief function was advising the Emperor on the more technical aspects of military and naval affairs.)

Agenda: Draft of the "Outline of National Policies" for Presentation to the Cabinet; Text of the Message to Germany; Draft of Communiqué by the Government; Draft of the Statement by the Foreign Minister to the Imperial Conference, etc.

[The Conference lasted from 5 P.M. to 9 P.M. For this particular meeting, Director of the Planning Board Suzuki, Minister of Finance Kawada [Isao], and Minister of Commerce and Industry Kobayashi Ichizo were also in attendance.

[*Summary:* Although it was planned to discuss only items on the agenda, the Foreign Minister proposed a six-month postponement of the occupation of southern French Indochina called for by "Acceleration of the Policy Concerning the South," which had been adopted by past Liaison Conferences and had obtained Imperial sanction. As a result, considerable time was spent on a discussion of this. In the end, it was decided to occupy French Indochina as planned. The draft of the document for presentation to the Cabinet and the draft of the communiqué by the Government were also approved. But the text of the message to Germany and the draft of the statement by the Foreign Minister were carried over until the next afternoon, when they would be reconsidered. The Imperial Conference was rescheduled for the morning of the 2d, and the meeting was adjourned. Thus the most urgent decision concerning national policy had to be postponed until the next day due to the Foreign Minister's revival of the Indochina occupation issue which had already secured Imperial sanction. Army Vice Chief of Staff Tsukada moved to stay all night to decide the issue; but the Foreign Minister demanded that the meeting be reconvened tomorrow because of his fatigued condition.

[The gist of the debate on the postponement of the occupation of French Indochina was as follows. The Foreign Minister strongly urged that we should not start a fire in the South, but should instead strike north. He made the following points:]

Until today Germany had asked us for no more than cooperation in the German-Soviet war; but today Ott showed me instructions he had received from his Government and asked that we enter the war.[52] Of course, the request to enter the war was appended to his

[52] In a telegram dated June 28, Ribbentrop sent Ott certain arguments to use in trying to persuade Matsuoka to work for a Japanese declaration of war against Russia. Among these points were that Russian military power would be destroyed in a short time; that removal of the Soviets from the Far East would facilitate a solution of the China problem and remove the pressure from the rear if Japan went south later; and that Japanese participation in the defeat of Russia

instructions and was expressed as his personal opinion and wish. In any case, the Empire must decide to enter the war. Why don't we stop building a fire in the South? Why not postpone occupying French Indochina, and instead proceed northward? How about postponing the occupation for six months? However, if the Supreme Command and the Prime Minister are determined to go through with it, I will not object, since I approved it previously.

[In response to this, Navy Minister Oikawa said to Army Chief of Staff Sugiyama, "How about postponing it for about six months?" Also, Navy Vice Chief of Staff Kondo whispered to Army Vice Chief of Staff Tsukada, "Let us think about postponing it for six months." But Army Vice Chief of Staff Tsukada told the Army Chief of Staff that the occupation must be carried out; and after conferring with Army Chief of Staff Sugiyama and Navy Chief of Staff Nagano, Tsukada, representing the Supreme Command, made it clear that the occupation must be carried out. Prime Minister Konoye stated that he would go ahead if the Supreme Command was in a position to do so. The Foreign Minister said that under the circumstances he was for it; but he asked the other Ministers whether they had objections. The various Ministers stated that they had none; and in the end it was decided to go through with the original plan. The following statements were made during the above discussion:]

FOREIGN MINISTER MATSUOKA: I have never made a mistake in predicting what would happen in the next few years. I predict that if we get involved in the South, it will become a serious matter. Can the Army Chief of Staff guarantee that it won't? Furthermore, if we occupy southern Indochina it will become difficult to secure oil, rubber, tin, rice, etc. Great men will change their minds. Previously I advocated going south, but I now favor the North.

CHIEF OF THE BUREAU OF MILITARY AFFAIRS MUTO: It is by occupying southern Indochina that we can acquire rubber and tin.

MINISTER OF HOME AFFAIRS HIRANUMA: I think we should go north. The question is whether we can. Here we must follow the thinking of the military.

NAVY CHIEF OF STAFF NAGANO: So far as the Navy is concerned, if we get involved in the North, it will be necessary to switch all preparations now being made in the South to the North; this will require fifty days.

---

would convince the United States of the senselessness of continuing the war on the British side. See State Department, *Documents on German Foreign Policy, 1918–1945*, XIII, 40–41.

[Regarding the statement to be issued by the Imperial Government, Prime Minister Konoye did not agree with the draft submitted by the Information Bureau.]

KONOYE: If you send out anything as abstract as this, I doubt that the people will be satisfied. I believe this was to be a public statement. Isn't there some better wording that might carry more weight?

ARMY CHIEF OF STAFF SUGIYAMA: How about adding that the Tripartite Pact will be basic, and that the China Incident will be settled?

KONOYE: Why doesn't the Supreme Command simply issue a statement that a decision on national policy has been made?

[Chief Secretary of the Cabinet Tomita made several suggestions. In the end, at the suggestion of the Prime Minister, the following statement was adopted: "Today an Imperial Conference was held, and a decision on important policies involving the Empire was made."

[As for the text of the message to Germany and the draft of the Foreign Minister's statement to the Imperial Conference, the Foreign Minister said he would like to go home and consider them further, since he was tired. Army Vice Chief of Staff Tsukada moved that they discuss it all night, but no discussion was held.

[In the course of the discussion noted above, the Foreign Minister talked about the fundamentals of diplomacy. The Army Chief of Staff and the Army Vice Chief of Staff earnestly told him that this was not the time to be talking about fundamentals, that they must make a decision on national policy that would harmonize high-level diplomacy and high-level military strategy. The Navy Minister, the Navy Chief of Staff, and the Navy Vice Chief of Staff made virtually no comments. The time was pretty much taken up by a debate between the Army Chief of Staff and the Foreign Minister.

[In retrospect, it would appear that there will be considerable difficulty in carrying out the occupation of French Indochina because of the Foreign Minister's hesitation and the idea of postponing the occupation proposed by Navy Minister Oikawa and Navy Vice Chief of Staff Kondo. Also, in view of the atmosphere at today's meeting and the attitude of the Navy toward the text of the message to Germany (the proposal to go either south or north), one can expect a great deal of controversy if a good opportunity to go north presents itself and we follow through. I am worried.]

[The Gist of the Meeting of the Supreme War Council on June 30 to Consider "Outline of National Policies in View of the Changing Situation." The Army Chief of Staff described the steps that had led to the adoption of "Outline of National Policies in View of the Changing Situation," and explained the main points of the document. A summary of the questions posed by the Supreme War Councillors and the answers to them follows:]

PRINCE HIGASHIKUNI:[53] What about plans to solve the Northern Question?

PRIME MINISTER KONOYE AND ARMY CHIEF OF STAFF SUGIYAMA: In concrete terms, it will be necessary to make a decision after further study of the strategic situation, both political and military. We have already studied this problem from the viewpoint of military strategy; but it will be necessary to decide on plans for the North only after we consider the demands of political strategy and assess the state of our preparations and the world situation.

PRINCE ASAKA:[54] It looks like we are sitting on the fence; which is first, North or South? I think it would be better to go north first.

[Army Chief of Staff Sugiyama replied as it is stated in the document.][55]

WAR MINISTER TOJO: Anybody can easily make a decision in the abstract. The difficulty comes from doing this while we are still engaged in the China Incident; if it weren't for the China Incident, it would be easy.

HIGASHIKUNI: What is the purpose of going south? What will we do if Britain, the United States, and the Soviet Union attack us?

SUGIYAMA: There are several possible timetables and methods for moving south; but for the purpose of survival and self-defense, we are thinking of going as far as the Netherlands East Indies. Territory is not our objective. We are going forward in such a way that the worst possible eventuality—i.e., Britain, the United States, and the Soviet Union attacking us simultaneously—will not happen. However, we cannot stop if we are confronted by Britain and the United States alone.

KONOYE: From what the Navy tells me, we are not going all the way in one stroke. For now we will go as far as French Indochina. After that we will proceed step by step.

[This was followed by an informal discussion.]

[53] Prince Higashikuni Naruhiko, a Supreme War Councillor and a relative of the Emperor.

[54] Prince Asaka Yasuhiko, also a Supreme War Councillor and head of an Imperial Princely house.

[55] Presumably he stated that Japan would go south first; but that, depending on changes in the situation, she might conceivably attack Russia also.

ASAKA: Aren't we being too careful, compared with the way Germany does things?

KONOYE: That's true, but this is a matter of grave concern to our national fate; and unlike hypothetical situations, it cannot be treated lightly.

GENERAL TERAUCHI:[56] As for exercising the rights of a belligerent, we must persuade the Navy to seize foreign vessels.

37TH LIAISON CONFERENCE
July 1, 1941

Japan had to make some answer to German pressure to enter the war against the Soviet Union. The Japanese reply, drafted by Foreign Minister Matsuoka, was discussed at this meeting. In essence, Matsuoka's reply stated that Japan was making preparations, was watching conditions in Eastern Siberia, and had in mind restraining Russia in the Far East. At the same time, it added that Japan found it absolutely necessary to secure bases in French Indochina in order to increase her pressure on Great Britain and the United States. By her actions in Southeast Asia, Matsuoka argued, Japan was restraining Britain and the United States, and this restraint was a contribution to the common cause "no less vital than Japan's intervention at this time in the German-Soviet war."[57]

The Conference indicated, as Matsuoka had suggested in his telegram to Ribbentrop, that the Japanese Army was indeed getting ready for action in Manchuria. In this connection, Minister of Commerce and Industry Kobayashi questioned Japan's ability to fight on two fronts simultaneously. Toward the end of the Conference, Army Vice Chief of Staff Tsukada and Matsuoka, who had been feuding, made their peace—at least on the surface.

Agenda: Text of the Message to Germany; Draft of the Foreign Minister's Statement.

[Participants: same as before. The text of the message to Germany, which was drafted by the Foreign Minister as indicated in the attached document, was studied and adopted as presented. In con-

---

[56] Terauchi Hisaichi, a Supreme War Councillor and formerly War Minister.

[57] The Japanese text of this statement is in *TSM, Bekkan*, pp. 462–63; an English translation of it appears in State Department, *Documents on German Foreign Policy, 1918–1945*, XIII, 75–76.

nection with the above, the following discussion took place between Army Vice Chief of Staff Tsukada and the Foreign Minister:]

TSUKADA: The message by the Foreign Minister should not refer to matters pertaining to the Supreme Command.

MATSUOKA: Since I am Chairman of the Joint Committee, I can refer to Supreme Command matters.[58]

TSUKADA: Even though you are Chairman of the Joint Committee, you cannot refer to Supreme Command matters because these are supposed to be negotiated by the military.

[The following discussion also ensued:]

MINISTER OF FINANCE KAWADA: Is the Army making war preparations?

SUGIYAMA: Yes, we are. First, we are putting our troops in Manchuria on a war footing.[59] Next we will prepare them for offensive action. We must exercise great care while doing this, so that they do not get out of hand.

TSUKADA: We are making preparations, all right, but our intention is to get the minimum number of troops ready for action. We have no idea of preparing an unnecessarily large number of troops.

KAWADA: What about the Navy?

NAVY VICE CHIEF OF STAFF KONDO: We must be prepared to lose 100 submarines.

WAR MINISTER TOJO: It will be necessary to put the units in Manchuria on a war footing. We must give careful thought to doing this secretly.

MINISTER OF COMMERCE AND INDUSTRY KOBAYASHI: I will say a word about resources. I do not think we have sufficient strength, so far as resources are concerned, to support a war. Both the Army and Navy can resort to force, but we do not have materials for war on both land and sea. The Army will probably mobilize quickly; the Navy will probably make preparations, too. Ships will be requisitioned, so we will not be able to transport materials. All this will greatly affect the expansion of our productive capacity and the replenishment of armaments. I think that we should consider ways to make sure we will not be defeated by Britain, the United States, and Soviet Russia. Do we go south or do we go north? I would like to have this studied carefully. The Empire does not have materials. What we should do at this point is consider how to make sure we

---

[58] I have not been able to identify this committee.

[59] In preparation for a possible war with the Soviet Union the number of Japanese troops stationed in Manchuria was increased from 400,000 to 700,000, and a vast quantity of war matériel was concentrated in that region.

will not be defeated and decide how to settle the China Incident.

[Director of the Planning Board Suzuki discussed the acquisition of vital materials from outside the area of self-sufficiency;[60] he asked the Supreme Command to study the matter also.]

TSUKADA: The Foreign Minister's drafts of the message to Germany and his statement to the Imperial Conference are well done, aren't they? If he had presented them earlier, I think things would not have been so prolonged.

MATSUOKA: It turned out well because I listened to the opinions of all of you.

IMPERIAL CONFERENCE
July 2, 1941

It was now time to give formal approval to the far-reaching policy decisions that had been hammered out in Liaison Conferences late in June. The usual group, augmented by President of the Privy Council Hara Yoshimichi and several others, assembled in the presence of the Emperor to discuss and approve the document on the agenda: "Outline of National Policies in View of the Changing Situation."

As a result of this Conference, the Army and Navy were given the green light to acquire bases in southern French Indochina and to take over the Foreign Settlements in China, enclaves of Western power, at an appropriate time. Foreign Minister Matsuoka and others who favored an immediate declaration of war on the Soviet Union were told to wait; but their feelings were assuaged by the knowledge that they had permission to get ready for military action in the meantime, and that depending on changes in the international situation, war against Russia would be reconsidered at a later date. (It is interesting that Hara strongly urged that Japan take this opportunity to attack the Soviets.) Finally, those who were more cautious about the use of force were somewhat reassured by repeated statements that every effort would be made to attain the objectives by diplomatic means rather than by military action.

The possibility of war with the United States and Britain was openly acknowledged. The participants agreed that Japan would go forward as planned in Southeast Asia, even if this ultimately led to war with the United States. The immediate problem was to assess the probability of the United States taking counteraction when Japa-

---

[60] This appears to refer to areas under direct Japanese control—Korea, Formosa, Manchuria, various Pacific islands, and parts of China.

nese troops moved into southern Indochina. Hara said he thought that "a war with Great Britain and the United States will occur if we take action against Indochina." Matsuoka agreed that this was a possibility. The Army Chief of Staff, however, took the position that the United States would not act because Germany was enjoying success in her war with the Soviet Union: Germany and Japan together could deter the United States from going to war.

Agenda: "Outline of National Policies in View of the Changing Situation." [This document follows:]

Policy

1. Our Empire is determined to follow a policy that will result in the establishment of the Greater East Asia Co-prosperity Sphere and will thereby contribute to world peace, no matter what changes may occur in the world situation.

2. Our Empire will continue its efforts to effect a settlement of the China Incident, and will seek to establish a solid basis for the security and preservation of the nation. This will involve taking steps to advance south, and, depending on changes in the situation, will involve a settlement of the Northern Question as well.

3. Our Empire is determined to remove all obstacles in order to achieve the above-mentioned objectives.

Summary

1. Pressure applied from the southern regions will be increased in order to force the capitulation of the Chiang regime. At the appropriate time, depending on future developments, the rights of a belligerent will be exercised against the Chungking regime, and hostile Foreign Settlements will be taken over.

2. In order to guarantee the security and preservation of the nation, our Empire will continue all necessary diplomatic negotiations with reference to the southern regions, and will also take such other measures as may be necessary.

In order to achieve the above objectives, preparations for war with Great Britain and the United States will be made. First of all, on the basis of "Outline of Policies Toward French Indochina and Thailand" and "Acceleration of the Policy Concerning the South," various measures relating to French Indochina and Thailand will be taken, with the purpose of strengthening our advance into the southern regions. In carrying out the plans outlined above, our Empire will not be deterred by the possibility of being involved in a war with Great Britain and the United States.

3. Our attitude with reference to the German-Soviet war will be based on the spirit of the Tripartite Pact. However, we will not enter the conflict for the time being. We will secretly strengthen our military preparedness vis-à-vis the Soviet Union, and we will deal with this matter independently. In the meantime, we will conduct diplomatic negotiations with great care. If the German-Soviet war should develop to the advantage of our Empire, we will, by resorting to armed force, settle the Northern Question and assure the security of the northern borders.

4. In carrying out the various policies mentioned above [in Section 3], and especially in deciding on the use of armed force, we will make certain that there will be no great obstacles to the maintenance of our basic posture with respect to war with Great Britain and the United States.

5. In accordance with established policy, we will strive to the utmost, by diplomatic and other means, to prevent the entry of the United States into the European war. But if the United States should enter the war, our Empire will act in accordance with the Tripartite Pact. However, we will decide independently as to the time and method of resorting to force.

6. We will immediately turn our attention to putting the nation on a war footing. In particular, the defense of the homeland will be strengthened.

7. Concrete plans covering this program will be drawn up separately.

[Participants: Army Chief of Staff Sugiyama, Army Vice Chief of Staff Tsukada, Navy Chief of Staff Nagano, Navy Vice Chief of Staff Kondo, Prime Minister Konoye, President of the Privy Council Hara, Home Minister Hiranuma, War Minister Tojo, Navy Minister Oikawa, Finance Minister Kawada, State Minister (concurrently Director of the Planning Board) Suzuki, Secretary of the Cabinet Tomita, and Chief of the Naval Affairs Bureau of the Navy Ministry Oka. Chief of the Military Affairs Bureau of the War Ministry Muto was absent owing to illness.]

Statement by Prime Minister Konoye:

I would like to explain the main points of today's agenda.

I believe that it is most urgent for our Empire to decide quickly what policies it should adopt in view of the present world situation —especially the outbreak of war between Germany and the Soviet Union and its subsequent development, the trends in the United States, the developments in the European war situation, and the settlement of the China Incident. Accordingly, the Government and the Army and Navy sections of Imperial Headquarters have deliberated at length; and as a result, the "Outline of National Policies in View of the Changing Situation," which is on the agenda today, was drawn up.

First of all, I will discuss the Policy Section. As has been repeatedly made clear in Imperial Rescripts, the basis of our national policy is to establish the Greater East Asia Co-prosperity Sphere, and thereby to contribute to the achievement of world peace. I believe, furthermore, that this national policy should not be altered in the least by changes and developments in the world situation.

It goes without saying that in order to establish the Greater East Asia Co-prosperity Sphere, it will be necessary to expedite the settlement of the China Incident, which is still pending. Moreover, I also believe that to lay the basis for the security and preservation of the nation we must proceed south, on the one hand; and, on the other, to get rid of our difficulties in the North we must settle the Northern Problem at an appropriate time, taking advantage of the world situation and especially of developments in the German-Soviet war. This [the Northern Problem] is of utmost importance, not only for the defense of our Empire but also for stability in all of Asia.

It is to be expected that in trying to achieve these objectives our Empire will encounter interference and obstruction from various quarters. But since our Empire absolutely must achieve these objectives, we are making clear our firm determination to remove all obstacles.

Next I will speak about the full-scale strengthening of our domestic wartime structure. In order to carry out the policies mentioned in the Summary it is vital that we quickly strengthen our domestic wartime structure as much as possible, and especially vital that we do our utmost to strengthen the defense of our homeland. The Government expects to remove all obstacles resolutely and put this policy into effect immediately.

The Army Chief of Staff and the Navy Chief of Staff will speak on matters pertaining to the disposition of the armed forces and to [military and naval] operations, while the Foreign Minister will speak on diplomatic matters.

With this I conclude my remarks.

Statement by Army Chief of Staff Sugiyama:
Let me explain the principal items.

On the settlement of the China Incident: Under present circumstances, I believe that in order to hasten the settlement of the Incident it will be absolutely necessary for our Empire to increase its direct pressure on the Chungking regime, and at the same time move southward and sever the links between the Chungking regime and the British and American powers, which support it from behind and strengthen its will to resist. The movement of our troops into southern French Indochina at this time is based on these considerations.

Moreover, I believe that in order to expedite the surrender of the Chungking regime it would be effective and appropriate for us to exercise the rights of a belligerent and take over the hostile Foreign Settlements in China at the appropriate time, which will be determined by an overall analysis of possible developments: for instance, the declaration of war against Germany by the United States, the imposition of an embargo against Japan by the United States, Great Britain, and the Netherlands, and the acquisition of a foothold in southern French Indochina by our Empire.

On the solution of the Northern Question: It goes without saying that we should act in accordance with the spirit of the Tripartite Pact with reference to the German-Soviet war; but it seems appropriate for us not to participate in that war for the time being, since we are presently acting to settle the China Incident, and since our relations with Great Britain and the United States are in a delicate state. Nevertheless, if the development of the German-Soviet war should turn out to be favorable to our Empire, I believe that we will have to decide on using force to settle the Northern Problem and assure the security of our northern borders. Therefore, it is vitally important for us to make in secret the necessary preparations for military operations, and to be in a position to act independently.

I further believe that in carrying out various measures for the solution of the Northern Problem, especially in using force, it is vital that we maintain, whatever the obstacles, our basic position of always being prepared for war with Great Britain and the United States, since the attitude of these countries toward Japan cannot be viewed with optimism.

Statement by Navy Chief of Staff Nagano:
Let me explain the principal items.

On the solution of the Southern Question: I believe that under present circumstances our Empire, in order to secure our defenses in the South and attain a position of self-sufficiency within the Greater East Asia Co-prosperity Sphere, must take immediate steps to push steadily southward by coordinating political and military action with reference to key areas in the South, in accordance with developments in the situation.

However, Great Britain, the United States, and the Netherlands are currently stepping up their pressure against Japan. If they obstinately continue to obstruct us, and if our Empire finds itself unable to cope with this, we may, it must be anticipated, finally have to go to war with Great Britain and the United States. So we must get ready, resolved that we will not be deterred by that possibility. As the first step, it will be necessary for us to carry out our policy with respect to French Indochina and Thailand in accordance with "Outline of Policies Toward French Indochina and Thailand" and "Acceleration of Policy Concerning the South," and thereby increase our ability to move southward.

On the attitude of our Empire regarding American participation in the war: It goes without saying that if the United States should enter the war in Europe, our Empire will act in accordance with the Tripartite Pact. This action should not be limited to fulfilling our obligations to assist Germany and Italy. I believe that we should also endeavor to carry out our policy to establish the Greater East Asia Co-prosperity Sphere, even if this ultimately involves the use of force.

However, it cannot be predicted when and under what circumstances the United States may enter the war in Europe. Therefore, I believe it will be necessary for us to decide independently when and in what manner we should use armed force against Great Britain and the United States, taking into consideration the situation at the time.

Statement by Foreign Minister Matsuoka:

Let me discuss matters relating to diplomacy.

It has been established, and remains unchanged, that our basic national policy consists of establishing the Greater East Asia Co-prosperity Sphere with the view of achieving permanent world peace. We have conducted our diplomacy in keeping with this national policy, taking into consideration such matters as the China Problem, relations with the United States, developments in the European situation, and the Southern Problem. However, a new situation has arisen with the outbreak of war between Germany and the Soviet Union. Hence I believe that it is vitally important in conducting our diplomacy to reaffirm our position regarding current national policy.

As the Army and Navy Chiefs of Staff have just stated, it is necessary in conducting our diplomacy to decide beforehand what circumstances will call for the use of force. Nevertheless, it is obvious that even though we may ultimately be compelled to resort to force, we must do our utmost until then to achieve our aims through diplomatic means. For example, in settling the China Incident we will, on the one hand, do our utmost to strengthen the National Government in Nanking; and on the other hand, we will endeavor, by various diplomatic measures directed at the Chungking regime on both domestic and foreign fronts, to force Chungking to capitulate, get her to merge with or form a coalition with the National Government, or persuade her to enter into peace negotiations. These measures will help us to carry out our policies toward French Indochina and Thailand and to satisfy our demands in the South in accordance with the "Outline of Policies toward French Indochina and Thailand" and "Acceleration of the Policy Concerning the South." Moreover, it goes without saying that our diplomatic policies in connection with the war between Germany and the Soviet Union should be based on the goals and spirit of the Tripartite Pact. However, it will be necessary for us to give full consideration in our diplomacy to the overall picture, embracing the entire area of Greater East Asia.

I further believe that it is important for us to be prepared to conduct our foreign policy vis-à-vis the Soviet Union in such a way that it conforms to the realities as seen by the Supreme Command and others. Furthermore, in our relations with the United States we must maintain a very cautious diplomatic attitude in order to prevent America from entering the European war, and to prevent her from clashing with our country.

Since it is difficult in our time to predict what will happen in international relations, we cannot exclude the possibility of totally unexpected developments in the international situation. Under the present circumstances, there is no alternative but to adhere firmly to the policy set forth in the Summary and to conduct our diplomacy with great care and caution. Even from the point of view of diplomacy, I believe that our Empire is confronted with a literally unprecedented danger; our people must see this clearly and deal with it in a truly determined and united manner.

[Proceedings:]

KONOYE: With your permission we will proceed with the meeting.

PRESIDENT OF THE PRIVY COUNCIL HARA: I have no questions or objections regarding the Policy portion of today's agenda as explained by the Prime Minister. I am going to raise some questions regarding the Summary.

First, in taking over hostile Foreign Settlements will we resort to force if necessary? Won't this raise problems with Great Britain and the United States? We have to be concerned with this matter, since we are going to adopt a strong policy toward French Indochina at the same time. I would like to know when and how the takeover will be made. Things would be different if it were to be done after we had begun a war with Great Britain and the United States. Otherwise, shouldn't we rely on peaceful diplomatic means? What is meant by "at the appropriate time"? I would like to know the relationship between the takeover of the Foreign Settlements and the war against Great Britain and the United States.

MATSUOKA: The words "depending on future developments" cover the entire sentence to the end. This problem is very important, and should be treated carefully. We hope to control the Foreign Settlements as a possible step in the settlement of the China Incident. Although we will have to resort to force if necessary, we will certainly try diplomatic means first. We want to avoid, if possible, the takeover of the Foreign Settlements by Japanese forces. We would rather have the National Government in Nanking take them over. We will consider a takeover by Japanese troops only as a temporary measure when no other solution is available. I believe the takeover of the Foreign Settlements will provoke Great Britain and the United States more than our action in French Indochina.

WAR MINISTER TOJO: We shall proceed carefully, as the Foreign Minister states. As you know, the Foreign Settlements stand in the way of settling the Incident. Foreign Settlements are found in Tientsin, Shanghai, and other places, and they all stand in the way. The Imperial Army has suffered heavily because of the need to stay out of the Foreign Settlements. During the four years of the China Incident the situation has changed, but I think that both diplomatic negotiations and military operations are needed to solve the problem. However, the matter should be handled carefully. I would especially call your attention to the fact that the Foreign Settlements constitute a serious obstacle to the settlement of the Incident.

SUGIYAMA: The Foreign Settlements in China obstruct our military operations, and we have suffered great losses during these four years. In order to settle the Incident quickly, we must act decisively and take over the Foreign Settlements in such cases, as I explained earlier. We might well deal with this problem when the United States has entered the war, or when Great Britain, the United States, and the Netherlands have imposed an embargo, or when the dispatch of our troops to southern Indochina, which is scheduled to be carried out soon, has been accomplished without greatly provoking Great Britain and the United States.

HARA: I asked the question because I wondered whether the words "will not be deterred by the possibility of being involved in a war with Great Britain and the United States" in Section 2 meant that we are prepared to go to war with Great Britain and the United States when we deal with the Foreign Settlements mentioned in Section 1. I think that we should deal with this problem after we have considered the possibility of a war against Great Britain and the United States, as the Army Chief of Staff has explained.

Another question: does the phrase "all necessary diplomatic negotiations" in Section 2 of the Summary refer to negotiations with the Netherlands East Indies?

MATSUOKA: It refers chiefly to French Indochina. It may also apply to Thailand and the Netherlands East Indies.

HARA: Since you state that French Indochina is included, I would like to ask about "Acceleration of the Policy Concerning the South." Section 3 [of that document] says that we might resort to force. I believe that this matter should be considered in connection with the settlement of the Incident. Is our policy [in Indochina] to be carried out chiefly by diplomatic means or by military action?

MATSUOKA: The chances are that diplomatic measures will not be successful.

We have asked Germany for her good offices, but we have received no answer yet. The reply is expected by about tomorrow. Germany seems to think that she would not be successful if she approached the Vichy regime. We have told Germany that we would not ask for her good offices if she were not certain of success in approaching the Vichy regime; but we have yet to receive her reply. We hope for Germany's good offices; otherwise it does not seem likely that diplomatic negotiations will succeed.

Therefore, we must tackle this problem determined to resort to military action. However, we will try until the last minute to solve it by diplomatic means. These may or may not prove to be successful. However, we managed to deal successfully with northern French Indochina last year, although the chances were only one in ten that diplomacy would be successful. This time I do not think that the situation is as favorable as it was last year, so I do not know whether or not we will succeed. We will try our best, since the Supreme Command prefers to avoid military action.

HARA: I agree that it will be difficult if we rely only on diplomatic negotiations. But military action is a serious matter. I regard a war against Great Britain and the United States, which is mentioned in Section 2 of the Summary, as a very serious matter.

The Foreign Minister has referred to Hakko Ichiu and he has frequently advocated the Imperial Way in diplomacy.[61] I do not think that the scheduled movement of our military forces into French Indochina is consistent with the circumstances: we assured Indochina last year that we would respect her territorial integrity, and we are just about to ratify the treaty between Japan and France. What does the Foreign Minister think about this? The situation would be different if Great Britain and the United States had used armed force against Indochina. Otherwise, isn't sending our troops inconsistent with the Imperial Way in diplomacy? The Foreign Minister says that he wishes to avoid military action. I think it is all right to persuade Indochina with armed force in the background; but I do not think it wise for Japan to resort to direct and unilateral military action and be called an aggressor. I offer my opinion to all of you, and will conclude this question.

Next, I believe all of you would agree that the war between Germany and the Soviet Union really represents the chance of a lifetime for Japan. Since the Soviet Union is promoting Communism all over the world, we will have to attack her sooner or later. Since we are now engaged in the China Incident, I feel that we cannot attack the Soviet Union as easily as we would wish. Nevertheless, I believe that we should attack the Soviet Union when it seems opportune to do so. Our Empire wants to avoid going to war with Great Britain and the United States while we are engaged in a war with the Soviet Union. The people are eager for a war against her. I want to see the Soviet Union attacked on this occasion. I ask you to try to give Germany whatever advantage we can in accordance with the spirit of the Tripartite Pact. Has Germany sent us any messages asking us to attack the Soviet Union?

MATSUOKA: I have carefully listened to your advice and opinion. The Imperial ratification of the agreement between Japan and French Indochina, which is now being acted on, is an important matter, and we must proceed with caution so that we will not be discredited. I will see to it that we will not appear to be engaging in an act of betrayal in the eyes of the world. As for cooperation with Germany in the German-Soviet war, Ribbentrop asked for our cooperation on

---

[61] Like most political slogans, "Imperial Way" does not have a precise meaning. In this particular context Hara appears to be referring to the Confucian concept of government by moral example. That is, when the Emperor possesses virtue and rules in a benevolent fashion, his subjects will consent to his rule freely, and therefore there will be little need for the use of force. Hara seems to be suggesting that the Asian peoples ought to be willing to accept the authority of the Japanese Emperor, and thus Japan should not have to use force.

the 26th, and he cabled us again on the 28th. At the time we were considering "Acceleration of Policy Concerning the South"; we were expecting a war between Germany and the Soviet Union. Consequently we do not want to give Germany the impression at this point that we are shirking our responsibility.

HARA: Has the Soviet Union indicated her wishes?

MATSUOKA: Four days after the outbreak of war between Germany and the Soviet Union, the Soviets asked us to clarify our attitude toward the Neutrality Pact between Japan and the Soviet Union. We replied that the war had nothing to do with the Tripartite Pact, and since then the Soviet Union has lodged no protest. She also asked what attitude Japan would take toward the present war, and we replied that we had not yet reached a decision.

A few more comments on this matter: Even if our Empire does not take part in the war between Germany and the Soviet Union, it will not be an act of betrayal according to the letter of the Tripartite Pact. In view of the spirit that led to the alliance, however, I think it would be proper for us to take part in the war.

HARA: Some people say that it would be improper for Japan to attack the Soviet Union in view of the Neutrality Pact; but the Soviet Union is notorious for her habitual acts of betrayal. If we were to attack the Soviet Union, no one would regard it as treachery. I am eagerly waiting for the opportunity to attack the Soviet Union.

I want to avoid war with the United States. I do not think that the United States would take any action if we were to attack the Soviet Union.

I have one more question. It is said that in carrying out our policy toward French Indochina, we are prepared to go to war, if necessary, with Great Britain and the United States. But the impending establishment of bases in Indochina is said to be preparation for a war with Great Britain and the United States. Haven't we already prepared for a war with them? I think that such a war will occur if we take action against Indochina. What is your opinion on this matter?

MATSUOKA: It is difficult to answer your question. The trouble is that the officers in the front lines are aggressive, convinced that we will use force. A war against Great Britain and the United States is unlikely to occur if we proceed with great caution. Of course, I have sanctioned the aggressive behavior of the officers, trusting in the wisdom of the Supreme Command.

Because of the war between Germany and the Soviet Union, Germany's invasion of Great Britain will be postponed. Great Britain and the United States, therefore, might think that Germany will not attempt an invasion of the British Isles; but I think it is probable that Germany will do so while she is still engaged in war with the Soviet Union. Even Ribbentrop did not know that war between Germany and the Soviet Union was imminent. It is Hitler alone who will decide whether or not to carry out an invasion of Great Britain during the German-Soviet war. If Germany invades Great Britain, the United States might be too astounded to take part in the war; or, on the other hand, she might take positive action against Japan from the north. I can envisage the latter possibility in view of the American national character, so it is very difficult to make a judgment.

HARA: What I want made clear is whether the United States would go to war if Japan took action against Indochina.

MATSUOKA: I cannot exclude the possibility.

SUGIYAMA: Our occupation of Indochina will certainly provoke Great Britain and the United States. After our successful mediation of the dispute in Indochina earlier this year, our influence has become quite strong there and in Thailand. At present, however, the intrigues of Great Britain and the United States in Thailand and Indochina have increased steadily, and we cannot tell what will happen in the future. At this juncture, Japan must resolutely carry out the policy she now has in mind: this policy is absolutely necessary in order to stamp out the intrigues of Great Britain and the United States.

Future developments in the German-Soviet war will have a considerable effect on the United States. If the Soviet Union is defeated quickly, the Stalin regime is likely to collapse, and the United States will probably not enter the war. If something goes wrong with German calculations, the war will be prolonged, and the probability of American entry into the war will be increased. Since the war situation is favorable to Germany, I do not believe that the United States will go to war if Japan moves into French Indochina. Of course, we wish to do this peacefully. We also wish to take action in Thailand; but that might have serious consequences, since Thailand is near Malaya. This time we will go only as far as Indochina. We will be careful in sending our troops into Indochina, since this will greatly influence our future policy with regard to the South.

HARA: I understand. I agree with you fully. I think that the Government and the Supreme Command are in agreement on this point: that is, we will try our best to avoid a clash with Great Britain and the United States. I believe that Japan should avoid taking belligerent action against the United States, at least on this occasion. Also, I would ask the Government and the Supreme Command to attack the Soviet Union as soon as possible. The Soviet Union must be destroyed, so I hope that you will make preparations to hasten the commencement of hostilities. I cannot help but hope that this policy will be put into effect as soon as it is decided.

For the reasons I have already given, I am in complete agreement with the proposal put before us today.

TOJO: I am of the same opinion as Mr. Hara, President of the Privy Council. However, our Empire is now engaged in the China Incident, and I hope that the President of the Privy Council understands this.

Foreign Minister Matsuoka just now expressed his opinion on the matter of the young officers. As a person responsible for supervising soldiers and military personnel, I wish to say a few words on the remarks made by the Foreign Minister in the presence of the Emperor.

Foreign Minister Matsuoka implied that some members of the Army in the front lines are intemperate; but I wish to say that the Army acts on orders issued by the Emperor. What the Foreign Minister implied has never happened. We took severe [disciplinary] measures when we sent troops to French Indochina. Coordination between military and diplomatic action is very difficult. I will try to avoid problems in this respect by cooperating with the Supreme Command.

SUGIYAMA: I completely agree with the War Minister. We will exercise strict supervision to prevent misconduct, so set your mind at ease. I will take this opportunity to describe the situation with respect to the Kwantung Army. Of the Soviet Union's thirty divisions, four divisions have already been sent to the West; but the Soviet Union still maintains an absolutely overpowering force, ready for strategic deployment. The Kwantung Army, on the other hand, is in the condition I have already described.[62] I want to reinforce the Kwantung Army, so that it can defend itself, can provide backing for diplomatic negotiations, can be prepared for offense, and can take the offensive when the opportunity comes. I think that the outcome of the war between Germany and the Soviet Union will become clear in fifty or sixty days. Until then we will have to mark time in the

---

[62] Here, as elsewhere, the transcriber of this record skips over matters that would presumably be well known to the Army High Command, for whom this set of notes was taken.

settlement of the China Incident and in the negotiations with Great Britain and the United States. This is why the phrase "will not enter the conflict for the time being" was inserted in the proposal.

SUGIYAMA: [Remarks after the conference.] Throughout the conference no one on the Navy side expressed an opinion. Nagano, Navy Chief of Staff, was once going to take the floor when there were questions on southern French Indochina, but he stopped when some other person stood up to speak.

The questions put by President of the Privy Council Hara were relevant and pointed. The Emperor seemed to be extremely satisfied. [The Imperial assent was given at one-thirty, immediately after lunch.] The answers by the Government and the Supreme Command were fluent and well done.

After the conference, the President of the Privy Council came to see me, and courteously explained that he had inquired about the phrase "without intervening" because he had not understood it, and that he had no intention of asking about military preparedness in Manchuria. He assured me that he had meant no offense.

TSUKADA, ARMY VICE CHIEF OF STAFF: This Summary is a state secret, and must not be divulged under any circumstances. I am going to give the official paper to each of you now, so please return the one given you earlier.

PART TWO

Prepare for War Now, but Continue to Negotiate

Prepare for War Now, but Continue to Negotiate

38TH LIAISON CONFERENCE
July 10, 1941

*The American note that Secretary Hull had given Ambassador No-
mura on June 21 had been set aside because of the debate within the
Japanese Government on the projected military occupation of French
Indochina and Japan's uncertainty regarding her response to the outbreak of the German-Soviet war. The Imperial Conference of July 2
had settled these matters for the time being; now the Liaison Conference took up the earlier American note.*

*The American note was accompanied by an "Oral Statement" from
Hull that aroused anger in Tokyo, particularly on the part of Foreign Minister Matsuoka; it was eventually returned to the American
Government by Nomura, who had been reluctant to accept it from
the very beginning for fear of adverse reaction in Tokyo. The "Oral
Statement" said that although Ambassador Nomura desired to bring
about peace between the two countries, there were "some Japanese
leaders in influential official positions" who were committed to the
support of Nazi Germany. "So long as such leaders maintain this attitude in their official positions and apparently seek to influence public opinion in Japan in the direction indicated, is it not illusory to
expect that adoption of a proposal such as the one under consideration offers a basis for achieving substantial results along the desired
lines?" An accompanying draft of "an exchange of letters" between
the Secretary of State and the Japanese Ambassador questioned, in
even harsher terms, Japan's attitude toward the negotiations, her
commitment to the Tripartite Pact, and her position in China. Ambassador Nomura, evidently on his own initiative, asked Secretary
Hull on June 22 for permission not to transmit these documents to
his Government. Although Hull did not withdraw the letters, Nomura was permitted to relay the points involved in whatever manner his discretion dictated.[1]*

---

[1] The proposed letters and subsequent conversations about them may be found
in *Papers Relating to the Foreign Relations of the United States: Japan, 1931–
1941*, II, 490–94.

It is not surprising that Foreign Minister Matsuoka's response to the Hull notes of June 21 and 22 should have been hostile, since Hull's reference to "certain Japanese leaders" was pointed at Matsuoka. In this Liaison Conference, however, Matsuoka, instead of making the attack himself, brought in Saito Yoshie, a confidant whom he had taken into the Foreign Office as an "Adviser," and had Saito undertake a critique of the Hull proposal. Matsuoka then added his own comments. Both declared that it would be impossible to continue the negotiations, given the American position as outlined in the Hull proposals.

Agenda: Adjustment of Japanese-American Relations, Especially the Statement of the Opinions of the Foreign Ministry Regarding the Reply of Secretary Hull, Dated June 21st.[2]

[Place: Official residence of the Prime Minister. Participants: Same as before (however, the Vice Chiefs of Staff were absent).]

FOREIGN MINISTER MATSUOKA: I really tried to accept whatever I could in Hull's reply; but this proposal is worse than the first proposal. According to Nomura's telegram, he is having a difficult time. Therefore, he has asked that we reconsider our position and try, if it is at all possible, to come to an agreement with the United States. But it is simply difficult to do that with this proposal.

[He then let Adviser Saito carry on the discussion.]

SAITO: I have studied the present proposal, and find many reasons, to be explained shortly, why it is unacceptable.

The present world, divided into those who are for the maintenance of the status quo and those who are for its destruction, the democracies and the totalitarian states, is in the midst of a war. Hull's reply is for the status quo and for democracy. It is obvious that America sent it after consultation with Britain and China. Thus I think the countries that are for the status quo are getting together to put pressure on Japan. On the matter of Sino-Japanese negotiations, the United States hopes to make us negotiate on the basis of conditions existing prior to the China Incident. In this proposal the phrase "Chinese Government" is used. I think this tricky wording is tantamount to saying that we should renounce the basic treaty between Japan and China.[3] Can-

---

[2] For the text of Hull's "Oral Statement" and the accompanying Draft Proposal, see Appendix B.

[3] Japan concluded a treaty with the puppet Nanking Government under Wang Ching-wei on November 30, 1940. The agreement provided for joint defense against communism and cooperation in economic development.

celling our recognition of the Nanking Government would mean reviving the moribund Chungking Government. We must consider and study this phrase "Chinese Government."

The Americans think that Manchuria should revert to China. This proposal says, in effect, that Japan and China should negotiate after Japan has renounced the joint declaration made by Japan, Manchukuo, and China.[4] If we begin negotiations by doing this at a time when Chungking is trying to regain lost territory, it is certain that from the very beginning things would go against us.

This proposal does not recognize the stationing of troops [in China] to maintain peace and order; it seeks the unconditional withdrawal of all troops. The stationing of troops to maintain peace and order is a most important element in our national policy. If we withdrew our troops unconditionally, the Chinese Communists, the Nationalists, the Nanking Government, and Chungking would fight, causing great disorder.[5] If this happened, Britain and the United States would intervene. Accordingly, the unconditional withdrawal of troops will deadlock our negotiations with the United States.

The proposal does not recognize the stationing of troops as a defense against Communism. Whereas the Japanese draft tries to recognize the treaties that have been concluded to date, the United States proposal tries to invalidate them. That the United States does not recognize the stationing of troops as a defense against Communism is indicated in Hull's Statement.

Japan aims at complete cooperation between Japan and China. By contrast, the United States is advocating nondiscriminatory treatment. This makes it impossible to establish a New Order in East Asia. Britain and the United States have continued to aid Chiang until the present time; and they are planning to obtain an advantageous position in China in the future. When an overall peace comes to China, the influence of American "dollars," which are backed by 80 per cent of the world's gold supply, will spread all over China, working from today's special position. America's intention is to bring about peace between Japan and China by means of an agreement

[4] The Japan-Manchukuo-China Joint Declaration was an annex to Japan's treaty with the Nanking Government. It pledged that the three countries would mutually respect each other's territories and sovereignties, cooperate in economic activities, and conduct a joint defense against communism.

[5] Saito was presumably thinking of the fact that the "Chungking regime" included not only the Nationalist Party but also warlords and others loosely associated with Chiang.

between Japan and the United States, and then to let Japan and China negotiate directly within the limits thus set. This procedure will transfer leadership in East Asia to the United States. It will interfere with the implementation of an independent policy by our Empire. It will give the United States the right to have a say in the China Problem.

The attitudes of Japan and the United States toward the European war differ greatly. Stated another way, we can only suppose that they mean to enter the war but are telling us to keep quiet. The United States has interpreted her right of self-defense very broadly. She has also practically said that Japan should renounce the Tripartite Pact. We must naturally reject such ideas.

As for trade between Japan and America, America plans to limit it to the pre-Incident level. In short, a maintain-the-status-quo mentality is evident. Moreover, the proposal talks about ordinary commercial transactions, but in the future we must increase trade in vital materials, such as steel and scrap iron; and by keeping trade at the pre-Incident level the United States will be legally preventing the development of Japan's foreign trade. That is, this action will interfere with Japan's future economic development, and the United States will freely control the markets of the Far East. The fact that the Americans have eliminated the word "Southwest" from "Southwest Pacific" is evidence that they are also greatly concerned with the North Pacific. They say "normal trade relations"; but Japan has in mind not only trade, but also mining and industry. The United States, by talking about "trade relations," is clearly limiting Japan's demands.

On the question of Japanese emigration to the United States, the previous draft stated that Japan would be treated the same as other countries; but this statement has been eliminated in the present draft.

We made a proposal regarding the independence of the Philippines; but the American proposal simply states that the Philippines have not yet developed to the point of independence.

Hull's "Oral Statement" contains especially outrageous language.[6] For instance, it says, "We have no intention of considering the stationing of troops a defense against Communism." Or again: "There are differences of opinion within the Japanese Government. I understand that there are Cabinet members who say Japan should ally herself with the Axis and fight side-by-side with Hitler. We cannot make

[6] See Appendix B.

an agreement with a Japanese Government of that kind. If you want to facilitate an improvement in Japanese-American relations, you had better change your Cabinet." His attitude is one of contempt for Japan. I have been in the foreign service for a long time. This language is not the kind one would use toward a country of equal standing: it expresses an attitude one would take toward a protectorate or a possession. These words are inexcusable.

MATSUOKA: In general, I am in agreement with Adviser Saito's report; but I would like to state one or two thoughts.

First of all, Hull's "Statement" is outrageous. Never has such a thing occurred since Japan opened diplomatic relations with other countries. Nomura and I are good friends, but it is inexcusable for him to transmit such an outrageous statement. I was truly amazed that he would listen without protest to a demand that Japan, a great world power, change her Cabinet. I sent a message to him right away, saying: "You should not have transmitted such a statement. Was there not some misunderstanding? Inform me of the circumstances at the time." But I have not yet received an answer from him.

Second, we cannot dissolve the Tripartite Pact.

Third, acceptance of the American proposal would threaten the establishment of a Greater East Asia Co-prosperity Sphere, and this would be a very grave matter.

Fourth, I think that Britain and the United States are trying to meddle in the settlement of the Sino-Japanese problem in one way or another. I am unhappy that among our people there are those who believe it would be better to achieve peace through the mediation of a third party, even though we have fought for four years trying to secure the leadership of East Asia. Such people use as a precedent the times when we sought the aid of third parties, including the United States, in the peace negotiations during the Sino-Japanese and Russo-Japanese wars; but they forget the position that the Empire occupies thirty years later. To put it in more down-to-earth terms, I am unhappy that there are quite a few people who are fed up with the China Incident, and who, abandoning their ideals, take the position of "dumplings rather than flowers."[7]

The United States has seized Iceland. Although this is tantamount to entering the war, she closes her eyes and says she is not entering the war. It is clear that were Japan to maintain the status quo and

[7] A Japanese proverb, which states that substance is more important than outward appearance.

return to the pre-Incident level of foreign trade, we would have no hope for economic expansion. In short, the United States is trying to destroy Japanese leadership in East Asia. If we shilly-shally over things like this, all that will happen is that the United States will take what we say and use it to attack us. One of these days a foolish question will be asked in the [U.S.] Senate, and that will have a great effect on our domestic politics.

Such being the case, I cannot accept the Hull proposal. I would like to come to an agreement somehow or other, but there is no hope for success. To begin with, the United States did nothing about our proposal for forty days. This proposal came on June 22, not two weeks ago; yet Nomura has already pressed me for an answer four or five times. It would be all right to keep prolonging the negotiations; but I absolutely cannot accept this proposal.

Furthermore, Hull's Statement said, "despite the efforts of the Ambassador and his associates"; so I have demanded that Nomura explain who his associates are. I have told him that the diplomatic state secrets are to go from the Foreign Minister to the Ambassador and from the Ambassador to Hull, and that it is improper to have a lot of people involved in it.[8]

[Thus the meeting was adjourned, after it was decided that the discussion would be continued on the 12th (Saturday).]

39TH LIAISON CONFERENCE
July 12, 1941

Foreign Minister Matsuoka, still angry at Secretary Hull's pointed remarks, wanted not only to reject the "Oral Statement," but also to discontinue the negotiations. However, the other members of the Liaison Conference were not yet ready to take so drastic a step. Prime Minister Konoye, disturbed by Matsuoka's outspoken position in the meeting on the 10th, had secretly met that evening with the Army, Navy, and Home Ministers in order to work out a common defense against the impulsive Foreign Minister.

Both the Army and Navy had their reasons for seeking to continue the negotiations. Since talks with French Indochina to obtain bases were about to begin, the Army did not wish to provoke the United States any more than necessary. It is true that in this Conference

---

[8] Matsuoka was probably referring to the unofficial negotiators, Ikawa and Iwakuro.

Navy Chief of Staff Nagano sided with Matsuoka; but he was more or less countermanded by Oka, Chief of the Naval Affairs Bureau of the Navy Ministry. Oka's remark about the "lower echelons" losing their "enthusiasm for their work" refers to the activities of a committee of middle-grade officers from both the Navy Ministry and the Naval General Staff, which had on June 5, 1941, drafted a lengthy document called "The Attitude the Navy Should Take in View of the Present Situation."[9] This document maintained that only the Navy held the key to a decision for war or peace, which must be made soon. As for the negotiations in Washington, the document stated: "Although the Nomura operation will be continued, it will be necessary to go forward with a forceful diplomatic policy [toward French Indochina and Thailand]; and it is anticipated that the Nomura operation will be gradually curtailed as the forceful diplomacy progresses."

Agenda: The Adjustment of Diplomatic Relations with the United States.

[Those present: Mr. Terasaki Taro, Chief of the American Bureau of the Foreign Office, was present by special invitation.]

[The gist of the discussion: As a result of deliberations carried over from our previous meetings regarding the future course of our attempts to adjust diplomatic relations with the United States, it was decided that even though we would hold firmly to our initial proposal, we would still leave room for negotiations. If some changes could be made in the wording, we would try to do so and would send a reply. It was agreed that for this purpose the three Bureau Chiefs of the War, Navy, and Foreign Ministries would prepare a draft this afternoon. Furthermore, it was decided that Secretary of State Hull's "Oral Statement" should be rejected. A brief summary of the discussion follows:]

FOREIGN MINISTER MATSUOKA: I just about exhausted this subject last time; but I will add that when I read the "Oral Statement," I really felt that we should reject it immediately. It is indeed absurd. I have thought about it for ten days, and I feel that the United States regards Japan as either her protectorate or her dependency; and that so long as we are not going to submit to this sort of judgment, we should not accept the "Statement." The reasons for the rejection are clear. So long as I am Foreign Minister, I cannot accept it. I am willing to consider anything else, but I cannot accept the "Oral State-

[9] The text of this document is in *TSM, Bekkan*, pp. 427–40.

ment." It is characteristic of Americans to be high-handed toward the weak. The "Statement" considers Japan a weak, dependent country. Among Japanese, there are some who are against me, and some who say that even the Prime Minister is against me. Such being the case, the United States thinks that Japan is exhausted; and for that reason it sent the "Statement." I propose here and now that we reject the "Statement," and that we discontinue negotiations with the United States.

Furthermore, I told Nomura to send Wakasugi[10] back in order to report on the situation; but Nomura replied that he himself would return, since even if he stayed in Washington, he could do nothing. Since it would not be appropriate for Nomura to return now, I asked him to stay on.

[After a period of silence the Army Chief of Staff spoke.]

ARMY CHIEF OF STAFF SUGIYAMA: I myself agree with the Foreign Minister's views. However, we among the military believe it is appropriate on this occasion to leave room for negotiation. It is not [yet] suitable to tell the United States that we might cut off diplomatic relations, since in the near future we plan to move troops into French Indochina, and since in the North we are directly faced with the grave necessity of strengthening the Kwantung Army.

MATSUOKA: I believe that the American attitude will not change, no matter what attitude Japan takes. It is the nature of the American people to take advantage of you if you show weakness. Therefore, I believe it is better to take a strong position on this occasion.

MINISTER OF HOME AFFAIRS HIRANUMA: At this point the most important thing for Japan is to prevent the United States from coming into the war. Ideally, Japan and the United States ought to cooperate to bring the present war to an end. However, if things continue as they have in the past, this war might last for fifty or a hundred years. From the point of view of Hakko Ichiu, Japan's great spirit, which the Foreign Minister is always talking about, Japan should not go to war. Japan is neither totalitarian nor liberal. I believe that the proper spirit of the Imperial Way is to rid the world of war. Perhaps the United States will not understand, but Japan really ought to stop the war; and shouldn't Japan try to get the United States to go along with this? Why don't we approach the United States in this spirit? If, as the Foreign Minister says, America's participation in the war is certain, there is no hope in what I say; still, the Foreign

10 Wakasugi Kaname, Minister at the Japanese Embassy in Washington.

Minister says that the American people go along because Roosevelt is pushing them, but that among Americans there are those who are opposed to war. I would like to proceed in the spirit of Japan's Imperial Way. As the Foreign Minister proposes, it is permissible to reject the "Oral Statement"; but with regard to the negotiations, even though the possibilities of success might be slight, I would like to see them carried on in the light of what I have just said. Of course, I would like to have him [i.e., Matsuoka] approach this in such a way that our great Empire will not lose face. It goes without saying that diplomacy is the job of the Foreign Minister; but there is a need to be earnest. If we let things go on this way, we will be fighting on two fronts. Our resources will be exhausted, and we will probably be unable to continue a great war. We must attack the Soviet Union, but under the present circumstances this is difficult. We must do so in the future. We must also strike in the South. But we cannot do both at the same time.

Given the present circumstances, Japan must acquire materials and strengthen her national power. There is, of course, the question of international integrity; but it would seem that we must avoid a break with the United States from the standpoint of the Empire's survival. As children of the Emperor, and in order to assist him, we must set his mind at rest. If the present Cabinet is bad, wouldn't it be better to change it, if necessary, to avoid getting into the war?

MATSUOKA: I completely agree with the Minister of Home Affairs. I would simply add that given the situation, the American President is trying to lead his country into the war. There is, however, one thread of hope, which is that the American people might not follow him. The President has even managed somehow to get things that appear rather difficult to get. He finally managed to get elected three times. Roosevelt is a real demagogue. We probably cannot prevent American entry into the war in the end. Our Empire has proceeded consistently on the basis of the Tripartite Pact. But let us try to the very end. Japanese-American accord has been my cherished wish ever since I was young. I think there is no hope, but let us try until the very end. We have not rejected the "Oral Statement." [He repeated what he had said previously.] In Japan there are some blockheads who revile me, perhaps in the belief that by so doing they are serving the State. Ever since I was young, I've had them figured out. Those people probably presume that the Prime Minister and those below him also think that I am a bad fellow.

WAR MINISTER TOJO: Even if there is no hope, I would like to persist to the very end. I know it is difficult; but it will be intolerable if we cannot establish the Greater East Asia Co-prosperity Sphere and settle the China Incident. Because of the Tripartite Pact, can't we at least prevent the formal participation of the United States in the war? Of course, since the "Oral Statement" affects the dignity of our national polity [*kokutai*],[11] I believe we cannot help but reject it, in line with the Foreign Minister's judgment. However, if we sincerely convey to the Americans what we, as Japanese, believe to be right, won't they be inwardly moved?

MATSUOKA: Since they are willing to say things like this to Japan without giving it much thought, it won't be serious if we reject the "Statement."

NAVY MINISTER OIKAWA: According to Navy reports, it appears that Secretary of State Hull and others are not prepared to provoke a Pacific war. Since Japan does not wish to engage in a Pacific war, isn't there room for negotiation?

MATSUOKA: Is there room? What will they accept?

OIKAWA: Well, something minor.

MATSUOKA: If we say we will not use force in the South, they will probably listen. Is there anything else they would accept?

OIKAWA: Won't they accept the security of the Pacific? The Open Door Policy in China?

MATSUOKA: Since the present American proposal is worse than the first proposal, it is difficult to go back to where we started. They sent this kind of letter because they believe that we give in easily. If we hold firmly to the original proposal and continue to negotiate, we will probably [have to] give up after we have been turned down a number of times.

[Addendum: Although Terasaki, Chief of the American Bureau, was told to draft a carefully worded reply rejecting the "Oral Statement," he said that he could not do so. The Foreign Minister said that he had some good ideas about it, and that he would revise Saito's draft and try his hand at writing the reply.]

[After the meeting:]

SUGIYAMA: Aren't we going to begin negotiations with French Indochina on the 14th? Therefore, if we send a rejection to the United States too early, we will provoke the United States. Vichy will be

---

[11] *Kokutai* was a prewar Japanese concept roughly equivalent to "national structure." It centered around the divinity of the Emperor and his position as "father of the nation."

unhappy with Japan's negotiations, and this will give the United States time to win over French Indochina to her side. Why don't we approach Vichy at once, and send our reply to the United States after we have reached the final stage in our negotiations?

MATSUOKA: The "Statement" is so outrageous that I would like to reject it immediately. Moreover, Nomura has asked many times for a reply. Well, I'll think about it.

NAGANO: Matsuoka, if it is true that the United States will not change its attitude no matter what Japan says, then won't it be all right to do as you propose?

CHIEF OF THE NAVAL AFFAIRS BUREAU OKA: It is one thing to say that we will try our utmost; but if we are going to break off negotiations, as His Excellency the Navy Chief of Staff proposes, won't those in the lower echelons lose all enthusiasm for their work?

NAGANO: There is something to what you say.

[The foregoing is what Nagano, Navy Chief of Staff, proposed out of the blue. It is completely different from the document "The Attitude Our Empire Should Take," which was presented this morning by the Navy. It appears that Oka, Chief of the Naval Affairs Bureau, indirectly retracted what the Navy Chief of Staff said. Today Minister of Home Affairs Hiranuma spoke particularly at length. The Prime Minister did not say a word.]

40TH LIAISON CONFERENCE
July 21, 1941

It had been decided at the previous Conference that those who had been acting as secretaries at the Conferences (Muto of the War Ministry; Oka of the Navy Ministry; Tomita, Chief Cabinet Secretary), together with Terasaki Taro and Saito of the Foreign Ministry, would draft a reply to the American proposal of June 21. Foreign Minister Matsuoka, however, refused to look at the draft prepared by the group. Finally, as a result of strong pressure from the armed forces, the Foreign Minister agreed on July 14 to take the earlier draft and revise it for eventual transmission to the United States.

The Prime Minister and others favored sending the final draft to Washington as soon as possible; but Matsuoka insisted that he must first send Hull a note to reject the "Oral Statement." Finally the Prime Minister and the armed forces agreed that under the circumstances the rejection of the "Oral Statement" should be sent together with the Japanese reply. Matsuoka, however, disregarding the wishes

*of his colleagues, went ahead and wired his rejection without at the
same time sending the Japanese counterproposal. When Terasaki,
Chief of the American Bureau, learned what had happened, he sent
the text of the Japanese counterproposal without first securing Matsuoka's permission. (Meanwhile, to add insult to injury, Matsuoka
had confidentially told the Germans the content of the Japanese reply.) In Washington, Ambassador Nomura decided not to deliver
the two documents to the State Department because of the Japanese
Cabinet change that occurred shortly thereafter.*

*Matsuoka's arbitrary action brought on a crisis that had been
building up as a result of the accumulated frustrations among those
who had tried to work with him. Earlier, Prime Minister Konoye
had told Kido, the Lord Keeper of the Privy Seal, that he was ready
to resign. The Army and Navy were convinced that Matsuoka had
become* persona non grata *in the United States, and that his presence in the Cabinet jeopardized the negotiations. They apparently
believed that if they could just get rid of the Foreign Minister, the
United States would be more willing to cooperate. However, Prime
Minister Konoye did not feel that he could simply fire Matsuoka—
partly because he feared that Matsuoka's admirers would charge
that the Japanese Government had bowed to American pressure, and
partly because he had brought Matsuoka into the Government despite the reservations that the Emperor had expressed at the time.
Therefore, Konoye, after consulting the War, Navy, and Home Ministers, as well as the Director of the Planning Board, asked for the
resignation of the Cabinet on July 16.*

*Two days later Konoye was authorized to organize a new Govern-
ment, the Third Konoye Cabinet. He invited the same people who
had been in the previous Cabinet to join him, except for Matsuoka.
The new Foreign Minister was Admiral Toyoda Teijiro, who, it was
believed, would be trusted by the United States. As the notes of this
Conference show, Toyoda verbally supported the Tripartite Pact;
but his remarks should not necessarily be taken at face value. It appears that his policy was actually aimed at reducing the Pact to a
dead letter.*

Agenda: The First Meeting of the Third Konoye Cabinet.

[Place: Imperial Headquarters in the Imperial Palace. It was de-
cided that hereafter the Conferences would be held at Imperial
Headquarters. Those present were Prime Minister Konoye, Foreign
Minister Toyoda, War Minister Tojo, Navy Minister Oikawa, Home

Minister Hiranuma, State Minister and Director of the Planning Board Suzuki, Army Chief of Staff Sugiyama, Navy Chief of Staff Nagano, Secretary of the Cabinet Tomita, Chief of the Military Affairs Bureau Muto, and Chief of the Navy Affairs Bureau Oka. It was decided that hereafter the participants would usually be the above persons.]

[After making known his desires (outlined in a separate document,[12] which was distributed at the same time), the Army Chief of Staff made the following additional comments:]

It appears that some of our citizens believe that the Tripartite Pact might be relaxed, and that we might revert to dependence on Great Britain and the United States. But this is absolutely not true. Since these ideas will have a great effect, not only on the people at home but also on the devotion of the soldiers at the front, I want the Government to pay special attention to this.

WAR MINISTER TOJO: The Government stated after the resignation of the previous Cabinet, and again after the formation of the present Cabinet, that it would not change national policies that had already been decided. It announced that it would carry out these policies promptly and resolutely. I believe that this is consistent with the desires of the Supreme Command. Moreover, both the War Minister and the Navy Minister have demanded in Cabinet meetings that there be no relaxation in national policies. I believe that this is also consistent with the desires of the Supreme Command.

FOREIGN MINISTER TOYODA: Since I did not wish to have the Ambassadors and Ministers to the various countries think that there might be a change in national policies, I sent telegrams saying that there would be no change in our policies that have been in effect. I took particular pains to tell this to Oshima, Tatekawa, Nomura, and Horikiri [Ambassadors to Germany, Russia, the U.S., and Italy, respectively], and I told them to carry on as before. At the same time, I summoned the German and Italian Ambassadors in Tokyo and told them that even though there had been a change in Foreign Ministers, there was no change in the attitude of the Imperial Government. Besides, since I was Vice Navy Minister at the time of the con-

---

[12] In this document the Army and Navy pledged their cooperation with the new Cabinet and reemphasized their determination to carry out the decisions reached at the July 2 Imperial Conference. They indicated that they would adhere firmly to the established policy in negotiations with the United States, especially avoiding any conflict with the spirit of the Tripartite Pact. The complete text is in *TSM, Bekkan*, p. 482.

clusion of the Tripartite Pact, I feel a responsibility to it. I was involved in its signing: I will not modify it.

[The opinion of the Army Chief of Staff: From the attitude indicated by the Foreign Minister, I believe that what he said is true.]

[Next the Army Chief of Staff explained what had happened so far in the occupation of French Indochina, and told of future plans to strengthen the Kwantung Army, the defense of the home islands, and the air defenses. Also, the Navy Minister spoke about the strength of the fleet that would be sent to the South.]

NAVY CHIEF OF STAFF NAGANO: As for war with the United States, although there is now a chance of achieving victory, the chances will diminish as time goes on. By the latter half of next year it will already be difficult for us to cope with the United States; after that the situation will become increasingly worse. The United States will probably prolong the matter until her defenses have been built up, and then try to settle it. Accordingly, as time goes by, the Empire will be put at a disadvantage. If we could settle things without war, there would be nothing better. But if we conclude that conflict cannot ultimately be avoided, then I would like you to understand that as time goes by we will be in a disadvantageous position. Moreover, if we occupy the Philippines, it will be easier, from the Navy's point of view, to carry on the war [against the United States].

I believe that our defenses in the South Sea Islands are strong, and that we can put up a good fight there.

[Next the Foreign Minister reported on the negotiations with Vichy since the 14th. On this occasion, he said the following with respect to the attitude of Ott:]

When I asked Ott for his cooperation in the occupation of French Indochina, he said that if the French consented to it, there was no need for him to do anything; but if they did not consent, he would do something. Since he gave this passive reply, I asked for another meeting; and on that occasion he took the position, citing the case of Syria, that since Germany was presently engaged in a war with the Soviet Union, she could not very well put pressure on France. From these two replies I got the impression that although Germany will help us, it will not be active help.

[The Navy presented a telegram from the Naval Attaché in France stating that the Japanese-French negotiations would be successfully concluded. With this, the meeting adjourned.]

[The impressions of the Army Chief of Staff:]

I got the impression that the exchange of information was facilitated, perhaps because there were many military people present. I believe that the value of the Liaison Conference has been increased, in contrast to the past.

[The following was decided with respect to the exchange of information between the Liaison Conferences, Imperial Headquarters, and the Government:

[At 10 A.M. on Monday, 11 A.M. on Wednesday, and 10 A.M. on Saturday [there would be] exchanges of information. At 10 A.M. on Thursday [there would be a] Liaison Conference.

[Place: Imperial Headquarters in the Imperial Palace. Those attending the Liaison Conferences will be the same as today. At the exchange of information there will be present in addition the Chief of the Second Section of the Army General Staff, the Chief of the Third Section of the Naval General Staff,[13] and the Bureau Chiefs of the Foreign Ministry.[14]]

41ST LIAISON CONFERENCE
July 24, 1941

One of Foreign Minister Matsuoka's last official acts had been to instruct Kato Sotomatsu, Ambassador to Vichy, to open negotiations for the peaceful occupation of southern Indochina. Japanese demands for bases and the entry of troops were to be met by July 20; otherwise force would be used. The Vichy Government signed a Mutual Security Pact with Japan on July 21.

Since the American Government had broken the Japanese diplomatic code, it was well aware of the July 2 Imperial Conference decision to move into French Indochina. On July 18 the American Cabinet discussed the situation, and decided in favor of some kind of action against Japan. The State Department began working on orders to freeze Japanese funds and restrict the export of petroleum to Japan.

As we have seen, the Japanese planners, especially in the Army, had predicted that the occupation of southern Indochina would not provoke a drastic reaction from the United States. By contrast, Nomura, from his vantage point in Washington, warned his Government on July 23 that a move south would lead to a situation just short of a break in diplomatic relations. The next day President

13 These were the intelligence sections.
14 East Asia, European, American, Commerce, and Treaty Bureaus.

Roosevelt saw Nomura personally, and told the Ambassador that he would endeavor to obtain a guarantee of the neutralization of French Indochina from the several powers concerned. For some reason, Nomura did not get this information through to his Government; it was not until Ambassador Joseph Grew in Tokyo relayed it to Foreign Minister Toyoda on the 27th that it was conveyed to the Foreign Ministry. By that time Japan had already moved her forces into Indochina, and it was too late. On the evening of July 25 the United States Government ordered all Japanese assets in the United States to be frozen. Although this was not a full embargo, it effectively halted trade between the two countries.

The possibility that the United States would freeze Japanese funds, among other things, was suggested by Foreign Minister Toyoda at this Liaison Conference.

Agenda: The Occupation of French Indochina; Adjustment of Japanese-American Relations; The Thai Embassy.

[At the outset the Army Chief of Staff said that the troops would set sail on the 25th, and would arrive at Nha Trang on the 28th and Cape Saint Jacques on the 29th.]

FOREIGN MINISTER TOYODA: The Vichy Government has asked that the occupation army maintain its discipline, and that no illegal measures be taken against the Annamese. I would like to have this understood. Since we are occupying for the purpose of mutual defense, I hope that the armed forces will be led in such a way that the foregoing things will not happen, and that they [the people of French Indochina] will support us.

ARMY CHIEF OF STAFF SUGIYAMA: There is no need to worry, since this has been explained carefully to the commanding officers. Also, we will pay full attention to this in the future.

[The draft of the Government's statement on the occupation of French Indochina was approved.[15] It was decided that the announcement would be made at noon on the 26th. The German and Italian Ambassadors were to be notified immediately, and the Chinese, Manchukuan, British, and American Ambassadors on the 25th.]

TOYODA: The occupation of Indochina will exert an influence on the United States; they will adopt a policy of putting an embargo on vital materials, freezing Japanese funds, prohibiting the purchase of gold, detaining Japanese vessels, etc.

[15] The statement indicated that Japan and France had reached a complete agreement of views and emphasized Japan's "solemn pledge" to respect the sovereignty and territorial integrity of French Indochina.

Among the items included in the embargo on vital materials will
be raw cotton, lumber, wheat, and petroleum. As for cotton and lumber, we have already taken steps. Since [America] is sending wheat
to China, we can somehow or other get around the embargo on
wheat. Although petroleum causes us some anxiety, it is unlikely that
the United States will impose a complete embargo on it.

As for the freezing of funds, Japanese cash in the United States
come to ¥200 million, and securities come to ¥350 million. Against
this, American funds in Japan come to ¥300 million. We lose ¥250
million when we balance off the two. This will create a shortage of
funds for importing petroleum, and will cause us a good deal of hardship. The prohibition on the purchase of gold is not of concern at the
present time because we are not sending gold to the United States.
Concerning the detention of Japanese ships: there are ten ships near
American waters; but since the Navy has told those ships that are not
yet in port not to go in for several days, all of them will not be de-
tained.

Finance Minister Ogura is of the opinion that the freezing of funds
will cause hardship, and he has said that he will send a letter to Mor-
genthau, the American Secretary of the Treasury, with whom he has
personal connections; but I have asked him to wait for a while.

[With regard to the adjustment of Japanese-American relations.]

TOYODA: Some time ago, Ambassador Nomura returned Secretary
Hull's "Oral Statement"; but our revised draft has not yet reached
Hull, and Nomura has made a report regarding this. We of the Foreign Office believe it would not be desirable to call off the Nomura
operation. I would like to get the United States to understand that the
present occupation of French Indochina is not a military occupation,
but something that is based on the Empire's need and was arranged
after agreement with the French. I would like to get them to stop the
freezing of funds and to lift the ban on the transit of Japanese ships
through the Panama Canal. And I would like to continue the Nomura
operation.

In the course of the Nomura operation, the United States has advocated two things: (1) the United States would like to handle the details of the peace negotiations with China; (2) on the problem of
peace in the Pacific, she does not want to be bound by Japan. I will
consult you again on the Nomura operation.

[Foreign Minister Toyoda raised a question regarding the eleva-
tion of our legation in Thailand to an Embassy, which was approved
by the Privy Council at yesterday's meeting. He asked whether we
should send an ambassador immediately. On this there were two

opinions: one was that we should send an ambassador right away, since there were many rumors occasioned by the occupation of French Indochina; the other was that there is a need to observe the American reaction to the occupation of Indochina, and for that reason it would be better to put this off to another day. In the end the Conference was adjourned without a decision.

[After the meeting there was a report by Ambassador Shigemitsu, who has returned to Japan.][16]

42D LIAISON CONFERENCE
July 29, 1941

The main topic at this Conference was the state of popular morale. The general view appeared to be that the domestic situation in Japan looked tranquil on the surface, but that constant vigilance was required to control groups and activities that were potentially subversive.

Agenda: Exchange of General Information.

[Participants: Today Minister of Home Affairs Tanabe was present by special invitation. First, the Army Chief of Staff spoke of the situation with regard to the landing of the occupation troops in southern Indochina. The War Minister spoke on the reactions of the Powers to the occupation. Then there was the following statement by the Foreign Minister:]

It appears that the British Minister to Thailand has told the Thai Government, "If Thailand hereafter grants military bases or special privileges to a third power, Britain will denounce the nonaggression pact." But even though Britain has said this, I do not believe that she will cross the border.

Thailand, as a result of a cabinet meeting, will shortly recognize Manchukuo. This was reported to us via Washington.

[When our Minister to Spain, Suma Yakichiro, visited the Italian Minister there, it was reported to him that the United States is planning to seize Dakar. The Army Chief of Staff stated, with respect to the attitude of the Empire toward the Annamese, that he would like to see the Government make up its mind and adopt a consistent policy. In connection with this, the War Minister raised the question of what should be done with the overseas Chinese. Although Bureau

---

[16] Shigemitsu Mamoru, Ambassador to Great Britain.

Chief Muto said that the matter was already under study, it was decided that it required further study.

[Suzuki, Director of the Planning Board, called attention to the
document "Attitudes toward Administration in Wartime," and noted
that it had been approved by the Cabinet.[17] He asked if the Supreme
Command had also approved it. At that point Minister for Home
Affairs Tanabe said that Paragraph 3 mentioned "making clear the
direction in which the people should go," and that this was very important; that it also declared we would endeavor to eliminate the uncertainty regarding the people's livelihood; and that this and Paragraph 4 were important, and hence required careful deliberation.

[Furthermore, at the Cabinet discussion Sakonji Masazo, Minister
of Commerce and Industry, and Yanigigawa Heisuke, Minister Without Portfolio, made the following remarks. SAKONJI: "We say we will
eliminate the uncertainty regarding the people's livelihood; but we
don't want the people to feel reassured. Under present conditions, the
people must not complain, even if they have nothing on but loincloths
and have to endure all sorts of hardships." YANAGIGAWA: "Regarding
the activities of the Imperial Rule Assistance Association,[18] they are
under good control and they are being taken seriously, so we seek
your cooperation."

[Next, Minister for Home Affairs Tanabe reported on the domestic
situation as follows:]

Ever since our national policy was decided at the Imperial Conference on July 2, the general public has shown increasing confidence in
the Government. Although there was previously much discussion
about going north or south, this has recently declined.

The Communist Party is not out in the open; but beneath the surface it is quite active, so we must be careful. It appears that quite recently there was a directive stating that Communists should take the
position that there is no connection between the Comintern and the

---

[17] The main points in the document were as follows: (a) administrative procedures must be tightened; (b) the Imperial Rule Assistance Association must be
encouraged, and national unity must be promoted; (c) "the Government must
indicate the action that the people should take, encourage their spirit, and endeavor to remove uncertainties about their livelihood"; (d) "those who take advantage of popular discontent, which is inevitable in wartime, for political purposes or for subversive social movements must be thoroughly suppressed; careful
investigation must be made of trends in left-wing and right-wing movements, and
they should be controlled when necessary."

[18] This organization was established under the Second Konoye Cabinet to re-
place all political parties, which were dissolved in October 1940.

State. Even though they are not openly active, they are continuing their movement; so we must be careful.

There are also some Koreans whom we must watch.

There are some returned soldiers whom we must watch, too. Especially among those in the small- and medium-size industries, there appear to be many ex-soldiers who are dissatisfied because they cannot find work, even though they have been discharged; or their business has declined during their absence, and at this point they don't know how to get along. The rich have become richer because of the China Incident, while the small and medium businessmen are in difficulties because they went to the front. There is nothing to be gained by talking about this, but we should take care of their livelihood.

The peasants on the whole are quiet, but it appears that the peasant movement is picking up. Generally speaking, there is no need to worry; but this is the situation if we go into the details, and I tell you this for your own information.

[The matter of diplomatic relations with Russia was raised by the War Minister, but the Foreign Minister said, "We should leave that for later," and the Navy Minister said, "We have to give that more study," so it was not pursued. The question of the "rights of a belligerent" was not taken up, and the meeting was adjourned.]

43D LIAISON CONFERENCE

August 1, 1941

The Imperial Conference of July 2, it will be recalled, had left open the question of attacking the Soviet Union. A few days later, on the strength of this decision, the Army began a large-scale movement of troops and matériel into Korea and Manchuria, resulting over a period of time in an unprecedented buildup of military might in that area. The aim, of course, was to move into eastern Russia if the German armies succeeded in overrunning the European portion of the Soviet Union. By the first of August, the time for decision was close at hand. Because winter operations in Siberia were not feasible, war against Russia would have to start no later than September 1, which necessitated a firm decision fairly early in August.

However, the international situation had changed somewhat since July 2. The move south had led the United States to freeze Japanese funds, and this was followed by similar moves on the part of Britain and the Netherlands. On August 1, the United States embargoed the export of oil to Japan. The economic squeeze was being put on Japan.

Meanwhile, the military had been watching German progress in Russia with great interest. Early in August Army Chief of Staff Sugiyama received a report from his intelligence officers, who predicted that Germany could not possibly defeat Russia during 1941, that thereafter the tide would very likely turn against the Germans, and that the war would probably be prolonged.

Quite independently of this, the Foreign Ministry had also concluded that Japan should not attempt a war against the Soviets, and its position was stated in a document entitled "Essence of Diplomatic Negotiations with the Soviet Union." This document declared that Japan should "make it clear that so long as the Soviet Union maintains neutrality and does not pose a menace to the Far East, Japan will respect the Japanese-Soviet Neutrality Pact." At this Conference, however, the Foreign Minister was unable to persuade his colleagues that his position was the right one. Interestingly enough, at the next Conference, on August 4, the group appears to have accepted in substance what the Foreign Minister had advocated.

Agenda: "Essentials of Diplomatic Negotiations with the Soviet Union."

[The gist: The Army Chief of Staff reported on the occupation of French Indochina, and on the dispatch of troops to the North. Next, there was a report by Suzuki, Director of the Planning Board, on "The Requirements for the Mobilization of Resources in Carrying On the War." Next, Foreign Minister Toyoda presented the "Essentials of Diplomatic Negotiations with the Soviet Union," and gave a general briefing. There was some exchange of opinions, but the decision was put off until next time, and the Conference was adjourned.

[A portion of Foreign Minister Toyoda's remarks follows:] [These remarks, referring to the different clauses in the document, have been omitted here.]

[However, almost everyone argued as follows: Our Empire must be guided by the Tripartite Pact. One could turn the rudder 90 degrees, or even 180 degrees; nevertheless, one must proceed straight ahead. The Tripartite Pact makes possible the establishment of the New Order in Europe and the establishment of Japan's New Order in East Asia, and we cannot give this up. Even though there may be obstruction from the outside, we must adhere to the Tripartite Pact. It is impossible to declare openly that we will respect the Neutrality Pact, or to make a firm promise to that effect. Moreover, former Foreign Minister Matsuoka had stated on this matter that the Neutrality Pact had no effect on the Tripartite Pact. It would be inappropriate to say this sort of thing now to the Soviet Union. The general trend of opinion was not to accept Matsuoka's position.

[In explanation of the document "Essentials of Diplomatic Negotiations with the Soviet Union" it was stated that the German-Soviet war would be a prolonged one. Both the Army Chief of Staff and the War Minister refuted this, saying: "That is not necessarily so. The fact that at the present time the fighting on the Western Front is not moving ahead rather means that the Soviets are playing into German hands, and the probability is high that the war will end in a quick German victory. It will become increasingly difficult for the Soviets to prolong the war as was stated in the explanation. To say that the German-Soviet war will be prolonged is to come to a hasty conclusion." The Navy Minister expressed agreement with these views.]

44TH LIAISON CONFERENCE
August 4, 1941

The question of Japanese-Soviet relations continued to plague the Conference members. Japan was allied with Germany and Italy, and she concurrently had a Neutrality Pact with the Soviets; and now Germany and Russia were at war. It was decided that Japan would observe the Neutrality Pact with Russia, at least for the time being.

Agenda: "Essentials of Diplomatic Negotiations with the Soviet Union."

[The Army Chief of Staff opened with remarks on his military telegram to the Kwantung Army concerning the attitude it should take in the event that Soviet planes penetrated the Manchurian border.[19] He also discussed the French Indochina occupation. Next the War Minister asked whether diplomatic overtures should not be made to the Soviet Union. The Foreign Minister stated that he wanted to have a discussion of the "Essence of Diplomatic Negotiations with the

---

[19] On August 3 the Kwantung Army reported indications of Soviet preparations for air attacks and sought advance permission to counterattack if they were actually launched. The Army General Staff responded that the counterattack should not extend into Soviet territory, and that the Kwantung Army should act with great caution. In short, the High Command was not anxious to provoke the Russians.

Soviet Union." Acting Vice Minister Yamamoto Kumaichi explained the views of the Foreign Office. The central question is the interpretation of neutrality. There is room for debate in terms of the treaty; but as a practical matter, do we [openly] promise to maintain neutrality, or do we agree [among ourselves] that we will maintain neutrality. We would like to adopt one view or the other.]

YAMAMOTO: How would it be if we negotiate with the Soviets along the following lines? Japan does not believe that East Asia is being threatened. The spirit motivating the two countries lies here.

NAVY MINISTER OIKAWA: It is a fact that the Empire has at the present time treaties of alliance and neutrality. The question is complicated. How would it be if no mention is made of the Neutrality Pact, and if we negotiate, saying, "Let us settle those problems that cause trouble between our two countries?"

WAR MINISTER TOJO [AND SEVERAL OTHERS]: The Tripartite Pact and the Neutrality Pact exist simultaneously. However, from the point of view of international relations, the Tripartite Pact comes first and the Neutrality Pact comes second. As a practical matter, all we need to do is figure out how we will deal with the question from the point of view of national policy, and so on.

[It was decided that the general procedure would be as follows: It is all right to tell the Soviet Union that if she strictly observes the Neutrality Pact and does not threaten the Empire in the Far East, we will observe the Neutrality Pact. If the Soviet Union does not observe neutrality and does not adopt a friendly attitude, or if she transfers the Maritime Provinces or Kamchatka to a third power, this Neutrality Pact will be void.

[There were several amendments to the proposal.]

[There followed an exchange between the Foreign Minister and Army Chief of Staff Sugiyama regarding reports that certain units in Manchuria were about to take the offensive. Sugiyama denied this.]

45TH LIAISON CONFERENCE
August 6, 1941

Representatives of the Army and Navy had previously met to try to reach an agreeemnt on how Japan should respond if Soviet forces invaded Manchuria. The Navy—as well as the Prime Minister and the Foreign Minister—did not want to go to war with Russia. They were afraid that the Kwantung Army might take unauthorized action and then confront the Government with a fait accompli, as had happened on previous occasions. The policy statement that was agreed upon at this Conference seemed to remove these fears.

In response to the German Ambassador's questions about Japanese relations with the United States, Foreign Minister Toyoda spoke about trying to calm down the United States. It might be noted in this connection that Nomura had reported to Toyoda: "The United States has suddenly established very close relations with the Soviet Union. In view of this fact, it is highly doubtful that the United States would merely watch from the sidelines if we should make any moves to the North."

Agenda: "Measures the Empire Should Take toward the Present Situation between Japan and the Soviet Union."[20]

[*Summary:* There was first a general exchange of views. Next, the Foreign Minister reported on his conversations with the German and Soviet Ambassadors. After that the "Measures the Empire Should Take toward the Present Situation between Japan and the Soviet Union," presented by the Army and Navy Sections of Imperial Headquarters, was discussed and approved in its original form.

[The gist of the Foreign Minister's report on his conversations with the German and Soviet Ambassadors was as follows:]

Yesterday I summoned the Soviet Ambassador and talked to him on the basis of the first paragraph of "Essence of the Diplomatic Negotiations with the Soviet Union."[21] The Ambassador said: "I had some doubts about the future, but what you have said has clarified things. I will report this matter to my Government. You are right in what you say about the problem of disputes. Up to now we have followed the wishes of Japan, and in the future we would like to continue to do so. As for the Maritime Danger Zone problem, we have

---

[20] *Measures the Empire Should Take toward the Present Situation between Japan and the Soviet Union:*

(1) Together with perfecting our precautionary defenses against the Soviet Union, we should strictly avoid provocative actions; moreover, even if disputes should arise, we should endeavor to prevent them from causing a Japanese-Soviet war and should try to keep them localized.

(2) In case of a frontal attack by the Soviet Union, we will fight back in order not to lose the initiative by adopting a totally defensive posture.

(3) The attitude of the Empire with respect to a Soviet attack will be promptly decided at a Cabinet meeting.

[21] The first paragraph demanded the removal of the Maritime Danger Zone, and elimination of the losses that this zone inflicted on Japan. Danger zones involved the laying of mines in certain areas of the Japan Sea and off the coast of Kamchatka; the Japanese had protested them, through their Ambassador in Moscow, as early as July. (Text in *TSM, Bekkan,* 489.)

already given you an answer; but we will think about it further. At any rate, both my Government and I appreciate the fact that you have touched on your basic foreign policies. I thank you from the bottom of my heart for your frank and clear comments." From this I got the impression that he felt relieved. I sent a wire to Ambassador Tatekawa regarding this conversation.[22]

Today, the 6th, at 9 o'clock, German Ambassador Ott came, and we talked as follows:

OTT: I understand that you spoke to the Soviet Ambassador. What did you talk about?

FOREIGN MINISTER TOYODA: We spoke about our hope that they will cooperate with us in connection with our concessions in northern Sakhalin, so that we can carry on our activities there without obstruction. We also discussed the Maritime Danger Zone.

OTT: What would Japan's attitude be if the United States should send arms to the Soviet Union via Vladivostok?

TOYODA: We would need to consider the matter.

OTT: What are you going to do about the United States?

TOYODA: The United States is excited. First of all, we will try to calm her down.

OTT: I have heard that Japan has been negotiating to secure the cession of the area east of Lake Baikal. How about this?

TOYODA: There is no truth to it.

[Then the discussion turned to "Measures the Empire Should Take toward the Present Situation between Japan and the Soviet Union," and the text was explained by Army Chief of Staff Sugiyama. Navy Minister Oikawa repeatedly warned that he did not want to see something serious come of this. In reply the Army Chief of Staff said that the commanding general of the Kwantung Army was very circumspect, and that instructions had also been sent from here warning him to be careful. He exhibited telegrams from the Kwantung Army, as well as telegrams sent to it by the Army Chief of Staff and Vice Chief of Staff.]

TOYODA: Does "frontal attack" mean a full-scale attack?

PRIME MINISTER KONOYE: From the explanations, it would appear that aircraft are the crucial thing. But what is the essence here?

ARMY CHIEF OF STAFF SUGIYAMA: The essence is attack by aircraft beyond our territory, and [also the point in] Paragraph 3.

KONOYE: In that case, how about changing Paragraph 2 to read "attack by aircraft beyond our territory?"

[22] Tatekawa Yoshitsugu, Ambassador to the U.S.S.R.

SUGIYAMA: In "fight back" in Paragraph 2, aircraft coming over the border are included.

SOMEONE: Then why did you put the part about aircraft in the explanation, and not in the document itself?

[There were questions and answers, and it appeared that the Army Chief of Staff, the War Minister, and the Chief of the Military Affairs Bureau would give in and accept a change in wording; but the Foreign Minister proposed: "If you read it carefully, it is very circumspect and tied together, so that there won't be any mistakes. I believe that the original draft should stand as is without revision." Everyone agreed, and the draft was adopted.

[Impression of the Army Chief of Staff:] I believe that there was much discussion because the document was written in too elaborate a style.

46TH LIAISON CONFERENCE
August 14, 1941

On August 1 the United States, worried by British reports of Japanese pressure on Thailand, had extended her proposal of neutralization for French Indochina to cover Thailand also. The Japanese reply to President Roosevelt's original proposal on neutralization was presented by Ambassador Nomura to the Secretary of State on August 6. In this note Japan offered to refrain from stationing troops in the Southwest Pacific region, except in French Indochina, and to withdraw from Indochina after the settlement of the war in China. In return the United States was asked to make concessions: (1) to suspend military activities in the Southwest Pacific; (2) to cooperate with Japan in acquiring materials from the Netherlands East Indies; (3) to use her good offices to get Japan and China to enter into direct negotiations; (4) to restore normal trade relations with Japan; (5) to recognize Japan's special status in French Indochina, even after the withdrawal of Japanese troops. Secretary Hull's reaction to all this was that in his view the Japanese were "lacking in responsiveness."

In Britain Anthony Eden, in a speech in the House of Commons, warned that a Japanese occupation of Thailand would have "grave consequences," and advised the Thais to resist aggression. More or less in reply, on August 8, Press Secretary Ishii Ko charged that Japan was being subjected to military, economic, and political encirclement by the "ABCD" powers (America, Britain, China, and the Dutch).

In an effort to reduce the developing tension between Japan and Great Britain, which had interests in Thailand, Foreign Minister To-yoda tried to develop a policy that would guarantee Thai neutrality in return for certain British concessions, including the shipment of materials to Japan from the British and Commonwealth territories in the Far East and the closing of the Burma Road, over which aid was being sent to Chiang Kai-shek. The Foreign Ministry draft of a policy statement was rejected by this Conference; but it was agreed that another statement, more or less similar in approach, should be drawn up by the Army, the Navy, and the Foreign Ministry.

Agenda: Diplomacy toward Britain, etc.

[Statement by the Foreign Minister:]

Negotiations with the United States are as in the telegram. As for the Soviet Union, Smetanin [Soviet Ambassador to Japan] called and replied as indicated in the attached letter [omitted in translation].

On the 12th, Craigie [British Ambassador to Japan] called, and the gist of our conversation was as follows:

CRAIGIE: Eden has said in England that a Japanese advance into Thailand poses a direct threat to Britain. However, Ishii Ko, the Press Secretary, has said that the ABCD alliance is being formed against Japan, and that this is an unfriendly act. What are the Foreign Minister's views? Moreover, the *Tokyo Nichi-nichi* states that Japan will demand military bases from Thailand, as well as an economic union. We do not want false reports, such as those of Ishii and the press, published.

FOREIGN MINISTER TOYODA: Where did you hear these reports?

CRAIGIE: From Germany and China; and though I hate to say it, from the Thai military attaché in Japan.

TOYODA: It is the British who are giving out false propaganda.

CRAIGIE: We are not doing anything that is threatening to Japan. We cannot increase our forces in Singapore and Malaya because we do not have the ships, although we are increasing aircraft. Hence we cannot advance into Thailand. Isn't it to our mutual disadvantage if both our countries engage in false propaganda?

In short, Britain is absorbed in defense. Isn't it said that Japan occupied French Indochina at the urging of a certain country?

TOYODA: That is what Chiang Kai-shek says; but wouldn't it be a good idea if you would caution him on that?

CRAIGIE: The British in Chungking cannot say anything to Chiang that would displease him. I believe that your entry into southern

French Indochina has nothing to do with the China Incident, and
that it is purely offensive.

TOYODA: If that is so, British aid to Chiang should be stopped.

CRAIGIE: You say "aid to Chiang," but we are not sending in much.
Isn't it Japan's aim to drive Britain out of Thailand? Britain is satisfied if she acquires rice, tin, and rubber. We must ask you to see to
it that this kind of material is not sent to Germany. Japan shouldn't
take all of it. It is most urgent that we settle these matters in Thailand. I also think that a certain amount of trade between Japan and
Britain is possible.

TOYODA: Why doesn't Britain make the first move?

CRAIGIE: I would like to have Japan make the first move.

My impressions of the results of the foregoing talk are as follows:

Britain's desire is to stop Japan's southward advance. Since she has
had friendly relations with Thailand for more than a century, she
would like to get rice, tin, etc. British troop strength along the border
is weak. Won't the matter of the freezing of Japanese funds be settled
if the military advance is stopped, irrespective of the economic advance?

The above also applies to the Netherlands East Indies.

[In this way the Foreign Minister presented the attached Foreign
Office draft on diplomacy toward Great Britain.]

WAR MINISTER TOJO: The acquisition of military bases in Thailand
has already been approved in Imperial Conferences on several occasions. It is not possible to change that at this point.

[Army Chief of Staff Sugiyama supported the above, and emphasized that the Foreign Office draft is unacceptable.]

TOYODA: This [pause in the southward advance] is a temporary
thing, and basically there is no change in policy.

PRIME MINISTER KONOYE: If it is temporary, it will be acceptable,
won't it?

[These were the questions and answers. It was decided that the
Army, Navy, and Foreign Office Bureau Chiefs would prepare a draft
[for understanding with Britain] along these lines: (a) guarantee of
Thai neutrality; (b) British cooperation with regard to Japan's acquisition of materials from the southern regions; (c) Britain should take
a friendly attitude toward the embargo and other matters; (d) Britain would stop aid to Chiang; (e) Britain would refrain from taking
military measures that would be disadvantageous to Japan.]

47TH LIAISON CONFERENCE
August 16, 1941

The Germans continued to urge their Japanese allies to attack the Soviet Union from the East; but by the middle of August Japan had pretty much abandoned the idea of a military campaign against the Russians. As the notes of this Conference show, however, Japanese leaders were not willing to admit this to the Germans, but chose instead to make evasive remarks.

The conflict between the Foreign Ministry and the armed forces, which was inherent in the theory of the independence of the Supreme Command, continued to create tension. Legally speaking, the Liaison Conference was an informal body, and its decisions were subject to the approval of the Cabinet; yet there was opposition to seeking such approval. Moreover, the Army was issuing statements on foreign policy matters, and when this practice was criticized by the Foreign Minister, War Minister Tojo stated in no uncertain terms that he did not intend to cooperate.

[Statement by the Foreign Minister:]
Yesterday I summoned the German and Italian Ambassadors, and reported to them what I had recently told the Soviet Ambassador. The gist was that since my appointment as Foreign Minister I had discussed with the Soviet Ambassador matters pertaining to concessions in northern Sakhalin and the abolition of Maritime Danger Zones, and that later I had conveyed our demands to the Ambassador. I added that in response the Soviets had said that they would observe the Neutrality Pact.

There were no questions from the Italian Ambassador, but there were a few from the German Ambassador. My answers were as follows:

OTT: On the granting of concessions in northern Sakhalin, has the Soviet Union made any guarantees? What has happened recently concerning the abolition of the Maritime Danger Zones?

FOREIGN MINISTER TOYODA: Sakamoto is currently negotiating with the Soviets.[23]

OTT: I don't remember clearly, but in former Foreign Minister

---

[23] Sakamoto Mizuo, Chief of the European Bureau of the Foreign Ministry.

Matsuoka's communication to Germany, he said that as soon as Japan felt prepared, she would overthrow the Communist system. What has happened to this plan?

TOYODA: The present state of our war preparations against the Soviet Union represents the first step in future operations against the Soviets; and I believe that this is in keeping with the spirit of the Tripartite Pact.

OTT: I believe that your statement that it is the first step in operations against the Soviet Union is highly significant. I understand clearly.

The Polish Legation is still in Tokyo; have any decisions been made on this?

[The Foreign Minister stated that this matter had been broached by the German Government, by Ambassador Oshima, and by Ott. The Germans are concerned that the Polish Legation is sending out hostile reports; but since at present the Privy Council is not meeting, we will have to wait until September to do something about this.]

[The Foreign Minister presented the draft statement on diplomacy toward Great Britain prepared by the Army, Navy, and Foreign Office Bureau Chiefs; and this was adopted as indicated in the attached document.[24] In discussing the foregoing, the Army people particularly stressed the closing of the Burma Road. In response to this, Chief of the Naval Affairs Bureau Oka said that the closing of the Burma Road was closely related to the United States. Therefore, he said that in carrying out diplomacy on this, care must be exercised in opening up the subject so that the approach will be consistent with the actual conditions. The Bureau Chief's remarks make one believe that he is very sensitive about the United States, and that he expresses the attitude of the Navy Ministry toward the United States.]

TOYODA: How about presenting the draft that was approved today to the Cabinet?

[The Supreme Command's position: There are matters [in the draft] that pertain to the Supreme Command; if they did not consult the Cabinet, it would be inappropriate, since they would be discourteous to the Ministers of State who bear the responsibility for affairs of state. They stressed the present suggestion, saying that it would be good to submit the decision of the Liaison Conferences to the Cabinet.]

SOMEONE: The main purpose of holding Liaison Conferences in the Imperial Headquarters Building was to discuss important mat-

[24] The text of this statement is not available, but presumably it was similar to the Foreign Ministry statement discussed at the previous Conference.

ters of state with the Supreme Command, with the Prime Minister
and other necessary Cabinet Ministers participating under the aus-
pices of Imperial Headquarters. We have had cases in the past where
secrets have leaked out because they were discussed in the Cabinet.
Except for those matters that because of their particularly grave nature should be presented to the Cabinet, in general the Cabinet
should not be consulted.

TOYODA: The other Ministers are also Ministers of State. Is it inappropriate to consult them too?

SOMEONE: You are right from the point of view of the Constitution.

TOYODA: Are you going to disregard the Constitution?

SOMEONE: Theoretically, what you say is correct; but if you present
something to the Cabinet, it always leaks out the next day. As a practical matter, you have to think both of theory and of the release of
secrets that should not be disclosed. When there is a need for it, the
Prime Minister can bring along the necessary Ministers of State.
Those Ministers who must be kept informed will be notified. That is,
I think it proper that the necessary Ministers be invited [to Confer-
ences].

[Next there was the following discussion:]

TOYODA: Regarding yesterday's joint announcement by Roosevelt
and Churchill, the Foreign Office wanted to act cautiously, since this
is a serious matter.[25] But since last evening there have been many
notices in the newspapers. According to what I hear, they originated
from the Chief of the Information Section of the Army. But this matter is a responsibility of the Foreign Minister and shouldn't be handled by the Army. I ask that you be careful.

TOJO: I am a Minister of State. What is wrong with my directing,
as a Minister of State, my Chief of Information in guiding public
opinion? There is a Director of the Information Bureau. Under him
are Chiefs of Foreign Office, Army, and Navy Sections. What is bad
about the Army making statements through its Minister of State? If
this matter was important, why didn't you get together with the Director and handle it? I don't think I am responsible. After all, I must
act in my capacity as War Minister. If it is a matter of who is [legally]
authorized [to take a certain action], you had better instruct the Director. I'm going to be frank from now on.

[25] This refers to the Atlantic Charter, issued by Churchill and Roosevelt after
their historic meeting. In a telegram dated August 16 Ambassador Nomura complained about the "scorching criticism" of this statement in the Japanese press
and said that in the "deteriorating atmosphere" he feared he could not accomplish
his mission of reaching an agreement with the United States.

[The Impressions of the Army Chief of Staff:]
It appears that the Foreign Minister has the feeling that the Foreign Office is being put under pressure in everything. He apparently feels strongly that the Liaison Conferences, news releases, and other things are controlled by the military. But he was put off in all matters.

48TH LIAISON CONFERENCE
August 26, 1941

Early in August Prime Minister Konoye had decided that he would make a final attempt to reach an agreement with the United States by arranging for a personal meeting with President Roosevelt. He feared that the opportune moment might be missed if negotiations were carried on through Ambassador Nomura. On August 4 he sounded out the Navy and War Ministers. The Navy leaders supported the idea, but War Minister Tojo, while not necessarily against it, imposed certain conditions. Tojo's judgment was that even if Konoye met with President Roosevelt, the probability of failure was eight out of ten; and he was insistent that in the event of failure Konoye must agree not to resign, but to lead the nation into war.

On instructions from Tokyo, Nomura suggested a meeting of the two heads of state to Secretary Hull; but the impact of his suggestion was blunted by Hull's reaction to the August 6 proposals.

On August 17, after President Roosevelt's return from the Atlantic Conference, Ambassador Nomura saw the President and proposed that he meet with Prime Minister Konoye. The President was more receptive to the idea than was his Secretary of State. Hence Prime Minister Konoye decided to send a message to President Roosevelt, and the content of the message was discussed at this Liaison Conference. The message was cordial, and indicated that the informal conversations, disrupted in July, did not meet the present situation, and that a conference involving the heads of state might save the situation. Konoye and the Foreign Ministry were especially anxious to avoid putting in anything that was too bellicose and therefore likely to provoke a hostile response from the United States. Ambassador Nomura delivered the message and statement to President Roosevelt on his visit to the White House on August 28. At that time the President suggested Juneau, Alaska, as a possible meeting place.

Agenda: Prime Minister Konoye's Telegrams Replying to the President of the United States and to Hull.

[The Prime Minister's telegraphic reply to the President of the United States:[26] Last night a meeting of the Army Chief of Staff, the Vice Chief of Staff, and the Chiefs of the First and Second Sections of the Army Staff was held in the official residence of the War Minister. A document studied at this meeting was presented [to this Conference] after the Prime Minister himself had made a few changes in wording. He also added the word "must," and the document was adopted.

[Regarding the telegraphic reply to Secretary of State Hull, it was adopted after being amended as indicated in red on the attached sheet. It was amended so as not to excite Hull so much that he might refuse to agree to a meeting. Moreover, with regard to this telegram, there were two views: one, that only the telegram to the President was needed; the other, that since Nomura had requested it, another telegram should also be sent to Hull. There were also two additional opinions: one, that the stronger the language the more effective it would be with Americans; the other, that it would be better not to say anything that they would dislike. That is, the arguments were that if the wording were too sharp we could not have a meeting, and, opposed to this, that if we refrained from saying anything the other party would dislike, the determined will of the Empire could not be indicated to them. It was decided that both of the telegrams would be sent today.]

PRIME MINISTER KONOYE: Neither the Tripartite Pact nor the East Asia Co-prosperity Sphere are mentioned, and it is necessary to make a decision on this.

FOREIGN MINISTER TOYODA: If we mentioned these matters, we could not get an improvement in diplomatic relations.

KONOYE: We must make a decision on the concluding section. [On this point there was an exchange of views, but no special decision was reached.]

[Admonitions by the Army Chief of Staff:]

It appears that Churchill has made some comments to the press about this negotiation.[27] Also, there are rumors that word has leaked

---

[26] The text of the Prime Minister's message to the President and the statement are in *Proceedings of the Joint Committee on the Investigation of the Pearl Harbor Attack* (U.S. Congress), Pt. 17, Exhibit 124, pp. 2776–78.

[27] The Japanese people had first learned of their Government's negotiations with the United States from Churchill's radio broadcast to the Empire. Churchill stated that if the negotiations failed, Britain would range herself "unhesitatingly at the side of the United States." David Lu, *From the Marco Polo Bridge to Pearl Harbor,* p. 195.

out to the public. All the officials present here should be especially careful to keep everything confidential.

49TH LIAISON CONFERENCE
August 30, 1941

News of Konoye's message to President Roosevelt upset the Germans, who feared that Japan might abandon the Tripartite Pact. Foreign Minister Toyoda tried to convince German Ambassador Ott that Japan's negotiations with the United States did not violate the spirit of the Tripartite Pact. The Foreign Minister also talked with Craigie, the British Ambassador, and complained about the so-called encirclement of Japan. Toyoda protested British aid to Chiang, among other things, and Craigie responded that the aid did not amount to much.

[Following an exchange of views, the Foreign Minister reported on his conversations with the German, Italian, and British Ambassadors.]

[Conversation with the German Ambassador:]

OTT: Although I had planned to be in Karuizawa[28] all this week, I changed my plans and returned last night; and I have now come to see you. Has there been a change in Japan's policy toward the Tripartite Pact?

FOREIGN MINISTER TOYODA: There has been no change.

OTT: Prime Minister Konoye has sent a message to the President of the United States. What did the message say?

TOYODA: Since it is a matter involving the United States, I cannot very well tell you about it now.

OTT: What was the reason for sending the message?

TOYODA: You are aware that ever since Matsuoka was Foreign Minister we have been attempting to improve Japanese-American relations. We think that in terms of peace in the Pacific it would lead to an unhappy situation if we were to leave Japanese-American relations in their present state. It is because both countries feel this way that the message has been sent. We are thinking about peace in the Pacific, and this is in keeping with the spirit of the Axis. I would like to make the atmosphere in the Pacific peaceful at this time.

OTT: You will be tricked by the United States, and negotiations will be drawn out; you had better break them off and avoid being tricked.

---

[28] A popular summer resort for the foreign community in Japan.

TOYODA: There are various ways of preventing American entry into the war. During Matsuoka's time, we tried to deter America with strong language. This aroused the Americans' hostility, and in the end they severed communications with Japan. Accordingly, we have to think carefully about the pros and cons of getting the United States even more excited. On this matter—and this is dwelling on the past —we would like to have Germany consider her own actions. As a matter of fact, when the United States occupied Iceland, when funds were frozen, and when the consulates were closed, isn't it true that Germany limited herself to one protest, and that she has said nothing more?[29] I wonder about the wisdom of Japan's being the only one to irritate the United States. As far as Japan is concerned, she cannot help but give some thought to the question of whether it is better to watch quietly, as your country is doing, or to go on a rampage. Wouldn't it be better for Japan to be patient and restrained, to calm American public opinion and not irritate the United States? If both countries assume a calm attitude, I believe relaxation will come naturally.

OTT: Have you proposed some conditions for the purposes of negotiation?

TOYODA: We merely put forward Prime Minister Konoye's views.

OTT: What are you going to discuss? Is Grew involved in this matter?[30]

TOYODA: The Prime Minister's message says nothing about what is to be discussed. Grew is not involved.

[With this the meeting was recessed. We agreed to meet again at 3:00 P.M. today.]

[At 3:00]

[In the main the conversation with the Italian Ambassador proceeded in about the same fashion as that with the German Ambassador. There were no matters of importance.]

[Conversation with the British Ambassador.]

I summoned the British Ambassador and reminded him that when I saw him on August 11 he had said that he would call immediately upon his return from Nikko.[31] He said that he had not come because

---

[29] On June 16, 1941, all German Consulates in the United States were closed by order of the American Government.

[30] Joseph C. Grew, United States Ambassador to Japan.

[31] A famous mausoleum that enshrines Iyeyasu, the founder of the Tokugawa Shogunate. An attraction for tourists, it is located in a mountainous area north of Tokyo.

he had understood that he would be summoned. Our questions and answers went as follows:

CRAIGIE: The British newspapers are at fault, too; but the Japanese press is playing up the encirclement of Japan. Can't something be done about this? The Japanese newspapers are carrying various reports; but I will state on my own responsibility that Great Britain is not allied to China, that she has not admitted Chinese troops to Burma, and that she has made no demands on Thailand. Again, it is said that the Commander in Chief of the [British] Far East Forces[32] discussed various things with the press; but it is a fact that between his appointment in November of last year and April 21 of this year he has granted only one press interview. Moreover, he did not touch on any Far Eastern matters. He did not meet with reporters on May 1. Again, it is reported that he said on July 11 that our defenses are all set; but there is no truth to this.

TOYODA: Although this is what Your Excellency says, isn't it true that the British side has put out quite a few false reports? For example, you frequently say that Japanese and Soviet troops have clashed on the Manchurian-Soviet border.

CRAIGIE: There is no one on our side who says things like that.

TOYODA: It is natural that Japan should be displeased about the British freezing of Japanese funds, and about other economic sanctions. As for the occupation of French Indochina, this was, as I have explained on several occasions, a peaceful occupation. Despite this, England says she is being threatened.

CRAIGIE: That is true. But it is clear, if you look at a map, that the airfields in southern French Indochina are directed toward the South.

TOYODA: If we both think that our countries are being threatened, we won't get anywhere.

CRAIGIE: British defense is the defense of the territory of both Malaya and Burma. But in the case of Japanese defense, haven't you occupied other countries?

TOYODA: We did that because Britain is engaged in aiding Chiang. I feel that it is most important that Britain stop this; how do you feel?

CRAIGIE: Britain's aid to Chiang is on a small scale, and at the present time it is not much. I myself have previously recommended the closing of the Burma Road to my Government; but today the situation is different. Hence I think it would be difficult for me to tell this to my Government today.

---

[32] Air Chief Marshal Sir Robert Brooke-Popham.

TOYODA: Hasn't Britain herself frozen our funds, stopped trade, and even induced the Netherlands East Indies to put economic pressure on Japan?

CRAIGIE: Britain is not putting pressure on the Netherlands. All measures against Japan are for the purpose of forcing you to consider the occupation of French Indochina. Japan says that the ABCD are forming a line to encircle Japan, but this is not something produced by joint action; it is the natural result of actions taken individually. I think that this encirclement will not change until Japan reconsiders certain basic issues. Originally French Indochina belonged to Vichy, which is a puppet of Germany; and Japan occupied it by threatening Vichy. Therefore, we regard Japan's occupation of French Indochina as a threat to us.

TOYODA: Japan, for her part, believes that Britain has promoted a conspiracy to encircle Japan; so feelings toward Britain are deteriorating more and more.

CRAIGIE: Britain's position is purely defensive, not offensive. So long as Japan occupies French Indochina, alleviation [of the tension] is difficult.

TOYODA: There is no point in talking further. As diplomats we both need to work for the peace of our countries. What about it?

CRAIGIE: Of course.

With this the meeting ended. It was agreed that we would meet again on September 1.

50TH LIAISON CONFERENCE
September 3, 1941

At this Conference a crucial policy document, "The Essentials for Carrying Out the Empire's Policies," was presented for discussion and adopted.[33] The key point in this document was the decision to carry on negotiations with the United States and simultaneously prepare for war. If negotiations were not successful by the last ten days of October, Japan would go to war.

As was usual with important policy statements of this kind, the document had been subjected to prior debate by the various Army and Navy agencies. The first draft of the document was presented by the Navy to a joint conference of Army and Navy Bureau and Section Chiefs on August 16. On August 18 it was sent to the War Guidance

---

[33] For the text of this document in its final form, see the Imperial Conference record of September 6 (herein, pp. 135–36).

Section of the Army General Staff, and then routed to the War Min-
istry. It was approved and sent on by the War Ministry with some
slight changes in wording, discussed on August 22 and 23 by the
Army General Staff, and then returned to the War Ministry. On
August 25, War Minister Tojo, Chief of the Military Affairs Bureau
Muto, Sato of the War Ministry, and Sugiyama and Tsukada, Army
Chief and Vice Chief of Staff, respectively, considered the revised
draft. Muto and Tanaka, Chief of the Operations Section of the Army
General Staff, met on August 26; and on the 27th and 28th the Bureau
and Section Chiefs of the Army and Navy conferred.

There is no evidence that the crucial question of Japan's chances
of winning a war against the United States and Britain was ever seri-
ously studied and discussed in any of these meetings. To begin with,
Sugiyama, Tsukada, and Tanaka, all on the Army General Staff, had
no previous experience in planning for and executing actual military
operations. Hence they were not prepared to make a critical study of
how Japan was likely to fare in a war against America and Britain.
In general, the Army planners felt that war against the United States
would be mostly the responsibility of the Navy; it was willing to leave
the business of assessing the chances of victory to the Navy Ministry
and the Naval General Staff. As we have seen, Navy Chief of Staff
Nagano had made some bellicose statements in previous Liaison Con-
ferences; and the general opinion in his group favored war.

Because of the serious character of the decision the 50th Confer-
ence was an extended one, lasting some seven hours. It is remarkable
that Prime Minister Konoye and Foreign Minister Toyoda, both of
whom opposed war with the United States, were willing to accept
the Army and Navy recommendations on the basis of one meeting.
It may be that they were so easily persuaded because they pinned
their hopes on a Konoye-Roosevelt meeting and believed that the
part of the decision having to do with war would never have to be
carried out.

Agenda: "The Essentials for Carrying Out the Empire's Policies."
[Participants: The Minister of Home Affairs attended. The Conference lasted from 11 A.M. to 6 P.M. First of all, Navy Chief of Staff
Nagano explained the reasons for the presentation of "The Essentials
for Carrying Out the Empire's Policies." The gist of his remarks was
as follows:]
In various respects the Empire is losing materials: that is, we are
getting weaker. By contrast, the enemy is getting stronger. With the

passage of time, we will get increasingly weaker, and we won't be able to survive. Moreover, we will endure what can be endured in carrying on diplomacy, but at the opportune moment we must make some estimates. Ultimately, when there is no hope for diplomacy, and when war cannot be avoided, it is essential that we make up our minds quickly. Although I am confident that at the present time we have a chance to win a war, I fear that this opportunity will disappear with the passage of time. Regarding war, the Navy thinks in terms of both a short war and a long one. I think it will probably be a long war. Hence we must be prepared for a long war. We hope that the enemy will come out for a quick showdown; in that event there will be a decisive battle in waters near us, and I anticipate that our chances of victory would be quite good. But I do not believe that the war would end with that. It would be a long war. In this connection, I think it would be good to take advantage of the fruits of [an initial] victory in order to cope with a long war. If, on the contrary, we get into a long war without a decisive battle, we will be in difficulty, especially since our supply of resources will become depleted. If we cannot obtain these resources, it will not be possible to carry on a long war. It is important to make preparations so that we will not be defeated, by getting essential resources and by making the best of our strategy. There is no set series of steps that will guarantee our checkmating the enemy. But even so, there will probably be measures we can adopt, depending on changes in the international situation.

In short, our armed forces have no alternative but to try to avoid being pushed into a corner, to keep in our hands the power to decide when to begin hostilities and thus seize the initiative. There is no alternative but to push forward in this way.

[Next there was the following statement by the Army Chief of Staff:]

With regard to making the last ten days of October the target date for completing our war preparations: even if we make up our minds right now, we will need until then to mobilize, and to arm ships and assemble them.

With reference to Paragraph 3, we must try to achieve our diplomatic objectives by the first ten days in October; and failing this we must push forward. We cannot let things be dragged out. The reason is that we cannot carry out large-scale operations in the North until February. In order to be able to act in the North, we have to carry out operations quickly in the South. Even if we start right away, operations will take until next spring. Insofar as we are delayed we will not be able to act in the North. Therefore, it is necessary to move as quickly as possible.

[Navy Minister Oikawa moved the following amendment to Paragraph 3:]

"In the event that there is no prospect of our demands being met by the first ten days in October, we will take the final measures for survival and self-defense."

[Various opinions were expressed concerning this; but in the end it was argued that it was inadequate. Then Oka, Chief of the Naval Affairs Bureau, moved the adoption of the following amendment:]

"In the event that there is no prospect of our demands being met by the first ten days in October, we will immediately decide to commence hostilities with the United States and Britain, and take final measures."

[There was opposition to this also. Finally the following was adopted:]

"In the event that there is no prospect of our demands being met by the first ten days in October through the diplomatic negotiations mentioned above, we will immediately decide to commence hostilities against the United States, Britain, and the Netherlands."

[In the meantime there was a discussion between Director of the Planning Board Suzuki, the War Minister, the Army Chief of Staff, and others concerning ships, oil, iron, etc. Next, there was the following discussion:]

SOMEONE: Is there a possibility that we will move into Thailand during the talks between Prime Minister Konoye and the President of the United States?

ARMY CHIEF OF STAFF SUGIYAMA: We will refrain from doing that sort of thing as much as possible. Moreover, we will prepare so as to avoid sending troops into French Indochina as much as possible; but we can't adhere to this completely.

WAR MINISTER TOJO: Are you going to build up military supplies in Indochina?

SUGIYAMA: We will send in military supplies.

TOJO: If you do that, our plans will become known.

SUGIYAMA: We can't help it.

CHIEF OF THE NAVAL AFFAIRS BUREAU OKA: Can't you pretend you are going into Kunming?

SUGIYAMA: We can't hide everything.

[It was agreed that Paragraph 4 of the Addendum, to the extent that a consensus on it could be reached, would be added at the end as a separate paragraph. Moreover, the phrase "on the basis of general international usage" was deleted at the insistence of Prime Minister Konoye. The reason was that defense and self-defense are ultimately interpreted in terms of power considerations, not on the basis of international usage of the terms. An example was [foreign reaction to] the exercise of the right of self-defense by the Empire in the Manchurian Incident. Hence it would be to the advantage of the Empire to delete this phrase.

[Then the phrase "Japan's interpretation and implementation of the Tripartite Pact" was amended to read: "Japan's interpretation of the Tripartite Pact and her actions therein." War Minister Tojo held that the amendment threw doubt on the Empire's carrying out its obligations under the Tripartite Pact, and moved the following as a note: "The above does not alter our obligations under the Tripartite Pact." The War Minister and Army Chief of Staff strongly advocated this, and it was adopted.

[It was decided that the foregoing [document] would be submitted to a Cabinet meeting on Friday, and to an Imperial Conference on Saturday. The Minister of Home Affairs and the Finance Minister would also participate in the Imperial Conference.]

IMPERIAL CONFERENCE
September 6, 1941

After the adoption of "The Essentials for Carrying Out the Empire's Policies" by the Liaison Conference, the Prime Minister went to see the Emperor to report this development. The Emperor expressed concern that the policy statement put emphasis on war rather than on diplomacy, but Konoye denied this. The Emperor then said he wanted to speak with the Army and Navy Chiefs of Staff about military matters, so they were summoned to the palace. During the audience, the Emperor asked Army Chief of Staff Sugiyama how long it would take the Army to finish the job in the event of a war with the United States. Sugiyama's reply was that operations in the South Pacific would be concluded in three months. The Emperor retorted that when the China Incident broke out Sugiyama, who was then War Minister, had said that the war would end in a month; but four years had gone by, and the war still had not ended. Sugiyama's defense was that the interior of China was huge; whereupon the Emperor, in great anger, said: "If the interior of China is huge, isn't the Pacific Ocean even bigger? How can you be sure that war will end in three months?" He then asked if the Supreme Command meant to put the emphasis on diplomacy, and Navy Chief of Staff Nagano came to Sugiyama's rescue and replied that that was the case.

Later the Emperor told his adviser Kido, the Lord Keeper of the Privy Seal, that he was dissatisfied with the lack of a real debate on issues in Imperial Conferences; and twenty minutes before the Imperial Conference was scheduled, he suggested to Kido that he wanted personally to ask questions. Kido did not approve of this procedure, and persuaded the Emperor that Hara, President of the Privy Council, should ask questions on his behalf, as was customary. The Emperor, however, did make a comment at the end.

Despite the assurances of Konoye and the military that diplomacy would come first, the very fact that a time limit had been placed on the decision for war or peace, and that in the meantime the armed forces would prepare for hostilities, tipped the balance in favor of war, just as the Emperor feared. In this sense, the decision marked a turning point.

In considering the possibility of war with the United States, the group naturally had to give thought to the chances of winning such a war. It was openly stated that great risks were involved, and that no sure victory was in view. In the end, however, the case boiled down to the argument that "there will never be a better time than now."

[Time: September 6, from 10 A.M. to 12 noon. Participants: Prime Minister Konoye, Foreign Minister Toyoda, Home Minister Tanabe, Finance Minister Ogura, War Minister Tojo, Navy Minister Oikawa, Army Chief of Staff Sugiyama, Navy Chief of Staff Nagano, Army Vice Chief of Staff Tsukada, Navy Vice Chief of Staff Ito, President of the Privy Council Hara, Secretary of the Cabinet Tomita, Chief of the Military Affairs Bureau of the War Ministry Muto, Chief of the Naval Affairs Bureau of the Navy Ministry Oka, Director of the Planning Board Suzuki.

[The conference was convened at 10:00 A.M. For one hour members heard statements by the Prime Minister, the Foreign Minister, the Director of the Planning Board, and the Army and Navy Chiefs of Staff. Then there were questions and answers, mainly conducted by the President of the Privy Council. The conference was adjourned at noon.

[Gist of the statement by the Foreign Minister: The Foreign Minister reported on the progress of the "Nomura" operation from the time of Foreign Minister Matsuoka until today. Then he read aloud and made some comments on the "Final Demands of Our Empire on

Great Britain and the United States to Be Attained Through Diplomatic Means, and the Maximum Concessions to Be Made by Our Empire," which was appended to "Essentials for Carrying Out the Empire's Policies."]

The Essentials for Carrying Out the Empire's Policies
[Adopted by the Imperial Conference, September 6.]

In view of the current critical situation, in particular, the offensive attitudes that such countries as the United States, Great Britain, and the Netherlands are taking toward Japan, and in view of the situation in the Soviet Union and the condition of our Empire's national power, we will carry out our policy toward the South, which is contained in the "Outline of National Policies in View of the Changing Situation," as follows:

I. Our Empire, for the purposes of self-defense and self-preservation, will complete preparations for war, with the last ten days of October as a tentative deadline, resolved to go to war with the United States, Great Britain, and the Netherlands if necessary.

II. Our Empire will concurrently take all possible diplomatic measures vis-à-vis the United States and Great Britain, and thereby endeavor to attain our objectives. The minimum objectives of our Empire to be attained through negotiations with the United States and Great Britain and the maximum concessions therein to be made by our Empire are noted in the attached documents.

III. In the event that there is no prospect of our demands being met by the first ten days of October through the diplomatic negotiations mentioned above, we will immediately decide to commence hostilities against the United States, Britain, and the Netherlands.

Policies other than those toward the South will be based on established national policy; and we will especially try to prevent the United States and the Soviet Union from forming a united front against Japan.

[Attached Document]

The Minimum Demands of Our Empire to Be Attained Through Diplomatic Negotiations with the United States (and Great Britain), and the Maximum Concessions to Be Made by Our Empire

ITEM ONE: The minimum demands of our Empire to be attained through diplomatic negotiations with the United States and Great Britain:

1. The United States and Great Britain shall neither interfere with nor obstruct the settlement of the China Incident by our Empire.

(a) They shall not obstruct our efforts to settle the Incident on the basis of the Fundamental Treaty between Japan and China, and the Joint Declaration of Japan, Manchukuo, and China.

(b) They shall close the Burma Road and cease to assist the Chiang Kai-shek regime militarily, politically, and economically.

Note: This does not prejudice the position that our Empire has been taking in relation to the settlement of the China Incident in the Nomura operation. We should particularly insist on stationing our troops under a new agreement between Japan and China. However, we have no objection to affirming that we are in principle prepared to withdraw our troops following the settlement of the Incident, except for those that are dispatched to carry out the purposes of the Incident. We have no objection to affirming that the economic activities of the United States and Great Britain in China will not be restricted, insofar as they are carried out on an equitable basis.

2. The United States and Great Britain shall refrain from actions that may threaten the defense of our Empire in the Far East.

(a) They shall not secure any military rights in the territories of Thailand, the Netherlands East Indies, China, and the Far Eastern section of the Soviet Union.

(b) They shall not increase their military forces in the Far East beyond the present strength [of those forces].

Note: Any demand to dissolve the special relations between Japan and French Indochina based on the agreement between Japan and France will not be accepted.

3. The United States and Great Britain shall cooperate in the acquisition of goods needed by our Empire.

(a) They shall restore commercial relations with our Empire and supply those goods from their territories in the Southwest Pacific that our Empire urgently needs to sustain herself.

(b) They shall amicably contribute to the economic cooperation between Japan, Thailand, and the Netherlands East Indies.

ITEM TWO: The maximum concessions to be made by our Empire:
If the demands indicated in Item One are met,

1. Our Empire will not advance militarily from the bases in French Indochina to the neighboring areas other than China.

Note: If we are asked about our attitude toward the Soviet Union, we will reply that we will not resort to military force unilaterally unless the Soviet Union violates the Japanese-Soviet Neutrality Pact and acts against the spirit of the Pact in such a way as to menace Japan and Manchukuo.

2. Our Empire is prepared to withdraw its forces from French Indochina after a just peace has been established in the Far East.

3. Our Empire is prepared to guarantee the neutrality of the Philippine Islands.

APPENDIX: Japan's attitude toward the European war will be governed by the ideas of protection and self-defense. Japan's interpretation of the Tripartite Pact and her actions therein in the event that the United States should enter the European war will be made by herself acting independently.

Note: The above does not alter our obligations under the Tripartite Pact.

[The gist of the Prime Minister's [informal] comments was as follows:]

With regard to the Note under Item One, Section 1, i.e., the "stationing of troops under a new agreement between Japan and China": the Imperial army will be stationed under a new agreement, which is to be concluded in the future between Japan and China; so on this matter there is no change in the principle that has already been indicated to the United States in the Nomura operation. [This comment deserves special attention.]

No agreement has been reached yet in the Nomura operation on "the economic activities of the United States and Great Britain in China" mentioned in the same Note.

As to the establishment of military rights [by the United States and Britain] in Section 2(a): there is no confirmed information that they have any in Thailand, the Netherlands East Indies, China, or the Far Eastern section of the Soviet Union. However, we have heard rumors that America has acquired a base for shipping in the Netherlands East Indies.

The special relations between Japan and French Indochina mentioned in the Note to Section 2(b) include joint defense, the Arsène-Henry–Matsuoka Agreement, and the Economic Agreement. We cannot have these agreements abrogated. They conflict with the freedom of trade advocated by the United States, but we cannot abrogate them because of Japan's special position.

Section 1 of Item Two has already been shown to the United States, and the Note to this Section has been informally conveyed to the United States.

Next, there is the problem of interpretation in the event of American participation in the war. The first paragraph [of the Appendix] makes it clear that Japan's attitude toward the European war is governed by the principle of refraining from positive participation in the war, and is based on protection and self-defense. With regard to our attitude in the event of American participation in the war, we have hitherto told the United States that we would immediately go to war; but this interpretation is a little too strict. Article 3 of the Tripartite Pact provides that the question of whether or not one signatory has been attacked shall be decided by consultation among the three nations; and the decision of the Special Committee provided for in Article 4 is to be put into effect subject to the approval of each of the governments concerned. Generalizing from all this, I do not believe we have to interpret the question as strictly as we have done up to now. Furthermore, we will act independently on military matters. That is why we have drafted the proposal this way.

[The formal proceedings of the Conference follow.]

Statement by Prime Minister Konoye:

May I call the conference to order. With your permission, I will take the chair in order that we may proceed.

As you all know, the international situation in which we are involved has become increasingly strained; and in particular, the United States, Great Britain, and the Netherlands have come to oppose our Empire with all available means. There has also emerged the prospect that the United States and the Soviet Union will form a united front against Japan as the war between Germany and the Soviet Union becomes prolonged.

If we allow this situation to continue, it is inevitable that our Empire will gradually lose the ability to maintain its national power, and that our national power will lag behind that of the United States, Great Britain, and others. Under these circumstances our Empire must, of course, quickly prepare to meet any situation that may occur, and at the same time it must try to prevent the disaster of war by resorting to all possible diplomatic measures. If the diplomatic measures should fail to bring about favorable results within a certain period, I believe we cannot help but take the ultimate step in order to defend ourselves.

The Government and the Army and Navy sections of Imperial Headquarters have discussed this matter on numerous occasions. They have now reached an agreement, and have drafted "The Essentials for Carrying Out the Empire's Policies," which is on today's agenda. I would like you to consider this proposal carefully.

The Navy Chief of Staff, the Army Chief of Staff, the Foreign Minister, and the Director of the Planning Board will explain the items that are under their jurisdiction.

Items explained by Navy Chief of Staff Nagano:

May I present my statement.

As the Prime Minister has explained in general terms, it is clear that our Empire must exert every effort to overcome the present difficult situation by peaceful means and must find a way to ensure her future prosperity and security. However, in the event that a peaceful solution is not attainable, and we have no alternative but to resort to war, the Supreme Command believes, from the standpoint of operations, that we cannot avoid being finally reduced to a crippled condition [if we delay for too long]. A number of vital military supplies, including oil, are dwindling day by day. This will cause a gradual weakening of our national defense, and lead to a situation in which, if we maintain the status quo, the capacity of our Empire to act will be reduced in the days to come. Meanwhile, the defenses of American, British, and other foreign military facilities and vital points in the Far East, and the military preparedness of these countries, particularly of the United States, are being strengthened with great speed. By the latter half of next year America's military preparedness will have made great progress, and it will be difficult to cope with her. Therefore, it must be said that it would be very dangerous for our Empire to remain idle and let the days go by.

Accordingly, if our minimum demands, which are necessary for the self-preservation and self-defense of our Empire, cannot be attained through diplomacy, and ultimately we cannot avoid war, we must first make all preparations, take advantage of our opportunities, undertake aggressive military operations with determination and a dauntless attitude, and find a way out of our difficulties.

As to our predictions of the way military operations are likely to go, the probability is very high that they [the United States] will from the outset plan on a prolonged war. Therefore, it will be necessary for us to be reconciled to this and to be prepared militarily for a long war. If they should aim for a quick war leading to an early decision, send their principal naval units, and challenge us to an immediate war, this would be the very thing we hope for. The naval units that Great Britain could send to the Far East would be rather limited because of the current war in Europe. Accordingly, if the combined American-British fleet should attack us in the areas of the ocean we have in mind, and when we take into consideration the role of aircraft and other elements, we can say with confidence that the probability of our victory is high. However, even if our Empire should win a decisive naval victory, we will not thereby be able to bring the war to a conclusion. We can anticipate that America will attempt to prolong the war, utilizing her impregnable position, her superior industrial power, and her abundant resources.

Our Empire does not have the means to take the offensive, overcome the enemy, and make them give up their will to fight. Moreover, we are short of resources at home, so we would very much like to avert a prolonged war. However, if we get into a prolonged war, the most important means of assuring that we will be able to bear this burden will be to seize the enemy's important military areas and sources of materials quickly at the beginning of the war, making our operational position tenable and at the same time obtaining vital materials from the areas now under hostile influence. If this first stage in our operations is carried out successfully, our Empire will have secured strategic areas in the Southwest Pacific, established an impregnable position, and laid the basis for a prolonged war, even if American military preparedness should proceed as scheduled. What happens thereafter will depend to a great extent on overall national power—including various elements, tangible and intangible—and on developments in the world situation.

Thus the outcome of a prolonged war is closely related to the success or failure of the first stage in our operations. The essential conditions that give a chance of success in the first stage of operations are: first, to decide quickly to commence hostilities in view of the realities of our fighting capacity and theirs; second, to take the initiative rather than to allow them to do so; third, to consider the meteorological conditions in the operational areas in order to make operations easier. It was in view of these considerations that the time when the crucial decision must be made, which is indicated in this proposal, was set. Of course we intend to proceed carefully with our war preparations, taking full account of the developments in diplomatic negotiations.

I would like to add a few more remarks. We must spare no efforts in seeking a way to settle the present difficult situation peacefully, and thus ensure the prosperity and security of our Empire. We must never fight a war that can be avoided. At the same time, I do not believe that a peace resembling that of the "Winter Battle at Osaka Castle,"[34] in which we would be forced to fight again during the following summer under unfavorable conditions, would contribute to the long-term prosperity of our Empire.

That part of my statement today concerning operations has reference to a situation that would arise if war became inevitable.

[34] Toward the end of 1614 there was a war between the Toyotomi family of Osaka and the Tokugawa family of Yedo (now Tokyo). This is called today "the Winter Battle at Osaka Castle." The shrewd Tokugawa Iyeyasu, seeing that the Toyotomi were almost invincible in the fortress of Osaka Castle, proposed to conclude peace on the condition that the outer moat of the Castle be filled in. However, Iyeyasu actually filled in both the inner and outer moats. Thus the Toyotomi were placed in a defenseless position, and were thoroughly defeated in the war of the following summer. Hence "the Winter Battle of Osaka Castle" refers to a temporary and apparently secure peace that in fact leads to one's downfall in the near future.

Items explained by Army Chief of Staff Sugiyama:

May I present my statement.

The Army is in complete agreement with the statement that has just been made by the Navy Chief of Staff. I am going to touch chiefly on the relationship between preparedness for war and diplomatic negotiations.

As is clear from the statement by the Prime Minister, the time is approaching when our Empire must choose between war and peace in view of the current critical situation, particularly the decline of reserve strength in our national power. The Supreme Command sees the need to make itself promptly ready for necessary military operations, so that it can be prepared for both peace and war.

If we remain idle and mark time in these pressing circumstances, and if we let ourselves be trapped by the intrigues of Great Britain and the United States, our national defense capability will decline as time goes on; by contrast, the military preparedness of Great Britain, the United States, and other countries will be gradually strengthened. Then it will become more difficult to carry out military operations, and it is likely that we might eventually be unable to overcome the obstacles posed by Great Britain and the United States. Therefore, in order to begin hostilities while we are still confident that we can carry on a war with the United States and Great Britain, we have selected the last ten days of October as the time to complete our preparedness for war—taking into account meteorological and other conditions in the expected operational areas and the time needed for the mobilization of manpower, the requisitioning and equipping of ships, and the deployment of our military forces at important strategic points by long-distance sea transport.

But it goes without saying that on this occasion we should exhaust all diplomatic measures before we choose between peace and war. While the diplomatic negotiations are being carried on, the Supreme Command will act carefully in getting ready for operations, so that its activities will not provoke the United States and Great Britain and thus interfere with the negotiations.

However, if there is no prospect that we will be able to achieve our aims through diplomatic measures by a certain time, it is necessary to decide promptly at that point to go to war with the United States and Great Britain, as well as to accelerate our war preparations. Thus we have to send reinforcements to southern French Indochina and complete other war preparations by the last ten days in October, the deadline. Therefore, I believe that when we take into account the movement of these forces, we must make the decision for war no later than the first ten days in October. With regard to the Northern Question while we are fighting in the South, I believe we need not worry. Ever since the outbreak of the German-Soviet war we have been strengthening our preparedness for a possible war with the Soviet Union, and we are ready for any unexpected development.

We can expect a coalition between the United States and the Soviet Union in the future. In winter, however, military operations on a large scale [in the North] are very difficult due to weather conditions; but even if in this season the United States and the Soviet Union should join hands and make use of a part of their aircraft and submarines, the probability of their being militarily effective is low. Therefore, if we could take advantage of the winter season and quickly finish our military operations in the South, I believe we would be in a position to deal with any changes in the Northern situation that might take place next spring and thereafter. On the contrary, if we should miss this seasonal opportunity, we will not be able to achieve security in the North during our operations in the South.

Finally, there is one more thing that I would especially like to mention. If it becomes necessary for us to wage a war in the South, our Empire should immediately disclose its intentions to Germany and Italy, enter into an agreement with them beforehand on the execution of the war, and see to it that Japan, Germany, and Italy can cooperate in achieving the aims of the war. In no case should we let Germany and Italy conclude a unilateral peace with the United States and Great Britain. I believe that this is particularly important in guiding the war.

Statement by Foreign Minister Toyoda [progress report on the negotiations concerning the "Draft Understanding between the Governments of Japan and the United States"]:

I would like to make a few remarks on developments in our negotiations concerning the so-called "Draft Understanding between the Governments of Japan and the United States."

After Nomura, our Ambassador to the United States, had met informally with Secretary of State Hull, Postmaster General Walker, and other officials, a tentative draft of an understanding between Japan and the United States was prepared. Ambassador Nomura reported on this draft in a telegram dated April 16.

In essence, the Draft Understanding sought to reach a broad agreement, in the form of a joint declaration by the Governments of Japan and the United States, on the basic conditions for improving relations between the two countries for the purposes of preventing the extension of the European war into the Pacific area, settling the China Incident, and promoting economic and commercial cooperation between Japan and the United States. It sought to arrive at an agreement on the details through Japanese-American talks following the joint declaration.

We carefully considered the draft, and sent our first amendment in a telegram dated May 12. On June 21 the United States submitted a counterproposal to our amendment mentioned above. Accordingly, we wired our second amendment on July 14, after careful consideration and study.

We repeatedly made sure that the highest authorities in Germany and Italy were informed confidentially of this matter through the German and Italian Ambassadors in Japan. The details of our second proposal were also conveyed confidentially to the German and Italian Ambassadors in Japan on the 15th [of July], but this proposal was not conveyed to the United States by our Ambassador there because the second Konoye Cabinet resigned on the 16th.

Shortly after that, the Imperial Army was sent to French Indochina. The United States Government mistakenly viewed this as the first step in Japan's military advance to the South. She took the attitude that this would destroy the principles for preserving peace in the Pacific that were to be the basis of the understanding between the Japanese and American Governments; and that she, therefore, could not find a basis for continuing negotiations on this matter. Moreover, she put into effect on July 26 an order freezing our assets. On July 28 we strengthened the law on the control of foreign exchange that had been in effect previously; and we put into effect a law to control transactions concerning foreigners, directed against the United States.

Then, on July 30, the *Tutuila* [a U.S. gunboat] was bombed and damaged at Chungking. Fortunately, as a result of peaceful negotiations, the United States officially stated on July 31 that this incident was settled and the matter was closed.

However, as I explained earlier, the Government of the United States regarded the stationing of our forces in southern Indochina as incompatible with the peaceful solution of international problems, which was the guiding principle in the negotiations to improve relations between Japan and the United States. Although the United States did not go so far as to propose that the negotiations be suspended, she implied that it was useless to continue the negotiations on the Draft Understanding as long as we did not alter such militaristic policies. On July 24 the American President told our Ambassador to the United States that he wanted us to give up our plans to send troops into French Indochina, or to withdraw our forces if the movement of our troops was already under way. He also proposed that upon the withdrawal of troops, he, the President of the United States, would guarantee to the Japanese Government that he was prepared to do his utmost to bring about a declaration by the United States, Great Britain, the Netherlands, and China on the neutralization of Indochina. The American Ambassador in Japan also conveyed this proposal to me on July 27.

As to the significance and nature of the present joint defense measures in Indochina: our Government explained to the American Ambassador that they were not only peaceful and self-defense measures, but also necessary measures in view of current public opinion, which had been provoked by the attitude that countries such as Great Britain, the United States, and the Netherlands had recently been taking toward Japan. We also explained that these measures had been taken in the belief that they would help to prevent the rupture of peace in the Pacific.

After the Government had carefully considered the American proposal, it instructed our Ambassador in the United States by cable on August 5 to explain in detail why we sent our troops into Indochina and to present this proposal to the United States Government:

I. The Japanese Government agrees:

(1) that in order to remove such causes as might constitute a menace of a military character to the United States, it will refrain from sending its troops into the Southwest Pacific areas except for French Indochina, and that the Japanese troops now stationed in French Indochina will be withdrawn immediately upon the settlement of the China Incident;

(2) that in order to remove such causes as might constitute a menace of a political and military character to the Philippine Islands, it will guarantee the neutrality of the islands at an appropriate time; however, the Japanese Government and Japanese nationals are to receive the same treatment as other countries and their nationals, including the United States and its nationals;

(3) that in order to remove such causes as might produce instability of economic relations between Japan and the United States in East Asia, it will cooperate with the Government of the United

States in the production and procurement of such natural resources as are required by the United States.

II. The Government of the United States agrees:

(1) that in order to remove such causes as might constitute a direct menace of a military character to Japan or to her transportation of materials from abroad, it will suspend its military measures in the Southwest Pacific area, and also that upon a successful conclusion of the present negotiations it will advise the Governments of Great Britain and the Netherlands to take similar steps;

(2) that in order to remove such causes as might be responsible for military, political, and economic friction between Japan and the United States, it will cooperate with the Japanese Government in the production and procurement of such natural resources as are required by Japan in the Southwest Pacific area, especially in the Netherlands East Indies, and in the settlement of the pending problems between Japan and the Netherlands East Indies;

(3) that in conjunction with the measures as set forth in (2) above, it will quickly take the steps necessary to restore the normal relations of trade and commerce that have hitherto existed between Japan and the United States;

(4) that in view of the action of the Japanese Government proposed in I(1) above, it will use its good offices to initiate direct negotiations between the Japanese Government and the Chiang Kai-shek regime for the purpose of a speedy settlement of the China Incident; and that it will recognize the special status of Japan in French Indochina even after the withdrawal of Japanese troops from that area.

Our Ambassador in the United States proposed these agreements to the United States Government on August 6, according to the instructions mentioned above. At that time the Secretary of State showed little interest in our counterproposal, saying that there was no point in continuing negotiations unless Japan gave up the policy of using force. The United States Government gave the impression of being prepared for any eventuality.

We feared that if nothing was done about the situation, the negotiations between Japan and the United States would collapse completely. Therefore, we strongly felt the need to improve Japanese-American relations from a broader standpoint; and the Prime Minister expressed to the President of the United States his opinions on Japanese-American relations and requested the President to talk with him at a suitable place as soon as possible.

The President of the United States, soon after he had returned from a trip abroad, asked our Ambassador in America to come to see him on August 17, although it was a Sunday, and proposed two items about which I informally reported to His Majesty the Emperor on August 22. The gist of his proposal was as follows:

The United States Government is willing to cooperate with Japan's request to resume informal and exploratory talks, and willing to hold a meeting of the heads of state of both countries. They feel, however, that it would be helpful in reaching an agreement on the proposals, in view of the circumstances that led to the cessation of the previous informal talks in July, if the Japanese Government would state its attitude and policy more clearly than it has before—as they have repeatedly requested it to do—since these bear heavily on the maintenance of peace in the Pacific and the adjustment of relations between Japan and the United States. [Japan should do so] prior to the resumption of the talks [and prior to] the planning of a meeting between heads of state.

After that, it was reported in both Japanese and American newspapers that American and Soviet ships were transporting oil and military goods from the West Coast harbors of the United States to Vladivostok, through the seas adjacent to Japan. This report aroused the feelings of our people, and the Imperial Government asked the Governments of the United States and the Soviet Union to abandon [this trade] voluntarily. The Soviet Government replied that it could not help regarding our protest as an unfriendly act. On the other hand, the United States Government replied that it could not understand our filing a protest, since the quantity of oil in question was almost negligible compared with that supplied to Japan. In the end, I believe, the United States Government will agree with our contentions, in view of the more important concern of the two governments with improving relations.

Furthermore, not only have American ships ceased to visit Japan for some time, but also no Japanese ships have left for the United States since July 26. Thus trade between Japan and the United States has virtually come to a standstill, and Japanese-American relations are becoming more and more strained. The Imperial Government, therefore, has increasingly felt the need to stabilize the precarious situation between the two countries, and to bring about an improvement in our relations. It tried, through our Ambassador in the United States and the American Ambassador in Japan, to persuade the high officials of the United States Government to agree to a meeting of the heads of state, which I mentioned earlier, as soon as possible. However, in answer to repeated requests from our Ambassador in the United States, the Imperial Government reached a decision on what might be called its basic conditions for the adjustment of relations with the United States; and on September 4 we asked the American Ambassador in Japan, Mr. Grew, to convey them to his Government. At the same time, the Imperial Government instructed our Ambassador in the United States to convey the same conditions to the American authorities, and to ask the United States to bring about as soon as possible a meeting of the two heads of state on the basis of the negotiations carried on to date.

Statement by Director of the Planning Board Suzuki: May I speak about the state of our national power.

With regard to manpower and the morale of the people, which are the sources of our Empire's national power, I believe we can rest assured, whatever situation our Empire may face in the future.

The only problem concerns material resources. Our economy developed by being traditionally dependent on trade with Great Britain, the United States, and the British Empire. Accordingly, we depend on foreign sources to supply many of our vital materials.

At the outbreak of the China Incident, we anticipated that eventually the present difficult circumstances would arise. So we tried to develop resources in the areas we controlled, and to increase the productive capacity of those areas. We tried to free our economy from dependence on foreign countries. The rapid change in the world situation after the outbreak of the war in Europe, and particularly the difficulties between Japan and the United States since last summer, led us to anticipate that we would soon have to make the decision to free ourselves quickly from dependence upon Great Britain and the United States, even though our productive capacity would not be sufficiently expanded. Since the latter half of last year, therefore, we have secured special imports equivalent to ¥660 million in order to acquire and accumulate vital materials. In addition, we have tried to make up the deficiency by making use of our economic agreements with Germany and the Soviet Union. However, since the outbreak of war between Germany and the Soviet Union in June of this year we have been compelled to give up this method of supplementing our needs.

At this stage our national power with respect to physical resources has come to depend entirely upon the productive capacity of the

Empire itself, upon that of Manchuria, China, Indochina, and Thailand, which are under the influence of our Imperial Forces, and upon vital materials stockpiled thus far. Therefore, as a result of the present overall economic blockade imposed by Great Britain and the United States, our Empire's national power is declining day by day.

Our liquid fuel stockpile, which is the most important, will reach bottom by June or July of next year, even if we impose strict wartime control on the civilian demand.

Accordingly, I believe it is vitally important for the survival of our Empire that we make up our minds to establish and stabilize a firm economic base. If it gets to the point where we must establish this base by the use of military force, we can anticipate that for a while our productive capacity will decline to one-half of what it is now, in view of [military demands on] our maritime shipping capacity and considering other relevant factors. Therefore, from the point of view of material resources, we must keep this period of decline in productive capacity as short as possible, and at the same time we must plan to make immediate use of our military successes to boost production. I believe that if important areas in the South were to fall into our hands without fail in a period of three or four months, we could obtain such items as oil, bauxite, nickel, crude rubber, and tin in about six months, and we would be able to make full use of them after two years or so.

However, where military action is involved, we have to be prepared for unexpected situations that may occur, and we are now studying in advance the means to cope with them.

With regard to a few items, such as high-grade asbestos and cobalt, it will be difficult for us to obtain some of them even if we occupy the Southern areas. However, we have been studying the use of substitutes; and I believe that we shall not run into serious difficulties in maintaining and strengthening our national power.

[Summary of questions and answers:]

PRESIDENT OF THE PRIVY COUNCIL HARA: I will put some questions and state my opinions.

I have heard the statements by the Prime Minister, the Army and Navy Chiefs of Staff, and others, and I understand the substance of this proposal. The Foreign Minister has explained that the relationship between Japan and the United States has reached a present state of great strain. Ordinary and conventional diplomacy will not do. Every possible means should be taken to resolve this difficult situation.

I appreciate the Prime Minister's resolution to meet Roosevelt and reach an agreement, and his loyalty and devotion to his country. [He seemed to strongly support the Prime Minister's visit to the United States.]

The people are watching the relations between Japan and the United States and fearing the worst, although they hope it won't come. At the last Conference I urged that an all-out effort be made in our diplomatic negotiations because it was said that we were prepared to risk a war with Great Britain and the United States. At present the Government and the two Chiefs of Staff seem to be of the same opinion as myself. However, if diplomacy should fail and worse comes to worst, there will be a war whether we like it or not, and the decision for war must be made at an appropriate time. I understand this to be the reason we must make preparations for war.

When I glance at Sections I, II, and III of the draft proposal, I notice that we are to make war preparations and carry on diplomacy simultaneously, in the interests of defense and self-preservation. Also, a determination to commence hostilities seems to be implied. There are some passages suggesting that it may not be possible to avoid an outbreak of war, but that we will try to solve the matter by diplomatic means if this is at all possible. It thus appears that war comes first and diplomacy second. However, I take it that starting now, we will prepare for war at the same time that diplomatic measures are being used; that is, everywhere we will try to break the deadlock through diplomacy, but if this should fail, we will have to go to war. The draft seems to suggest that the war comes first, and diplomacy second; but I interpret it to mean that we will spare no efforts in diplomacy and we will go to war only when we can find no other way.

NAVY MINISTER OIKAWA: President Hara's interpretation and the feelings I had when I wrote the draft are the same. In fact, the Imperial Government has been devoting a good deal of effort to [improving] relations between Japan and the United States. I put into the draft the provision that when confronting the present situation we will resort [to armed force] with firm determination only if we can find no other way.

There is no difference in emphasis between the preparations for war in Section I and the diplomacy in Section II. And we mean that if there is no prospect of achieving what is stated in Section III, we will go so far as to decide on war. However, in deciding this matter we will have to be given Imperial Assent at a Conference in the presence of the Emperor. I repeat that the substance expressed in the draft is similar to President Hara's opinion, and that we will carry diplomatic negotiations as far as possible. I believe that Prime Minister Konoye's decision to visit the United States stems from the same feelings.

HARA: The substance of this proposal has been made clear to me by your comments.

Since this proposal was adopted at a Liaison Conference between the Government and the Supreme Command, I feel reassured that the Supreme Command also thinks in the same way as the Navy Minister does, as indicated in his reply. When the Prime Minister visits the United States in the near future, it is necessary that he be determined to improve relations by using all conceivable diplomatic measures, even though we will be making preparations for war as a matter of policy. If this proposal is given Imperial Assent, I ask everybody to cooperate in promoting the object of the Prime Minister's visit to the United States, and in avoiding the worst possible development in the relations between Japan and the United States.

Now I would like to ask about relations between the United States and the Soviet Union in the event of a Japanese-American war.

[In reply to this question the Army Chief of Staff discussed in detail, one point after another, the position of the Soviet Far Eastern Army, the Soviet attitude toward Japan, the position of our Army, the facts about military and economic assistance given so far by the United States to the Soviet Union and possible developments along this line in the future, and the relationship of these factors to military operations in the South.]

HARA: As a result of the report by the Supreme Command, I am now fully informed as to our relations with the Soviet Union. As to the decision to go to war: I have been told that it will be subject to careful deliberation; but if in the end the Prime Minister's efforts do not bear fruit, we will face the worst possible situation, namely war. In that event, we will have to decide to go to war as the Supreme Command suggests. Since I have been told that this war decision will be subject to careful deliberation, I will not ask any further questions.

I shall be satisfied if the diplomatic negotiations can be carried out under the conditions indicated in the attached papers, and I give my complete consent to this proposal.

Lastly, I would like to make a few remarks.

After the China Incident was expanded, it was said that our

hundred million people were completely united; but reality betrays this assertion. Even at the present time some people are opposed to the adjustment of relations between Japan and the United States.[35] They might be patriots, but I feel a great anxiety when I see that some people are opposed to what the Government is doing. It is indeed deplorable that some people will resort to direct action when our nation has its very destiny at stake. It is most regrettable that an enemy fifth column exists. This may lead to destruction of the country from within; and it will benefit the enemy even if it stems from patriotism. If these terroristic actions should continue, I doubt that what is decided at this Conference in the presence of the Emperor can be effectively carried out. At the time of the Russo-Japanese war the people really were of one mind; but as the war approached its end Foreign Minister Komura was sometimes in danger, and there were riots in Hibiya Park. Now, despite the fact that we are engaged in war, acts of terror are perpetrated.

I wonder if the decisions of this Conference in the presence of the Emperor can be put into effect? I would like to see courageous and drastic action taken, so that the decisions of the Imperial Conference can be carried out even if worse comes to worst.

[In reply, the Home Minister stated in detail that this was very regrettable; and that he would investigate the organizations and individuals concerned, so that he would be able to take the appropriate measures when necessary.

[Thus the proposal was approved.

[Finally, the Emperor graciously made some remarks. (They are contained in the Memorandum of the Emperor's questions, which is not reproduced here).[36]]

[35] Ultranationalistic individuals and organizations were actively promoting expansionist policies and a war against the United States. Minister of State Hiranuma was shot and wounded in the neck and jaw, apparently for his failure to leave the Konoye Cabinet when Matsuoka was ousted. A plot to assassinate Prince Konoye was discovered, and the guard assigned to Lord Keeper of the Privy Seal Kido and his family was doubled. "Continuing arrests during this unsettled period also thwarted ultranationalistic plots to attack the American Embassy, the Home Ministry, the Metropolitan Police Headquarters, and other key points.... The mood of the ultranationalists was consequently a factor which could not be ignored by members of the ruling elite." Butow, *Tojo and the Coming of the War,* pp. 252–53.
[36] We know from other sources that the Emperor read a poem composed by his grandfather, the Emperor Meiji: "All the seas in every quarter are as brothers to one another. Why, then, do the winds and waves of strife rage so turbulently throughout the world?" Nagano and Sugiyama, acknowledging these remarks as Imperial censure, indicated that diplomacy would be stressed.

[Attached Document]

Reference Materials for Answering Questions at the Imperial Conference on September 6 Regarding "The Essentials for Carrying Out the Empire's Policies." (Note: These materials were prepared in advance for answering questions at the Imperial Conference, after an exchange of views at meetings attended by the three secretaries of the Liaison Conferences: Tomita Kenji, Chief Secretary of the Cabinet; Muto Akira, Chief of the Military Affairs Bureau of the War Ministry; and Oka Takasumi, Chief of the Naval Affairs Bureau of the Navy Ministry. Thus they are not the views of the Supreme Command alone, but those prepared after consultation between the Government and the Supreme Command.)

Is war with Great Britain and the United States inevitable?

Our Empire's plan to build a New Order in East Asia—the central problem of which is the settlement of the China Incident—is a firm policy based on the national principle of Hakko Ichiu. The building of the New Order will go on forever, much as the life of our State does.

However, it appears that the policy of the United States toward Japan is based on the idea of preserving the status quo; in order to dominate the world and defend democracy, it aims to prevent our Empire from rising and developing in East Asia. Under these circumstances, it must be pointed out that the policies of Japan and the United States are mutually incompatible; it is historically inevitable that the conflict between the two countries, which is sometimes intense and sometimes moderate, will ultimately lead to war.

It need not be repeated that unless the United States changes its policy toward Japan, our Empire is placed in a desperate situation, where it must resort to the ultimate step—namely, war—to defend itself and to assure its preservation. Even if we should make concessions to the United States by giving up part of our national policy for the sake of a temporary peace, the United States, its military position strengthened, is sure to demand more and more concessions on our part; and ultimately our Empire will have to lie prostrate at the feet of the United States.

What are the aims of a war against the United States, Great Britain, and the Netherlands?

The purposes of war with the United States, Great Britain, and the Netherlands are to expel the influence of these three countries from East Asia, to establish a sphere for the self-defense and self-preservation of our Empire, and to build a New Order in Greater East Asia. In other words, we aim to establish a close and inseparable relationship in military, political, and economic affairs between our Empire and the countries of the Southern Region, to achieve our Empire's self-defense and self-preservation, and to build up at the same time the New Order of co-existence and co-prosperity in Greater East Asia. Accordingly, we must resolutely expel the hostile powers of the United States, Great Britain, and the Netherlands, which interfere with the above purpose.

What is the outlook in a war with Great Britain and the United States; particularly, how shall we end the war?

A war with the United States and Great Britain will be long, and will become a war of endurance. It is very difficult to predict the termination of war, and it would be well-nigh impossible to expect the surrender of the United States. However, we cannot exclude the possibility that the war may end because of a great change in American public opinion, which may result from such factors as the remarkable success of our military operations in the South or the surrender of Great Britain. At any rate, we should be able to establish an invincible position: by building up a strategically advantageous position through the occupation of important areas in the South; by creating an economy that will be self-sufficient in the long run through the development of rich resources in the Southern regions, as well as through the use of the economic power of the East Asian continent; and by linking Asia and Europe in destroying the Anglo-American coalition through our cooperation with Germany and Italy. Meanwhile, we may hope that we will be able to influence the trend of affairs and bring the war to an end.

What about the military alliance between the United States, Great Britain, the Soviet Union, China, and the Netherlands?

There seems to be a tacit agreement on the common use of naval and air bases in the Southern Regions, particularly in Malaya, the East Indies, and Australia. It is also reported that the air force specialists of the United States, Great Britain, and China met in Chungking at the end of July to discuss the use of existing air bases in the hinterland of China.

It is widely known that the United States has been supplying China with military goods. In addition, it is worth noting that the movement of United States Army personnel, who are going to China a few at a time and bringing weapons with them, particularly airplanes, shows that a military coalition actually exists between the United States and China.

It seems that in the meeting between the United States President and the British Prime Minister, they discussed what military steps they should take to thwart our Empire's advance to the South. The action of the United States in sending military materials by way of the northern Pacific Ocean under the pretext of assisting the Soviet Union is worth our close attention; by these methods, the United States could acquire military bases, especially air and maritime-shipping bases, in the Far Eastern section of the Soviet Union if circumstances should require them, and would thus establish the northern segment of a ring around our Empire. Furthermore, our Empire cannot overlook the fact that a meeting between the United States, Great

Britain, and the Soviet Union is going to be held in Moscow soon, and that the Chungking Government also hopes to attend.

Military alliance in China between the United States, Great Britain, the Soviet Union, and China.

In spite of maneuvering by China, both the United States and Great Britain are not very interested in this matter; and we have not been able to detect any military alliance that unites the United States, Great Britain, the Soviet Union, and China. However, partial agreements are being reached on specific matters concerning military alliance between the United States, Great Britain, and China. They are as follows: (1) between the United States and China, assistance to the Chinese air force; (2) between Great Britain and China, formation of mobile guerrilla units; (3) against Japan's advance southward, use of Chinese bases by American and British air units.

Why have we set the last ten days of October as a tentative deadline for war preparations?

We need not repeat that at present oil is the weak point of our Empire's national strength and fighting power. We are now gradually consuming oil that has been stockpiled. If things continue as at present, we will be self-sufficient for a two-year period at the most. This period will be further shortened if we undertake a large-scale military operation. As time passes, our capacity to carry on war will decline, and our Empire will become powerless militarily.

Meanwhile the naval and air forces of the United States will improve remarkably as time goes on; and defensively, the United States, Great Britain, and the Netherlands will gradually grow stronger in the South. Hence the passing of time not only means that we will face more difficulties in military operations, but also means that the increasing military prepared-ness of the United States Navy will surpass the naval power of our Empire after next autumn, and that we will finally be forced to surrender to the United States and Great Britain without a fight.

In view of the meteorological conditions in winter, it is very difficult for both Japan and her enemies to undertake large-scale winter operations in the North. Accordingly, it is necessary to fully prepare for war in the shortest possible time, so that we can conclude the main operations in the South quickly during this season and preserve our freedom of military action in the North after the spring of next year.

If we begin preparations for war immediately, it will be about the last ten days of October before we complete mobilization, the requisitioning and equipping of ships, and the deployment of forces in the main strategic areas by means of long-distance sea transportation.

What is the difference between military preparations until about the first ten days of October and preparations from then to the last ten days of October, and how are they related to diplomatic negotiations?

Military preparations until the first ten days of October will include mobilizing and organizing troops, assembling and deploying them, and establishing bases. Since we will be making every effort in diplomatic negotiations during this period, we must try not to interfere with these negotiations: we must carry out military preparations as secretly as possible, conceal our intentions, and refrain from sending additional forces to southern French Indochina. Military action thereafter (i.e., after we decide to commence hostilities) until the last ten days of October will aim at completing and coordinating all necessary military preparations, with the use of military force scheduled for the beginning of November. Diplomatic negotiations during this period should be conducted with a view toward facilitating the switchover from political to military methods.

"If diplomatic negotiations fail to produce a prospect of achieving our demands, we will immediately decide to commence hostilities." When will we resort to military force?

Military force will be used after military preparations have been completed and coordinated, that is, in the early part of November.

What is meant by the words "we will decide to commence hostilities" in Section III of the document?

This is the final step; the use of military force will follow immediately. Diplomatic negotiations, military affairs, and other matters should be ready for this step. In short, military force should be used promptly if there is no prospect of diplomatic success. It is expected that the United States and Great Britain will try to delay us with diplomatic negotiations. We must be careful not to be inveigled into this trap. We can overcome the intrigues of the enemy only if we are wise and resolute enough to foresee before the enemy does whether or not we can succeed in attaining our demands through diplomatic negotiations.

How can we prevent cooperation between the United States and the Soviet Union?

There can be no satisfactory diplomatic solution unless we are determined to go to war with the United States and the Soviet Union. We have already asked the Soviet Union and the United States to suspend the flow of aid to the Soviet Union through the Soviet Far East, but to no avail.

What are our policies, other than those toward the South?

There are policies contained in the "Outline of National Policies in View of the Changing Situation" that are not within the scope of the Southern Question. Among them are: the settlement of the China Incident, the Northern Question, the attitude of our Empire toward American participation in the war, and the establishment of a wartime national structure.

Why will we discontinue diplomatic negotiations after our decision in the first ten days of October to commence war against the United States? Is it not advisable to continue diplomatic negotiations until immediately before the use of military force?

To make final military preparations for commencing war against the United States and Great Britain while continuing negotiations with the United States is tantamount to destroying those negotiations. Hence such actions as sending additional forces to southern French Indochina should be done after we decide to commence war, and we should not take the initiative in diplomatic negotiations during this period. However, it goes without saying that we may respond to diplomatic overtures, and not resort to war if the United States and Great Britain should accept all of our demands.

What effect will the Southern operations have on the settlement of the China Incident?

More pressure can be brought to bear on the Chungking regime by immediately exercising the rights of a belligerent against it and by getting rid of hostile Foreign Settlements, both of which we have hitherto refrained from doing out of consideration for the United States and Great Britain.

The occupation of Hong Kong and the closing of the Burma Road will completely sever Chungking's connecting link with the United States and Great Britain; it will prevent assistance from going to Chiang Kai-shek, and will thus force the surrender of the Chungking regime. In particular, the resolute execution by our Empire of a war against the United States and Great Britain will destroy the sense of dependence on the United States and Great Britain exhibited by the Chungking regime and the people who follow it; this will very probably weaken their will to fight and cause the collapse of organized resistance. Accordingly, there is great likelihood that we will have a chance to bring Chungking to her knees while we are fighting with the United States and Great Britain. However, if our national power should become exhausted, and if the morale of our people should drop, the Chungking regime's will to resist will be raised instead, and the prospects of settling the Incident will become increasingly slim. Attention should be paid to this fact in guiding the war.

What are the recent developments in the Chungking regime? And what is the actual state of the Chinese Army?

The Chungking regime is paying close attention to present developments in our Empire, and is preparing countermeasures. However, it depends wholly on a favorable development in the situation, which it hopes will be brought about by the withdrawal and redeployment of our Empire's forces in China and by the increased pressure of the United States and Great Britain on Japan; and it is merely intriguing and propagandizing in order to bring this about.

Chinese military forces consist of about two million men, organized in some three hundred divisions, and an air force of about 110 planes in the front lines. In view of the resistance that we met the other day in the Third War Zone on the lower Yangtze River, it is clear that at present the Chinese Army by itself cannot carry out a general counteroffensive of a decisive nature. They are now rebuilding their air force, in which they have placed their hope, but they are still not in a position to present us with a menace.

With regard to its internal structure, the Chungking regime has not yet been perturbed or dislocated in the least by the attacks from the Communist Party on the Left or the Nanking Peace Group on the Right. However, it is badly pressed in financial and economic matters, and there are unmistakable signs that it is gradually approaching a catastrophe. It has adopted the "ABCD" procedure as the central theme of its national policy for war and diplomacy. It is striving hard to strengthen and carry out this policy, both from within and without, but the policy does not seem to have had a great effect as yet.

How are the American and British military policies toward French Indochina and Thailand actually progressing?

Great Britain has implied that if our Empire should exert military pressure on Thailand, Britain would counter with military force. She threatens Thailand by stating that if Thailand offers military bases or military assistance to a third party, the Nonaggression Treaty between Great Britain and Thailand will be nullified. At the same time, she is pressuring Thailand to grant her military bases, and is trying to persuade Thailand to do this with the proposal that Britain will consider supplying Thailand with oil and supporting Thailand's wishes to regain lost territory. It is reported that the British battleship *Warspite* was in the Bay of Siam on August 4. Although Britain has no direct military involvement in French Indochina, she is obstructing everything that our Empire intends to do there.

The United States has issued a statement on the French Indochina problem, and has criticized the French Government on the joint defense of French Indochina. She has ordered Americans in French Indochina to return home. It is reported that she has urged Thailand to take a strong position on the defense of her territory, and that she has offered to supply arms (this is a proposal to guarantee neutrality).

What is the outlook on the German-Soviet war and the anticipated operations of the German Army?

The probability is high that the German Army will destroy the main field armies of the Soviet Union by the end of October or the beginning of November, occupy the principal European sections of the Soviet Union, engage the defeated Soviet Army with one part of its powerful force, and then begin operations in the Caucasus, the Near East, and North Africa. Therefore, we judge as follows:

The expected front line this autumn will be a line connecting the White Sea, eastern Moscow, and the Donets basin. Around the time the above-mentioned operations in European Russia are being completed, the Caucasus operation will be launched and will be followed, sooner or later, by the Near Eastern and North African operations. With regard to operations against Great Britain, the air raids will be stepped up with the redeployment of the air force now being used in the war with the Soviet Union. The war to destroy commerce will also be strengthened. However, the invasion of the British Isles will be put off until next spring or summer, when the Near Eastern and North African operations will have been completed.

What sort of relationship with Germany and Italy should we have in order to carry out war with the United States and Great Britain?

Since the most likely development of the war is that mentioned above, our Empire should naturally be prepared to carry on while relying only on its own power; but it is essential to maintain a strong and solid union with Germany and Italy. Accordingly, an agreement must be reached that Germany and Italy shall not conclude a unilateral peace treaty with the United States and Great Britain; and that Japan, Germany, and Italy shall cooperate in bringing Great Britain to her knees. However, we should be careful not to be restrained from launching the Southern Operation just because it might be inconvenient for Germany and Italy.

In connection with the South, how should we think of the North?

While we are militarily engaged in the South, we should do our best in the North to prevent the war from developing into a two-front operation. We must especially prevent the formation of a joint front against Japan by the United States and the Soviet Union. As a result of the use of force in the South, our Empire should anticipate cooperation between the United States and the Soviet Union as a matter of course. However, this cooperation is regarded as militarily difficult during the winter, owing to weather conditions.

However, if developments in the German-Soviet war should turn out to be favorable to our Empire, or if the threat from the North that would result from cooperation between the United States and the Soviet Union should become very serious, or if the Soviet Union should take the offensive and we could no longer allow it from the point of view of national defense, it is possible that we might use military force to settle the Northern Question during, or even before, our use of force in the South.

Is it possible that developments in the German-Soviet war will turn out to be favorable to us, so that we can use military force in the North this year?

It is believed that the situation will no doubt become more favorable as time passes; but it is our judgment that the kind of favorable situation we hope for is unlikely to come before the middle of winter.

It is almost certain that Germany will conquer most of European Russia, and that the Stalin regime will evacuate eastward to the Urals and beyond. But the Stalin regime will probably not collapse immediately. At present the Far Eastern portion of the Soviet Union is generally depressed, but there is no sign of unrest. It will require a certain period of time before the influence of defeat in European Russia will extend to the Far East and cause the general situation in the Far East to become unstable, and to change.

However, the middle of this winter will prove to be the time of greatest peril for the Soviet Union; the shortage of food and oil, and the problems of rationing them, might abruptly alter the situation. Further, it is evident that the Stalin regime, robbed of European Russia, will weaken, and will lose its power to carry on the war. There is no doubt, therefore, that a situation favorable to our Empire will develop sooner or later. We judge that it will probably be after the middle of this coming winter.

However, it is difficult to conduct operations in the severe winter season, even if we are presented with a good opportunity; so force will be used in late winter, early next year.

What is the relationship between the Southern Operation and shipping?

In carrying out the Southern Operation, the number of ships available to satisfy the civilian demand will be reduced to the minimum for a period of some three months; this will have an effect on production for a time. However, our Empire must put up with this situation for the time being, since it is unavoidable in carrying on the war. The military has made several studies of the most economical way to operate ships, keeping especially in mind the relationship between strategic needs and the need to increase productivity during a prolonged war.

Is not the demand for the cessation of assistance to Chiang Kai-shek in "The Minimum Demands," I(b), incompatible with the proposal in the Nomura Operation?

(In the Nomura Operation we will advise that aid be discontinued, but will demand it if our advice is not followed. In the "Minimum Demands" paragraphs (a) and (b) stand side by side.)

This matter refers to the demand at the final stage. It is not contrary to the attitude of our Empire on the settlement of the China Incident, which has hitherto been stressed in the Nomura Operation.

What is the present status of the defense of our homeland?

For the purpose of defending our homeland, the Army has lately organized and deployed a number of defense units, and has been steadily educating and training men, as well as strengthening facilities. But we have not yet reached the stage of complete and secure readiness. In addition, the cities of our Empire do not have strong defenses against air raids, and countermeasures to build stronger defenses have not been completed.

With things as they are now, we have to be prepared for considerable damage if we begin a war. However, the Army and the Navy will try to destroy the enemy air forces by taking the offensive. Therefore, it is believed that if the military, the Government, and the people cooperate fully and try to deal with the situation determined not to give an inch, the losses from air raids can be limited to a point where no great difficulties will be encountered in carrying on the war.

What is the outlook for negotiations with the United States under "The Minimum Demands and Maximum Concessions," which is separately attached?

The negotiations will be successful only if a spirit of mutual concession exists between Japan and the United States. If the United States should demand, as it does now, concessions by Japan alone—and in particular, if she should ask us to give up the settlement of the China Incident and the construction of the Greater East Asia Co-prosperity Sphere, and force us to renounce the Tripartite Pact—the negotiations are unlikely to prove successful.

The minimum demands and maximum concessions:

The maximum concessions mean those that can be safely acceded to when the United States and Great Britain accept our minimum demands, and we should not disclose the limit to which we can make concessions at the outset. At the same time, the minimum limit to our demands should not be changed in terms of fundamentals, although we do not mean it should not be modified by even a letter or phrase. As a matter of diplomatic technique, of course, there is no problem if we submit larger demands first and then reduce them gradually. However, this matter is related to the Supreme Command in a number of points, and it is necessary to maintain close coordination between political and military strategies.

Are the diplomatic negotiations to be brought to an end if all of the conditions in Item One of the attached document are not accepted?

The acceptance of Sections 1 and 2 of "The Maximum Concessions to Be Made by Our Empire" will in fact mean the suspension of our Empire's military advance to the South, which is a great threat to the United States and Great Britain, and will thus benefit them greatly.

Our Empire, on the other hand, will be able to use the resources of the Asian continent, and of the United States, Great Britain, and the Netherlands; so we cannot back down an inch on this point. In particular, since we promise not to use military force in the South, we must put China under the complete control of our Empire. To do that, it is absolutely essential to station the necessary forces there. China will not listen to us if we withdraw all our forces. Japan will not be able to survive, [even though] our Army has sacrificed hundreds of thousands of men. Furthermore, if we promise not to use military force in the South, it is quite reasonable to make the Americans refrain from such actions as might menace the defense of our Empire. If they do not accede to the conditions that we propose, we must regard it as disclosing their true intention, which is to bring Japan to her knees. If we make concessions on this point, it is evident that we will soon fall prey to the United States.

What is the meaning of guaranteeing the neutrality of the Philippine Islands, which are the territory of the United States?

It is intended that both Japan and the United States guarantee the neutrality of the Philippine Islands after they have gained their independence.

Item Two, Section 2, of the attached document says that "our Empire is prepared to withdraw its forces from French Indochina after a just peace has been established in the Far East." What will become of the joint defense with French Indochina? Where does the joint defense with French Indochina stand now?

If a just peace (including a peaceful settlement of the China Incident) is established in the Far East, the menace to French Indochina from the United States, Great Britain, and China will end as a matter of course, and the withdrawal of our forces will present no inconvenience to French Indochina.

Until now no measures have been taken except for the stationing of our Empire's Army in southern Indochina under the Protocol of Joint Defense between Japan and Indochina. Negotiations have not yet begun on concrete matters of military cooperation.

What is the military strength in the enemy territories in the Outer Southern Regions?

INDIA

Ground forces: A little more than 300,000 Regular Army; in addition, over 150,000 men that may be sent abroad.

Airplanes: 200.

Changes since our advance into southern Indochina: It appears that they have sent forces to Malaya and the Middle East, but no details of their strength are available.

AUSTRALIA

Ground forces: 250,000 Regular Army; in addition, 120,000 men that may be sent abroad.

Airplanes: 250.

Changes since our advance: Australia also sent forces to Malaya, and she is expected to send more.

NEW ZEALAND

Ground forces: 11,000 Regular Army; in addition, over 20,000 men that may be sent abroad.

Airplanes: 100.

Changes since our advance: No change.

BURMA

Ground forces: 14,000 Regular Army; about 20,000 reserve forces and other paramilitary forces.

Airplanes: 50.

Changes since our advance: About 150 pilots and ground personnel arrived from Singapore and Calcutta at the beginning of August.

TOTAL: Over 885,000 ground forces and 600 airplanes.

What is the strength of the enemy (excluding navy) in the Southern Regions? What changes have recently been made?

GUAM (U.S.)

Ground forces: 300 Marines and 1,500 Defense Forces.

Airplanes: Seaplane base, but no planes.

Changes since our advance into southern Indochina: No change.

PHILIPPINE ISLANDS (U.S.)

Ground forces: (1) 42,000 Regular Army, (2) 900 Marines, (3) 140,000 Philippine Defense Forces.

Airplanes: About 160 Army and Navy planes.

Changes since our advance: (1) The Philippine Defense Forces have come under the control of the Commander, U.S. Far East Forces; (2) about 20,000 men of the Philippine Defense Forces have been enlisted in the Regular Army Native Corps; (3) Patrol Corps have come under the control of the Commander, U.S. Far East Forces.

MALAYA (BRITISH)

Ground forces: (1) About 60,000 Regular Army—11,000 British, 15,000 Australian, and 35,000 Indian; in British Borneo, 1,000 Regular Army. (2) There are 20,000 Volunteer forces in Malaya, and 2,500 in British Borneo.

Airplanes: 200 to 250 Army and Navy planes.

Changes since our advance: (1) Australian forces increased by 4,000–5,000 in the middle of August; (2) Indian forces seem to have been considerably increased, although the exact figures are not available.

THE NETHERLANDS EAST INDIES

Ground forces: 70,000 Regular Army (50,000 in Java and 20,000 in other territories).

Airplanes: About 200 Army and Navy planes.

Changes since our advance: The first recruitment under the Native Personnel Conscription Order (alleged to be 150,000, but this figure seems exaggerated) will occur at the beginning of September, and armed training will be inaugurated then.

TOTAL
Ground forces: 334,700.
Airplanes: 560 to 610 Army and Navy planes.

What is the general strength of the United States Army (as of the end of August 1941)?
There are 500,000 men in the Regular Army, 300,000 in the National Guard, and 50,000 in organized reserve forces. In addition, about 540,000 men are currently being recruited and enrolled in the Regular Army and National Guard. The total numerical strength is about 1.4 million.

American ground forces comprise: 11 infantry divisions (9 on the mainland and 2 in the territories), 4 armored divisions, and 2 cavalry divisions. There are also 18 National Guard divisions.

The Army Air Corps has 17 squadrons on the mainland and 5 in the territories, with about 3,500 planes in the hands of fighting units.

How do we assess the Atlantic Conference?
The conference between the American President and the British Prime Minister is supposed to have reconsidered future policies, paying special attention to policies toward the Axis countries and toward Japan in particular, in view of the inevitable situation following the freezing of our assets in America and the end of the war between Germany and the Soviet Union. It seems that the United States and Great Britain, anticipating the situation after the termination of the German-Soviet war, have also studied these items: (1) assistance to Great Britain, and United States participation in the war; (2) how to increase the Soviet capacity to wage war against Germany; and (3) problems regarding Japan.

With regard to problems relating to Japan, they are supposed to have foreseen the inevitability of our Empire's advancing to the South with military force. They also discussed: (1) how to prevent Japan from using force in the South and/or North; (2) the guiding principles of the United States and Great Britain for war with Japan in case Japan should use force in the South and/or the North; and (3) how to make use of the Soviet Union.

PART THREE

"The Time for War Will Not Come Later"

"The Time for War Will Not Come Later"

51ST LIAISON CONFERENCE
September 11, 1941

The Japanese were afraid that the clash between the United States and Germany over the German submarine attack on the destroyer Greer might cause the Germans to invoke the Tripartite Pact. Hence they hoped that President Roosevelt would not involve them in his speech on the subject. The President's Fireside Chat of September 11 did not mention Japan or the Far East, but strongly warned Germany and Italy that in the future their ships entered the established American defense zone at their own risk.

On September 3, President Roosevelt gave Nomura a letter replying to Prime Minister Konoye, together with an Oral Statement. In the letter Roosevelt stated that there existed in some quarters in Japan concepts that appeared to raise obstacles to a successful meeting of the heads of state; and that in order to ensure that the proposed meeting would be a successful one, there should be a "preliminary discussion of the fundamental and essential questions on which we seek agreement." In the Oral Statement the President reiterated Hull's Four Principles, recalled that in the notes exchanged in the past there had been differences in views on certain fundamental questions, and sought "an indication of the present attitude of the Japanese Government with regard to the fundamental questions under reference."

In the meantime, Foreign Minister Toyoda had been working on a communication to Secretary Hull. The note from Washington arrived after he had prepared his message, so in the communication that he gave Ambassador Grew on September 4, he noted the arrival of the American statement and said that the "present communication will serve as my Government's reply to the American Government concerning the preliminary discussions mentioned in its Oral Statement as well as in the President's message."

As was reported during this Liaison Conference, Hull was dissatis-

fied with the Japanese note. He viewed the note as narrowing the scope of the talks: it eliminated the United States as a negotiator between Japan and China, and it asked the United States to abstain from actions prejudicial to the settlement of the China Incident and to suspend any military measures in the Far East and the South Pacific. Toyoda pointed out to Grew that there was a new approach to the Tripartite Pact: that is, Japan would no longer go to war immediately if the United States entered the European war, but would decide independently. Grew was doubtful that these proposals could form a basis for a Roosevelt-Konoye meeting.

Prime Minister Konoye, meanwhile, had met secretly with Grew to urge him that time was of the essence in arranging a meeting with Roosevelt. He even said that he was prepared to go along with Hull's Four Principles, but this statement was later withdrawn.

Agenda: Japanese-American Negotiations.

[The Foreign Minister gave an account of Japanese-American negotiations:]

On the morning of the 10th, Nomura talked with Hull and told him: "I hear that the President is going to speak over the radio. I think it would be better if he would not talk about the Japanese question." Hull, however, did not agree. He only promised to be careful, as before, about keeping everything secret. [This matter was conveyed to Grew by the Foreign Minister as well.]

Nomura asked Hull if we could have an answer to the proposal we had made to Grew. Hull said that he would reply after he had met with Roosevelt following the President's speech the next day, the 11th. Therefore, we may receive their answer today, the 11th, at the earliest. At that time Hull indicated displeasure that our answer to the United States was less forward-looking than our previous replies. Nomura felt that Hull's view was that while the United States had presented for discussion a number of problems, Japan had confined herself to a portion of them; so he said to Hull: "We have selected only controversial problems, omitting those we have already agreed upon informally."

Today's speech by Roosevelt will probably last fifteen minutes, although it was originally scheduled for ten minutes. He will probably speak strongly against German attitudes.

Yesterday, September 10, Grew called on me. [The memorandum that he gave to the Foreign Minister is attached.[1]]

---

[1] This was not included in the Japanese version of the documents.

52D LIAISON CONFERENCE
September 13, 1941

*By this time the outstanding issue in the negotiations between Japan
and the United States was the question of peace in China. On September 10 Ambassador Grew gave Foreign Minister Toyoda a note
that specifically stated the American position on this subject. The
United States insisted that: (1) there must be a fair and just settlement between Japan and China; (2) Japan must not discriminate
against American business interests in China; (3) the United States
would make no agreement that would restrict its aid to nations resisting aggression. The American note sought clarification on these
and other points relating to China.*

*In essence, the American position was that there must be an in-
dependent Chinese government under the leadership of Chiang Kai-
shek. But political reality was much more complicated. There were
in fact three regimes in China in this period: the Nationalist Government under Chiang, with its temporary capital in Chungking in
southwestern China; the Chinese Communist regime in the north
and northwest; and a Japanese-sponsored puppet regime in the north
and along the eastern seaboard. Japan was willing to withdraw its
troops from certain sections of China following peace talks with
Chiang but not from Inner Mongolia and northern China, where the
Communists were strong. The Japanese Army's position on the issue
of troop withdrawal was very firm.*

*In Washington, Ambassador Nomura felt that there was little
chance of a Roosevelt-Konoye meeting unless the Japanese Government made its position clear on the China Question, especially on
the withdrawal of troops. For instance, he cabled his Government
on September 11 to say that the American Government would take
a stubborn position on the stationing of Japanese troops in China.
He urged, therefore, that Japan agree to withdraw troops within two
years after the restoration of peace. He reasoned that this topic would
be discussed by the heads of state when they met, taken up by Japan
and China, and followed by a cease-fire and a peace conference. He
calculated that all this would take more than a year: so even if Japan
promised now to withdraw its troops two years after the signing of
the peace, the actual withdrawal would take place some years later;
in the meantime the situation could change. He sought a firm decision on the troop withdrawal issue.*[2]

[2] Nomura gives a summary of his telegram in his *Beikoku ni Tsukai Shite,*
p. 118.

As a result of the American note and Nomura's telegrams, the Army, the Navy, and the Foreign Ministry prepared a statement setting forth the conditions for peace between Japan and China and presented it for approval at this Liaison Conference. The Japanese position called for the stationing of troops in Inner Mongolia and certain areas in North and South China, the merging of the Chiang Kaishek regime with the puppet Nanking regime under Wang Chingwei, and the recognition of the puppet state of Manchukuo—all of which proved to be unacceptable to the United States.

The Liaison Conference was also asked to approve the draft of a telegram to be sent to Nomura. However, the contents of the telegram and of the "Basic Terms of Peace between Japan and China" were somewhat different. For example, probably in deference to Nomura's plea, no mention was made of the decision to station troops in Inner Mongolia and certain parts of North China. Although Nomura received the telegram on September 13, he did not deliver the message to Secretary Hull until September 23.[3]

Agenda: "Basic Terms of Peace between Japan and China."

[Since it had become necessary for the sake of the Nomura Operation to make clear to the other side our attitude on the conditions for peace between Japan and China, the document "Basic Terms of Peace between Japan and China" (Attached Paper 1), which resulted from studies made by the Army, the Navy, and the Foreign Ministry, was approved. Then the draft of a telegram (Attached Paper 2) to answer the telegrams from Nomura sent on September 10 and 11 was approved. However, the content was a little different from the "Terms of Peace" stated above. These terms were thought to be damaging to future negotiations.]

[Attached Paper 1]

Basic Terms of Peace between Japan and China
1. A good-neighbor policy.
2. Respect for national sovereignty and territorial integrity.
3. Mutual defense by Japan and China: Japanese-Chinese cooperation in the suppression of Communism and other movements disruptive of peace and order, which threaten the security of both Japan and China. For the above purpose, Japanese forces shall be stationed for the required period in Inner Mongolia and certain areas in North China; and Japanese

---

[3] The text of the message sent to Nomura on September 13 is in his *Beikoku*, appendix, pp. 132–34.

warships and troops shall be stationed for the required period on Hainan Island and Amoy, in conformity with previous agreements and conventions.

4. Withdrawal of troops: Troops sent to China to carry on the China Incident, other than those mentioned above, will be withdrawn as soon as the Incident is settled.

5. Economic cooperation: Japan and China will cooperate economically, chiefly in order to develop and exploit natural resources that have important military value; this will not limit any economic activities that are conducted on a legitimate basis by third parties.

6. Merger of the Chiang and Wang governments.

7. No annexation of territory.

8. No reparations.

9. Recognition of Manchukuo.

[Attached Paper 2]

Draft of a Telegram Replying to Telegrams from Nomura on September 10 and 11

Regarding your telegram No. [unavailable]:

1. A.[4] The Draft Understanding, which has been the basis of previous negotiations, will continue to form the basis of negotiation. However, in regard to the handling of the Draft, as indicated in previous telegrams (particularly No. ——), our position is that in our informal discussions we have agreed on the Preamble, on the concepts of international relations and the essential nature of the State, and on the United States' offering its "good offices"[5] between Japan and China, as set forth in the Draft Understanding. Incidentally, the United States seems to have the mistaken view that we do not want the "good offices" of the United States; we have not rejected them, but desire them as before.

B. The phrase "without reason" modifies only the last half of the paragraph, and does not affect the first half.

[No comment was made on C.]

D. Japan and China will cooperate and undertake a common defense to suppress Communism and other movements disruptive of peace and order (which threaten the security of both Japan and China) and to maintain peace and order. The common defense mentioned above will include the stationing of troops for the required period in certain areas, in accordance with "agreements" between Japan and China. Troops which have been sent to China to carry on the China Incident shall be withdrawn as soon as the Incident is settled.

---

[4] The letters A, B, etc., refer to the paragraphs in the Japanese proposal of September 6.

[5] The Japanese term used here is *hashi-watashi*: literally, "putting a bridge across." It could be translated as either "good offices" or "mediation."

E. The reason for this paragraph is that it appears that the United States is fearful that we will trample on her interests in China; in order to dispel this fear we state that we have no intention of stopping legitimate economic activities.

It goes without saying that the Empire does not deny the principle of non-discrimination in commerce in China, as well as in the Southwest Pacific region; and we shall respect the interests of the United States in China. However, we believe that it is natural that, in view of the territorial proximity of Japan and China, especially close economic relations—which will be developed quite naturally—should be recognized to exist between them, as they exist between other countries that are geographically close to each other. Accordingly, we affirm: that economic cooperation between Japan and China, which will be close and of a special character, will not involve the creation of so-called monopolies or preferential rights; that such cooperation is a natural phenomenon of mankind; and that recognition of this natural order of things is an important factor in world economic prosperity, as well as a shortcut to the maintenance of world peace.

F. Since China is covered by a separate item as indicated above, we have made clear our position on the Southwest Pacific region, which, of the regions in the Pacific area, is of most concern to the United States.

2. A. We refer to the various kinds of aid to Chiang Kai-shek. As for the "good offices," we have mentioned them above.

53D LIAISON CONFERENCE
September 18, 1941

Time was running out, but as yet no agreement had been reached with the United States. Hence, on September 17, the Foreign Ministry (aided by Muto, Chief of the Military Affairs Bureau of the War Ministry) drafted a statement that would hopefully form the basis of another attempt to arrive at an overall settlement of the issues. But the Army General Staff refused to have this document presented to the Liaison Conference on the 18th because Army Staff personnel had not had an opportunity to study it.

From the comments expressed at this Conference, it is evident that the Army believed that Japan's position had not been fully conveyed to the United States by the Foreign Ministry and Ambassador Nomura. As a matter of fact, both the Foreign Ministry and Nomura had toned down some of Japan's demands in an effort to reach an understanding with the United States.

Agenda: The Clarification of the Empire's Attitudes toward the Nomura Operation.

[In the course of the Nomura Operation, the expression of the Empire's attitudes has varied from time to time; and this has resulted in a failure to sufficiently convey the determination of the Empire to the other side. For example, the drafts of May and July vary. Moreover, even though the Imperial Conference draft of "Essentials for Carrying Out the Empire's Policies" was adopted by the Liaison Conference on September 3, the Foreign Office draft of a telegram to Nomura on the resumption of the Nomura Operation, which was adopted by the Conference on the same day, differs in content from "Essentials for Carrying Out the Empire's Policies," which was attached. Again, even though the "Basic Terms of Peace between Japan and China" was adopted by the Liaison Conference on September 13, the draft of the reply wired to Ambassador Nomura differs from that document. And so on.

[Two weeks have now passed since the decision of the Imperial Conference on September 6; but the prospects of a Japanese-American conference remain unclear. There is the likelihood that if we allow things to go on this way, the prospects of successful diplomacy will not be clear by the first ten days of October, and we will be the victims of America's delaying tactics. Perhaps because of this, the Army Chief of Staff spoke today, and was strongly supported by the Navy Chief of Staff. The following was adopted: "The final position of the Empire concerning the Nomura Operation must be quickly decided, and this must be made known to the United States."]

54TH LIAISON CONFERENCE
September 20, 1941

After the previous Liaison Conference, the Section Chiefs of the Army General Staff met, and their views were conveyed to the Foreign Ministry by Muto of the War Ministry. The Foreign Ministry produced a draft statement, but this document was not acceptable to the Army Staff. Finally, an Army document setting forth Japan's final position was prepared by representatives of the Army General Staff and the War Ministry; it was discussed and approved at this Liaison Conference. The document, a lengthy one, reviewed the outstanding issues; it was to be a response to the American Draft Understanding of June 21. The "Basic Terms of Peace between Japan and China" adopted on September 13 were incorporated into this document with some changes. It was a much stronger statement than the one that the Foreign Ministry had presented on September 4.

*It would appear from the discussion at this Conference that the
Army had not yet completely given up the idea of an invasion of
Russia.*

Agenda: The Final Decision on the "Draft Understanding between
Japan and the United States."

[*Summary:* Amendments to the "Draft Understanding Regarding
the Adjustment of Diplomatic Relations between Japan and the
United States" were proposed by the Army General Staff. All were
adopted, and a final decision was made. On this matter, the Prime
Minister and his associates stood by yesterday waiting for the Liaison
Conference to be called; but the Army General Staff demanded a delay on the ground that they had something to say.

[The important points discussed at the meeting were as follows:
On the attitude toward the Tripartite Pact in Article II:][6]

CHIEF SECRETARY TOMITA: Since the Japanese Government has often explained that the Tripartite Pact is defensive, I would like to
see sentences or phrases with that meaning added here.

SOMEONE: The idea of its being defensive was expressed as the
Japanese view; the United States has not said anything to indicate
her attitude. Therefore, I believe an all-inclusive expression like "protection and self-defense" would be appropriate. [Thus the second
opinion was approved.]

[On the amendment of the phrase in Article III,[7] "measures by the
Government of Japan directed toward a peaceful settlement" to read
"measures by the Government of Japan directed toward the settlement of the China Incident":]

YAMAMOTO, CHIEF OF THE ASIAN BUREAU OF THE FOREIGN MINISTRY:
"Peaceful settlement" has a broader meaning.

ARMY CHIEF OF STAFF SUGIYAMA: The purpose of the "good offices"

[6] "Both Governments maintain it is their common aim to bring about peace
in the world, and, when an opportune time arrives, they will endeavor jointly for
the early restoration of world peace.

"With regard to developments of the situation prior to the restoration of world
peace, both Governments will be guided in their conduct by considerations of
protection and self-defense; and in case the United States should participate in
the European War, Japan would decide entirely independently in the matter of
the interpretation of the Tripartite Pact between Japan, Germany, and Italy, and
would likewise determine what actions might be taken by way of fulfilling the
obligations in accordance with the said interpretation."

[7] Article III was entitled "Action toward a Peaceful Settlement between Japan
and China."

is to terminate fighting, as well as to create a peaceful relationship. "Peaceful settlement" seems to exclude the termination of fighting. Therefore it would be better to say "the settlement of the China Incident."

[On the note to Article III:][8]

CHIEF OF THE NAVAL AFFAIRS BUREAU OKA: I would prefer not to specify the place where and the period for which our troops would be stationed. That is, I would prefer to delete the names of the places where troops would be stationed and simply state, "in certain areas for a necessary period." [Because of this opinion, the draft adopted previously by the Liaison Conference was amended.][9]

[On the deletion of Article VI, non-advance to the North:][10]

PRIME MINISTER KONOYE: We have already told the other side that we do not intend to advance north without good reason. Hence it would be awkward not to mention it. Moreover, they will most certainly inquire about it. Therefore, it would be better to leave it in. [There were many expressions of view in support of this.]

SUGIYAMA: The main concern of Article VI is French Indochina and the Southwest Pacific. It has no direct relationship to the North. On questions concerning the North, we only need to reply if the other side asks; and there is certainly no need to include the matter in the Draft Understanding. I would be especially dubious about saying that we will not advance militarily to either the South or the North. Although it is agreed in principle that we will not advance to either the South or the North without good reason, I would prefer not to mention the North. There is no need to mention the North again in the Draft Understanding. It will be sufficient to reply if the other side asks. [Because of the above, it was resolved to delete Article VI.]

[Miscellaneous:]

DIRECTOR OF THE PLANNING BOARD SUZUKI: Is this the final draft? Is there room for additional amendments? If there is sufficient time, we do not have to regard this as final.

WAR MINISTER TOJO: We do not have the time. We are already behind schedule, and circumstances are pressing.

[8] The note referred to "Basic Terms of Peace between Japan and China," which had been adopted by the Liaison Conference on September 13.

[9] The "Basic Terms of Peace between Japan and China" specifically mentioned stationing troops in Inner Mongolia and certain areas in North China.

[10] The note handed to Grew on September 4, from the Foreign Minister to the American Government, stated that Japan would not, "without any justifiable reason, resort to military action against any regions lying north of Japan."

KONOYE: It is necessary to arrange things so that negotiations will proceed as rapidly as possible. Therefore, it would be better to state it [the policy toward the North] so that there will be no exchange of questions and answers.

TOYODA: A law to restrict travel by foreigners is being proposed, but this gives the impression of something new. How about this point? From the point of view of diplomacy, the sudden adoption of new measures is undesirable.

TOJO: This measure is necessary to protect military secrets.

TOYODA: They say that young officers in the Army are fuming about the southward advance. How about this?

SUGIYAMA: No doubt there are those among the young officers who are worried about national defense and discussing it. But what has been decided as national policy is being carried out by the Ministers and the Chief of Staff; there is no need to be concerned all the time about what the young men say.

55TH LIAISON CONFERENCE
September 25, 1941

The Army and Navy had now set October 15 as the deadline for negotiations with the United States. Meanwhile, the proposed meeting between the two heads of state had not yet materialized. The American leaders were reluctant to have a meeting without prior agreement on fundamental issues because such a meeting might be interpreted as an American endorsement of the Japanese position; if it failed, the militarists would be provided with an opportunity to convince the Japanese people that the United States was responsible for its failure.

It was revealed at this Conference that the Foreign Minister had not yet transmitted the Draft Understanding adopted on September 20. After the meeting, however, he did hand the note to Grew; and on September 27, the Japanese Embassy in Washington presented the same note to the State Department.

Two days after this Conference Foreign Minister Toyoda talked with Ambassador Grew and urged a quick reply to the proposal of a meeting between President Roosevelt and Prime Minister Konoye. Incidentally, the Foreign Ministry had wired Nomura that any time between October 10 and 15 was acceptable. Grew urged the State Department to take a risk and agree to a meeting with Konoye. On September 29, Nomura met with Hull and suggested that if the pro-

posed meeting was not held, the Konoye government was likely to fall and be succeeded by a less moderate Cabinet.

Actually, Konoye was shocked by the deadline of October 15, which the Armed Forces insisted upon. He threatened to resign, "retired" to his home in Kamakura, and refused to come to Tokyo.

Agenda: The Deadline for Determining the Prospects for Success or Failure of Diplomatic Negotiations with the United States, and its Relation to the Opening of Hostilities.

[Following reports by the Army and Navy Chiefs of Staff, the Army Chief of Staff explained the need, as seen by the Supreme Command, to set October 15, at the latest, as the deadline for political strategy against the United States. The Navy Chief of Staff made supplementary remarks from the point of view of the Navy. Although no direct opinions were expressed on the above, the following comments were made:]

FOREIGN MINISTER TOYODA: I fully understand the need for decision by October 15 at the latest. I told Grew that I would reply before the 27th. I told him "before the 27th" because that day is the first anniversary of the Tripartite Pact, and also because it is not good to delay this matter indefinitely. Shall we shorten the time limit for the reply in view of the demands of the Supreme Command? That would make it look like a final ultimatum, and so would be undesirable.

ARMY CHIEF OF STAFF SUGIYAMA: At any rate, I want it done quickly.

SOMEONE: There will be no problem if the Konoye-Roosevelt talks cannot be held. But if they are to be held, our delegation would have to leave here about October 1 if a decision is to be made by October 15. Is this possible?

WAR MINISTER TOJO: We can decide by calculating our chances.

SUGIYAMA: It would be undesirable if our talks with the other side provided no more than a few years' temporary peace, and were then followed by disputes. We must reach an agreement that will produce tranquility for several decades.

[It may be concluded that with this the matter won the approval of the Government; but it was not discussed in detail.]

[On the handling of the "Draft Understanding between Japan and the United States," approved by the Liaison Conference on the 20th:]

SUGIYAMA: What has happened to the Draft Understanding? Has it been sent to the United States?

TOYODA: It has not been sent yet. It will be wired this afternoon.

SUGIYAMA: Why hasn't it been wired yet?

TOYODA: There is nothing new, so all we need to do is to reply to their past questions. If we were to present this Draft Understanding now, it would be taken that we were proposing some new conditions; so I have not sent it yet.

[The impressions of the Army Chief of Staff:]

I'm very glad that I asked about the disposition of the Draft Understanding today.

56TH LIAISON CONFERENCE
October 2, 1941

Ambassador Nomura had wired on September 27 that he believed many of the points in the Japanese draft would be unacceptable to the United States. The Foreign Minister then sent a reply that did not meet with the approval of the Supreme Command, and he was forced to amend it. The military were annoyed because they believed that the Foreign Minister was not faithfully conveying to the United States the decisions made in the Liaison Conferences.

Agenda: The Adjustment of Diplomatic Relations between Japan and the United States.

[The Foreign Minister commented on the amendment to the telegram sent to Ambassador Nomura regarding adjustment of diplomatic relations between Japan and the United States. This was a wire replying to Ambassador Nomura's telegram concerning the Draft Understanding that was approved by the Liaison Conference on September 20. Although this wire was sent on the 30th, it was then amended on the demand of the Supreme Command because it was not consistent with the intent of the Liaison Conference decision. With regard to the above, the following comments were made:]

ARMY CHIEF OF STAFF SUGIYAMA: I'm glad that it has already been amended, as reported by the Foreign Minister. But the two items on our obligations under the Tripartite Pact and the settlement of the China Incident were not satisfactory in the original telegram. The Supreme Command is greatly interested in these two items, so in the future please pay careful attention to them. [War Minister Tojo made additional remarks on this.]

[Concerning the above, on September 23 the Foreign Minister sent

Ambassador Nomura a wire on the problem of stationing troops;[11] but the Foreign Minister asked that the Vice Chief of the Army Command wire the Military Attaché in the United States [Maj. Gen. Isoda Saburo] in detail about the need for stationing troops and about other matters, and that he have the Attaché explain this to Nomura and obtain his understanding.[12] Both Chiefs of Staff agreed to this.]

57TH LIAISON CONFERENCE
October 4, 1941

On October 2 Secretary Hull gave Ambassador Nomura a note, ostensibly the American reply to the Japanese note of September 6. It was actually a long note that reviewed the developments to date. It reiterated the "Four Principles," and stated that the Prime Minister had indicated to the American Ambassador that he would subscribe to these principles. However, it continued, the September 6 note seemed to indicate a divergence of views between the two governments. The American note specifically mentioned Japan's intention to station troops in China: "It is believed that a clearcut manifestation of Japan's intention in regard to the withdrawal of Japanese troops from China and French Indochina would be most helpful in making known—in particular to those who might be inclined to be critical —Japan's peaceful intentions and Japan's desire to follow courses calculated to establish a sound basis for future stability and progress in the Pacific area." The note expressed doubt that a meeting of the heads of state would contribute to peace, given the apparent divergence of views between the two governments on fundamental questions.

It is little wonder that Ambassador Nomura, after receiving the note from Hull, wired his Government that the negotiations had reached a "deadlock." Nevertheless, Foreign Minister Toyoda pre-

[11] This note argued that Japan must station armed forces in certain sections of China after the restoration of peace between China and Japan, for the following reasons: (1) The activities of the Communists and the lack of internal stability necessitate the presence of Japanese troops. (2) Internal stability affects the economic situation, which in turn affects Japan's defense and existence. (3) Japan is prepared to withdraw her troops whenever her presence is no longer required; the maintenance of peace by using international forces is unacceptable to Japanese public opinion.

[12] In a telegram to the Foreign Minister on October 15, Nomura said: "The Military Attaché here has been instructed by Headquarters in Tokyo to advise us not to yield an inch in our stand regarding the evacuation of troops."

pared a reply to the note and presented it for consideration at this Liaison Conference; but it was rejected by the representatives of the armed forces.

Agenda: On the Attitude of the Empire Toward the American Reply.

[Participants: the Prime Minister, the War, Foreign, and Navy Ministers, both Chiefs of Staff, and Terasaki, Chief of the American Bureau of the Foreign Ministry.]

FOREIGN MINISTER TOYODA: Because important national policy will be discussed today we have asked the important Ministers and the two Chiefs of Staff to come, unaccompanied by their secretaries. [The Minister of Home Affairs, the Director of the Planning Board, the Chief Secretary of the Cabinet, and the two Bureau Chiefs were not present.]

Last night the American reply arrived. There were 12 parts altogether; No. 8 came before No. 6, and so on, and the translation has just been completed.

[Next Bureau Chief Terasaki explained the important points as he read the telegrams. He said that the American note states in effect: "Since it appears that although Japan agrees with the United States regarding principles, she differs on their application, the United States is doubtful about holding a meeting of the two heads of state." He presented a draft of a telegram replying to this.]

WAR MINISTER TOJO: The American reply ought to be "yes" or "no" or something in between; but the reply that has come is neither "yes" nor "no." The Imperial Government must make some forecasts about diplomacy on this occasion. Since the matter is extremely critical, there is a need to put aside our reply to the United States for a while and give it serious study.

ARMY CHIEF OF STAFF SUGIYAMA: I agree with the War Minister. But the Supreme Command would be opposed to further delay. If we delay, both the South and the North will be left hanging in the air. We need not decide today. We had better decide after further study.

NAVY CHIEF OF STAFF NAGANO: There is no longer time for discussion. We want quick action.

[The War Minister explained the Empire's exceptions to the "Four Principles." He said, "I would like to have the foregoing exceptions to the handling of the principles considered."]

[It was proposed that there be no further discussion today, that the secretaries study the question of how to reply, and that another meeting be held as soon as possible. In response to this, the Navy Chief of Staff stated that the Supreme Command wished to proceed as quickly as possible; and that when the secretaries studied the matter he would like to have the Chief of the First Section of the Naval General Staff join them. There was unanimous approval, and the meeting was adjourned.]

58TH LIAISON CONFERENCE
October 9, 1941

The American note of October 2 precipitated a flurry of conferences within the Japanese Government and the armed forces. The Army felt that there was no point in continuing the negotiations, and that Japan should decide to go to war. However, some Navy leaders— particularly the Navy Minister—were reluctant to see the negotiations broken off. Their reluctance stemmed from their lack of confidence in Japan's ability to win a prolonged war with the United States. Prime Minister Konoye and Foreign Minister Toyoda also sought to continue the negotiations; and toward that end Nomura was instructed to seek clarification of some of the points raised in the American note. Ambassador Nomura met with Secretary Hull on October 9, but this meeting did not result in satisfactory answers. The next day Foreign Minister Toyoda, distrusting the management of events in Washington and feeling the pressure of the impending deadline, complained to Grew and asked that he try to get the necessary information for him.

The American Ambassador took the occasion of this meeting to emphasize that the movement of additional troops to Indochina, which had been reported, could adversely affect the course of Japanese-American negotiations. Reports were coming in that the Japanese, with threat of force, were demanding more air bases and military facilities in southern Indochina. Earlier the State Department had instructed Grew to state that the American Government found it "especially difficult at this time to reconcile the reported Japanese actions in Indochina with recent declarations of high Japanese officials that Japan's fundamental policy is based upon the maintenance of peace and courses of peace."[13]

[13] State Department, *Foreign Relations of the United States, 1941: The Far East*, V, 304.

Agenda: On the Attitude of the Empire Toward the American Reply.

[For an hour, starting at 3 P.M., there was a report by the Intelligence Chiefs of the two General Staffs regarding the interpretation of the situation. After that the Liaison Conference began. The Foreign Minister and Terasaki, Chief of the American Bureau, gave what was primarily the Foreign Ministry's account of the American reply. Although there was some discussion of this, the meeting was adjourned without reaching a decision.]

FOREIGN MINISTER TOYODA: On the 7th we pressed Ambassador Nomura for a reply regarding the three points that were not clear in the American reply; but none came. Accordingly, at 9 o'clock today [the 9th] we talked with him on the telephone and pressed him again. He replied that he had been promised a reply when he met with Hull tomorrow morning at 9 o'clock [9 P.M. on the 9th, Tokyo time]. Hence I will wait for this reply, and consult you as soon as possible.

ARMY CHIEF OF STAFF SUGIYAMA: Regarding the American question, from our point of view the Supreme Command cannot extend the deadline beyond October 15. If the matter can be settled within this time period, I would like to have it pushed ahead as fast as possible. How about calling a Liaison Conference when the answer comes tomorrow? [He spoke only of the time, and not of what would be discussed.]

[Navy Chief of Staff Nagano was about to present the following memo, but was prevented from doing so by Navy Minister Oikawa. He showed it to the Foreign Minister after the meeting. The Foreign Minister nodded his head in approval.]

1. It will be difficult from the point of view of operations if the negotiations are prolonged.

2. If you are going to negotiate, do so with the conviction of sure success. If you reach a stalemate in the course of it and come to me, I won't have anything to do with it. From now on, one should not make any test shots without this conviction.

[Gist of the private talks between Terasaki, Chief of the American Bureau, and Grew and Dooman:][14]

TERASAKI: Grew said the following with great circumspection, and with the understanding that it was on his own responsibility:

---

[14] The American account of these conversations, which differs in certain respects from what is reported here, can be found in State Department, *Foreign Relations of the United States: Japan, 1931–41*, II, 666ff. Eugene Dooman was Counselor at the American Embassy in Tokyo.

"Both Dooman and I believe that the United States' view is that we want to proceed with the negotiations. I believe the important points in the note are: (a) the stationing of troops in China and French Indochina; (b) economic problems in the Southwest Pacific area; (c) Japan's advantageous position in China due to her proximity. I do not have the authority to speak on the interpretation of the withdrawal of troops—that is, on whether what is required is an expression of the intent to withdraw troops or the actual withdrawal of troops. Since this is a problem that the President himself wants to deal with, I would prefer that you negotiate directly with my Government." (He thus avoided getting into it too deeply.)

"In my own [Grew's] thinking, the withdrawal of troops mentioned in the note would appear to cover both firm agreement and actual withdrawal of troops."

The following is what Dooman said:

"In addition to the chief points in the note mentioned by Grew, there is the 'right of self-defense.' It is not clear from the language whether the withdrawal of troops involves actual withdrawal or a firm commitment to do so.

"The real problem is Japan's attitude toward French Indochina rather than the withdrawal of troops from China. You have seized houses of Indochinese, imprisoned the nationals of other countries, acted as though you were in Japan itself, and engaged in illegal actions from the point of view of the international community. I believe that the actions of the Japanese armed forces in French Indochina are a great obstacle to the future progress of Japanese-American negotiations. I think things will calm down, since Ambassador Yoshizawa[15] is to go there; but, in any case, Japan's actions are outrageous.

"On the self-defense question, I would prefer to have you think of [American] entry into the European war as self-defense."

[The attitude of the Japanese armed forces toward French Indochina:]

TOYODA: On the 7th I met with Arsène-Henry,[16] and he presented a protest, as indicated in the attached document, under orders from his Government. He spoke about the actions of the Japanese armed forces, so I replied in an appropriate fashion.

BOTH BUREAU CHIEFS: We have told the armed forces on the spot to be very careful on this matter, so there is no need to worry. As for the

---

[15] Yoshizawa Kenkichi, after his recall from the Netherlands East Indies, was appointed to a post in French Indochina.

[16] Arsène-Henry was the Vichy French Ambassador to Japan.

population survey that is being protested, we must undertake it from the point of view of mutual defense.

TOYODA: If this sort of thing continues, we will run into trouble; so please be careful.

With regard to our request for ¥65 million worth of piasters, the Foreign Ministry officials have told Indochina that this sum is required for airfields, warehouses, and buildings in southern French Indochina. Yet Lieutenant Colonel Hayashi[17] has stated that 50,000 troops will move into northern Indochina, and this makes it difficult from the point of view of diplomacy.

SUGIYAMA: We are sending out propaganda to the effect that our troops will not be going into southern French Indochina, and that many troops will go into northern Indochina for the purpose of attacking Kunming.

59TH LIAISON CONFERENCE
October 23, 1941

Alarmed by the trend toward war, Prime Minister Konoye summoned the Foreign, War, and Navy Ministers to his residence in the Ogikubo section of Tokyo on October 12. At this meeting, known as the Ogikubo Conference, Konoye tried to persuade War Minister Tojo that there was hope for negotiations with the United States, but without success. If at this meeting the Navy Minister had unequivocally stated that the Navy was not prepared to go to war, the outcome might have been different; but he refused to take this stand, and said instead that the issue of war or peace ought to be decided by the Prime Minister. But neither the Prime Minister nor the Foreign Minister could guarantee to the War Minister that an agreement with the United States was likely to result if negotiations were continued. Under the circumstances, Konoye could not make the War Minister change his mind.

At the Cabinet meeting the next day, War Minister Tojo reiterated his stand, stressing the importance of the operational considerations that had played so large a part in the decision of September 6. Tojo indicated to Konoye that if the decision of September 6 was to be repudiated, all who had taken part in that decision should resign, having failed in their obligation to the Emperor. A new Cabinet might then in conscience reconsider the September 6 decision.

Since he was unwilling to lead the nation into war, Konoye resigned. Both he and Tojo felt that the best man to head the new Gov-

---

[17] I have not been able to identify this person.

ernment would be Prince Higashikuni, an Army officer and a blood relative of the Emperor. Konoye felt that the Prince was opposed to war and would continue the negotiations; Tojo supported Higashikuni because he felt the Prince could unify the Army and Navy behind the Government's policies. However, Kido, the Lord Keeper of the Privy Seal, and other elder statesmen opposed Higashikuni's appointment. They felt he had little political experience, and were reluctant to have a relative of the Emperor lead the nation into war because this might threaten the position of the Emperor if Japan were defeated.

In the end War Minister Tojo was recommended for the Prime Ministership on the ground that he was strong enough to control the military. Tojo himself was unaware of his nomination until summoned to the Imperial presence. The Emperor told him: "We direct you to form a Cabinet and to abide by the provisions of the Constitution. We believe that an exceedingly grave situation confronts the nation. Bear in mind, at this time, that cooperation between the Army and Navy should be closer than ever before." The Emperor also summoned the Navy Minister and ordered him to cooperate with the Army. Finally, he directed the Lord Keeper of the Privy Seal to tell the two Service Ministers that they should study the situation at home and abroad without being bound by the Imperial Conference decision of September 6. Under these conditions, Tojo Hideki felt he could accept the Prime Ministership. He also served concurrently as War Minister. Admiral Shimada Shigetaro was named Navy Minister.

Tojo asked two new men to fill the key posts of Foreign Minister and Finance Minister. Togo Shigenori, an experienced diplomat, was named Foreign Minister, and Kaya Okinori was appointed Finance Minister. Before accepting the posts, both felt it necessary to assure themselves that efforts would be continued to find a diplomatic settlement if at all possible.

It was against this background that the first Liaison Conference of the new Cabinet began to restudy the question of war or peace.

Agenda: Reconsideration of the "Essentials for Carrying Out the Empire's Policies."

[The first meeting between the Cabinet and the Supreme Command was held at 2 P.M. It ended at 5:30 P.M.

[To provide information, there were briefings by Section Chiefs Okamoto and Maeda on "The Prospects of the European War."][18]

---

[18] Maeda Minoru, Chief of the Intelligence Section, Naval General Staff; Okamoto Kiyofuku, Chief of the Intelligence Section, Army General Staff.

REAR ADMIRAL MAEDA: Because of Germany's success in the German-Soviet war and the growing strength of England, the probability of the European war gradually becoming a long-term war [between England and Germany] is very high.

England is stressing the defense of Suez and Singapore. With the advance of Germany into the Near East, there will be military operations in the Near East before long.

The United States will probably try to prevent Japan from getting into the war until the end of 1942, when the United States will be sufficiently prepared to fight on two oceans.

[After the above briefing ended, the Liaison Conference commenced at 4 P.M. Navy Chief of Staff Nagano reported on the present situation in the Navy, and said forcefully: "We were to have reached a decision in October, and yet here we are. So I want to see our study and discussion kept concise. The Navy is consuming 400 tons of oil an hour. The situation is urgent. We want it decided one way or the other quickly." Army Chief of Staff Sugiyama discussed the Army's war situation since the French Indochina occupation and emphasized: "Things have already been delayed one month. We can't devote four or five days to study. Hurry up and go ahead."]

PRIME MINISTER TOJO: I well understand why the Supreme Command emphasizes the need to hurry. The Government would prefer to give the matter careful study and do it in a responsible way, since there are new Ministers of the Navy, Finance, and Foreign Affairs. I would like to have us decide whether the Government can assume responsibility for the September 6 decision as it stands, or whether we must reconsider it from a new point of view. Does the Supreme Command have any objections?

SUPREME COMMAND: No objections.

TOJO: In that case, what is the best method [for study]? How about having the secretaries draft a proposal?

CHIEF OF THE MILITARY AFFAIRS BUREAU MUTO: It will be difficult for the secretaries to agree on a draft proposal. In the main these are problems we have already studied.

CHIEF OF THE NAVAL AFFAIRS BUREAU OKA: How would it be if the various Ministries give their points of view at some length here, others voice their opinions regarding these views, and the various secretaries then put everything together?

ALL: We agree.

FINANCE MINISTER KAYA: I would like to be informed in such a way that I can understand the problem. What will happen to our resources if we undertake a war? What will happen if we leave things as they are and do not go to war? What will happen if negotiations with the United States are unsuccessful? These are the questions we should study. The budget can be decided once the relationship between the supply and demand of resources is set. I don't believe the budget itself presents much of a problem.

SOMEONE: If we study these thirteen questions one after the other, all this will become clear.[19]

TOJO: This will be all for today. I would like to consider these questions on Friday afternoon, Saturday morning, and Monday afternoon.

[The meeting was adjourned. A reexamination of the "Empire's Policies" was not undertaken today.]

60TH AND 61ST LIAISON CONFERENCES
October 24 and 25, 1941

Following the installation of the Tojo Cabinet, the Liaison Conference met almost daily to reexamine the Imperial Conference decision of September 6. For this purpose papers that posed questions and set forth answers were prepared. It is important to note that the preparation of these papers was entrusted to the Army and Navy officers who (except for the new Navy Minister, Shimada) had been involved in the earlier decisions; so it was a foregone conclusion that a radically different policy orientation was not likely to emerge. It is also important to note that the instruction from Lord Keeper of the Privy Seal Kido not to be bound by the September 6 Imperial Conference decision was not formally conveyed to the Army and Navy Chiefs of Staff. Hence preparations for war continued to go forward in high gear in the armed forces.

At these Conferences (the notes for the October 24 and 25 meetings seem to have been combined), and those that followed, much attention was paid to assessing Japan's capacity to wage war—especially in terms of vital war materials, including steel and oil, and in terms of shipping and shipbuilding capacity. Here certain facts confronted the decision makers. Japan's steel capacity was only about one-thirteenth of that of the United States, and Japan could not produce all the ships she needed. As for oil, 60 per cent of Japan's supply had come from

---

[19] A paper in the form of questions and answers had been prepared to serve as a basis for discussion. Actually there appear to have been eleven rather than thirteen questions.

*the United States in 1940; but since the freezing of Japanese funds in
July 1941 no oil had been imported from America. Efforts had been
made all along to build up stockpiles, but at best the supply of oil
would last only eighteen months.*

*One of the problems in assessing Japan's war capability was the
limitation on information available to those charged with decision
making. For instance, General Suzuki Teiichi, the Director of the
Planning Board, was unable to obtain information about petroleum
stored by the armed forces until about October 1941. Foreign Minister Togo later complained: "I was astonished at our lack of the statistical data required for a study of this sort; but even more, I keenly
felt the absurdity of our having to base our deliberations on assumptions, since the high command refused to divulge figures on the num-
bers of our forces, or any facts relating to operations."*[20]

Agenda: Reexamination of the "Essentials for Carrying Out the
Empire's Policies."

[The meeting began at 2 P.M. and ended at 8:20 P.M. on October
24. It began at 9 A.M. and ended at noon on October 25.]

Question Two:[21] "What are the prospects of operations in the beginning, and after a few years, in a war against the United States,
Great Britain, and the Netherlands?"

[The Army gave the same explanation as in the questions-and-
answers paper.]

NAVY: We will be all right at the beginning; but if the war is prolonged, our chances will depend on the international situation and
the determination of the people. The Navy has asked several times
for the necessary resources.

NAVY MINISTER SHIMADA, FINANCE MINISTER KAYA: Do you have any
idea of liquidating the China Front?

ARMY VICE CHIEF OF STAFF TSUKADA: We would like to maintain this
front if possible; but we will liquidate it if the situation requires us to
do so. Especially if something develops in the North, we will be
forced to liquidate it.

ARMY CHIEF OF STAFF SUGIYAMA: Military operations in the South
will for the most part require four to five months.

NAVY VICE CHIEF OF STAFF ITO: The Navy will need from six to eight
months.

[20] Togo Shigenori, *The Cause of Japan* (New York, 1956), p. 127.
[21] There are no notes on the discussion of Question One, which referred to the
outlook with respect to the war in Europe.

[This gave everyone the impression that there were differences between the Army and Navy regarding their understanding of the operations.]

Question Three: "If we begin hostilities in the South this autumn, what situation will we face in the North?"

[On this question the Army, Navy, and Foreign Ministers were mostly in agreement. There will be no aggressive action [in the North] after the beginning of war; but the United States might use Soviet military bases, or the Soviet Union, enticed by the United States and Britain, might engage in machinations. If the war is prolonged, depending on conditions, a Japanese-Soviet war cannot be ruled out.]

Question Four: "What will be the attrition rate of ships?"

[The Army gave the same explanation as in the paper. The General Director of the Ship Management Section of the Navy[22] gave a report, the gist of which follows.]

The following are the prospects for new ships:[23] first year, 400,000 tons; second year, 600,000 tons; third year, 800,000 tons. But the following conditions must be met: (1) priorities on needed materials; (2) guaranteed repairing of damages to facilities; (3) priorities on labor and transportation; (4) improvement in shipbuilding facilities; (5) the Army's continuing needs to be reduced to 900,000 tons;[24] (6) centralization of administrative machinery relating to ships; (7) mass production to be made possible by using a standard 3,000-ton, 12-section ship.

Also, to build 600,000 tons of new ships, 360,000 tons of steel are required. The Navy also needs considerable amounts of steel [for warships]. Will this be supplied? Also, will it be possible to expand manufacturing facilities; will there be an allocation of machinery for repairs; will a labor force for transport be guaranteed—all to the extent desired?

PRIME MINISTER TOJO: What is the general shipbuilding capacity?

GENERAL DIRECTOR: By and large, 400,000 tons the first year and 600,000 tons the second year.

NAVY MINISTER SHIMADA: Young people are too optimistic. There is the problem of repairing warships, too; so ship construction will probably be 200,000 to 300,000 tons, one-half of what the General Director says.

---

22 I have not been able to identify this person.
23 This presumably refers to merchant shipping.
24 This presumably refers to steel.

Question Five: "What are the prospects for the acquisition of vital materials?"

[The study report of the Planning Board is explained.]

KAYA: The budget can be managed in any way, so long as we have the materials and the manpower.

If we can maintain the people's livelihood while prosecuting the war, and bring up the next generation besides, we need not worry.

In the occupied territories we can get rid of the banks and use military currency. By contrast with our problems in China, our task will be unexpectedly easy.

SHIMADA: The Navy will require a budget of ¥9.4 billion in 1942, ¥9.5 billion in 1943, and ¥10 billion annually after that. Is this all right?

[Today Questions Four and Five were unresolved. On Question Two, the prospects of the war, there were the following comments on the method of making the enemy surrender after we win the first phase of the war: this cannot be achieved merely through the use of force; it must depend on diplomacy. The British fleet must not be active in the Far East after Britain surrenders. Moreover, Germany's power can be relied upon, and many have great confidence in Germany's national strength. (However, on cooperation with Germany: in the event that our policies greatly affect German interests, we must be careful of German moves. There are many people who believe that Germany cannot be trusted.)]

62D LIAISON CONFERENCE
October 27, 1941

The appraisal of Japan's warmaking capacity continued. The picture that began to emerge was not one that warranted great optimism. It became clear that despite this outlook the Army was building up strength in Manchuria to prepare for possible military operations against the Soviet Union. The Army was not satisfied that the build-up was adequate, but Army Chief of Staff Sugiyama argued that the deficiencies could be overcome by good luck and clever strategy. This kind of approach seems to be typical of many of the decision makers.

Agenda: Reexamination of the "Essentials for Carrying Out the Empire's Policies."

[The Conference began at 2 P.M. and ended at 6:20 P.M.]

Question Five: "What are the prospects for the acquisition of vital materials?"

FINANCE MINISTER KAYA: I would like to raise the following questions with respect to materials vital to the State in the event of operations in the South:

1. Does the required amount include everything [military, government, and civilian]? Especially in the case of military needs, does the amount anticipate needs during the coming years?

2. Has the ability of the State to supply these needs been considered [includes productive capacity, stockpiles, etc.]?

DIRECTOR OF THE PLANNING BOARD SUZUKI: Concerning the first question, in Japan we do not have a national defense state. There is no long-term plan for materials. Every fiscal year we compare the productive capacity of the country and the production desired, and then allocate production.

Our ability to supply the natural resources needed in 1942 will probably be 90 per cent of our ability in 1941. In doing this, we will be using up all of our stockpiles. However, only in the case of raw cotton can we manage until 1943 by using what is left in our stockpiles and by buying some from China.

As for production, measures to restrict government and civilian demand have already been carried as far as possible. If the demand is restricted further, the productive power of the country will decline.

If 3 million tons of shipping can be provided continuously, it would be possible to maintain the material strength of our country at present levels. But to maintain 3 million tons, it will be necessary to build 400,000 tons in 1942 and 600,000 tons in 1943. But if, as Navy Minister Shimada says, shipbuilding capacity should be cut in half, in the third year there would be only 190,000 tons for supplying all the needs of the people, and it would be questionable whether our national power could be maintained.

[Discussion of Suzuki's second question:]

PRIME MINISTER TOJO: The Army is making preparations, with emphasis on getting ready for the Soviet Union. The materials to be used in the South represent only a small part of the total required. The Army has been using 60 per cent of the past budgets for armaments and has been stockpiling them. We can manage somehow in 1942 and 1943 if the Army has the same allocation as before. But this does not meet the demands of the Supreme Command, and on this point we have asked for their indulgence. We do not know what will happen after 1944.

ARMY CHIEF OF STAFF SUGIYAMA: The Army has been making preparations on the assumption that many of the 170 Soviet divisions would be sent to the Far East. We are still in the midst of these preparations, and they are inadequate. But the deficiency of materials can be overcome by taking advantage of changes in the situation, and by clever strategy. It isn't true that we can't make war because we don't have as many materials as we had counted on.

[A résumé of the exchange between the Vice Minister of the Navy, Bureau Chief Oka, the Chief of the Bureau of Supplies and Equipment, and Finance Minister Kaya follows:]

[So long as the Navy is undertaking operations in the South, we must be able to keep up with the present expansion plans of the United States; so a supply of steel at the 1941 level would be inadequate.

[The proposed plan for building new warships calls for: 180,000 tons in 1942, 250,000 tons in 1943, 270,000 tons in 1944, 300,000 tons in 1945, 370,000 tons in 1946, 340,000 tons in 1947, 330,000 tons in 1948. Bureau Chief Oka said that this is a plan proposed by the Naval General Staff, and that the Navy Ministry does not necessarily agree with it. In any case, steel production at the 1941 rate will not be sufficient.]

YAMADA, CHIEF OF THE NAVY BUREAU OF SUPPLIES AND EQUIPMENT: If war begins in November, aircraft gasoline, plus what we will get from the Netherlands East Indies, will last 30 months. If war begins in March, it will last 21 months. If we maintain the status quo, aircraft gasoline will be exhausted in 34 months, and automobile fuel in 26 months.

KAYA: The point I would raise is that, according to what the Navy Minister has said, the Navy budget will be ¥9 billion. Hence the Army will probably demand ¥15 billion. This would make a big budget of ¥15–20 billion in excess of the fixed expenses of the Army and Navy. We would then need more than twice that in material resources. Hence we cannot avoid asking about materials. Without materials we can't make up a budget.

Question Seven: "What is the extent to which we can get cooperation from Germany and Italy?"

[Although the Foreign Minister said that we could not expect too much, the draft of the Army Chief of Staff was approved by the majority. Its gist is as follows:]

Resolution: Although we do not have great expectations [of aid from Germany and Italy], in the event that we let them know about our determination, and propose military cooperation, we should first of all get them to agree to the following provisions: (a) declaration of war against the United States; (b) no separate peace [Nagano suggested that the draft by the Army Chief of Staff should be adopted]; (c) to act in concert with Japan through stepped-up operations in the Near East; (d) cooperation in warfare to destroy commerce.

[As for attacking the Soviet Union: since they are already doing so, if we make strong demands on them, they may demand that we attack the Soviets. So it was decided that we should omit this. As for invading the British Isles: it was decided that we would get them to agree to this later, and that for the moment we would not mention it.

[According to statements made by the Navy, it is understood that the respective spheres of responsibility of Germany and Japan on the high seas are separated at Colombo.]

Question Eight: "Can the United States, Britain, and the Netherlands be separated, or can they not be separated?"

[The Foreign Ministry and the Navy explained this. The Army added the comment that from the point of view of strategy it is not necessarily impossible to separate them; but if it is impossible from the point of view of naval strategy, then it would be the same for the Army.

[Today the Army Chief of Staff said that from the point of view of the Supreme Command time is running out; so he asked that the study be speeded up. The Prime Minister replied that the Government understood the desire of the Supreme Command to hurry things; but the Government would like to study this thoroughly and take responsibility for it. He said he wanted this point understood. The Army Chief of Staff repeated his demand: although the Government, it goes without saying, has responsibility, in reality so does the Supreme Command; so he wanted special attention paid to moving forward quickly.

[Our observations are: (a) it appears that the determination of the Prime Minister is unchanged; (b) as before, the Navy Minister is not clear; most of his statements are negative; (c) there is a tendency for the whole Navy to engage in propaganda to secure more materials; (d) it appears that the Foreign Minister is frank, brief, and has considerable self-confidence; most of his arguments are consistent.]

63D LIAISON CONFERENCE
October 28, 1941

At this Conference Finance Minister Kaya posed the question, "Suppose you have war, and suppose you don't have war; which is better

*in terms of the supply of materials?" The question does not appear to
have been answered directly, but the discussion indicated that the
situation seemed to be bad either way.*

*The possibility of delaying the war until March of 1942 was con-
sidered, but discarded. Next, the question of producing synthetic oil
to solve the oil problem was taken up; but this, too, was found to be
impractical.*

Agenda: Reexamination of the "Essentials for Carrying Out the
Empire's Policies."

[The Conference began at 2 P.M. and ended at 6 P.M.]

Question Nine (a): "In the event war begins in March, what would
be its effect on our foreign relations?"

[After considering the draft by the Army Chief of Staff, the Foreign Minister came to the conclusion that, from the point of view of
international relations, the time was not propitious for the beginning
of hostilities. A better time might come later.]

FOREIGN MINISTER TOGO: The Soviet threat from the North will be
less than it is now.

ARMY CHIEF OF STAFF SUGIYAMA: That is not necessarily so. They
could make preparations during the winter, and next spring they
could get together with the United States and take positive action.
It is the same as our studies of Question Three.

TOGO: Depending on the situation, there might be a German-Soviet
peace.

SUGIYAMA: That is possible.

TOGO: Even though the United States might not enter the war until
next March, it would be prepared for entry. On the other hand, it
would use most of its forces in the Atlantic. Also, various difficult
problems would arise on the domestic scene. Ultimately there would
not be much difference.

SUGIYAMA: However, the harm would become greater: that is, the
alliance that is encircling Japan would get stronger. Also, Japan's relations with the Soviets would become more uneasy. Oil and other
materials would diminish, while the other side's military preparedness would be improved. [When Italy entered the war Germany was
not pleased, they say. Even if we postponed beginning the war until
next March, considering that the other party [Germany] has not
asked us to go ahead, it would probably not be enough to cool them
down. Hence it was decided to delete this question.]

Question Nine (b): "In the event war begins in March, what are the prospects for the supply of materials?"

[We reached the same conclusion as yesterday.]

Question Nine (c): "In the event war begins in March, what are the advantages and disadvantages from the point of view of strategy?"

[The beginning of war must come in November. That is, it is necessary to decide on commencing hostilities by the 30th of this month. The Army and Navy Chiefs of Staff emphasized that for the Navy this is imperative because of the problem of materials.

[Thus, the Army and Navy draft was adopted almost without change.]

Question Nine (d): "Can't the oil problem be solved by producing synthetic oil?"

DIRECTOR OF THE PLANNING BOARD [SUZUKI]: A project to produce 4 million tons would require for construction of facilities 1 million tons of steel, 25 million tons of coal, and expenditures of ¥2.1 billion. The plant facilities would not be completed for three years. Obviously, the State would have to take extraordinarily strong measures.

Although we plan to produce 340,000 tons in 1941, 550,000 tons in 1942, 1.61 million tons in 1943, and 4 million tons in 1945, there are serious difficulties in achieving this.

YAMADA, CHIEF OF THE NAVY BUREAU OF SUPPLIES AND EQUIPMENT: If this synthetic petroleum plan is undertaken, the Navy's preparations will take twice as long. We can't have this sort of thing done, which disregards international relations. It is difficult to carry out. Moreover, the oil shortage cannot be relieved by synthetic petroleum alone.

FINANCE MINISTER KAYA: Suppose you have war, and suppose you don't have war: which is better in terms of the supply of materials? I would like to know in quantitative terms.

Question Eleven: "What will be the effect [of the Southern Operation] on Chungking?"

[After the draft by the Army Chief of Staff, the War Ministry, and the Foreign Ministry was considered, it was adopted.]

KAYA: When we go south the Armed Forces will take what is needed; but the problem is whether this will enable us to replenish the fighting power of the Army and Navy from the point of view of materials. I would like to see a precise judgment made, rather than a statement of generalities.

[Today the Prime Minister apologized to the two Chiefs of Staff for the slow progress that was made in the deliberations.]

64TH LIAISON CONFERENCE
October 29, 1941

[The Conference lasted from 1 P.M. to 10 P.M. The text is not available.]

65TH LIAISON CONFERENCE
October 30, 1941

The complex task of reexamining the problem of war or peace was concluded at this Conference. No new paths lay clearly before the decision makers. The choices were limited: peace (at any price), war, or war qualified with continuing negotiations until the absolute deadline of November 30.

The leaders felt that, given the gravity of the decision, they needed time to think. The price for peace, as they saw it, was high: the loss of Japan's position in China and leadership in Asia, reduction to a third-rate power, and economic stagnation leading to increased dependence on the Great Powers—the very things they wanted to avoid. War, on the other hand, was risky. No one was willing to say what might lie ahead if war was prolonged. At the same time a few leaders, notably the Foreign Minister, wished to continue to try for a diplomatic solution to avoid launching a risky war. No one, however, was able to challenge the deadline set by the Army and Navy.

[The Conference lasted from 9 A.M. to noon. Question Five was studied, together with Question Nine, "Prospects for Materials," and Question Ten, "Prospects for Diplomacy."]
Questions Five and Nine:
[Explanations by Director Suzuki:]
(1) *"How much of the liquid fuel will depend on synthetic petroleum?"* This cannot be manufactured in a hurry; we cannot expect to assure the security of the State, insofar as fuel is concerned, by this.
(2) *"What about liquid fuel in the event of operations in the South?"* If we manage it right, there will be 2,550,000 tons left in the first year, 150,000 tons in the second year, and 700,000 tons in the third year. However, fuel for aircraft might be in short supply toward the end of the second year and going into the third year.

(c) *Steel:* The requirement for 1942 can be met with the 1941 production level. However, 3 million tons of shipping will be needed; and to maintain 3 million tons of shipping, 600,000 tons of new ships will need to be built. For this 300,000 tons of steel will be required. We would like to inquire about the Navy's Plan Five.

CHIEF OF THE GENERAL AFFAIRS SECTION OF THE SHIP ADMINISTRATION BUREAU: The Navy seeks a gradual increase in the building of warships as follows:

1942	950,000 tons
1943	1,000,000 tons
1944	1,200,000 tons
1945	1,000,000 tons
1946	1,000,000 tons

There is some uneasiness with respect to steel. Moreover, if we are to build 600,000 tons of warships, our seven conditions must be met.[25]

FINANCE MINISTER KAYA: I'm uneasy about steel and ships. It is necessary to give the matter further thought.

Question Ten:

(1) "What are the prospects of Japanese-American negotiations?"

[There is no hope of success over the short term. The Navy Ministry says that there is no hope even within two weeks.]

(2) "What are the limits to the concessions that can be made?"

[There was much discussion on this point. In the end the topic was changed to "How much can we concede?"]

[The results of the discussions:

[a. The Tripartite Pact: the same as in the past, no change.

[b. On the application of the Four Principles: what has been said to the United States in the past cannot be helped; but Tojo noted that he felt that "agreement in principle but with conditions" was not possible.

[c. Regarding equal opportunity for commerce in China: it was decided that there would be a condition that "the principle of equal opportunity would be applied throughout the world." It was further decided that "Southwest" would be excluded. On this point, the Army Chief of Staff strongly held out against any changes; but the Prime Minister expressed the strong opposition of the Government, and presented this compromise proposal. Nagano, Navy Chief of Staff, sud-

---

[25] This refers to the seven conditions enumerated in the 61st Liaison Conference, p. 189.

denly said: "How about proposing nondiscrimination in commerce? Let's show our generosity."

[d. No change in the question of withdrawing troops from French Indochina.

[e. Withdrawal of troops from China: same as before. However, it was decided that as a diplomatic gesture it will be permissible to reply that the necessary period will be about 25 years.

[On this point Army Chief of Staff Sugiyama and Army Vice Chief of Staff Tsukada took a strong stand and disagreed with the others over and over again. Foreign Minister Togo, forgetting reality, stated that "Even though we withdraw troops we can still do business; indeed it would be better to withdraw troops right away." The Navy also was not enthusiastic about stationing troops. The Army Chief of Staff strongly advocated the stationing of troops. The discussion was heated.

[The Prime Minister proposed that a certain number of years "close to being forever" be mentioned. He suggested that of the various common diplomatic expressions—99 years, 50 years, 30 years, 25 years—25 years be adopted. The Army Vice Chief of Staff made a strong objection to showing weakness by naming a definite number of years, such as 25. Many guessed that even if the deadline were 25, 20, or as little as 10 years away, the United States would not accept it.]

(3) "What would happen to Japan if the American proposals were accepted in their entirety?"

[All except the Foreign Minister judged that the Empire would become a third-rate country. The Foreign Minister judged that if conditions were softened and accepted, everything would turn out for the better; he gave everyone a strange feeling.]

[Next it was urged that another meeting be held tomorrow, the 31st. But Finance Minister Kaya said, "Let me think about it for a day"; and Foreign Minister Togo said, "I want to get my mind in order," etc., indicating a wish to postpone it one day. The Prime Minister took about thirty minutes to explain why every minute counted. Nagano also urged speed.

[The Prime Minister said that a decision must be reached on November 1, even if we have to meet all night, and suggested that the following items be studied:]

Proposal One: Avoid war and undergo great hardships.

Proposal Two: Decide on war immediately and settle matters by war.

Proposal Three: Decide on war but carry on war preparations and diplomacy side by side. [We would like to do it in such a way that diplomacy will succeed.]

[At today's meeting:

[The Foreign Minister suggested that he would like to proceed with diplomacy. As usual the Navy Minister was vague. Although Finance Minister Kaya has many questions, he is serious.

[Nagano said: Make preparations for war, but also go ahead with diplomacy.

[As for the deadline, the Government said that it understood the position of the Supreme Command; but at the same time it was in a difficult position. The doubts must be resolved. The Government imploringly asked that there be no meeting tomorrow, since it wanted to settle the issue even if it took all night on the 1st. It was not easy to deny this.

[In the discussion, the Army Chief of Staff and the Vice Chief in particular advocated strong measures, but they were isolated and failed to get support. Tojo had difficulty in distinguishing between his remarks as War Minister and as Prime Minister. He only supported the Army Chief of Staff in his capacity as War Minister. In the end, he more often proposed compromise measures between the Army General Staff and the Government, instead of supporting the Army Chief of Staff as War Minister.]

66TH LIAISON CONFERENCE
November 1, 1941

This was a historic conference. It lasted 17 hours, amid great tension and angry exchanges between the participants. Prior to the meeting on October 31, the War Ministry and the Army General Staff personnel had met separately to decide what position they should take toward the three alternatives that had been posed in the previous Liaison Conference.

The War Ministry decided to support the third proposal, which was to decide on war but to continue negotiations with the hope that war might be avoided. The Army Staff, however, favored Proposal Two, which called for war and no further negotiations. General Tojo, acting in his capacity as Prime Minister, conferred with Navy Minister Shimada, Foreign Minister Togo, Finance Minister Kaya, and Director of the Planning Board Suzuki. The group—except for the Foreign Minister, who was uncertain—favored Proposal Three. Next Prime Minister Tojo met with Army Chief of Staff Sugiyama in an attempt to reach an agreement, but was unsuccessful; Tojo favored Proposal Three, while Sugiyama insisted on Proposal Two. Thus the two were forced to go to the Liaison Conference without having reached a prior agreement, a rare occurrence.

Meanwhile, the Navy came forward with a demand for a large allocation of steel, which appeared to be the price it demanded in return for its support of the war decision. The Prime Minister, among others, did not know quite how to interpret this demand; in any case, the group went along with it.

As these notes of the Liaison Conferences suggest, the alternative of assuring peace by making concessions to the United States was never seriously considered. Yet the prospect of war, whose outcome was uncertain, continued to trouble both Foreign Minister Togo and Finance Minister Kaya, who tried unsuccessfully to get the war decision postponed. They were overwhelmed by the argument that "it is better to go to war now rather than later" put forward by Navy Chief of Staff Nagano on strategic grounds, and by Director of the Planning Board Suzuki on grounds of availability of materials. Both Togo and Kaya refused to take part in the decision of this Conference (so the decision was by majority vote); but afterwards they did give their assent to the Prime Minister personally, thus making it unanimous.

The Liaison Conference adopted Proposal Three, which stipulated that war would begin on December 1. Diplomacy would continue until midnight November 30; and if diplomacy were successful by that deadline, war would be called off. This meant that some way of continuing the negotiations had to be found. For this purpose, the Foreign Minister presented two proposals labeled A and B.[26] *Proposal A would be tried, and if it was unsuccessful, Japan would retreat to B. In essence, B was a "modus vivendi," seeking to restore conditions to those existing before Japan had pushed into southern Indochina in July and provoked American economic sanctions, etc.*

Reexamination of "Essentials for Carrying Out the Empire's Policies."

[This was the final meeting to reach a decision; it lasted 17 hours, extending to 1:30 A.M. on the 2nd.

[Prior to reaching a decision, the Navy demanded a large allocation of materials, especially steel, as its share. There was the follow-

[26] For details see Imperial Conference record of November 5.

ing demand from the Navy for steel and other materials; it was approved for 1942 (by the Army, Navy, and Planning Board), provided there were operations in the South:

Steel

Navy....................1,100,000 tons
Army .... 790,000 tons
Civilian.................2,610,000 tons

However, in the event that production is more than 4.5 million tons the Army's share will be increased to 900,000 tons. Oil for sailing vessels with auxiliary engines will be supplied by the Navy. The above ratios will also govern the allocation of materials other than steel.

[Diplomatic measures will be taken as soon as possible toward Germany and Italy. The necessary steps will also be taken toward Thailand.

[On the true relations of ruler and subjects, the 20th Group [in the Operations Section of the Army General Staff] draft and the Section Two [Intelligence, Army General Staff] draft will be the basis.][27]

[The conclusions were as follows. On Proposal One (not to engage in war):]

FINANCE MINISTER KAYA: If we go along, as at present, without war, and three years hence the American fleet comes to attack us, will the Navy have a chance of winning or won't it? [He asked this several times.]

NAVY CHIEF OF STAFF NAGANO: Nobody knows.

KAYA: Will the American fleet come to attack us, or won't it?

NAGANO: I don't know. I think the chances are 50–50.

KAYA: I don't think they will come. If they should come, can we win the war on the seas? [He could not very well ask the Supreme Command whether we would lose.]

NAGANO: We might avoid war now, but go to war three years later; or we might go to war now and plan for what the situation will be three years hence. I think it would be easier to engage in a war now. The reason is that now we have the necessary foundation for it.

KAYA: If there were chances of victory in the third year of the war, it would be all right to go to war; but according to Nagano's explanation, this is not certain. Moreover, I would judge that the chances of

---

[27] The text of these documents does not appear to be available.

the United States making war on us are slight, so my conclusion must be that it would not be a good idea to declare war now.

FOREIGN MINISTER TOGO: I, too, cannot believe that the American fleet would come and attack us. I don't believe there is any need to go to war now.

NAGANO: There is a saying, "Don't rely on what won't come." The future is uncertain; we can't take anything for granted. In three years enemy defenses in the South will be strong, and the number of enemy warships will also increase.

KAYA: Well, then, when can we go to war and win?

NAGANO: Now! The time for war will not come later! [He said this with great emphasis.]

DIRECTOR OF THE PLANNING BOARD SUZUKI: Kaya feels uneasy because we are short of materials. He appears to feel that if we go to war, we will be at a disadvantage in terms of materials in 1941 and 1942. But there is no need to worry. In 1943 the materials situation will be much better if we go to war. We have just been told that with the passage of time the Supreme Command's strategic position will deteriorate. So we can conclude that it would be better to go to war now. [In this way he again tried to persuade Kaya and Togo.]

KAYA: I still have my doubts. [With this he stopped asking questions about Proposal One.]

[On Proposal Two (go to war): There was a detailed explanation of the attached proposal by the Army Chief of Staff.[28] No views in opposition were expressed.]

KAYA AND TOGO: Before we decide on this, we would like somehow to make a last attempt at diplomatic negotiations. This is a great turning point in the history of our country, which goes back 2,600 years; and on it hangs the fate of our country. It's outrageous to ask us to resort to diplomatic trickery. We can't do it.

ARMY VICE CHIEF OF STAFF TSUKADA: The first things to decide are the central issues: "to decide immediately to open hostilities," and "war will begin on the first of December." Unless these are decided, the Supreme Command cannot do anything. I would like to see diplomacy studied after these have been decided. Even if you are going to engage in diplomacy, decide on these points first.

---

[28] In essence, this document took the following position: Japan gives up hope of success in negotiations, and is determined to begin war against the United States, Britain, and the Netherlands at the beginning of December. Negotiations with the United States will be continued until then in order to gain an advantage in war. An attempt will be made immediately to strengthen ties with Germany and Italy.

NAVY VICE CHIEF OF STAFF ITO [he suddenly says at this point]: As far as the Navy is concerned, you can negotiate until November 20.

TSUKADA: As for the Army, negotiations will be all right until November 13, but no later.

TOGO: You say there must be a deadline for diplomacy. As Foreign Minister, I cannot engage in diplomacy unless there is a prospect that it will be successful. I cannot accept deadlines or conditions if they make it unlikely that diplomacy will succeed. You must obviously give up the idea of going to war. [Thus Togo from time to time speaks of no war and the maintenance of the status quo.]

[As indicated above, it became necessary to discuss the deadline and conditions for diplomatic negotiations. The Prime Minister proposed that the discussion also include Proposal Three, decision for war combined with diplomatic efforts.

[On Proposal Three (to be studied along with Proposal Two): Army Vice Chief of Staff Tsukada repeated what is in the draft by the Army General Staff, and demanded that "diplomacy must not obstruct military operations. The deadline will not be changed in the light of diplomatic developments; the deadline will be November 13." The deadline, November 13, became an important issue.]

TOGO: November 13 is outrageous. The Navy says November 20.

TSUKADA: Preparations for military operations are tantamount to military operations. Airplanes, surface vessels, and submarines are going to collide, I tell you. Thus the time for ending diplomatic negotiations must be the day prior to the time when preparations for military operations will be so intense as to be tantamount to military operations. That day is November 13.

NAGANO: Small collisions are incidents, and not war.

TOJO AND TOGO: We are going to undertake both diplomacy and military operations simultaneously; so you must give your word that if diplomacy is successful we will give up going to war.

TSUKADA: That's impossible. It will be all right until November 13; but after that you will throw the Supreme Command into confusion.

SUGIYAMA AND NAGANO: This will endanger the Supreme Command.

NAVY MINISTER SHIMADA [to Navy Vice Chief Ito]: It will be all right to negotiate until two days before the outbreak of war, won't it?

TSUKADA: Please keep quiet. What you've just said won't do. What deadline does the Foreign Minister want?

[Thus the deadline for diplomatic negotiations became the subject of heated debate. A twenty-minute recess was called. At this point,

Tanaka, Chief of Section One, was called in.[29] The Army Chief of Staff, the Vice Chief of Staff, and the Chief of Section One studied the matter and concluded that "it would be all right [to negotiate] until five days prior to the outbreak of war." Accordingly the Army Chief of Staff decided that "it would be all right to carry on negotiations until November 30." Meanwhile, the Navy Chief of Staff also called in his Section One Chief [Fukutome] and discussed the matter. The meeting was reconvened.]

TOJO: Can't we make it December 1? Can't you allow diplomatic negotiations to go on even for one day more?

TSUKADA: Absolutely not. We absolutely can't go beyond November 30. Absolutely not.

SHIMADA: Mr. Tsukada, until what time on the 30th? It will be all right until midnight, won't it?

TSUKADA: It will be all right until midnight.

[In this way the deadline was set at midnight, November 30 (Tokyo time). Thus: (a) a decision for war was made; (b) the time for the commencement of war was set at the beginning of December; (c) diplomacy was allowed to continue until midnight, November 30, and if diplomacy were successful by then, war would be called off.

[Next there was discussion of the conditions under which negotiations would proceed. Proposals A and B presented by the Foreign Ministry were studied. Proposal A was a somewhat reduced version of the past proposals presented in negotiations with the United States (based on reexamination). Proposal B was limited to the South. Proposal B, the Foreign Ministry draft, is attached; it has Paragraphs 1, 2, and 3, relating to the "Rescinding of the Freezing of Funds," no Paragraph 4, on "Relations with China," and two notes.][30]

SUGIYAMA AND TSUKADA: Proposal B does not refer to the China Problem and agrees to the withdrawal of troops from French Indo-

[29] Tanaka Shin'ichi, Chief of Section One (Operations), Army General Staff.

[30] (1) Both Japan and the United States will pledge not to make an armed advance into Southeast Asia and the South Pacific area, except French Indochina.

(2) The Japanese and American Governments will cooperate with each other so that the procurement of materials they need in the Netherlands East Indies will be assured.

(3) The United States will promise to supply Japan with one million tons of aviation gasoline.

Notes: (a) Japan is prepared to move her troops presently in the southern part of French Indochina to the northern part in the event an agreement along these lines is reached. (b) If necessary, those provisions relating to nondiscrimination of commerce and the interpretation and application of the Tripartite Pact that have been proposed before may be added.

china; from the point of view of national defense this will be disastrous for our country. The stationing of troops in Indochina will enable us to make China do what we want her to do, and will enable us to acquire materials from the South on a 50–50 basis. Moreover, it will strengthen the strategic situation vis-à-vis policy toward America and the settlement of the China Incident. Even if we reach an agreement with the United States, she may not give us materials. We are opposed to Proposal B. Also we don't have much time left; so go forward with Proposal A rather than with Proposal B, which is a new one.

TOGO: Since the way we negotiated in the past was not satisfactory, I would like to narrow the area of negotiation, settle just the Southern Question, and arrange to settle the China Question by ourselves. We cannot allow the United States a voice in the China Question. From this point of view, our past negotiations with the United States incorporated to a large degree the revival of the Nine-Power Treaty. It was a distasteful procedure. As I have said before, it was absurd to agree in principle to the Four Principles. Therefore, I would like to proceed with Proposal B. I believe that there is no hope for Proposal A in the short time that is left. I'm put in a difficult position if you tell me to do something that I can't do.

TSUKADA: We absolutely cannot withdraw our troops from southern Indochina [on this point he repeats his opposition]. In the Foreign Ministry draft of Proposal B nothing is said about China; the situation there would remain as is. Also, if we withdrew our troops from French Indochina, our supply routes for materials from the South would come completely under the control of the United States, and we would be subject to American obstruction at any time. Moreover, American aid to Chiang Kai-shek will not stop. The mere rescinding of the order freezing funds will hardly enable us to carry on commerce as before; and oil especially will not come in. In this way, six months from now the opportunity for war will have come and gone. The Empire must be able to do what she wants with China. Hence Proposal B is out. Go ahead with Proposal A.

[In the discussion, Paragraph 3 [of Proposal B] was amended to read that the commercial situation prior to the freezing of funds would be restored, and the shipping of oil would be resumed. A new Paragraph 4 was added, saying there would be no obstruction to the settlement of the China Incident. But the question of the withdrawal of troops from southern French Indochina was not resolved.]

TOGO: If we amend the part on commerce, add a paragraph on "no obstruction to the settlement of the China Incident," and remove our concession on withdrawing troops from southern Indochina, it will be impossible to negotiate. This won't do. We can't engage in diplomacy, yet it's best not to go to war.

TSUKADA: That's why we should go forward with Proposal A.

NAGANO: We ought to go ahead and negotiate with Proposal A.

[In this way, the Army Chief and Vice Chief argued with Togo in a loud voice about the transfer of troops from southern Indochina to northern Indochina, and about Proposal B. Togo refused to agree, and held to his own views, at times threatening to block any decision for war. There was fear that if the discussion continued in this way, it would lead to Togo's resignation and the almost certain fall of the Cabinet. Bureau Chief Muto proposed a recess; the meeting recessed for ten minutes.

[During the recess Sugiyama, Tojo, Tsukada, and Muto conferred in another room [and they agreed to the following]: "Since China has been added to the conditions, we will go along with Proposal B. If we conclude that diplomacy cannot succeed, and reject the section on withdrawal of troops from southern Indochina, the resignation of the Foreign Minister—that is, a change in Government—is conceivable. In that event, the probability of the new Cabinet being opposed to war is high. Also, time would be required to reach a decision on starting the war. At this juncture, a political change as well as a delay cannot be permitted."

[A summary of the above would cover the following points:

[a. This discussion cannot be allowed to last any longer. From the point of view of the Supreme Command, the first ten days in December are absolutely fixed [as the deadline].

[b. The Cabinet cannot be permitted to fall. This would result in the appearance of an antiwar cabinet; more time would be required for debate.

[c. Should the conditions be softened?

[Points (a) and (b) were definite. The big problem was what to do about (c). The Army gave careful consideration to whether it should give in and agree to a softening of the conditions, or let everything fall apart. It finally agreed to soften the conditions. Otherwise there would have been a disagreement with the Foreign Ministry, and a change in the Government could have been anticipated. There would have been a return to the antiwar, maintenance-of-the-status-quo position. The Army Chief and Vice Chief of Staff unenthusiastically agreed. Army Vice Chief of Staff Tsukada's impressions were as follows:]

Nagano, Navy Chief of Staff, is clearly determined that we must go to war now. Navy Minister Shimada, who has said that the future prospects of a war are not clear, appears to think, like Nagano, that there is no alternative but to go to war now. But he does not state this in a positive manner. Army Chief of Staff Sugiyama states strongly that now is the best time for war. He says he is confident that Army operations, given Navy protection of transportation on the high seas, would assure control of the occupied areas. Finance Minister Kaya and Foreign Minister Togo are completely unable to decide, on grounds that we don't know what would happen several years hence if we went to war. They give the appearance of being among those who are willing to endure great hardships. Director of the Planning Board Suzuki is worried about Kaya and Togo, but argues that there is no alternative but to decide on war now; and that from the point of view of materials it would be better to go to war now.

In general, the prospects if we go to war are not bright. We all wonder if there isn't some way to proceed peacefully. There is no one who is willing to say: "Don't worry, even if the war is prolonged. I will assume all responsibility." On the other hand, it is not possible to maintain the status quo. Hence one unavoidably reaches the conclusion that we must go to war.

I, Tsukada, believe that war cannot be avoided. Now is the time. Even if we don't go to war now, we must do so next year, or the year after that. Now is the time. The moral spirit of Japan, the Land of the Gods, will shine on this occasion. It is more effective, from the point of view of carrying out our national defense policy, to go to war now and take the South. Moreover, when it comes to bringing the war to a close, the probability of Japan's push southward enabling Germany and Italy to defeat Britain is high, and the probability of forcing China to capitulate is even higher than it is now. Then we could even force Russia to capitulate. If we take the South, we will be able to strike a strong blow against American resources of national defense. That is, we will build an iron wall, and within it we will destroy, one by one, the enemy states in Asia; and in addition, we will defeat America and Britain. If Britain is defeated, America will have to do some thinking. When we are asked what will happen five years from now, it is natural that we should not know, whether it is in military operations, politics, or diplomacy.

IMPERIAL CONFERENCE
November 5, 1941

After the long Liaison Conference, Tojo had an audience with the Emperor to report the decision of the Government and the armed forces. The Emperor accepted the decision that it was necessary to decide on war and to make preparations, but asked that every effort be made to break the deadlock through diplomatic negotiations. Upon his return to the War Ministry, Tojo told one of his subordinates: "Proposal B is not an excuse for war. I am praying to the Gods that somehow we will be able to get an agreement with the United States with this proposal."[31] Tojo appears to have felt that there was still some hope of avoiding war. In his more optimistic moments he assessed the probability of success through diplomacy as 50–50, and at other times three chances out of ten.[32]

The Imperial Conference met to give formal approval to the decision of the Liaison Conference. As usual the leading Ministers made their statements and later answered questions put to them by President of the Privy Council Hara. The Emperor made no statement, and the documents on the agenda were approved. Although the negotiations were to continue, the dice were loaded in favor of war. Actually, on November 3 Admiral Yamamoto Isoroku, Commander in Chief of the Combined Fleet, had approved Secret Operations Order No. 1, which said in part:

"The Japanese Empire is expecting war to break out with the United States, Great Britain, and the Netherlands. War will be declared on X day. This order will become effective on Y day."[33]

[Editor's note: The Conference was convened at 10:30 A.M. and adjourned at 3:15 P.M. with a one-hour recess between 12:30 and 1:30 P.M. The participants were as follows: Tojo Hideki, Prime Minister and War Minister; Hara Yoshimichi, President of the Privy Council; Shimada Shigetaro, Navy Minister; Togo Shigenori, Foreign Minister; Kaya Okinori, Finance Minister; Suzuki Teiichi, Director of the Planning Board; Nagano Osami, Navy Chief of Staff; Sugiyama Gen, Army Chief of Staff; Ito Seiichi, Navy Vice Chief of Staff; Tsukada Ko, Army Vice Chief of Staff. The Secretaries were: Hoshino Naoki,

---

[31] Quoted in *TSM*, VII, 320.
[32] *Ibid.*, pp. 320–21.
[33] Herbert Feis, *The Road to Pearl Harbor* (New York: Atheneum, 1963), p. 296.

Chief Secretary of the Cabinet; Muto Akira, Chief of the Military Affairs Bureau of the War Ministry; and Oka Takasumi, Chief of the Naval Affairs Bureau of the Navy Ministry.]

Agenda: "Essentials for Carrying Out the Empire's Policies" [This document, which of course differs from the September 6 document of the same title, follows].

I. Our Empire, in order to resolve the present critical situation, assure its self-preservation and self-defense, and establish a New Order in Greater East Asia, decides on this occasion to go to war against the United States and Great Britain and takes the following measures:

1. The time for resorting to force is set at the beginning of December, and the Army and Navy will complete preparations for operations.

2. Negotiations with the United States will be carried out in accordance with the attached document.

3. Cooperation with Germany and Italy will be strengthened.

4. Close military relations with Thailand will be established just prior to the use of force.

II. If negotiations with the United States are successful by midnight of December 1, the use of force will be suspended.

[Attached Document]

Summary of Negotiations with the United States of America

We will negotiate with the United States and seek to reach an agreement on the basis of attached Proposal A or attached Proposal B, both of which express, in a more moderate and amended form, important matters that have been pending between the two countries.

PROPOSAL A:

We will moderate our position on the most important matters pending in the negotiations between Japan and the United States: (1) stationing and withdrawal of troops in China and French Indochina; (2) nondiscriminatory trade in China; (3) interpretation and execution of the Tripartite Pact; (4) the Four Principles. This will be done as follows:

1. Stationing and withdrawal of troops in China:

We will moderate our position on this point as follows (in view of the fact that the United States—disregarding for the time being the reason for the stationing of troops—attaches importance to the stationing of troops for an indefinite period, disagrees with the inclusion of this item in the terms for peace, and urges us to make a clearer statement of our intentions regarding withdrawal):

Of the Japanese troops sent to China during the China Incident, those in designated sections of North China and Inner Mongolia, and those on

Hainan Island, will remain for a necessary period of time after the establishment of peace between Japan and China. The remainder of the troops will begin withdrawal simultaneously with the establishment of peace in accordance with arrangements to be made between Japan and China, and the withdrawal will be completed within two years.

Note: In case the United States asks what the "necessary period of time" will be, we will respond that we have in mind 25 years.

Stationing and withdrawal of troops in French Indochina:

We will moderate our position on this point as follows, since we recognize that the United States is apprehensive that Japan has territorial ambitions in French Indochina and is building a base for military advance into neighboring territories:

Japan respects the sovereignty of French Indochina over her territory. Japanese troops currently stationed in French Indochina will be immediately withdrawn after the settlement of the China Incident or the establishment of a just peace in the Far East.

2. Nondiscriminatory trade in China:

In case there is no prospect of an agreement on the basis of the proposal that was presented on September 25, we will proceed on the basis of the following:

The Japanese Government will recognize the application of the principle of nondiscrimination in the entire Pacific region, including China, if this principle is applied throughout the world.

3. The interpretation and execution of the Tripartite Pact:

On this point we will respond as follows: We do not intend to broaden unreasonably the interpretation of the right of self-defense. Regarding the interpretation and execution of the Tripartite Pact, the Japanese Government, as it has stated on previous occasions, will act independently. Our position will be that we assume that the United States is fully aware of this.

4. Regarding the so-called Four Principles put forward by the United States, we will make every effort to avoid their inclusion in official agreements between Japan and the United States (this includes understandings and other communiqués).

PROPOSAL B:

1. Both Japan and the United States will pledge not to make an armed advance into Southeast Asia and the South Pacific area, except French Indochina.

2. The Japanese and American Governments will cooperate with each other so that the procurement of necessary materials from the Netherlands East Indies will be assured.

3. The Japanese and American Governments will restore trade relations to what they were prior to the freezing of assets. The United States will promise to supply Japan with the petroleum Japan needs.

4. The Government of the United States will not take such actions as may hinder efforts for peace by both Japan and China.

Notes:

1. As occasion demands, it is permissible to promise that with the conclusion of the present agreement Japanese troops stationed in southern Indochina are prepared to move to northern Indochina with the consent of the French Government; and that the Japanese troops will withdraw from Indochina with the settlement of the China Incident or upon the establishment of a just peace in the Pacific area.

2. As occasion demands, we may make insertions in the provisions on nondiscriminatory trade and on the interpretation and execution of the Tripartite Pact in the abovementioned proposal (Proposal B).

Statement by Prime Minister Tojo:

The Conference is now opened. With His Majesty's permission I will take charge of the proceedings.

At the Imperial Conference of September 6 "Essentials for Carrying Out the Empire's Policies" was discussed, and the following was decided by His Majesty: our Empire, determined not to avoid war with the United States, Great Britain, and the Netherlands in the course of assuring her self-preservation and self-defense, was to complete preparations for war by late October. At the same time it was decided that we would endeavor to attain our demands by using all possible diplomatic measures vis-à-vis the United States and Great Britain; and that in case there was no prospect of our demands being attained through diplomacy by early October, we would decide immediately on war with the United States, Great Britain, and the Netherlands.

Since then, while maintaining close coordination between political and military considerations, we have made a special effort to achieve success in our diplomatic negotiations with the United States. In this interval we have endured what must be endured in our efforts to reach an agreement, but we have not been able to get the United States to reconsider. During the negotiations, there has been a change in the Cabinet.

The Government and the Army and Navy sections of Imperial Headquarters have held eight Liaison Conferences in order to study matters more extensively and deeply on the basis of the "Essentials for Carrying Out the Empire's Policies" adopted on September 6. As a result of this, we have come to the conclusion that we must now decide to go to war, set the time for military action at the beginning of December, concentrate all of our efforts on completing preparations for war, and at the same time try to break the impasse by means of diplomacy. Accordingly, I ask you to deliberate on the document "Essentials for Carrying Out the Empire's Policies."

There will be statements by participants on matters for which they are responsible.

Statement by Foreign Minister Togo:

I respectfully submit that the essence of our Empire's foreign policy is to establish a system of international relations based on justice and fairness, and thereby contribute to the maintenance and promotion of world peace.

The successful conclusion of the China Incident and the establishment of the Greater East Asia Co-prosperity Sphere would assure the existence of our Empire and lay the foundations for stability in East Asia. To achieve these objectives, our Empire must be prepared to sweep away any and all obstacles.

With the conclusion of the basic treaty between Japan and China on November 30 of last year, our Empire recognized the Nanking Government, marking a great step in the China Incident. Since then we have cooperated with that government to foster its growth and add to its strength. On the other hand, we have continued to put military pressure on the Chiang Kai-shek regime, in an effort to get it to reconsider. Its continued resistance after four and a half years of our holy war depends a great deal, it is clear, on aid from the United States and Great Britain.

Since the outbreak of the China Incident, both the British and American Governments have obstructed our advance on the continent. On the one hand, they have aided Chiang; on the other hand, they have checked our activities in China or have stepped up their economic measures against us. Needless to say, Great Britain, which has acquired more interests than anyone else in East Asia, took all kinds of measures to obstruct us from the beginning. The United States, cooperating with her, abrogated the Japanese-American Trade Agreement, limited or banned imports and exports, and took other measures to increase her pressure on Japan. Particularly since our Empire concluded the Tripartite Pact, the United States has taken steps to encircle Japan by persuading Great Britain and the Netherlands to join her and by cooperating with the Chiang regime. Since the start of the German-Soviet war, she has taken unfriendly action against us by supplying oil and other war materials to the Soviet Union through the Far East, despite warnings from our Government. As soon as our Empire sent troops into French Indochina after concluding a treaty on the basis of friendly negotiations with the French Government for the purpose of defending ourselves and bringing the

China Incident to a conclusion, America's actions became increasingly undisguised. Not only did she cut off economic relations between Japan and the United States, with Central and South America going along with her, under the guise of freezing our assets; but also, in cooperation with Great Britain, China, and the Netherlands, she threatened the existence of our Empire and tried harder to prevent us from carrying out our national policies. Accordingly, our Empire, which is the stabilizing force in East Asia, was compelled to try to overcome the impasse by showing firmness and determination.

President Roosevelt has stressed, as his national policy, the rejection of "Hitlerism"—that is, policies based on force—and he has continued to aid Great Britain, which is almost tantamount to entering the war, by utilizing the economically superior position of the United States. At the same time, as I have stated before, he has adopted a policy of firm pressure on Japan. In the middle of April of this year unofficial talks were begun, seeking a general improvement in relations between Japan and the United States. Our Imperial Government, desirous of promoting stability in East Asia and peace in the world, has since then continued the negotiations with a most sincere and fair approach. For a period of more than six months we have tried to reach an amicable settlement by showing patience and a spirit of compromise. In particular, the previous Cabinet tried hard to break the deadlock by suggesting a conference of the two heads of state, and in this way it displayed its sincerity. Late in September it presented a compromise proposal for the improvement of relations between the two countries. The American Government, however, maintained an extremely firm attitude, stuck to the proposal of June 21, which might be considered its original position, and refused to make any concessions. Recently, in discussions since the formation of the previous Cabinet, there have been some optimistic reports that the United States has shown a willingness to compromise substantially; but in fact, she has not made any concessions. Moreover, she has taken many measures to tighten the encirclement of Japan—strengthening of military facilities in the South; encouragement to Chiang through economic assistance, supplying arms, and sending military missions; meetings with military leaders in Singapore and Manila; and holding frequent military and economic conferences in Batavia, Hong Kong, etc. There has been nothing to demonstrate her sincerity. Hence we cannot help but regretfully conclude that there is no prospect of the negotiations coming to a successful conclusion quickly if things continue as they have in the past.

A close study of the June 21 proposal shows that it contains some points that we could accept. But in general it is a reaffirmation of the Nine-Power Pact; and it was feared that it might destroy the policy we have pursued at great sacrifice since the Manchurian Incident; this in turn might block the creation of a New Order in East Asia and endanger our position as the leader in that area.

In the final analysis, the present international situation is this: In East Asia the British and American policy of aiding Chiang Kai-shek and Japan's encirclement by a coalition of Great Britain, the United States, the Netherlands, and the Chiang regime have been continuously strengthened; and it is possible that the Soviet regime might extend its influence in the Far Eastern area with aid from Great Britain and the United States. Therefore, it cannot be denied that there is a danger that the basis for both the settlement of the China Incident and the construction of the New Order in East Asia at which our Empire is aiming, might be seriously threatened. In Europe, although Germany and Italy will be able to achieve their first goal, the conquest of the Continent, we cannot anticipate an overall conclusion soon, and the war there is likely to be prolonged. In reality we could not expect Germany and Italy to give us much co-operation.

As I see it, the situation is becoming more and more critical every day, and negotiations with the United States are very much restricted by the time element; consequently, to our regret, there is little room left for diplomatic maneuvering. Moreover, the conclusion of a Japanese-American understanding would necessitate great speed in negotiations, partly because of the time required for domestic procedures on the American side. For this reason we have been required to carry on negotiations under extremely difficult circumstances. The prospects of achieving an amicable settlement in the negotiations are, to our deepest regret, dim. However, the Imperial Government will endeavor on this occasion to make every effort to arrive at a quick settlement in our negotiations. We would like to negotiate on the basis of the two proposals in the attached document, which assure the honor and self-defense of our Empire. The first proposal is one that has considered and acceded to as much as possible American wishes concerning stationing and withdrawal of troops in China, interpretation and execution of the Tripartite Pact among Japan, Germany, and Italy, and nondiscrimination in international trade, all of which were unsettled questions in the proposal of September 25. The second proposal, on the whole, is an agreement not to undertake a military advance in the Southwest Pacific areas, to promise each other cooperation in the procurement of materials in that area, to agree that the United States will not obstruct the establishment of peace between Japan and China, and to mutually abrogate the freezing of assets. Finally, I should like to add that we are going to negotiate on the basis of an understanding that in the event our present negotiations lead to a settlement, all emergency measures that have been taken by the Imperial Government will be rescinded.

In case the present negotiations should unfortunately fail to lead to an agreement, we intend to strengthen our cooperative arrangements with Germany and Italy, and to take a variety of measures so as to be prepared for any situation.

Statement by President of the Planning Board Suzuki:

I am going to give a summary of the outlook with regard to our national strength, particularly in vital materials, in case we go to war against Great Britain, the United States, and the Netherlands.

First, if we can constantly maintain a minimum of 3 million tons of shipping for civilian use, it will be possible to secure supplies in the amount called for by the Materials Mobilization Plan for the fiscal year of 1941, except for certain materials.

That is, with the exception of some materials, at least 3 million tons of shipping are needed in order to secure materials from the Zone of Self-support and the First Supplementary Zone in the amount specified in the Materials Mobilization Plan of 1941. We judge that on the average it will be possible to transport 4.8–5 million tons per month, using 3 million tons of shipping and assuming a 15 to 20 per cent decline in shipping during wartime. The above transportation capacity is equal to the average monthly amount of 5 million tons of materials actually transported in the first half of the Materials Mobilization Plan of 1941.

Second, if the yearly loss in shipping is estimated to be between 800,000 and 1 million tons, the maintenance of the 3 million tons of shipping mentioned above should be possible if we can obtain an average of about 600,000 gross tons of new construction each year. In other words, I think we can constantly maintain 3 million tons of shipping if we build 1.8 million gross tons of shipping in three years, or an average of 600,000 tons a year, provided we lose [no more than] 800,000 to 1 million tons of shipping a year. Building the foregoing 600,000 tons of shipping is considered possible if we rationally utilize the present civilian shipbuilding capacity of 700,000 gross tons and the engineering and forging capacity of about 600,000 gross tons and if we take such measures as standardizing and lowering the quality of the ships to be built, giving overall control of shipbuilding operations to the Navy, and securing a labor force, as well as allocating 300,000 tons of steel, copper, and other necessary materials.

Third, in order to build 600,000 gross tons of new ships, more than 300,000 tons of ordinary steel will be needed. This can be secured if steel available for civilian use can be maintained at 2.61 million tons and this is allocated on a priority basis, with the allotment being kept to a minimum.

In order to provide 2.61 million tons of steel for civilian use, there will need to be a steel program whose implementation, on the whole, is within our capability, as follows:

The production goal will be more than 4.5 million tons (in 1941, 4.76 million tons). The Navy will be allotted 1.1 million tons (in 1941 a little more than 0.95 million tons), and the Army will be allotted 0.79 million tons (in 1941 a little more than 0.9 million tons).

However, in case production exceeds 4.5 million tons, the excess will be given to the Army until its share reaches 0.9 million tons. The allocation for civilian use will be 2.61 million tons (in 1941 a little more than 2.95 million tons). In 1942, in order to secure the above production level, we must take all possible measures, such as increased consumption of ore previously stockpiled on a compulsory basis, and increased transportation of coal by presently idle sailing ships with auxiliary engines. The Navy is to help supply fuel for these ships.

Fourth, in order to maintain the shipping needed for production, it will be necessary to follow the plan agreed upon between the Army, Navy, and the Planning Board when it comes to determining the amount of shipping and the length of time such shipping will be needed for the Southern Operation.

The amount of shipping and the length of time such shipping will be needed for the Southern Operation is as follows [in gross tons]:

Army		*Navy*
First month	2,100,000	Each month 1,800,000 gross tons, in-
Second month	2,100,000	cluding small vessels as follows:
Third month	2,100,000	Tankers 270,000
Fourth month	2,100,000	Fishing boats 94,000
Fifth month	1,700,000	Freight-passenger boats 336,000
Sixth month	1,650,000	Freighters 110,000
Seventh month	1,500,000	Small boats 15,000
After the eighth month	1,000,000	

Since it is estimated that for a certain period of time during the 1942 operation in the South ships for civilian use would be reduced to a minimum of 1.6 million gross tons, and civilian shipping capacity to around 2.6 million tons [for this period], it is expected that steel production during this period would decline to 3.8 million tons in terms of yearly production, and that other important materials would decline by around 15 per cent.

Consequently, steel production in 1941 would come to about 4.5 million tons as against the 4.76 million tons in the Plan. Steel production in the first half of 1941 was 95.6 per cent of the Plan, representing a reduction of 96,000 tons.

In the second half of 1941, particularly in the fourth quarter, transportation capacity will decline because of operations in the South; so we plan to hold the decrease in production to 150,000 tons by mobilizing sailing ships with auxiliary engines, utilizing iron foundries that can use coal shipped by rail, increasing the use of stored iron ore, collecting more scrap iron, and so on. Thus we estimate that actual production will be about 4.5 million tons, as against the 4.76 million tons called for in the Plan.

Fifth, concerning rice, I think it will be necessary to consider substitute food, such as soybeans, minor cereals, and sweet potatoes, and to exercise some control over food in case the expected imports of rice from Thailand and French Indochina called for in the Food Supply Plan for the 1942 rice year (from October 1941 to September 1942) are reduced owing to operations in the South. That is, if the expected imports from Thailand and Indochina are reduced by 50 per cent, the food supply will be down to 93 per cent of the amount called for in the Plan; and if the imports decrease by 75 per cent, the supply will go down to 91 per cent. However, if imports from Thailand and French Indochina can be increased by using more ships after the completion of the first phase of military operations, it may be possible to prevent the reduction from becoming too large.

As a rough estimate we plan to supply food by producing about 3.1 million *koku* of rice in Formosa, about 6.28 million *koku* in Korea, and 59.13 million *koku* in the home islands; and also by importing about 3 million *koku* from Thailand and about 7 million *koku* from Indochina [one *koku* is approximately 5.13 bushels].

Sixth, if we can occupy important points in the Netherlands East Indies in a short period of time, we can expect to obtain the following major items in these amounts (I will discuss petroleum later under liquid fuel):

[MAJOR ITEMS OBTAINABLE FROM NETHERLANDS EAST INDIES,
EXCLUDING PETROLEUM]

[Percentages are percentages of monthly average of Materials Mobilization Plan of 1941]

Item	Tons
Nickel ore (purity 3.5%)	6,000 (62%)
Tin (for anti-friction alloy and gilding)	1,200 (144%)
Bauxite (raw ore for aluminum)	17,000 (42%)
Crude rubber	17,000 (400%)
Cassava root, theriac (for industrial alcohol)	15,000[a]
Copra, palm oil (glycerin, substitute machine oil)	13,000[a]
Sisal (substitute for Manila hemp)	3,000[a]
Corn (animal feed and foodstuff)	20,000 (26%)
Industrial salt	7,000 (8%)
Sugar	20,000 (25%)

[a] A very small amount of import is expected in 1941.

Among the above items, crude rubber, tin, and bauxite would most seriously affect the United States if their supply is cut off.

Seventh, the total supply of petroleum, in case of operations in the South, will be 850,000 kiloliters in the first year, 2.6 million kiloliters in the second year, and 5.3 million kiloliters in the third year. If an estimate is made of the future supply and demand of petroleum, including 8.4 million kiloliters in our domestic stockpile, I believe we will just be able to remain self-supporting, with a surplus of 2.55 million kiloliters in the first year, 150,000 kiloliters in the second year, and 700,000 kiloliters in the third year. Concerning aviation fuel: it is expected that, depending on consumption, we might reach a critical stage in the second or third year.

That is, according to a study of the supply and demand of petroleum resulting from the occupation of the Netherlands East Indies, which was made jointly by the Army and the Navy at Liaison Conferences, the quantity expected to be obtained from the Netherlands East Indies is 300,000 kiloliters in the first year, 2 million kiloliters in the second year, and 4.5 million kiloliters in the third year. A breakdown of the above follows:

	First year	Second year	Third year
Borneo:			
Army	200,000 kl.	600,000 kl.	1,500,000 kl.
Navy	100,000	400,000	1,000,000
Sumatra:			
Southern	———	750,000	1,400,000
Northern	———	250,000	600,000
TOTAL	300,000	2,000,000	4,500,000

Expected production of aviation gasoline is 75,000 kiloliters in the first year, 330,000 kiloliters in the second year, and 540,000 kiloliters in the third year, the breakdown being as follows:

	First year	Second year	Third year
Netherlands East Indies	———	140,000 kl.	290,000 kl.
Iso-octane (in Japan)	15,000 kl.	40,000	60,000
Hydrogenolysis and cracking (in Japan)	60,000	150,000	190,000
TOTAL	75,000	330,000	540,000

The total of oil stockpiled by Army, Navy, and civilian authorities as of December 1, 1941, will be 1.11 million kiloliters.

The oil surplus or shortage each year:

The surplus or shortage, calculated with a presumed loss of 100,000 kiloliters in the first year, 50,000 kiloliters in the second year, and 20,000 kiloliters in the third year, is given below. Estimate One [assumes a demand of] 800,000 kiloliters in the first year, 750,000 kiloliters in the second year, and 620,000 kiloliters in the third year. Estimate Two is based on a calculation of 700,000 kiloliters, 650,000 kiloliters, and 620,000 kiloliters respectively. If a reserve of 200,000 kiloliters, equivalent to approximately two months' need, is taken into account, the supply-and-demand relationship is as follows: in Estimate One, 180,000 kiloliters surplus the first year, 440,000 kiloliters shortage the second year, and 28,000 kiloliters shortage the third year; in Estimate Two, 280,000 kiloliters surplus the first year, 240,000 kiloliters shortage the second year, and 28,000 kiloliters shortage the third year.

Overall supply and demand of liquid fuel:

If civilian demand is assumed to be 1.4 million kiloliters each year, and military demand is added to it, the overall demand is 5.2 million kiloliters in the first year, 5 million kiloliters in the second year, and 4.75 million kiloliters in the third year.

On the other hand, the potential supply, including stockpiles, production, and expected procurement from the Netherlands East Indies, less a minimum of 150,000 tons for reserve, is: 7.75 million kiloliters in the first year, with a remainder of 2.55 million kiloliters; 5.15 million kiloliters in the second year, with a remainder of 150,000 kiloliters; and 5.45 million kiloliters in the third year, with a remainder of 700,000 kiloliters. In this estimate, domestic production is calculated at 250,000 kiloliters in the first year, 200,000 kiloliters in the second year, and 300,000 kiloliters in the third year, while synthetic petroleum is estimated at 300,000 kiloliters, 400,000 kiloliters, and 500,000 kiloliters respectively.

In brief, it is by no means an easy task to carry on a war against Great Britain, the United States, and the Netherlands—a war that will be a protracted one—while still fighting in China, and at the same time maintain and augment the national strength needed to prosecute a war over a long period of time. It is apparent that the difficulty would be all the greater if such unexpected happenings as natural disasters should occur. However, since the probability of victory in the initial stages of the war is sufficiently high, I am convinced we should take advantage of this assured victory and turn the heightened morale of the people, who are determined to overcome the national crisis even at the cost of their lives, toward production as well as toward [reduced] consumption and other aspects of national life. In terms of maintaining and augmenting our national strength, this would be better than just sitting tight and waiting for the enemy to put pressure on us.

Next I will speak briefly on the outlook, both domestic and foreign, and on the situation with respect to vital materials in the event that we avoid war, maintain our present domestic and foreign posture, and suffer unspeakable hardships and privations.

First, materials in the Zone of Self-support will be in good supply, since the Government will guide the social situation in the proper direction. That is, maritime shipping capacity will necessarily be increased. If we assume that the amount of shipping to be requisitioned will be maintained at 2.15 million gross tons, and 500,000 gross tons of new ships will be built in the first year, 700,000 gross tons in the second year, and 900,000 gross tons in the third year, the average monthly civilian transportation capacity will be about 5.77 million tons in the first year, about 7.77 million tons in the second year, and about 8.97 million tons in the third year. If this amount of transportation is available, it is estimated that steel production will be around 4.82 million tons in the first year, about 4.97 million tons in the second year, and about 5.2 million tons in the third year. Like steel, other materials will also be in good supply.

Second, the probability that we will experience increased difficulties in obtaining materials from the First Supplementary Zone owing to pressure from the Anglo-American bloc is high. Nonetheless, it will be necessary to obtain the expected materials in the anticipated amounts from this area. Here, I believe, lurks a danger that we will enter into a war even though we wish to avoid it. That is, in order to meet our domestic needs we must obtain a supply of such materials as tungsten ore, tin ore, crude rubber, rice, corn, phosphate rock, pine resin, raw Japanese lacquer, oxhide, vegetable oil, and fat; but there is a danger that it will become difficult to obtain them because of pressure from Great Britain and the United States.

Third, serious shortages might develop in our domestic stockpiles, especially in liquid fuels. The kinds and quantities of liquid fuels necessary to insure our national security cannot possibly be supplied solely by the synthetic petroleum industry.

That is, when we look at crude petroleum, domestic production of natural petroleum will be about 360,000 kiloliters in the first year, about 400,000 kiloliters in the second year, and about 440,000 kiloliters in the third year. The production of synthetic petroleum will be 300,000 kiloliters in the first year, 500,000 kiloliters in the second year, and 700,000 kiloliters in the third year if a rational construction program, which considers the limitations inherent in various conditions (the distribution of materials and labor resources, as well as technology necessary to stimulate the industry against a background of stepped-up military production), is carried out.

If we estimate that civilian demand will be 1.8 million kiloliters, and that shortages will be met by disbursements from military supplies, it will be barely possible to meet civilian needs. It is anticipated that in that event the military will also have difficulty in meeting its own needs at the end of the third year.

The foregoing is a view of the crude petroleum situation in terms of the overall quantity; but when we examine the picture with respect to specific items we note an imbalance. There will be difficulties in meeting the demand for kerosene for civilian use (in agriculture and forestry), ordinary machine oil (all industries), high-quality machine oil (railroads), and diesel oil (ships, fishing boats).

It is extremely difficult to overcome these shortages by means of the synthetic petroleum industry, in view of the present status of hydrogenolysis, cracking, iso-octane (aviation gasoline), synthetic fuel (diesel oil), and polymerization (machine oil). We fear that by the fourth year there will be nothing we can do.

In case we seek to increase our synthetic petroleum capacity by 5.2 million kiloliters, we will need 2.25 million tons of steel, 1,000 tons of cobalt, 30 million tons of coal, expenditure of ¥3.8 billion, 380,000 coal miners, and a minimum construction period of six months for low-temperature carbonization plants and about two years for synthetic hydrogenolysis plants. Therefore, we will need more than three years to complete all plants.

If we examine closely the foregoing conditions, as well as the engineering skills necessary for their completion—particularly the ability to manufacture reacting cylinders, tubes, and the like—we must conclude that it is well-nigh impossible to achieve self-sufficiency in liquid fuels in a short period of time, depending only on synthetic petroleum. It is estimated that even if we take strong measures, at least seven years will be required. Consequently, if we go forward with our national policy depending solely on synthetic petroleum, there will be a very serious defect in our national defense picture within a certain period of time. This is very dangerous, given a world torn by wars and a situation in which we are trying to conclude the China Incident.

Fourth, there will be an imbalance in vital strategic materials, and shortcomings in our military preparedness and industrial production will be aggravated.

Fifth, in order to secure production necessary for maintaining and strengthening our defensive power, extraordinary effort will be necessary because of the need to unify the minds of the people. We fear that there is a danger that one misstep might divide public opinion.

Sixth, it is evident that as a result of permitting the United States to freely obtain materials necessary to build up her defense, there will develop differences in defensive power between the United States and Japan.

In conclusion, it would appear that if we go forward maintaining the present state of affairs, it would be very disadvantageous from the point of view of strengthening the material aspects of our national defense, if nothing else.

Statement by Finance Minister Kaya [summary of his statement giving his judgment on the sustaining power of finance in connection with war against Great Britain, the United States, and the Netherlands]:

Although the budget of our country has constantly increased since the beginning of the China Incident and has reached more than ¥7.99 billion in the general account and ¥5.88 billion in extraordinary military expenditures (agreed upon by the 76th Diet Session), or a total of over ¥13.2 billion, we have been able to secure large amounts in taxes and assure large savings, thanks to the efforts of various institutions and of the people. On the whole, we have been able to carry on operations smoothly. However, it is clear that when we begin military operations in the South, additional large expenditures of Government funds will be needed to cover them. Can our national economy bear the burden of such large military expenditures? Especially, are they feasible when the probability is high that the war will be protracted? Will there not be unfavorable effects on finance? Isn't there danger of a vicious inflation as a result of these expenditures?

However, war expenditures are mostly used to obtain vital materials, utilize facilities, and employ technology and labor. Therefore, the first question to be asked is whether there is a sufficient supply of materials to meet the need, and whether a minimum standard of living for the people can be maintained. So long as the material needs can be met, money and finance can go on for many years if that portion of national income designated for [civilian] consumption does not exceed the supply of consumer goods; surpluses are siphoned off by taxes and national savings, with the result that military expenditures put into circulation will end up as financial resources for military expenditures and production activities.

The above-mentioned absorption of funds by taxation or national savings will be possible if the Government's economic policies are adequate, and if the people are fully aware that the destiny of their country is at stake and are willing to exert every effort and make extreme sacrifices. Moreover, we anticipate that the Government's policies will not be in error because the Government itself will carry them out. We believe the people will make every effort and endure sacrifices because they are the subjects of our Empire. Hence we must judge that it is possible. After all, if we cannot supply the materials necessary to carry on military activities and maintain the people's livelihood, the national economy must collapse no matter how perfect the Government's financial and monetary policy might be. This is why I would judge that if the necessary materials, facilities, technology, and labor can be supplied, our money and finance can go on for many years.

The areas in the South that are to become the object of military operations have been importing materials of all kinds in large quantities. If these areas are occupied by our forces, their imports will cease. Accordingly, to make their economies run smoothly, we will have to supply them with materials. However, since our country does not have sufficient surpluses for that purpose, it will not be possible for some time for us to give much consideration to the living conditions of the people in these areas, and for a while we will have to pursue a so-called policy of exploitation. Hence even though we might issue military scrip and other items that have the character of currency in order to obtain materials and labor in these areas, it would be difficult to maintain the value of such currency. Therefore, we must adopt a policy of self-sufficiency in the South, keep the shipment of materials from Japan to that area to the minimum amount necessary to maintain order and to utilize labor forces there, ignore for the time being the decline in the value of currency and the economic dislocations that will ensue from this, and in this way push forward. Of course it is to be recognized that the maintenance of the people's livelihood there is easy compared to the same task in China because the culture of the inhabitants is low, and because the area is rich in natural products.

Statement by Navy Chief of Staff Nagano:
I respectfully make my statement.

The Government has made every effort to break through the present critical situation, while the Naval General Staff, in cooperation with the Army and in keeping with the Government's policies, has continued to make war preparations, which will be almost completed by the end of November.

Hereafter we will go forward steadily with our war preparations, expecting the opening of hostilities in the early part of December. As soon as the time for commencing hostilities is decided, we are prepared for war.

We are planning and getting ready with great care because success or failure in the initial phases of our operations will greatly affect success or failure in the entire war. It is very important that we carry out our initial operations ahead of the enemy and with courageous decisiveness. Consequently, the concealment of our war plans has an important bearing on the outcome of the war; and so, in putting our whole nation on a war footing in the future, we would like to maintain even closer relations with the Government and attain our desired goal.

Statement by Army Chief of Staff Sugiyama:

I respectfully make my statement.

First I will discuss [enemy] army strength in the several countries in the South.

Army strength in the several countries in the South is gradually being increased. Roughly speaking, Malaya has an army of about 60,000 to 70,000 and about 320 airplanes, the Philippines have about 42,000 men and about 170 airplanes, the Netherlands East Indies have about 85,000 men and about 300 airplanes, and Burma has about 35,000 men and about 60 airplanes. Compared to strength before the outbreak of the war in Europe, enemy strength has been increased about eight times in Malaya, four times in the Philippines, two and one-half times in the Netherlands East Indies, and five times in Burma; it totals well over 200,000 in these countries. It is anticipated that the rate of increase will rise as the situation changes.

The ground forces in these regions, although varying from one region to another, are composed for the most part of native soldiers, with a nucleus of about 30 per cent white, "homeland" soldiers. They do not have sufficient education and training, and their fighting ability is generally inferior. It should be remembered, however, that they are thoroughly acclimatized, and used to tropical conditions. As to the fighting ability of the enemy air force, I assume that it cannot be taken lightly when compared to the ground force, since the quality of the aircraft is excellent and their pilots are comparatively skilled.

I will comment on the following matters: (1) timing of the commencement of war; (2) prospects of the operations in the South; (3) situation in the North resulting from operations in the South; (4) relationship between operations and diplomacy.

1. On the timing of the commencement of war:

From the standpoint of operations, if the time for commencing war is delayed, the ratio of armament between Japan and the United States will become more and more unfavorable to us as time passes; and particularly, the gap in air armament will enlarge rapidly. Moreover, defensive preparations in the Philippines, and other American war preparations, will make rapid progress. Also, the common defense arrangements between the United States, Great Britain, the Netherlands, and China will become all the more close, and their joint defensive capability will be rapidly increased. Finally, if we delay until after next spring, the weather will permit operational activities in the North, and also there will be a higher probability that our Empire will have to face simultaneous war in the South and in the North. Thus it would be very disadvantageous for us to delay; and it is to be feared that it might become impossible for us to undertake offensive operations.

In addition, weather conditions in the area where important operations are going to take place are such that no delay is possible. Accordingly, in order to resort to force as soon as preparations for the operations we contemplate are completed, we would like to set the target date in the early part of December.

2. On the prospects of the operations:

Since the principal Army operations in the initial stages in the South will be landing operations against fortified enemy bases, conducted after a long ocean voyage in the intense heat of the sun while repelling attacks from enemy submarines and aircraft, we expect to face considerable difficulties. However, if we take a broad view of the situation, the enemy forces are scattered over a wide area and moreover separated by stretches of water, making coordinated action difficult. We, on the other hand, can concentrate our forces, undertake sudden raids, and destroy the enemy piecemeal. Therefore, we are fully confident of success, given close cooperation between the Army and the Navy. As for operations after we land, we have complete confidence in our victory when we consider the organization, equipment, quality, and strength of the enemy forces.

After the initial stage in our operations has been completed, we will endeavor to shorten greatly the duration of the war, using both political and military strategies, particularly the favorable results from our naval operations. Nevertheless, we must be prepared for the probability that the war will be a protracted one. But since we will seize and hold enemy military and air bases and be able to establish a strategically impregnable position, we think we can frustrate the enemy's plans by one means or another.

We will firmly maintain in general our present posture with respect to defense against the Soviet Union and operations in China while we engage in operations in the South. In this way we will be able to strengthen our invincible position vis-à-vis the North, and there will be no problem in carrying on in China as we have been doing. With regard to China, the favorable results of the operations in the South should particularly contribute to the settlement of the China Incident.

3. On the situation in the North resulting from operations in the South:

The Red Army has suffered massive losses at the hands of the German Army; and there has been a marked decline in the productivity of the Soviet armament industry. In addition, the Red Army in the Far East has sent westward to European Russia forces equal to 13 infantry divisions, about 1,300 tanks, and at least 1,300 airplanes since last spring. Its war potential, both materially and spiritually, is declining. Consequently, the probability of the Soviet Union taking the offensive, so long as the Kwantung Army is firmly entrenched, is very low.

However, it is possible that the United States may put pressure on the Soviet Union to permit America to utilize a part of the Soviet territory in the Far East for air and submarine bases for use in attacking us; and the Soviet Union would not be in a position to reject these American demands. Hence we must anticipate the possibility that we might see some submarines and aircraft in action against us from the North. Consequently, it cannot be assumed that there is no danger of a war breaking out between Japan and the Soviet Union as a result of such causes and changes in the situation. Thus our Empire must conclude its operations in the South as quickly as possible, and be prepared to cope with this situation.

4. On the relationship between operations and diplomacy:

Up to now, in accordance with the decision of the Imperial Conference of September 6, we have limited our preparations for operations so that they would not impede diplomatic negotiations. But from now on, given the decision for war, we will take all possible measures to be ready to use force at the beginning of December. This will have the effect of goading the United States and Great Britain; but we believe that diplomacy, taking advantage of progress in war preparations, should be stepped up. Needless to say, if diplomatic negotiations succeed by midnight of November 30, we will call off the use of force. If they do not succeed by that time, however, we would like to receive the Imperial Assent to start a war in order not to miss our opportunity, and thereby to fully achieve the objectives of our operations.

[A summary of the question-and-answer session between President of the Privy Council Hara and others follows.]

HARA: The topic of today's Imperial Conference is the extension and execution of the decision of the Imperial Conference of September 6. The decision of September 6 was primarily on the development of Japanese-American negotiations; but, to my regret, the negotiations have not led to agreement. I know nothing of their contents. I cannot reach a conclusion merely from the documents presented here today. First of all, I should like to ask the Foreign Minister what had been achieved before the present proposals were drawn up.

TOGO: The Japanese-American negotiations were initiated in April. Then the revised proposal of June 21 was made. The proposal contained wording not previously used toward Japan by another country, and it differed in many respects from usual treaties. I shall omit the details.

HARA: I should like to skip over the technical points of diplomacy and ask what is the present status of the negotiations. What are the important points? What has been definitely agreed upon, and what has not?

TOGO: I shall omit theoretical matters.

Concerning attitudes of both countries toward the European war: The two parties have virtually agreed upon the matter of preventing the expansion of the war. On this matter, what the United States wants is to exert military power against Germany as a right of self-defense, while Japan promises not to exert military force in the Pacific region.

Concerning the question of peace between Japan and China: The two parties have not agreed upon the question of stationing and withdrawing troops. Japan shall station troops in necessary places for the necessary period of time, and shall withdraw other troops under certain conditions in a certain period of time. Nevertheless, the United States demands that we proclaim the withdrawal of all troops; but we cannot accept the demand.

Concerning activities of both countries in the Pacific region: The United States demands that there be no discrimination in trade in the entire Pacific region, including China; whereas Japan cannot agree to the demand unconditionally because of the problem of obtaining resources in China, and so on. On the other hand, since the United States contends that this principle [of nondiscriminatory trade] should be maintained throughout the world, we have said in the negotiations that we would agree to their demand if it is possible to maintain the principle throughout the world.

Both parties have agreed not to solve political problems in the Pacific region by military force. Concerning this, the withdrawal of troops from French Indochina is a problem we have not agreed on.

The above is a summary of negotiations between Japan and the United States.

TOJO: Since the Foreign Minister might be unfamiliar with some matters pertaining to the previous Cabinet, I will make some supplementary remarks.

The American reply received on October 2 does endeavor to force upon Japan the Four Principles: (1) respect of territorial integrity and sovereignty; (2) noninterference in internal affairs; (3) nondiscriminatory trade; and (4) disapproval of changing the status quo by force. The Four Principles are a condensation of the Nine-Power Treaty. If we agree to (1), the agreement will involve even Manchukuo, which the Americans have not recognized, to say nothing of the China Incident. If we agree to (2), there is a danger that this might lead to the abolition of agreements with the Nanking regime: i.e., the Japanese-Chinese treaty for trade and communications. Although (3) might be regarded as proper from a common-sense viewpoint, we cannot concede it where it concerns the self-preservation and self-defense of our Empire. This would also be the attitude of the United States and of Great Britain. Nondiscrimination would also change our rights in nearby areas, which are prescribed by Article 6 of the Japanese-Chinese treaty. Concerning (4), we think that we could probably accept it in the Southwest Pacific, but not in the areas vital to our national defense and vital for procuring resources, such as China. The United States demands that we accept these principles. We cannot do so, because we carried out the Manchurian Incident and the China Incident in order to get rid of the yoke that is based on these principles. The new Foreign Minister and the new Finance Minister say that it is dangerous to agree to these principles. The previous Cabinet conceded what should not have been conceded for the sake of reaching an agreement in the Japanese-American negotiations. Although the American proposal of October 2 uses flowery words, the spirit and attitude expressed in the proposal remain unchanged. The United States has not conceded a single point; it simply makes strong demands on Japan.

The important points are as the Foreign Minister has stated. In concrete terms:

With reference to our attitudes toward the European war, they "appreciate Japan's attitudes" and add, "If Japan would reconsider the matter, it would be most beneficial." That is to say, they are demanding that we clarify our attitude toward the Tripartite Pact. Approval of the Four Principles and their local application are serious questions. More serious is the question of the stationing and withdrawal of troops. What they insist upon is Japan's acceptance of the principle of withdrawal of troops. They urge us to proclaim the withdrawal both at home and abroad, while suggesting that we could probably make some arrangements for stationing troops secretly. As I understand it, withdrawal of our troops is retreat. We sent a large force of one million men [to China], and it has cost us well over 100,000 dead and wounded, [the grief of] their bereaved families, hardship for four years, and a national expenditure of several tens of billions of yen. We must by all means get satisfactory results from this. If we should withdraw troops stationed in China under the Japanese-Chinese treaty, China would become worse than she was before the Incident. She would even attempt to rule Manchuria, Korea, and Formosa. We can expect an expansion of our country only by stationing troops. This the United States does not welcome. However, the stationing of troops that Japan insists upon is not at all unreasonable.

Concerning the Japanese-American conference of heads of state, we do not agree with each other. The United States insists that the meeting be held after the major questions have been agreed upon; whereas Japan proposes to settle the major questions at the talks.

HARA: I have acquired a preliminary understanding of the contents of Proposals A and B as a result of the explanation just given. I shall now ask questions in detail.

Under (1), "Stationing of troops," does "disagrees with the inclusion of this item in the terms for peace" mean that it is not acceptable to include the stationing of troops in the Japanese-Chinese peace treaty?

TOJO: Yes. That is, the United States makes it a principle that troops must be withdrawn, and objects to including stationing of troops in the terms.

HARA: Do they mean that we should write the withdrawal of troops into the treaty, but still negotiate with China on stationing troops?

TOJO: The United States seems to be suggesting that we negotiate with China on stationing troops, which she maintains should be dealt with as an unofficial matter.

HARA: I assume that the United States knows about the treaty we have concluded with the Nanking Government. I wonder if she is telling us this without knowledge of the treaty; or does she know about it and intend to obstruct Japan?

TOJO: I would judge that they know about it. This is because Hu [Shih], T. V. Soong, and others stationed in the United States are very active. The first two persons know about it, judging from the "To" operation some years ago.[34]

[34] This refers to informal talks in 1939 between Japanese and Chinese representatives in Hong Kong, undertaken in the hope of ending the war in China. The talks were not successful. Hu Shih was the Chinese Ambassador to the United States; T. V. Soong was a brother-in-law of Chiang Kai-shek and a well-known Chinese banker.

HARA: What do you mean by "in case there is no prospect of an agreement on the basis of the proposal [of] September 25" under (3), "nondiscriminatory trade"?

TOGO: The proposal of September 25 does not include China; we should not include China in light of Japan's special relations with her. But the United States has not conceded this point. Therefore, in our final proposal, we intend to approve China's inclusion on the condition that nondiscrimination be applied throughout the world.

HARA: Concerning (4), the question of the Tripartite Pact: The United States wants its own way about the right of self-defense. What is the significance of the phrase "to broaden unreasonably the [. . .] right of self-defense"?

TOGO: The draft has some peculiar phrases. This refers to American attitudes.

HARA: Item 3 of Proposal B reads "to restore [trade relations] to what they were prior to the freezing of assets." What about sanctions imposed prior to the freezing of assets?

TOGO: Our sending of troops into French Indochina directly caused the issuance of the order freezing our assets. The situation should be restored to what it was before the Indochina incident. Japan would prefer that we returned to the state of affairs prior to the abrogation of the trade treaty, but I think it would be better to seek first of all a relaxation of tension. Since the United States will not be completely satisfied because this item is conditional, as stated in Note 1, we think we should first proceed to return to the situation prior to the freezing order, and after this has been achieved carry on negotiations with the United States on various matters. However, in the case of oil, its export was prohibited even before the freezing order; so I would like to make an agreement whereby Japan would be able to buy the amount she needs, and not be limited to the amount prior to the freezing order.

HARA: It was because of the China Incident that the United States put restrictions on trade with us. The freezing order resulted from our advance into French Indochina. Nonetheless, we want to settle the China Incident; therefore, I think we should negotiate and settle all these questions, including the China Incident, with the United States at one and the same time. Aren't our demands in Proposal B too weak? We plan to proceed with negotiations first on the basis of Proposals A and B, and then go on to other questions. How is the United States likely to react to these proposals?

TOGO: I shall explain what led us to put in Point 3 in Proposal B.

Although we desire to return to the situation prior to the abrogation of the trade treaty in one stroke, as you have said, a most serious situation—namely, war—would result if the United States did not agree with us. Therefore, if we offer as many concessions as we can afford, and still the United States does not agree with us, then we will know that she intends to go to war, and at the same time our moral position will be made clear both at home and abroad. Answering your question on the overall situation, we cannot expect to settle matters quickly by means of Proposal A. I am afraid we cannot settle matters even with Proposal B. Take, for example, the withdrawal of troops from French Indochina. The United States, I think, will not agree to the China Question in (4) of Proposal B either, for she has never agreed to it. I suppose it will also be very difficult for her to agree to Item 2 of the Notes, since she has been requiring us to observe it. I, however, do not think that Japan's demands are unreasonable. If the United States wants peace in the Pacific, or if she reflects on the fact that Japan is determined, I think that the United States must give some consideration to our demands. But since this means that Japan will coerce the United States with force [in the background], it is not impossible that she may resist us. Moreover, we have only a short time left. Since we will send instructions to begin negotiations after His Majesty has made the decision, and because we must conclude them by the end of November, we have only two weeks for negotiations. This cannot be helped because of other needs. Consequently, I think the prospect of success in the negotiations is small. As Foreign Minister, I hope to do my best. To my regret, there is little hope for success in the negotiations.

HARA: I should like both the Army and Navy Chiefs of Staff to explain what will happen if the negotiations break down. Please state it in such a way that it can be understood with the use of common sense. Regarding operations in the South, the field of battle in the map we have here covers the entire region. What is the scope of operations, and how successful are our military operations likely to be?

SUGIYAMA: Targets of this operation are military and air bases in Guam, Hong Kong, British Malaya, Burma, British Borneo, Dutch Borneo, Sumatra, Celebes, the Bismarck Islands, and small islands southwest of the Bismarck Islands. The numerical strength of the enemy in these places is more than 200,000, while the number of enemy aircraft is 800. There are other forces in India, Australia, and New Zealand, which I assume would participate sooner or later. The Army will carry out operations under these conditions in cooperation with the Navy, and its major efforts will be made in the Philippines and Malaya. The operation is planned to start in Malaya and the Philippines simultaneously, and then to move toward the Netherlands East Indies. In this way, it is estimated that it will take 50 days to complete the operation in the Philippines, 100 days in Malaya, and 50 days in the Netherlands East Indies; and that the entire operation will be completed within five months after the opening of the war. However, in case the American fleet comes to attack us, and our Navy goes out to meet it, or in case the United States and the Soviet Union attack us in the North—although the probability of this is low—the periods mentioned above would probably be extended for some time. I believe, however, that we would be able to carry on a protracted war if we could bring under our control such important military bases as Hong Kong, Manila, and Singapore, and important areas in the Netherlands East Indies.

HARA: India and Australia are excluded from this map. Although it is said that there is a force of well over 200,000 men and some aircraft in these areas, there are also warships. Can we destroy their fleet in a short period of time?

NAGANO: The ratio of our fleet to that of the United States is 7.5 to 10; but 40 per cent of the American fleet is in the Atlantic Ocean, and 60 per cent is in the Pacific. I do not believe that Great Britain will be able to send a large fleet against us; probably her fleet would consist of a battleship, ten or more cruisers, and some aircraft. As to the method of fighting battles, the United States would need considerable time if she should withdraw ships from the Atlantic Ocean and come to attack us. However, a part of their naval force might be able to obstruct our operations in the South, although the strength of that naval force would probably be insufficient to engage in a decisive battle. Consequently, they would have to bring the Atlantic Fleet into the Pacific. Great Britain might send a part of her fleet because she would not want to lose Singapore. In this case it is possible that Great Britain and the United States might combine their fleets. Our navy has plans for this contingency, although the method of fighting battles would be different from the other case. The combined force of Great Britain and the United States has weak points. We are, therefore, confident of victory. We can destroy their fleet if they want a decisive battle. Even if we destroy it, however, the war will continue long after the Southern Operation.

HARA: Although the Army Chief of Staff has stated that the operation would last 50 to 100 days, I would imagine that landings could not be carried out unless we could deal with the enemy fleets now in the South Pacific. What is your opinion on this?

NAGANO: I assume that, among enemy fleets, the surface fleets operating in the vicinity of our fleets would temporarily retreat. We would destroy them if possible; even if we could not, they would not be able to do much. But it is submarines that we would attempt to overwhelm. It would not be difficult to dominate the enemy fleets now in the Pacific Ocean.

HARA: I shall ask about the Soviet Union. While it is stated that our plans are to occupy the greater part of the South Pacific in about 100 days, it is usual for predictions to turn out wrong. Although at the time of the Russo-Japanese war the capture of Port Arthur was expected to be accomplished in the summer of the 37th year of Meiji (1904), it was actually achieved on January 1 of the following year. The same is true of German plans in the war between Germany and the Soviet Union. Although I believe that our Supreme Command's plan is most realistic, would you transfer some troops in the South to the North in case the war is prolonged, and the Soviet Union starts a war against us? What would happen in the Chinese theater? I should like to hear your views on this, just to be certain.

SUGIYAMA: It is difficult for the Soviet Union to conduct a major operation in winter. In light of the present situation, the probability of the Soviet Union entering the war is low. Even if the Soviet Union and the United States should combine forces, they would be unable to carry out a major operation. Even if there were combined operations, they would be only nominal ones for the Soviet Union. We are prepared to deal with their winter operations.

What we are most concerned with is a possible United States-Soviet alliance concurrent with a delay in our plans to occupy Malaya in 100 days and to complete occupation of the Netherlands East Indies in five months. This is dangerous. I think we should be able to meet this situation adequately by using Army corps now in the home islands and forces to be transferred from China.

HARA: I think it is clear that the Soviet Union would not attack us immediately. I also assume that the alliance between the United States and the Soviet Union would be as you have described it. I should like to ask further if we can ignore the possibility that our trade and maritime commerce might be hindered by the activities of the Soviet Navy, and by the enemy fleet stationed in the South Seas. Can we assume that the transportation of materials and other goods would not be affected by interference from the Soviet Union and enemy ships in the South Seas?

NAGANO: If the Soviet Union starts a war, and if her submarines become active, we would not be able to send sufficient forces against her, since our Navy would be carrying out operations in the South Seas. We would put up a defense against her activities; and then, as our operations in the South Seas progressed, we would fight actively against them. In the South Seas there are enemy warships, submarines, and aircraft. We are, therefore, prepared to suffer considerable damage once we have begun operations. Since our operation in the South would be the major one, we would devote our efforts to it. Consequently, we expect to suffer considerable damage. With aircraft, for example, our losses might reach one-third or one-half. Merchant ships would naturally suffer considerable damage. However, since maritime transportation is of vital importance to the life of our country, we would take all possible means to protect it. Nevertheless, I expect that we would suffer considerable losses every year. If we could protect the ships and make up the losses, I assume that our marine transportation would be all right.

HARA: Am I to understand that materials can be secured even if the Soviet fleet and the navies of Great Britain, the United States, and the Netherlands interfere?

SUZUKI: The Army and the Navy have already made studies concerning the loss of ships.

HARA: Although (4) under I in "Essentials for Carrying Out the Empire's Policies" discusses relations with Thailand just prior to resorting to arms, it would seem that we will not be able to confer with her if this must be done just before we use force. What do you think about this point? If we allow time for negotiations, Great Britain will learn about them. In that event, the intentions of the Supreme Command will become known to the enemy. What is meant by "just prior"? If you are going to use coercion, it will be coercion, and not negotiation for a close military relationship. This approach would affect our relations with Thailand in the future.

TOJO: Since diplomatic and military affairs are closely interrelated here, I will answer. With the idea of winning Thailand over to our side we have been working on [Prime Minister] Pibun Songgram to set up close military relations ever since the time of our advance into southern French Indochina. As you have pointed out, there are delicate points. It is necessary from an operational point of view for us to make landings in Thailand. It will not do to let this be known too early. Therefore, we cannot do other than push the matter by force if they do not agree with us at the talks just before we act.

HARA: Although the description of our relations with Thailand has been softened by the use of the word "establish," I recognize that in actuality we are using coercion, as the Prime Minister has mentioned. I shall not comment, since I only know what I have heard from the Government and the Supreme Command; I do not have any additional data to go on.

It would not be desirable to fail to get an agreement on Japanese-American negotiations. We have endured hardships for four years because we are a unified nation under an Imperial family with a history of 2,600 years. It seems that Britain already has war weariness. I wonder about Germany. It also seems that there is an antiwar movement in Italy. I believe that the favorable situation in our country results from our national polity with the Imperial family as its head. Nonetheless, our people want to settle the China Incident quickly. Statesmen must give serious consideration to the wisdom of waging war against a great power like the United States without the prospect of the China Incident being settled quickly. At the last Imperial Conference it was decided that we would go to war if the negotiations failed to lead to an agreement. According to the briefings given today, the present American attitude is not just the same as the previous one, but is even more unreasonable. Therefore, I regret very much that the negotiations have little prospect of success.

It is impossible, from the standpoint of our domestic political situation and of our self-preservation, to accept all of the American demands. We must hold fast to our position. As I understand it, the Japanese-Chinese problem is the important point in the negotiations, and there is suspicion that the United States is acting as spokesman for the Chungking regime. If Chiang, relying on American power, should negotiate with us, I doubt that the negotiations could be completed in two or three months. It would be nice if he would capitulate in the face of Japan's firm determination; but I think there is absolutely no hope for this.

On the other hand, we cannot let the present situation continue. If we miss the present opportunity to go to war, we will have to submit to American dictation. Therefore, I recognize that it is inevitable that we must decide to start a war against the United States. I will put my trust in what I have been told: namely, that things will go well in the early part of the war; and that although we will experience increasing difficulties as the war progresses, there is some prospect of success.

On this occasion I would like to make one comment to the leaders of the Government. Although the China Incident is one cause for war between Japan and the United States and Great Britain, another is the German-British war. I do not believe that the present situation would have developed out of just the China Incident. We have come to where we are because of the war between Germany and Great Britain. What we should always keep in mind here is what would happen to relations between Germany and Great Britain and Germany and the United States, all of them being countries whose population belongs to the white race, if Japan should enter the war. Hitler has said that the Japanese are a second-class race, and Germany has not declared war against the United States. Japan will take positive action against the United States. In that event, will the American people adopt the same attitude toward us psychologically that they do toward the Germans? Their indignation against the Japanese will be stronger than their hatred of Hitler. The Germans in the United States are considering ways of bringing about peace between the United States and Germany. I fear, therefore, that if Japan begins a war against the United States, Germany and Great Britain and Germany and the United States will come to terms, leaving Japan by herself. That is, we must be prepared for the possibility that hatred of the yellow race might shift the hatred now being directed against Germany to Japan, thus resulting in the German-British war's being turned against Japan.

Negotiations with the United States have failed to lead to an agreement. A war against the United States and Great Britain is inevitable if Japan is to survive. However, we must give serious consideration to race relations, exercise constant care to avoid being surrounded by the entire Aryan race—which would leave Japan isolated—and take steps now to strengthen relations with Germany and Italy. Paper agreements will not do. I would like to call the attention of the officials in the Government to the following point: don't let hatred of Japan become stronger than hatred of Hitler, so that everybody will in name and in fact gang up on Japan. I hope that our officials will deal adequately with international affairs in the future.

TOJO: The points of the President of the Privy Council are well taken. Ever since the previous Imperial Conference, the Government has not given up its earnest desire to somehow break the impasse in our negotiations with the United States. It is natural for the Supreme Command to devote itself exclusively to military operations, since it sees little hope for the negotiations' success. However, in the hope that there might be some way to break the impasse, the Government sought a settlement, even though it meant some sacrifice of freedom in military operations. That is, we pursued diplomacy and military planning at the same time. There is still some hope for success. The reason the United States agreed to negotiate with us is that they have some weaknesses: (1) they are not prepared for operations in two oceans; (2) they have not completed strengthening their domestic structure; (3) they are short of materials for national defense (they have only enough for one year); and so on.

They will learn how determined Japan is from the deployment of our troops, which we will carry out on the basis of the present proposal. The United States has from the beginning believed that Japan would give up because of economic pressure; but if they recognize that Japan is determined, then that is the time we should resort to diplomatic measures. I believe this is the only way that is left for us. This is the present proposal. This is the last measure we can take that is in line with what President Hara has called "going by diplomacy." I cannot think of any other way in the present situation.

If we enter into a protracted war, there will be difficulties, as mentioned before. The first stage of the war will not be difficult. We have some uneasiness about a protracted war. But how can we let the United States continue to do as she pleases, even though there is some uneasiness? Two years from now we will have no petroleum for military use. Ships will stop moving. When I think about the strengthening of American defenses in the Southwest Pacific, the expansion of the American fleet, the unfinished China Incident, and so on, I see no end to difficulties. We can talk about austerity and suffering, but can our people endure such a life for a long time? The situation is not the same as it was during the Sino-Japanese War [1894–95]. I fear that we would become a third-class nation after two or three years if we just sat tight. We agreed upon the present proposal as a result of a careful study in the light of the possibility just mentioned. The President should share our views on this point.

I intend to take measures to prevent a racial war once war is started. I should like to prevent Germany and Italy from making peace with Great Britain or with the United States by taking advantage of the results of campaigns in the South. I think the sentiments of the American people are as the President of the Privy Council has indicated, and so I intend to take precautions.

As to what our moral basis for going to war should be, there is some merit in making it clear that Great Britain and the United States represent a strong threat to Japan's self-preservation. Also, if we are fair in governing the occupied areas, attitudes toward us would probably relax. America may be enraged for a while, but later she will come to understand [why we did what we did]. In any case I will be careful to avoid the war's becoming a racial war.

Do you have any other comments? If not, I will rule that the proposals have been approved in their original form.

67TH LIAISON CONFERENCE
November 12, 1941

After the Imperial Conference of November 5, increasing attention was paid to the problem of conducting the war that was expected to break out, and to Japan's relations with her Axis allies. In the meantime, of course, negotiations with the United States were continued; but the diplomats were confronted by a firm deadline, which, as the Foreign Minister reported in this Liaison Conference, made things difficult.

[Time: 1:30 P.M. to 4 P.M.

[The draft of the proposal "Basic Plan for a Wartime Economy,"[35] submitted by the Director of the Planning Board, was discussed and approved as submitted.

[Navy Chief of Staff Nagano proposed that an agreement be reached on the document "Limiting the Use of Civilian Personnel and Facilities in the Occupied Areas to a Level Absolutely Necessary from the Point of View of Military Operations." With reference to this, War Minister Tojo and Army Chief of Staff Sugiyama explained the need for moving civilian personnel forward with the military forces. It was agreed after discussion that this matter must be treated with great care in order to maintain secrecy; and that it would be discussed again in the future if there should arise a need for new regulations.

[In connection with the presentation and discussion of a proposal, "The Foreign and Domestic Implementation of the 'Essentials

[35] In essence this Basic Plan covered the following points:

1. Steps will be taken to step up procurement and development of natural resources—oil, coal, iron, etc.—and to stop the flow of vital war materials to the enemy.

2. Attempts will be made to achieve self-sufficiency in petroleum, iron, and shipbuilding by the end of 1943.

3. Industrial reorganization to achieve these ends will be attempted.

4. Efforts will be made to maintain the people's livelihood at a minimum level.

for Carrying Out the Empire's Policies'[36] adopted by the Imperial
Conference on November 5," the Navy suggested that the Foreign
Ministry's draft be used, and Bureau Chief Yamamoto[37] made some
comments on it.

[Moreover, Foreign Minister Togo spoke [as follows] on measures
that Foreign Ministers have taken in the past:]

Negotiations with the United States have run into considerable
difficulties because of the need to conclude them in a short time.
They are also difficult because, on the one hand, we are taking measures on the assumption that the negotiations will be successful; and
on the other hand, we must prepare for the possibility that they will
end in failure.

In our negotiations with the United States, we would like to sign
an agreement sometime this month; but I think this would be difficult. As for Great Britain, we are carrying on talks with her
through the United States, and we are also negotiating with her directly; hence I would like to sign an agreement with her at the same
time we sign an agreement with the United States; but I think this
would be difficult. I have told Nomura to speed up the negotiations.

I summoned the American and British Ambassadors the day before
yesterday, told them about our wishes, and asked them to transmit
this information to their governments.

[The British Ambassador conveyed to the Foreign Minister the
reply from his Government, which said, in essence: "Since the present Japanese-American negotiations relate to basic principles, Great
Britain cannot get involved in them; but she will consider concrete
proposals." The Foreign Minister responded that the current negotiations between Japan and the United States were not preliminary
talks but real negotiations, and hence they must be concluded quickly.
It appeared that he understood this. It would seem that the American
Ambassador also understands the need to hurry and is taking this
seriously.]

On the basis of the way recent conversations between Nomura
and Hull have gone, I would judge that on the Sino-Japanese problem the two countries [Japan and China] are to negotiate directly,
and that an agreement between Japan and the United States is possible. In that event, it is conceivable that even though Japan and
the United States may come to an agreement, Japan and China may

---

[36] Document attached.
[37] Yamamoto Kumaichi, Chief of the Asian Bureau of the Foreign Ministry.

not. As Foreign Minister, I believe that it would not be proper to deal with the China problem using the United States as an intermediary; it would be more appropriate for Japan and China to negotiate directly, and this would be more profitable.

I have urged both Nomura and Grew to try to get an agreement within ten days.

In the event that we decide to use force in the South, I thought it would be better to inform Germany and Italy of our intentions beforehand, so that Germany would be prepared, rather than tell them all of a sudden without prior warning. Accordingly I told the German Ambassador the following:

When Toyoda was Foreign Minister, Germany asked that Japan tell the United States: "If the United States should undertake warlike actions against Germany, Japan would have to declare war against the United States. Therefore, the United States should exercise restraint in her actions in the Atlantic." Japan replied: "It would not be appropriate for us to make statements of this kind right now. I believe it would be better for Japan to stand firm."

In response, Ott asked: "I hear that in the negotiations between Japan and the United States, the two sides are far apart. Is this so?" Then I said: "That is so. There may be developments, Mr. Ambassador, that I will need to tell you about."

Thus without referring to specifics, I hinted that depending on the circumstances, we might have some things to discuss with Germany.

The Foreign Ministry's draft was drawn up with the foregoing considerations in mind.

[Following this the proposal on "Foreign and Domestic Implementation" was discussed, amended, and approved.]

[Attached Document]

The Foreign and Domestic Implementation of the "Essentials for Carrying Out the Empire's Policies" Adopted by the Imperial Conference on November 5

1. Toward Germany and Italy:

In the event that Japanese-American negotiations fail, and it is recognized that war is inevitable (it is assumed that this will be after November 25th), Germany and Italy will be notified without delay that the Empire intends to declare war on Great Britain and the United States as soon as preparations have been completed. As part of the above-mentioned preparations, the following necessary agreements will be negotiated: (a) The participation of Germany and Italy in the war against the United States; (b) neither of the two parties will make peace separately.

Note: In case Germany demands that we participate in the war against the Soviet Union, we will respond that we do not intend to join the war for the time being. Even if this should lead to a situation whereby Germany will delay her entry into the war against the United States, it cannot be helped.

2. Toward Great Britain:

As to those items that might be agreed on as a result of negotiations with the United States that affect Great Britain, we will get Great Britain to accept them; moreover, we will take steps to get her to cooperate immediately in a positive manner by negotiating either directly or through the United States.

In order to keep our plans secret, no other special diplomatic measures will be taken.

3. Toward the Dutch East Indies:

In order that our plans may be kept secret and deceptive, we will gradually begin diplomatic negotiations, ostensibly in the form of continuing our earlier negotiations, for the purpose of acquiring vital materials for our Empire.

4. Toward the Soviet Union:

In general we will continue our negotiations on the basis of Paragraph One of "The Essentials of Diplomatic Negotiations with the Soviet Union,"[38] adopted by the Liaison Conference between Supreme Headquarters and the Government on August 4, 1941.

5. Toward Thailand:

(a) Just before we occupy the country we will demand the following and secure Thailand's immediate agreement (even if Thailand does not accept our demands, our troops will enter the country as planned; however, efforts will be made to limit armed clashes between Japan and Thailand): (1) that the transit of Japanese troops and the use of facilities be allowed, and that other aid also be provided; (2) that immediate steps be taken to prevent clashes between Japanese and Thai troops in connection with the transit of Japanese troops; (3) that a mutual defense pact be signed if Thailand wishes it.

Note: There should be no particular change in our approach to Thailand before we enter into these negotiations; great care must be taken to keep secret our plans to begin war.

(b) Immediately after our occupation, agreements will be made on the spot regarding the following points: (1) the transit and stationing of Japanese troops; (2) providing military facilities and building new ones; (3) providing the necessary transportation and communications facilities and factories, etc.; (4) providing billets and provisions for troops in

[38] See pp. 113–14.

transit and for troops on occupation duty; (5) loaning the necessary military funds. Note: Negotiations regarding Points (1) and (2) will be on the basis of the "Essentials of Policy toward French Indochina and Thailand,"[39] adopted by the Liaison Conference between the Government and the Supreme Headquarters on February 1, 1941. We will promise to respect the sovereignty and territorial integrity of Thailand; in order to facilitate our negotiations and depending on Thailand's attitude, she may be secretly told that in the future she might be given a part of Burma, or perhaps Malaya.

6. Toward China:

The following steps should be taken in order to limit consumption as much as possible so as to prepare for a protracted world war, to assure the preservation of Japan's overall war-making capacity, and to prepare for the possibility that her war-making ability might be reduced in the future:

(a) Eliminate British and American forces in China.

(b) Place enemy Foreign Settlements (including the Foreign Legation Quarter in Peking) as well as principal foreign interests (customs, mines, etc.) under effective Japanese control. However, care should be taken to keep to a minimum the burden placed on Japan's human and material resources. Note: Enemy forces will be removed from the International Settlement and the Peking Legation Quarter, and these areas will be placed under our control; but since the interests of friendly foreign powers are also involved, these areas will not be taken over.

(c) In order to conceal our plans, the foregoing paragraphs will not become effective until war begins with the United States.

(d) The exercise of the rights of a belligerent against Chungking will not take the form of a special declaration, but for practical purposes will go into effect with the opening of hostilities against the United States.

(e) As for enemy rights in China, even those relating to the National Government will, depending on the need, be placed for the time being under the control of Japan. Special steps will be taken to adjust them.

(f) In the occupied areas, the Chinese leaders will be encouraged as much as possible to carry on activities, and efforts will be made to secure the support of the people through joint Sino-Japanese efforts. In this way peace will gradually be restored in local areas wherever possible.

(g) With respect to economic relations with China, emphasis will be placed on the acquisition of vital materials; and for this reason rational adjustments will be made in the restrictions presently in force.

[39] This document established the objective of "a close and inseparable military, political, and economic union between Japan, Thailand, and Indochina." Pressure would first be applied, and if this was not successful, military force would follow.

68TH LIAISON CONFERENCE
November 13, 1941

[Time: From 10 A.M. to noon.
[The document "Hastening the End of the War in the South" was discussed and studied. It was decided that the document would be considered a draft; and that it would be adopted, with some amendments, at the next meeting on Saturday.]

69TH LIAISON CONFERENCE
November 15, 1941

Foreign Minister Togo had sent the text of Proposals A and B to Ambassador Nomura on November 4, one day prior to the Imperial Conference; immediately after that Conference he had instructed the Ambassador to proceed with the negotiations on the basis of Proposal A. Along with the Proposals, Togo sent a long cable in which he stressed the urgency of the situation. He stated his view, moreover, that the Japanese Government had made many concessions but the United States had not reciprocated.

Following instructions, Nomura presented Proposal A to Secretary Hull on November 7; he pressed for a quick reply, but without success. Hull, however, did offer a personal suggestion that a mutual pledge of friendship and cooperation might be made between Japan and China. This suggestion raised the hope among the Japanese that it might help remove the difficult Chinese Question from the Japanese-American negotiations. However, this hope died when Nomura saw Hull again on November 12. The Secretary indicated that any pledge of friendship given by Japan to China would have to be linked to the American principles that Japan had been unwilling to accept all along.

By November 15 the United States had rejected Proposal A, although the rejection was accompanied by a proposal for an economic agreement, which the United States hoped would have an ameliorating effect.

Meanwhile, Foreign Minister Togo carried on parallel negotiations with Ambassador Grew in Tokyo because of the pressure of time. Togo told Grew that economic pressure might be more of a menace to Japan's national existence than force. Togo also talked with British Ambassador Craigie because he wanted a simultaneous agreement with Britain if an accord with America materialized.

At the same time, Togo, who was not hopeful of success in nego-
tiations with the United States, began to approach Germany in an
effort to strengthen ties with her.

Finally, at this Liaison Conference, a document called "Draft
Proposal for Hastening the End of the War against the United States,
Great Britain, the Netherlands, and Chiang" was presented. The
document shows, among other things, that the Japanese military were
still counting on a German invasion of Britain, despite the fact that
the Japanese Naval Attaché in Berlin had reported as early as April
and May that a German landing on Britain seemed unlikely.[40]

[Time: From 10 A.M. to noon.

[First, Foreign Minister Togo reported on recent developments in
Japanese-American negotiations. Next, the document on "What to
Call the War in the South" was discussed, the substance of the
amendments was agreed on, and it was decided that the amendments
drafted by the secretaries would be adopted at the next meeting.

[Report by the Foreign Minister on Japanese-American negotiations:]

With reference to Japanese-American negotiations: After the Imperial Conference on the 5th our proposal was sent to Ambassador
Nomura. On that occasion the following was appended:

"We have endured what is difficult to endure for more than half
a year. Our endurance up to now stems from our desire for peace.
But there is a limit to our patience. We would like you to inform the
United States that she should reflect seriously on [whether it is wise]
to continue to ignore Japan's demands, and that the present situation cannot be overlooked even for a day."

Nomura called on Hull and conveyed to him exactly what we had
wired. The United States responded that the present negotiations
were preliminary discussions. Accordingly, we told Nomura, "That
won't do." At the same time we put pressure on the American Ambassador, saying: "There is a danger that we will let an opportunity slip
if we delay too long. Please send an early reply." I said to Grew,
in effect: "These negotiations are being conducted in Washington;
but we would also like to carry them on in Tokyo in order to facilitate
the negotiations in Washington." Grew indicated his agreement.

I also told Grew: "The United States has delayed and delayed.
Japan has made concession after concession. It appears that the prob-

[40] *TSM,* VII, 333.

lem of Japanese immigration and other differences have become more
aggravated. The feelings of the Japanese people won't allow this situation to continue. The Diet is in session, and the situation is critical.
Hence we must find a solution quickly and should not call the present
talks 'preliminary discussions.'

"Since the United States is applying economic pressure on us,
which is even stronger than military pressure, we may have to act in
order to defend ourselves. For the United States to insist that Japan
disregard the sacrifices she is making in China is tantamount to telling us to commit suicide. Please convey this to your Government."

Grew replied: "I understand. I will convey it to my Government.
I am most anxious to find a solution." And he went home in a tearful
mood.

When I was talking with Craigie, the British Ambassador, the
other day, he said that Britain believes that Japan and the United
States are still discussing fundamentals and have not taken up concrete problems. I replied: "These are not preliminary discussions;
we are at the final stages." Craigie realized that the matter was
urgent.

In looking over the report of Nomura's meeting with Hull on November 13, I realized that the United States has stated a series of
demands she is making on Japan; but she has not mentioned anything that she herself will do. Hence if we are going to reply, we
must add, by way of a preface, the phrase "if all Japan's demands are
accepted."

Furthermore, the more I look at the documents relating to Japanese-American negotiations to date, the more I believe that they leave
something to be desired. We have given the other side all of our
IOU's, and we have not received anything from them. Hence we are
in serious difficulties.

Given the pattern to date, it appears that Japanese-American negotiations are likely to go on for a while. I think that if the negotiations
end in failure, it will be necessary to strengthen our ties with Germany. It may well be that Germany will not be prepared to come in
fully on our side, judging from her disapproval when Italy entered
the war. I believe it may be a bit early for negotiations with Germany,
but I would like to get started on the preliminaries right away; and
I would like to have this point understood.

[Regarding "What to Call the War in the South," it is written in
a way to emphasize throughout the document the demands we are
making on others. There is also a view that it would be necessary to

stress that we are forced to act because of China's anti-Japanese views. As to whether we should declare war, or whether we should begin the war without declaring it, the majority opinion is that the problem needs to be studied.

[After the meeting, the Foreign Minister asked the Army Chief of Staff the following regarding an informal approach to Germany:]

In case Japanese-American negotiations end in failure, it will be necessary to strengthen immediately the alliance with Germany, and I would like to make preparations for this. However, it would be awkward for me as Foreign Minister to talk directly with Germany through Ambassador Oshima while I am negotiating with the United States. Wouldn't it be possible for the Army Chief of Staff to get Major General Okamoto to carry on informal talks indirectly, either through Sakanishi, the Military Attaché, or through Ott?

[To this request, Army Chief of Staff Sugiyama replied: "I am in favor of having Major General Okamoto undertake this.[41] I will tell him to keep in close touch with you."]

[Attached Document]

Draft Proposal for Hastening the End of the War Against the United States, Great Britain, the Netherlands, and Chiang
[Approved at this Conference]

POLICY

1. We will endeavor to quickly destroy American, British, and Dutch bases in the Far East, and assure our self-preservation and self-defense. We will endeavor at the same time to hasten the fall of the Chiang regime by taking positive measures, to work for the surrender of Great Britain in cooperation with Germany and Italy, and to destroy the will of the United States to continue the war.

2. We will do our utmost to prevent an increase in the number of countries at war against us; and we will endeavor to influence the countries not presently involved.

SUMMARY

1. Our Empire will engage in a quick war, and will destroy American and British bases in Eastern Asia and in the Southwest Pacific region. At the same time that it secures a strategically powerful position, it will control those areas producing vital materials, as well as important transportation routes, and thereby prepare for a protracted period of self-sufficiency.

---

[41] Okamoto Kiyofuku, Chief of the Intelligence Section.

At the appropriate time, we will endeavor by various means to lure the main fleet of the United States [near Japan] and destroy it.

2. First of all, Japan, Germany, and Italy will cooperate and work for the surrender of Great Britain.

(a) The Empire will adopt the following policies: (1) the connection between Australia and India and the British mother country will be broken by means of political pressure and the destruction of commerce, and their separation will be achieved; (2) the independence of Burma will be promoted, and this will be used to stimulate the independence of India.

(b) We will endeavor to get Germany and Italy to adopt the following policies: (1) to carry out operations against the Near East, North Africa, and Suez, and at the same time carry out measures against India; (2) strengthen the blockade of Great Britain; (3) if conditions permit, carry out the invasion of the British Isles.

(c) The three countries will cooperate and adopt the following policies: (1) endeavor to establish contact among the three countries through the Indian Ocean; (2) strengthen naval operations; (3) stop the shipment of vital materials from the occupied countries to Great Britain.

3. Japan, Germany, and Italy will cooperate and endeavor to deal with Great Britain, and at the same time endeavor to destroy the will of the United States to fight.

(a) The Empire will adopt the following policies: (1) In dealing with the Philippines, for the time being the present policy will be continued, and thought will be given to how it can hasten the end of the war. (2) An all-out attempt will be made to disrupt commerce to the United States. (3) The flow of materials from China and the South Seas to the United States will be cut off. (4) Strategic propaganda against the United States will be stepped up; emphasis will be placed on enticing the American main fleet to come to the Far East, persuading Americans to reconsider their Far Eastern policy, and pointing out the uselessness of a Japanese-American war; American public opinion will be directed toward opposition to war. (5) Attempts will be made to break the ties between the United States and Australia.

(b) We will endeavor to get Germany and Italy to adopt the following policies: (1) to set up naval attacks against the United States in the Atlantic and Indian Oceans; (2) to step up military, economic, and political offensives against Central and South America.

4. In China we will stop support going to Chiang by utilizing the results of our military operations (especially against the United States, Great Britain, and the Netherlands), and will destroy Chiang's power to resist. We will also work for the collapse of the Chiang regime by vigorously undertaking various strategies—the seizure of the Foreign Settlements, utilization of the overseas Chinese in the South Pacific, stepping up military operations, etc.

5. The Empire will endeavor to the utmost to prevent the outbreak of

a war with the Soviet Union while we are engaged in military operations in the South.

We will keep in mind the possibilities of arranging a peace between Germany and the Soviet Union, depending on the wishes of these two countries, and bringing the Soviet Union within the Axis camp; of improving Japanese-Soviet relations; and, depending on circumstances, of encouraging the Soviets to push into Iran and India.

6. We will continue our present policy toward French Indochina. We will persuade Thailand to cooperate with us by restoring to her territory she has lost to the British.

7. While paying full attention to changes in the war situation, the international situation, and popular feelings in enemy countries, we will endeavor to seize the following opportunities in order to bring the war to a close: (a) conclusion of the principal military operations in the South; (b) conclusion of the principal military operations in China, especially the capitulation of the Chiang regime; (c) favorable developments in the war situation in Europe, especially the conquest of the British Isles, the end of the war between Germany and the Soviet Union, and the success of the policy vis-à-vis India.

For this purpose we will step up our diplomatic and propaganda activities directed against Latin America, Switzerland, Portugal, and the Vatican.

The three countries—Japan, Germany, and Italy—agree not to sign a separate peace agreement; at the same time, they will not immediately make peace with Great Britain when she surrenders, but will endeavor to use Great Britain to persuade the United States. In the planning to promote peace with the United States, attention will be paid to supplies of tin and rubber in the South Pacific region, and to the treatment of the Philippines.

70TH LIAISON CONFERENCE
November 20, 1941

In anticipation of the occupation of Southeast Asia, this Liaison Conference took up a policy document prepared by the Army and Navy. As might be expected, the armed forces proposed a military occupation. Evidently the Foreign Minister pushed the idea of converting military government into civilian government, but did not get very far.

The Foreign Minister reported on the latest developments in Washington. There Ambassador Kurusu Saburo, who had just been sent by the Foreign Ministry to assist Nomura, paid his first formal call on President Roosevelt on November 17. The next day, during a lengthy conversation with Hull that seemed to be getting nowhere, the Japanese representatives, without prior authorization from Tokyo, suggested that to clear the air the two nations should return to the situation that existed before July—Japan to evacuate southern Indochina, and the United States to restore trade to its former levels. When this was reported to Tokyo, the Foreign Minister replied strongly that the Ambassadors should present Proposal B, and that "no further concessions can be made."

[Time: 9 A.M. to 11:30 A.M.

[There was a discussion of the "Essentials of Policy Regarding the Administration of the Occupied Areas in the Southern Regions," followed by a statement on the steps taken by the Foreign Minister on the 19th regarding Nomura's telegram of the 18th.

[The "Essentials of Policy Regarding the Administration of the Occupied Areas in the Southern Regions" was discussed, using as the basis the Army-Navy draft with amendments proposed by the Foreign Ministry. At the beginning of the discussion, Army Chief of Staff Sugiyama indicated the following desiderata:]

Our experience in the China Incident has shown that often in the administration of occupied areas there is fragmentation of leadership that leads to undesirable consequences. We are suffering from its harmful effects even now. In view of this, I would like to have sufficient attention paid in our discussions to the problem of creating a unified administration in the South.

[The details follow:

[With regard to "changing agencies for military government in the occupied areas into [civil] government agencies," even though the Foreign Minister forcefully urged that this provision ought to be written into the policy statement, nothing was done except to take note of it, on the ground that such a change should not be made too early.

[There was much discussion of the phrase in 10(a) reading "Important provisions relating to military government in the occupied areas will be decided by the Liaison Conference"; but it was decided that the Foreign Ministry draft would be adopted. Also, with reference to the clause "Decisions made in Tokyo will be transmitted to the occupied areas by the Army and Navy," the Army-Navy draft was approved and adopted.

[Although the Foreign Minister urged the adoption of a provision that "personnel for civilian government will be chosen by the respective Government agencies," it was eliminated. The clause "the details would be decided by agreement among the agencies concerned" was eliminated because it is obvious.

[The draft was adopted with the foregoing changes.]

[Negotiations with the United States: The Foreign Minister reported on Nomura's meetings with Hull on the 17th and 18th, and gave his opinions on the matter as follows:]

On the 18th, Nomura stated: "Since time will be required to settle the problem of trade, it would be more appropriate to first settle those matters that could lead to a reduction of tension on both sides. I would like to have troops withdrawn from southern Indochina, and in return have the order freezing Japanese assets rescinded."

I felt that such a proposal was an attempt to solve in a piecemeal fashion what should be solved by means of an overall agreement, and that this wouldn't do. So without delay I wired him this morning, "Postpone meeting with Hull until we send instructions," since I felt that we should convey our views to him before he met with Hull. Later I sent Ambassador Nomura the following telegram: "There will be trouble later if we proceed in a piecemeal fashion to settle problems. This method is not satisfactory. Indicate clearly to the United States that when you sent your personal suggestion to Tokyo, Tokyo instructed you that Proposal B must be agreed upon in its entirety. Hereafter proceed with negotiations on the basis of Proposal B. When we say, 'do not obstruct efforts to achieve peace between Japan and China,' we mean that America should suspend aid to Chiang. We will proceed independently with regard to the Tripartite Pact. That is, tell the other party that although the United States says that Japan will be a tool of Germany, Japan intends to act on her own."

Moreover, the feeling of tension that now exists in our country has not been sufficiently reflected in Ambassador Nomura. Also, recently one sees signs that the United States is coming to the view that it does not desire war if an agreement can be reached; but the United States faces the problem of public opinion, and I believe that it is difficult for her to give in and compromise with Japan.

[Attached Document]

*Essentials of Policy Regarding the Administration of the
Occupied Areas in the Southern Regions*

POLICY

In the occupied areas military government will first be established. It will work for the restoration of peace and order, for the rapid acquisition of vital war materials, and for assuring the self-support of our forces.

The question of what nation will finally control the occupied areas, as well as their disposition in the future, will be decided later.

SUMMARY

1. In the functioning of military government, every effort will be made to utilize existing organs of government; existing organizations and popular customs will be respected.

2. The occupying forces will take steps to promote the acquisition and development of vital war materials to the extent that it does not interfere with military operations. Vital war materials developed or acquired in the occupied areas will be included in the planning for materials in Tokyo. We will adopt the principle that whatever is needed by the forces in the field will be allocated to them on the basis of this planning.

3. The Army and Navy will assist in every way in shipping materials to Japan. Moreover, the Army and Navy will endeavor to use fully all vessels that have been requisitioned.

4. Railroads, shipping, harbors, airfields, communications, and postal services will be controlled by the occupation forces.

5. The occupation forces will establish controls over foreign trade and foreign exchange operations; they will especially prevent the flow to the enemy of certain vital materials, such as oil, tin, rubber, tungsten, cinchona, etc.

6. We will endeavor in principle to use currency that has been in circulation in that particular area. When necessary, military scrip printed to look like local currency will be used.

7. In order to acquire war materials and to enable the occupying forces to be self-supporting, our people will be compelled to endure pressures that cannot be avoided; measures for promoting their welfare will be limited to an amount compatible with the objectives stated above.

8. The treatment of Americans, the British, and the Dutch will be such as to get them to cooperate with the military government; those who do not so cooperate will be evacuated or dealt with in other appropriate ways.

The existing interests of Axis nationals will be respected, but efforts will be made to limit the subsequent expansion of such interests.

We will get the overseas Chinese to forsake the Chiang regime and cooperate with us.

The native population will be guided in such a way that they will increase their confidence in the Imperial forces. Premature attempts to encourage independence movements among them should be avoided.

9. Japanese who go to these areas for the first time after the commencement of hostilities should be carefully checked beforehand as to their character. Japanese now in Japan who previously resided in these areas and who wish to return should be given preference.

10. The following provisions will apply in the establishment of military government:

(a) Important provisions relating to military government in the occupied areas will be discussed and decided by the Liaison Conferences between Imperial Headquarters and the Government. Decisions made in

Tokyo will be transmitted to the forces in the occupied areas by the Army and Navy.

(b) Planning and control of the acquisition and development of materials will be vested for the time being in Tokyo agencies under the Planning Board. In carrying out the above provision, Paragraph (a) will be followed.

(c) Our policy toward French Indochina and Thailand will be based on that already adopted, and military government will not be established. What to do in case the situation changes will be decided later.

Note: As Japanese policy toward the occupied areas makes progress, the military governmental structure will either be merged with or converted into a new structure, which will be under the Government.

71ST LIAISON CONFERENCE
November 22, 1941

At this Conference the Foreign Minister tried to get authority to handle the details of the negotiations in the event that the United States accepted Proposal B. Included in Proposal B was a requirement that the United States agree to provide Japan with oil. Foreign Minister Togo had already wired Washington that the amount of oil to be provided must be settled before an agreement would be signed. In the same telegram he informed Nomura that the requirement that the United States not hinder a Japanese-Chinese settlement meant specifically that no aid be sent to Chiang.

Secretary Hull found this last item particularly hard to accept when the two Ambassadors, following instructions, presented Proposal B on November 20. The Secretary was glum, for he knew from intercepted and decoded messages that this was Japan's last try at a settlement. He later wrote that the things America was asked to do "were virtually a surrender."

⟦Time: 2 P.M. to 4 P.M.

⟦The "Wording of the Announcement on the Commencement of Hostilities," the "Essentials of Policy toward Thailand," and "Guaranteeing Proposal B in Negotiations with the United States" were discussed.

⟦"Wording of the Announcement on the Commencement of Hostilities":

⟦The term, "Chuka Minkoku" [Republic of China] is inappropriate. "Kokuri" [National Interest] appears in the Imperial Rescripts on the Sino-Japanese war and the Russo-Japanese war, so further study is needed.

[There is need to exercise caution with regard to China and the United States, so that we will not reach an impasse in the future; hence the last paragraph under 2 and the first paragraph under 3 require some revision. For reasons stated above, the revisions should be made by specialists on documentary language; and these revisions will be adopted later.

[In connection with this, it was agreed that the question of whether there should be a declaration of war was to be studied carefully in terms of methods, legalities, and realities. The majority view was that even though in the end it might be decided that there should be a declaration of war, the method of declaring war required thorough study.]

[Draft of the "Essentials of Policy toward Thailand" (This was adopted unanimously).]

["Guaranteeing Proposal B in the Negotiations with the United States":

[The Foreign Minister stated, "I would like to handle this administratively, since amounts [of oil], etc. are involved"; so the matter was not discussed.

[Army Chief of Staff Sugiyama made a demand as follows: "We need to move quickly on this matter, since there is no time left from the point of view of the Supreme Command."]

[The text of the "Essentials of Policy toward Thailand" has been omitted in this translation. The texts of the other two documents were not available.]

72D LIAISON CONFERENCE
November 26, 1941

The Foreign Minister's report to this Liaison Conference of his conversations with Ambassador Grew differs somewhat from the report that Grew sent to the State Department. Grew reported that Togo said: "The withdrawal of Japanese troops at present stationed in French Indochina to the northern part is in any event the maximum concession Japan can make." Grew also reported that Togo expected American aid to Chiang to cease as soon as Japan and China began negotiations.[42]

Japanese-Soviet relations were touchy at this point. On November 6 the Japanese Government had lodged a protest over the sinking

[42] Grew's version is in State Department, *Foreign Relations of the United States: Japan, 1931–41*, II, 762–63.

of the Kehi Maru *by Soviet mines in the Maritime Danger Zone. Furthermore, the renewal of the Anti-Comintern Pact did not exactly please the Russians.*

Secretary Hull, in a meeting with Ambassadors Nomura and Kurusu on November 22, said he had been in consultation with other governments about possible relaxation of the freezing order if the Japanese Government "could assert control of the situation in Japan as it related to the policy of force and conquest." He made it clear that the embargo on oil would be relaxed gradually, if at all, because of existing stockpiles in Japan. The Japanese armed forces, by contrast, were pressing for an American commitment to provide a large amount of oil. This was one way to make sure that the negotiations could not succeed.

Agenda: Statement of Recent Developments in Negotiations between Japan and the United States; Discussion of the Amount of Oil Guaranteed in Proposal B.

[Time: From 10 A.M. to 12 noon.

[Statement on Japanese-American negotiations by the Foreign Minister:]

The day before yesterday, the 24th, I summoned Ambassador Grew and told him quite clearly that the American position regarding the suspension of aid to Chiang was not clear. I also said:

"The United States has stated that the Japanese army in southern Indochina must not stay in northern Indochina, but must withdraw from that area, too. However, Japan will withdraw completely from French Indochina only when peace has been established between Japan and China. What prompted our forces to move into northern Indochina is different from their reasons for going into southern Indochina.

"It is all right for the United States to act as a mediator for establishing peace between Japan and China; but we cannot agree to anything unless the United States stops interfering in the settlement of the China Incident. In our talks in Washington we want to reach an overall agreement, rather than to settle things piecemeal."

The only reply Grew made to this was, "I will convey that to my Government." [It appears that Grew has not been given any authority in the present negotiations.]

On November 24 there was a report from Ambassador Nomura that the meeting in Washington had been postponed until the 25th. According to newspaper reports, the British, Dutch, and Chinese Ambassadors have been summoned, and they are conferring. I would judge on the basis of this that they will decide what position to take vis-à-vis Japan and send us an answer. I anticipate that the reply will give us a good idea of what to expect.

[The Foreign Minister's statement on the Soviet problem:]

I have asked the Soviet Ambassador the following regarding the *Kehi Maru* incident: "Find out whether the safety devices on the mines were working; and if the safety devices were inoperative, then you must agree to Japan's demands." We have not yet received a reply from the Soviet government.

[Furthermore, on that occasion the Foreign Minister asked him about the Neutrality Pact with the Soviet Union. "Will you grant bases to a third party?" he asked. The Soviet Ambassador replied: "We will not. However, the Neutrality Pact has no provision for third parties, so we will study this matter."]

In the future Japan will have to pay attention to the fact that Litvinov[43] has been sent to the United States. Also, the agreement to continue the Anti-Comintern Pact was signed yesterday, and I think that this will have considerable effect on diplomatic relations.

[Study of guarantees in Proposal B sent to the United States:]

ARMY CHIEF OF STAFF SUGIYAMA: I have spoken about this previously, and I think it is of vital importance. There is need to undertake an immediate study of the guarantees regarding Proposal B. Of course, I believe that negotiations on the basis of Proposal B will not succeed. But in case they should, we must have concrete guarantees written in at the time an agreement is signed. Otherwise there is a danger that our wishes will not be met after an agreement is reached. There is a danger that even if an agreement is reached, time will be spent on the details and we will miss our opportunity. Hence we need to incorporate guarantees in the agreement. Otherwise there is a danger that we will be tricked and that we will fall into an American trap. What has the Foreign Minister done about this?

FOREIGN MINISTER TOGO: Our staff is studying it.

SUGIYAMA: There is no time for staff study. It is necessary to present our demands to the other side.

TOGO: I don't believe it will be possible to get an agreement within the stated period on the figure of ten million tons of oil contained in that proposal. Moreover, hasn't it been said that the Navy has a considerable amount of oil?

DIRECTOR OF THE PLANNING BOARD SUZUKI: I think we will need at least 8 million tons.

[43] Maxim Litvinov, Soviet Ambassador to the United States.

[It was said that it would not be a good idea to make unreasonable demands at this time. The following was decided after an extended discussion: For the time being, oil for next year will be set at the following figures, and it will be gradually increased: 4 million tons from the United States, including aviation gasoline (note: last year 3.3 million tons were imported); 2 million tons from the Dutch East Indies, including aviation gasoline (note: last year Yoshizawa demanded 1.8 million tons). The foregoing figures will be wired to Nomura immediately.]

73D LIAISON CONFERENCE
November 27, 1941

Ambassador Nomura had been told earlier that he should get an agreement by November 25. That day had come and gone, and the reports from Washington suggested that there was practically no chance of Proposal B's being accepted in toto. The next day (Washington time), Secretary Hull had handed the Japanese Ambassadors a document entitled "Outline of Proposed Basis for Agreement between the United States and Japan." Instead of being an American response to Proposal B it was an extreme statement of the American position. It called for the complete withdrawal of Japanese troops from Indochina and China, the abandonment of extraterritorial rights in China, and so on. It was regarded by the Japanese as an ultimatum.

Reports about the Hull note had come in from the naval and military attachés in Washington shortly before this Liaison Conference began. The decision makers in Tokyo assumed that the end of the road had been reached so far as negotiations were concerned; and attention was now focused completely on the war that was about to break out. This meant that another Imperial Conference formally sanctioning war was necessary. On November 26 the Emperor told Prime Minister Tojo that if Japan went to war, it was essential that the country be unified; he inquired whether the Senior Statesmen (i.e., all former Prime Ministers) were in favor of war. He suggested to Tojo that the Senior Statesmen take part in the Imperial Conference scheduled for December 1. Tojo objected to their inclusion in the Imperial Conference on the ground that men who were not vested with political authority should not participate in decision making. One might speculate that he also knew that many of them were apprehensive about the risks involved in a war with the United States. In any case, a compromise arrangement was made, and Tojo met separately with the Senior Statesmen.

[Time: from 2 P.M. to 4 P.M.

[Today the following were discussed: whether or not the Senior Statesmen should participate in the Imperial Conference that will make the final decision on national policy; "Administrative Procedures to be Taken Regarding the Declaration of War"; "Essentials for Guiding Domestic Opinion"; and the draft of the Imperial Rescript announcing the outbreak of war.

[The problem of Senior Statesmen participating in the Imperial Conference: Prime Minister Tojo asked whether a meeting limited to the Senior Statesmen should be held (for details see report of conversations with the Emperor on November 26), or whether there is some other appropriate method. The discussion on this point was as follows:]

As the Prime Minister has stated to the Emperor (according to the report of the conversations between the Emperor and the Prime Minister), it would be inappropriate for the Senior Statesmen to participate in the Imperial Conferences, since those without responsibility would be carrying on discussions with those who bear responsibility. Also, they should not carry on discussions in the presence of the Emperor, since, as the Prime Minister said in his conversations with the Emperor, this would involve responsibility. At the time of the Russo-Japanese war, the decision for war was made by the Cabinet, and then the Emperor sought the advice of the Elder Statesmen. Ito, Matsukata, and others were true Elder Statesmen and different from the present Senior Statesmen.[44] The only qualification the present Senior Statesmen possess is that they once held the post of Prime Minister, and they are not necessarily able men. The recent meetings of the Senior Statesmen were convened on the initiative of the Lord Keeper of the Privy Seal. From the standpoint of secrecy they are not good; for example, information about the proceedings of the Senior Statesmen's conference at the time of the Tojo Cabinet's formation has leaked out. Moreover, it would be a serious matter if, without knowledge of what has transpired and on the basis of abstract thinking, they should overturn policy that the Government and the Supreme Command have adopted after careful deliberation. Accordingly, our conclusion is that the Prime Minister should summon the Senior Statesmen, explain the situation to them, and get them to agree [informally]."

[44] Ito Hirobumi and Matsukata Masayoshi were among the handful of leaders instrumental in modernizing Japan in the late nineteenth and early twentieth centuries. In time they gave up active direction of the Government and became "Elder Statesmen."

[That is, it was unanimously agreed that on November 29 the Senior Statesmen should be summoned to the Imperial Palace, where they would hear explanations by the Prime Minister (the Emperor would not be present). Depending on the convenience of the Palace officials, they would be invited to lunch afterwards. (During the discussions, the Foreign Minister was the only one who stated that the Senior Statesmen could meet in the presence of the Emperor.) The foregoing decision was made in spite of precedent and prevailing opinion, which were contrary to it, and to set the Emperor's mind at ease.

["Administrative Procedures to be Taken Regarding the Declaration of War" and the "Essentials for Guiding Domestic Opinion" were approved.

[Draft of the Imperial Rescript announcing the outbreak of war: It was decided that this should be studied further; and that the Chief Secretary of the Cabinet would first collect suggestions from those who wished to make them and would then revise it.]

[Attached Documents]

Administrative Procedures to Be Taken Regarding the
Declaration of War

In general, the administrative procedures to be taken regarding the declaration of war are as follows:

1. The Liaison Conference will determine the agenda for the Imperial Conference, which will arrive at a decision on the national will to declare war (prior to the Cabinet meeting on November [sic] 1).

2. The agenda for the Imperial Conference decided upon by the Liaison Conference will next be approved by the Cabinet. (December 1, A.M.)

3. The Imperial Conference will decide on the national will to declare war. (December 1, P.M.)

4. On Day Y (X plus 1), after the Cabinet has declared war, the matter will be submitted to the Privy Council for its advice to the Emperor.

5. The Cabinet will decide the following items: (a) after the decision of the Privy Council on the declaration of war has been conveyed to the Emperor, the Emperor will be asked to grant his approval; (b) the Government's statement on the declaration of war; (c) the Cabinet's proclamation indicating the time when a state of war exists; (d) memoranda to all Government offices regarding the publication of "Outline of Developments to Date, and the Policies Adopted by the Government."

6. The following will be put into effect at the same time: (a) the publication of the Imperial Rescript on the declaration of war; (b) publication of the Government's proclamation on the declaration of war; (c) the Cabi-

net's proclamation indicating the time when a state of war exists; (d) memoranda to all Government offices regarding publication of "Outline of Developments to Date, and the Policies Adopted by the Government" (it can be issued immediately after the declaration of war).

Outline for Guiding Domestic Opinion in Connection with Carrying On the War

1. Guidance: Summary [omitted by the transcriber].
2. The following are the specific measures that should be taken: (a) Asking the Emperor to issue the Imperial Rescript on the declaration of war. (b) Indication of the determination of the Government; Government proclamation. (c) An announcement giving the diplomatic background. (d) Convening an emergency session of the Diet, depending on the need; mobilizing the Imperial Rule Assistance Association.

74TH LIAISON CONFERENCE
November 29, 1941

At this Conference the agenda for the Imperial Conference formally sanctioning war was agreed on. There remained the question of what to do about the United States in the interval before the first shot was fired. Foreign Minister Togo understandably wanted to know when the fighting would start, and he finally got this information for the first time at this Conference (from Navy Chief of Staff Nagano). Having gotten this information, the Foreign Minister then proposed to inform the diplomats, but the Conference ruled against him.

[Time: from 4 P.M. to 5 P.M.

[The following were discussed: the agenda for the Imperial Conference that will decide on war; diplomatic policy toward Germany and Italy; domestic and foreign policy with reference to the determination to open hostilities.

[Agenda for the Imperial Conference: Delete "accordingly" from "accordingly, we will commence war against the United States, Great Britain, and the Netherlands" in Paragraph 2 of the draft. The statement by the Minister of Education scheduled to be given during the proceedings will be omitted because it has little direct bearing on the problem.]

[Policy toward Germany and Italy. The Foreign Minister made the following proposal:]

I would like to have the two Ambassadors, Oshima and Horikiri, tell Germany and Italy the following: Japanese-American negotiations are certain to be broken off. We believe that the danger of Japan and the United States resorting to force as a result of this is very great. This might happen unexpectedly in the near future, so we would like to agree on the following:

1. The Empire expects Germany and Italy to declare war against the United States immediately. Germany and Italy will take steps to prepare for this.

2. Japan and Germany, and Japan and Italy, agree not to make peace separately with the United States and Great Britain. [The Foreign Minister said that it would be more advantageous to make separate agreements between Japan and Germany and between Japan and Italy not to conclude a separate peace than to say, "The three countries will not make peace separately." It would be better to have an arrangement whereby, even if Italy should make peace separately in violation of this agreement, Japan and Germany would still be bound by it. This way is more convenient in the light of precedents.]

[There was general agreement regarding the foregoing, and no one was opposed to sending a telegram that evening. However, there were two views concerning the phrase "common enemy." From the point of view of Germany and Italy the phrase would include the Soviet Union, whereas it would not be advantageous for Japan to include the Soviet Union. Still, if the phrase "common enemy" were left in, Germany and Italy would be more likely to find the agreement acceptable; and in this sense it would be to Japan's advantage to leave it in. Finally, it was agreed that there should be a clarifying statement to the effect that the phrase "common enemy" referred to Great Britain and the United States.

[How should diplomacy toward the United States be carried out?]
FOREIGN MINISTER TOGO: It can't be helped.[45]

SOMEONE: I would like to see diplomacy carried out in such a way that we can win the war.

TOGO: Is there enough time left so that we can carry on diplomacy?
NAVY CHIEF OF STAFF NAGANO: We do have enough time.

TOGO: Tell me what the zero hour is. Otherwise I can't carry on diplomacy.

NAGANO: Well, then, I will tell you. The zero hour is ———.[46] There

---

[45] The meaning of Togo's remark is not evident because the person who took these notes has not given us a summary of the debate that preceded it. It may be that Togo had been arguing in favor of sending a final note to the United States declaring war.

[46] He said, in a low voice, "December 8." See *TSM*, VII, 368–69.

is still time, so you had better resort to the kind of diplomacy that will be helpful in winning the war.

SOMEONE: The Japanese people are very excited. If we raise their spirits any more, we will force the United States to step up war preparations; so we should take steps to restrain their excitement.

SOMEONE: That won't do. If we do that, the people will become dispirited.

SOMEONE: Do it only to the extent that they won't get discouraged. It is particularly bad for Government leaders to talk about lowering the spirit of the people.

SOMEONE: I think that the best way to restrain them is to utilize foreign news dispatches.

[Nagano, Shimada, Oka, and others from the Navy strongly urged that "diplomacy should be sacrificed in order to win the war."]

TOGO: I understand. Can't we tell our representatives [in Washington] that our minds are made up? We have told the attachés [he hints that he means the Naval Attaché] that we have made up our minds, haven't we?

NAGANO: We have not told the Naval Attaché.

TOGO: We can't continue to keep our diplomats in the dark, can we?

SOMEONE: Our diplomats will have to be sacrificed. What we want is to carry on diplomacy in such a way that until the very last minute the United States will continue to think about the problem, we will ask questions, and our [real] plans will be kept secret.

TOGO: The situation is critical; I think there is no possibility of a settlement. I will tell our representatives to exert their efforts in diplomacy so that the United States will continue to consider the problem and we will continue to ask questions.

SOMEONE: On this occasion the entire population will have to be like Oishi Kuranosuke.[47]

IMPERIAL CONFERENCE
December 1, 1941

The November 25 deadline for an agreement with the United States had passed. The task force whose mission was to attack Pearl Harbor had set sail, under sealed orders, from Hitokappu Bay in the remote

---

[47] Oishi is one of the principal figures in the celebrated story of the 47 *Ronin* (masterless samurai). Oishi and his fellow conspirators set out to avenge the death of their feudal lord. In order to deceive the intended victim, so that he would not be on his guard, Oishi posed as a dissolute samurai.

Kuriles at 6 P.M. on November 26. The issue of war or peace had been debated at length, and now it was time to formalize the decision that had been reached in the Liaison Conferences.

Agenda: Failure of Negotiations with the United States Based on the "Essentials for Carrying Out the Empire's Policies" approved on November 5; Declaration of War on the United States, Great Britain, and the Netherlands.

[Time: 2:05 P.M. to 4 P.M.]

Statement by Prime Minister Tojo:

With your permission, I will begin the proceedings today.

On the basis of the Imperial Conference decision of November 5, the Army and Navy, on the one hand, devoted themselves to the task of getting everything ready for military operations; while the Government, on the other hand, used every means at its disposal and made every effort to improve diplomatic relations with the United States. The United States not only refused to make even one concession with respect to the position she had maintained in the past, but also stipulated new conditions, after having formed an alliance with Great Britain, the Netherlands, and China. The United States demanded complete and unconditional withdrawal of troops from China, withdrawal of our recognition of the Nanking Government, and the reduction of the Tripartite Pact to a dead letter. This not only belittled the dignity of our Empire and made it impossible for us to harvest the fruits of the China Incident, but also threatened the very existence of our Empire. It became evident that we could not achieve our goals by means of diplomacy.

At the same time, the United States, Great Britain, the Netherlands, and China increased their economic and military pressure against us; and we have now reached the point where we can no longer allow the situation to continue, from the point of view of both our national power and our projected military operations. Moreover, the requirements with respect to military operations will not permit an extension of time. Under the circumstances, our Empire has no alternative but to begin war against the United States, Great Britain, and the Netherlands in order to resolve the present crisis and assure survival.

We have been engaged in the China Incident for more than four years, and now we are going to get involved in a great war. We are indeed dismayed that we have caused His Majesty to worry.

But, on further reflection, I am thoroughly convinced that our military power today is far stronger than it was before the China Incident; that the morale of the officers and men of the Army and Navy is high; that unity in domestic politics is greater; that there is willingness on the part of individuals to make sacrifices for the nation as a whole; and that, as a result, we can anticipate that we will overcome the crisis that confronts the nation.

I should, therefore, like to have you discuss the proposal on the agenda today. I now turn the meeting over to other Ministers and to officers of the Supreme Command, who will make statements about diplomatic negotiations, military affairs, and other matters.

Statement by Foreign Minister Togo on Japanese-American Negotiations:

I will confine my remarks today mostly to the developments in Japanese-American negotiations since the Imperial Conference of November 5. But, if I may, I will first summarize briefly our negotiations prior to that—that is, up to the end of October. They were as follows:

The basis of America's international relations was to adhere firmly to the Four Principles and to demand their application. They were: (1) respect for the territorial integrity and sovereignty of all nations; (2) non-interference in the internal affairs of other countries; (3) non-discrimination in commercial matters; (4) non-disturbance of the status quo in the Pacific, except by peaceful means. Moreover, the United States indicated that she doubted the peaceful intentions of our Empire, objected to our stationing troops in China, advocated the unconditional application of the principle of nondiscrimination in commercial matters in China, and demanded that we make the Tripartite Pact effectively a dead letter. As a result, the negotiations ran into difficulties and finally came to a standstill.

What produced these differences in views between our two countries was the fact that the United States, in the conduct of international relations, adhered firmly to abstract principles that she had traditionally maintained, and urged their application to China and other areas without considering the actual situation in East Asia. We recognized that it was extremely difficult to reach an agreement as long as the United States did not revise her attitude.

However, the present Cabinet believed that it should attempt to improve Japanese-American relations and reach a just settlement. Our Empire made every concession it could, and thereby made a final effort to avert a clash between Japan and the United States. That is, in this spirit we retreated from our proposal of September 25 regarding the three points that had presented the greatest difficulties in our previous negotiations: the interpretation of the right of self-defense under the terms of the Tripartite Pact; the principle of nondiscrimination in commerce; and the withdrawal of troops from China and French Indochina. With reference to the problem of self-defense under the Tripartite Pact, we got the United States to affirm that she would not improperly expand her interpretation of the right of self-defense, and we decided to make a similar affirmation. As for the principle of nondiscrimination in commerce, we stated that we would have no objection to its application in China, as long as it was [uniformly] applied throughout the world. As for the withdrawal of troops, we revised our position as follows: Japanese troops sent to China as a result of the China Incident were to remain for a certain necessary period after the conclusion of peace between Japan and China, but only in a section of North China and Inner Mongolia and on Hainan Island; the troops elsewhere were to begin withdrawal as soon as peace was restored by an agreement between Japan and China, and this was to be completed within two years after the establishment of law and order. With regard to French Indochina: we agreed to respect its territorial integrity, and to withdraw our troops either after the settlement of the China Incident or after the establishment of a just peace in the Far East.

All this was approved by the Imperial Conference of November 5. On the basis of this decision, the Government instructed Ambassador Nomura that at this critical juncture, in order to turn the tide in Japanese-American negotiations that were on the verge of ending in failure, there was no alternative but to arrive at a quick settlement on the basis of this proposal; and that he should inform the United States that our Empire, having endured great hardships to make the maximum concessions possible, earnestly desired the United States to reconsider and cooperate with us for the sake of peace in the Pacific. Following this, negotiations were carried out in Washington. In order to facilitate these negotiations, I met frequently with the American Ambassador in Tokyo. Ambassador Nomura met with Secretary of State Hull on the 7th, with President Roosevelt on the 10th, and again with Secretary of State Hull on the 12th and the 15th. In this way he did his best to press forward with the negotiations. Meanwhile, the Government, in view of the gravity of the situation and in order to do everything possible diplomatically, dispatched Ambassador Kurusu to the United States on the 5th. He arrived in Washington on the 15th; starting on the 17th, he assisted Ambassador Nomura in the negotiations.

The negotiations had already reached their climax. The United

States, starting on the 7th, raised questions on many points, and it appeared that she was trying to sound out our true intentions. Very early in the negotiations the United States had declared her opposition to "Hitlerism," and had demanded that we renounce the use of force. It appeared that the United States continued to doubt our policy regarding the Tripartite Pact; and on this occasion, questioning our peaceful intentions, she demanded that we reaffirm the declaration of peaceful intent that we had made on August 28. In addition, she repeated forcefully that if a Japanese-American agreement were concluded, our Empire would no longer need to continue the Tripartite Pact; and that she wished us either to abandon it or to render it a dead letter.

As for nondiscrimination in commerce, she wanted to eliminate the Japanese provision regarding it—namely, "its application to the whole world." She stressed that the United States had been exerting efforts to restore the freedom of trade. At the same time, she suggested a "Joint Declaration on Economic Policy." This document proposed that the two countries cooperate to restore freedom of trade throughout the world, and that normal trade be restored between the two countries on the basis of a Japanese-American commercial treaty. Moreover, it proposed that complete control of the economy, finance, and money of China be restored to the Chinese Government; and that joint economic development of China be undertaken by the Powers on a cooperative basis.

There was no extended discussion of the problem of withdrawing troops from China. The United States merely indicated disapproval of our maintaining troops perpetually, or for an indefinite period. She indicated her willingness to act as a mediator in establishing direct negotiations between Japan and China if Japan decided to pursue a peaceful policy.

Our Government responded to these proposals in the following manner:

The American desire for a reaffirmation of the declaration of peaceful intentions that we made on August 28 is satisfied in our proposal of September 25, and the present Cabinet has no objection to confirming that proposal now.

We attached a condition to the principle of nondiscrimination in commerce because we wished to see the principle applied throughout the whole world; it is our intention to admit its application in China to the degree that it is applied elsewhere. As for the "Joint Declaration," we find it difficult to accept the proposal because it ignores the actual situation in China. Since we are afraid that the proposal for the joint development of China will mark the beginning of an international control of China, we also find it difficult to accept this. However, we do not object to the American offer of mediation to bring peace between Japan and China.

Ambassador Kurusu participated in the negotiations at this stage; and the two Ambassadors, Nomura and Kurusu, met with the President on the 17th, and with Secretary of State Hull on the 18th, 20th, 21st, 22d, and 26th. During the meetings on the 17th and 18th[48] President Roosevelt indicated a desire to see peace between Japan and the United States. He said that he had no intention of meddling with the China Question, and that he merely wished to act as a go-between. On the other hand, Secretary of State Hull stressed time and again that as long as Japan was allied with Germany, Japanese-American negotiations would be difficult; hence this basic difficulty must first be removed. Although the two sides discussed matters fully, it became evident that the obstacles were still the Tripartite Pact, the principles of nondiscrimination in trade, and the China Question.

On the 20th we presented a new proposal. We simplified our earlier proposal, which had formed the basis of negotiations, because it had a propagandistic tone; and we removed the question of non-discrimination in trade, since it had been difficult to reach an agreement on this principle. We also eliminated mention of the Tripartite Pact from our proposal, on the theory that we would wait for the other side to make a suggestion on this question. Regarding the China Question, we simply tried to prevent the United States from interfering in the achievement of peace between Japan and China, on the theory that this problem should be taken up by means of direct negotiations between these two countries. That is, the details of our proposal were as follows:

1. The Governments of Japan and the United States agree that neither of them shall undertake an armed advance into the regions of South Asia and the Western Pacific, except for French Indochina.

2. The Governments of Japan and the United States shall cooperate to assure the acquisition of materials they both need in the Netherlands East Indies.

3. The Governments of Japan and the United States shall mutually restore their commercial relations to those that existed prior to the freezing of assets. The Government of the United States agrees to supply Japan with a required quantity of oil.

4. The Government of the United States will refrain from actions

[48] The Ambassadors saw the President only on the 17th.

prejudicial to Japan's endeavors to restore peace between Japan and China.

5. The Government of Japan agrees to withdraw its troops now stationed in French Indochina, either upon the restoration of peace between Japan and China or upon the establishment of a just peace in the Pacific area. The Government of Japan declares that it is prepared to move its troops now stationed in the southern part of Indochina to the northern part of that territory if the present draft proposal is agreed upon.

In response to this proposal the United States said that unless Japan clarified her attitude toward the Tripartite Pact and affirmed her peaceful intentions, it would be difficult for the United States to stop giving aid to Chiang. The President's offer to act as a go-between was conditional on Japan's adopting a policy of peace.

Our reply to this was that it was inconsistent for the United States to continue to give aid to Chiang and obstruct the establishment of peace, even though direct negotiations between Japan and China would begin if the United States were to act as an intermediary for peace, the President bringing the two parties together; and we asked them to reconsider the matter.

However, the United States, even though she voiced no objection to the idea that Japan and the United States would assume positions of leadership in East Asia and the Western hemisphere respectively and stated that she desired to arrive at a peaceful settlement in the Pacific area, refused to discontinue aid to Chiang. In addition, she reiterated her stand toward the Tripartite Pact. She gave no indication of a willingness to compromise.

Meanwhile, the American Government conferred with representatives of Great Britain, Australia, the Netherlands, and Chungking. On the 22nd, Secretary Hull stated that these countries might restore normal trade relations if it became evident that Japan would pursue a policy of peace; but that for the moment they intended to proceed slowly in this matter. He said, moreover, that the withdrawal of troops only from French Indochina would not be sufficient to improve the critical situation in the South Pacific area. He also disclosed that the time was not ripe for the President to serve as an intermediary between Japan and China.

After that the United States Government continued to confer with the representatives of the other countries; and on the 26th Secretary Hull told our two Ambassadors that he had carefully studied our new proposal of the 20th and conferred with the various countries concerned, but that he regretfully concluded that he could not agree to it. As a compromise between the American proposal of June and our proposal of September, he first suggested that the so-called Four Principles (however, the fourth Principle was changed to "international cooperation and conciliation for the prevention of disputes") be affirmed; and secondly, he sent us a proposal containing the following provisions, which were to form the basis for future negotiations:

1. The two Governments of Japan and the United States will endeavor to conclude a multilateral nonaggression pact between the British Empire, the Netherlands, China, the Soviet Union, and Thailand.

2. The two Governments of Japan and the United States will endeavor to conclude an agreement among the Japanese, American, British, Chinese, Dutch, and Thai Governments to respect the territorial integrity of French Indochina and to confer immediately on the steps that should be taken if the territorial integrity of French Indochina were threatened. Each of the governments party to the agreement will endeavor to avoid seeking preferential treatment in trade and economic relations with French Indochina and to establish the principle of nondiscrimination.

3. The Government of Japan will withdraw all forces (military, naval, air, and police) from China and French Indochina.

4. The two Governments will not support, militarily, politically, or economically, any government in China except the Chungking Government.

5. The two Governments will give up extraterritorial rights (including International Settlements and rights based on the Boxer Protocol) in China, and will persuade other countries to do the same.

6. The two Governments will negotiate a commercial treaty based on reciprocal most-favored-nation treatment and reduction of trade barriers (raw silk will be put on the free list).

7. The two Governments will mutually end the freezing of assets.

8. The two Governments will confer on the stabilization of the yen-dollar rate, and each country will provide one-half of the funds for that purpose.

9. The two Governments agree that no agreement that has been concluded with a third power will be interpreted by them in such a way as to contradict the basic objective of this treaty—that is, the maintenance of peace in the entire Pacific region.

10. Other countries will be persuaded to adhere to the above principles.

I understand that our two Ambassadors pointed out the unreasonable character of these provisions and lodged a strong protest; but Secretary Hull indicated no willingness to compromise. It appears that when our two Ambassadors met with the President on the 27th, the President stated that he still hoped that Japanese-American negotiations could be brought to a successful conclusion; but he added that cold water had been dashed on the efforts because Japanese forces had moved into southern Indochina in July while the negotiations were going on, and he felt that negotiations were still hampered, according to recent reports. He said that even if the two countries should attempt to break the deadlock with a *modus vivendi*, such a temporary solution would ultimately be useless as long as the two countries did not agree on basic principles.

There are several provisions in the American proposal that we could accept: the problem of commerce (Provisions 6, 7, and 8) and the abolition of extraterritoriality in China (Provision 5). But our Empire could not agree to those on China and French Indochina (Provisions 2 and 3), withdrawal of recognition of the National Government (Provision 4), non-recognition of the Tripartite Pact (Provision 9), and the multilateral nonaggression pact (Provision 1). Compared to previous American proposals, this one is a conspicuous retrogression; and we had to recognize that it was an unreasonable proposal, which completely disregarded the negotiations that had gone on for half a year.

In short, the United States Government has persistently adhered to its traditional doctrines and principles, ignored realities in East Asia, and tried to force on our Empire principles that she herself could not easily carry out. Despite the fact that we made a number of concessions, she maintained her original position throughout the negotiations, lasting for seven months, and refused to budge even one step. I believe that America's policy toward Japan has consistently been to thwart the establishment of a New Order in East Asia, which is our immutable policy. We must recognize that if we were to accept their present proposal, the international position of our Empire would be reduced to a status lower than it was prior to the Manchurian Incident, and our very survival would inevitably be threatened.

First, China under Chiang's control would increasingly come to rely on Britain and the United States; our Empire would betray its faith toward the National Government of China, and our friendship with China would be marred for a long time to come. We would be forced to retreat completely from the mainland, and as a result our position in Manchuria would necessarily be weakened. Any hope of settling the China Incident would be swept away, root and branch.

Second, Britain and the United States would gain control over these regions. The prestige of our Empire would fall to the ground, and our role as stabilizer would be destroyed. Our great undertaking, the establishment of a New Order in East Asia, would be nipped in the bud.

Third, the Tripartite Pact would be reduced to a dead letter, and the reputation of our Empire abroad would decline.

Fourth, the attempt to control our Empire by including the Soviet Union in a multilateral agreement would magnify our problems along the northern border.

Fifth, the principle of nondiscrimination in trade, and other principles, should not necessarily be rejected out of hand; but the attempt to apply them only to the Pacific area is nothing but a way of carrying out a policy to benefit Britain and the United States, and this limited application would present a great obstacle to our acquiring vital materials.

In short, one must say that it was virtually impossible for us to accept their proposal; and even if we were to continue negotiations on the basis of this proposal in order to get the United States to withdraw it, it would be almost impossible for us to obtain what we seek.

[A document tracing the course of Japanese-American negotiations from April to November 1941, which was drafted by the Foreign Office on November 28, 1941, is omitted—Editor.]

Statement by Navy Chief of Staff Nagano:
I respectfully make my statement, on behalf of the two Chiefs of Staff.

The Army and Navy sections of the Supreme Command, on the basis of "Essentials for Carrying Out the Empire's Policies," approved on November 5, and in close coordination with the policies of the Government, have pushed forward preparations for military and naval operations. We are now in a position to begin these operations, according to predetermined plans, as soon as we receive the Imperial Command to resort to force.

Meanwhile, the United States, Great Britain, and the Netherlands have steadily strengthened their defenses; and they have gradually become better prepared, especially in the South Pacific. However, we judge that their present state of preparedness is not greatly different from what we had anticipated; and hence we are convinced that it will present no hindrance to our launching military and naval operations, and that we will be able to proceed as we have planned.

With regard to the Soviet Union, we are maintaining strict vigilance, along with appropriate diplomatic measures; but at present, judging from the deployment of their forces, we need not feel a sense of insecurity.

In this most serious crisis since the founding of our country all of the officers and men in the task forces of the Army and Navy have extremely high morale and are prepared to lay down their lives for their country. Once the Imperial Command is given, they will undertake their assignments. I hope Your Majesty will feel assured on this point.

Statement by Minister for Home Affairs Tojo [concurrently Prime Minister and War Minister]:

I would like to speak on popular movements relating to Japanese-American problems and on measures for dealing with these movements.

When we take an overall view of popular opinion relating to Japanese-American problems, we conclude that the people in general are aware that our nation, in view of the present world situation, stands at a crossroad, one road leading to glory and the other to decline. They have shown an extraordinary interest in the diplomatic negotiations being carried out by the Government. Even though the Americans have given no indication that they would reconsider, and even though this has led to a rupture in diplomatic negotiations and to the outbreak of war, they are prepared to accept this as an inevitable development. They are displaying the spirit characteristic of the Japanese people; and they are truly determined to undergo all manner of hardships, and to overcome adversity by united action.

The so-called nationalistic organizations have advocated a strong foreign policy; and once diplomatic negotiations end in failure, they will very likely demand that we move southward at once. Even the owners of small and medium-sized enterprises, whose livelihood has been much affected by the recent strengthening of economic controls —to say nothing of the laboring and peasant classes—are clearly aware of the position in which our country finds itself, and their spirits are high. It appears that they tend to want the Government to take an unambiguous position in executing a strong policy. There are, however, some within our large nation who would like to avoid war as much as possible at this time; but even these people have made up their minds that as long as the United States refuses to acknowledge our legitimate position, does not remove the economic blockade, and refuses to abandon her policy of oppressing Japan, our moving southward is inevitable; and if this action leads to a clash between Japan and the United States, this also cannot be helped.

To ensure that we will be able to maintain internal security in case an emergency situation arises following the rupture of Japanese-American negotiations, we have begun to make detailed plans for the more stringent measures that will be taken. Preparations for some of these are completed, and we are beginning to implement them:

First, we have especially strengthened our controls over those who are antiwar and antimilitary, such as Communists, rebellious Koreans, certain religious leaders, and others who we fear might be a threat to the public order. We believe that in some cases we might have to subject some of them to preventive arrest.

Second, there are the nationalistic organizations. Some of these tend to be very excitable; they are rash, and they may resort to violence. We believe they should be kept under observation and control; it may be necessary to temporarily detain those who would disturb the public peace. Accordingly, we plan to do everything to provide adequate protection for the Senior Statesmen and those political and financial leaders who are regarded by extremists as being pro-British and pro-American, as well as for foreign diplomats and their staffs, and for law-abiding foreigners.

Third, there is the control of rumors. We must be prepared for many rumors, given the serious nature of the situation. To stabilize the views held by the people, it will be necessary to guide public opinion, and at the same time to exercise rather strict controls over it.

Fourth, as for foreigners of whom there is some suspicion, we have completed all of our investigations; we believe it will be necessary to round them up and detain them when the time comes.

Fifth, with respect to various crimes that will arise in the confusion of war, we have finished conferring with the Minister of Justice. We have given thought to various measures, especially making penalties more stringent, simplifying criminal trial procedure, and so on.

Sixth, we have already completed plans and preparations for the mobilization and deployment of police officials and firemen, who will be responsible for dealing with emergencies.

Seventh, we can anticipate that in a period of emergency the people are bound to be uneasy for a time because of food and monetary problems. We are paying particular attention to trends in attitudes among the people.

We have touched on the main points concerning the maintenance of public peace and security. We officials of the Ministry of Home Affairs are cooperating with other agencies concerned, and we anticipate that all measures for dealing with the emergency will prove to be adequate.

Gist of the Statement by Minister of Finance Kaya Concerning the Estimate of Our Long-Term Financial and Monetary Capacity in Connection with a War Against Great Britain and the United States:

Ever since the outbreak of the China Incident, the national budget has gradually grown; and this fiscal year the budget has reached ¥7.99 billion for ordinary expenditures plus ¥5.88 billion in emergency military expenditures (portion approved by the 76th Diet Session), making a total of more than ¥13.2 billion (excluding the expenditure approved by the 77th Diet Session). However, we have maintained large tax collections and public savings, thanks to the efforts of various institutions and the people, and thus we have been able to manage successfully. However, now that we are going to begin military operations in the South, it is evident that we will need large supplementary military appropriations; and many have expressed doubt that our national economy can bear such large military costs, especially when the probability of a prolonged war is high, and have speculated on the danger of harmful changes in the monetary situation, especially the vicious effects of inflation.

However, to begin with, a substantial portion of war expenditures is used to secure needed materials, utilize equipment, and employ skilled labor. That is, what is required is that we will be able to supply the needed materials and at the same time be able to maintain the people's livelihood at the minimum level. As long as the necessary materials can be supplied, and as long as the portion of the national income directed toward [civilian] consumption does not exceed the amount of goods available for the people's livelihood (we arrange this by absorbing surplus buying power through increased taxes and savings and consequently making sure that war expenditures put into circulation are recovered and used as a source of funds for more war expenditures and for welfare), the financial and monetary system can continue to operate for any number of years.

Moreover, the recovery of funds through increases in taxes and savings is possible, provided the Government's policy regarding the national economy is appropriate, and provided the people, aware that the State hovers between glory and decline, will exert great effort. We would anticipate that the Government would not institute a bad economic policy. As for the people making a great effort, we cannot say that the subjects of this Imperial State are incapable of it. Therefore, our judgment must be that it is possible [to carry on the war financially]. In short, if we are unable to supply the necessary materials to carry on military operations and at the same time maintain the people's livelihood, the national economy cannot help but go bankrupt regardless of the fiscal and monetary policies of the government. This is the reason we conclude that if it is possible to meet the demand for vital materials, equipment, and skilled labor, our fiscal and monetary system can be sustained.

In the past the southern areas that will be the scene of military operations imported a considerable quantity of goods; when we occupy these areas the imports will cease. Accordingly, to enable their economies to function smoothly, we should provide them with goods; but our country does not have enough reserve capacity to do this. Hence for quite a long time it will not be possible for us to be concerned with the livelihood of the peoples in these areas. It must be said that even if we issue military scrip and other types of currency to secure goods and labor in these areas, it will be difficult to maintain their value. That is, it will be necessary for us to adopt a policy of self-sufficiency in these areas as much as possible, to keep the shipment of goods from our country to the minimum amount necessary to maintain peace and order and to secure labor services there, and to disregard the decline in the value of paper money and the economic dislocation that will result from it. Of course, we realize that in these areas the cultural level of the people is low, and the areas are rich in natural products, so the maintenance of the people's livelihood should be easy, compared to the same problem in China.

On fiscal and monetary measures to be taken during the emergency:

In the event that the outbreak of war seems imminent, or in the event that war has broken out and certain parts of our country are attacked by enemy planes, we should pursue the following emergency fiscal policies in order to prevent disruption of our national economy, to enable industry to go forward and funds to be accumulated, to maintain order among the people living in a wartime situation and thereby to keep the people in a state of tranquility.

(1) Policy for dealing with bank deposits: There will be no restrictions on withdrawal of bank deposits (bank moratorium). The Bank of Japan, the Bank of Korea, and the Bank of Formosa will take positive steps to supply financial institutions with the funds necessary to pay their depositors, and at the same time will guarantee the obligations of these financial institutions. In this way we will endeavor to eliminate feelings of insecurity among depositors.

(2) On dealing with obligations of war-damage victims to financial institutions: In the event that there are air raids, and those who own enterprises in the affected areas suffer either direct or indirect losses and cannot honor the promissory notes they have issued or repay loans from financial institutions, there will be undesirable effects on the industrial and financial communities. Consequently, in order to make these promissory notes liquid, the Bank of Japan, the Bank of Korea, and the Bank of Formosa will actively make funds available by discounting these notes and by other means. In this way the stability of the economic system will be assured.

(3) Financial protection for vital industries: If firms engaged in vital manufacture suddenly lose their credit standing through no fault of their own, causing lending institutions to demand repayment of loans, and if this might result in spreading a sense of economic insecurity and in lowering production levels, the Japan Industrial Bank or the Japan Hypothec Bank will underwrite or guarantee such loans. In this way the stability of the industrial world will be assured.

(4) Facilitating withdrawal of deposits in war-damaged areas or in places of refuge in order to assure funds for the maintenance of [the people's] livelihood: we must avoid the inconvenience that would be caused if the places of business of financial institutions were bombed, or if residents of an area under attack moved to a safe area, and depositors lost contact with banks with which they had done business and could no longer withdraw their deposits. Accordingly, all banks will assume the financial obligations of other banks and financial institutions located in areas specified by the Minister of Finance, and will pay out funds (the amount will be limited to what is necessary to maintain the livelihood of the depositor). In this way, depositors in war-damaged areas will be protected, and the threat to their livelihood will be removed.

(5) Stock market policy: If there is a danger that prices on the stock exchange will tumble (because of general fear and lessened appeal) and cause dislocations in stock transactions, the present pol-

icy of unlimited buying by the Japan Joint Securities Corporation will be stepped up. Everything will be done to provide the necessary funds for this operation. Depending on the need, a law regulating stock prices will be put into effect.

Moreover, in dealing with the above matter, regulations governing the circulation of funds and guarantee of obligations, as stated in Article 11 of the National Mobilization Law, will be put into effect.

We are presently negotiating with various Government agencies regarding emergency steps to be taken to protect the shipment of currency and to relax restrictions on communications among financial institutions. We will take other appropriate steps when necessary.

Gist of the Statement by Minister of Agriculture Ino:
In strengthening our determination in light of the worsening international situation, our basic premise must obviously be to assure that our people will have the minimum of nourishment necessary to maintain life, given the present food situation.

It is natural that in considering food resources we should stress rice and wheat; but it is absolutely necessary that we secure supplies of protein and fat, as well as starches, for the health of the nation. Accordingly, we must take an overall look at the food situation from this point of view.

This is the present situation with respect to food supply: First, when we look at rice and wheat, we see that in the 1942 rice year (November 1, 1941 to October 31, 1942) it is estimated the supply will be about 73.9 million *koku* (of which 8.39 million *koku* will represent carry-over, plus estimated second crop of 55.45 million *koku*[49] and anticipated import of 10 million *koku* from Korea and Formosa), while the demand will be about 85 million *koku* (of which 79 million *koku* will be consumed, 900,000 *koku* will be exported, and 5 million *koku* will be carried over into next year); so there will be a deficit of about 11.1 million *koku*. It will be necessary to solve this problem by securing foreign rice, and consequently we are currently working out concrete measures to do this. Nevertheless, one can imagine that the import of foreign rice would become difficult as the international situation becomes more tense; hence we conclude that we will need

[49] In the southern parts of Japan the weather makes it possible to harvest two crops of rice a year. Ino presumably means that the carry-over is that left from the first crop. However, the second rice crop is seldom larger than 30 per cent of the first crop (since only part of the cultivated area is used), so it would seem that the transcriber of the Conference misunderstood the breakdown of rice sources.

to try to become self-sufficient. We have therefore decided on war-time emergency food controls. In concrete terms, we plan to increase the production of wheat, sweet potatoes and white potatoes, and at the same time strengthen regulations pertaining to consumption, such as reducing rice grown for sake brewing. We will try to make up the deficit in this way, but it will still be absolutely necessary to make sure of the supply of rice from Korea and Formosa. Accordingly, I need not emphasize on this occasion that the establishment of a uni-fied food policy, embracing the home islands and overseas territories, together with better coordination and the procurement of adequate shipping, are prerequisites.

Furthermore, regarding the import of foreign rice, we must take various steps. It is very important in dealing with the problem of im-proving food supply to provide the people with a sense of economic stability. Hence at this point we must make a determined effort to im-port foreign rice by securing cooperation from many quarters. If we are assured the desired amount of foreign rice, we will be able to stockpile an equivalent amount of rice.

Second, when we look at the sources of protein and fat, it is evident that the supply of fish products and animal products, which provide them, will be greatly diminished because of regulations restricting the consumption of petroleum, the requisitioning of fishing vessels, the decline in the supply of animal feed, and the shortage of ships to bring soybeans, seeds, and nuts for making oil from Manchuria and China. Therefore, we must attempt to increase the output of fish products as much as possible by using substitute fuels, securing fuel from the Navy, and exploiting inland waters. In the case of animal products, we must endeavor to increase the number of cows and pigs by using home-produced animal feed. As for soybeans, seeds, and nuts for making oil, we must try to secure the anticipated amount from Manchuria and China by getting priorities on shipping.

The above are emergency measures to cope with the present food situation. Permanent measures appropriate for a long-term war are embodied in "Facilities for Strengthening Self-Sufficiency in Food-stuffs," which has already been approved; "Overall Food Plan," em-bracing Japan, Manchuria and China, which is presently being worked out; and "Plan to Increase Fisheries Production." If the co-operation of various Government departments can be obtained, and these plans are carried out fully, we will be able to assure the long-term supply of food at a minimum level necessary to sustain the life of the nation.

[There followed questions and answers:]

PRESIDENT OF THE PRIVY COUNCIL HARA: We are discussing a very grave subject; but it was previously taken up by an Imperial Conference, and every step that could be taken has been taken. Therefore, I have nothing in particular to add. Still, since the subject is a grave one, I will ask a few questions.

First of all, the reply that the American Secretary of State handed to our two Ambassadors is indeed an unreasonable one. I understand that the two Ambassadors argued with him about the unreasonable points in it. Now the United States, in supporting the Chungking regime, has demanded that we withdraw troops from all of China; I would like to know whether Manchukuo is included in the term China? Did our two Ambassadors confirm this point? What is their understanding of it?

FOREIGN MINISTER TOGO: The point that you have now raised was not discussed in the meeting held on the 26th. However, as to whether Manchukuo would or would not be included in China, the American proposal of April 16 stated that they would recognize the state of Manchukuo, so Manchukuo would not be part of China. On the other hand, if we look at this in light of the fact that there has been a change in their position, that they look upon Chungking as the one and only legitimate regime, and that they want to destroy the Nanking regime, they may retract what they have said previously.

HARA: It appears, according to a radio broadcast, that our two Ambassadors are to confer with Hull today. If this is true, who took the initiative in these negotiations? If I assume that our side sought to confer with Hull, then why did we take this step?

TOGO: They have not told us when the meeting is to take place. Having studied the American proposal, we cannot let it go by without taking further action. I have ordered the two Ambassadors: "Tell the United States that the Japanese proposal of November 25 was a just one; that we find it difficult to understand the position the United States has taken in the past, and that she ought to reexamine her stand."[50] Because of this, I think it is quite conceivable that our Ambassadors might have sought a meeting with Hull.[51]

HARA: I would like to question the Supreme Command. It is indeed

[50] This must be in error. Togo was probably referring to the Japanese note of November 20.

[51] The Japanese Ambassadors met with Secretary Hull that day and discussed the possibility that the United States might reexamine her position; but Hull firmly stated that the American proposal of November 26 must stand.

gratifying that preparations for commencing hostilities have been completed. According to recent reports from Britain and the United States, those countries are stepping up their military preparedness in the Far East. It appears that they are increasing the number of warships. If this is so, how much of an increase is there? Will it have an adverse effect on our operations?

NAGANO, NAVY CHIEF OF STAFF: The distribution of American strength is still 40 percent in the Atlantic and 60 percent in the Pacific. Recent activity is confined to Great Britain. The present British naval strength in the Indian Ocean area is as follows: at Hong Kong, 1 B-class cruiser and 3 destroyers; at Singapore, 4 B-class cruisers, 6 destroyers, and 1 submarine; in Australia, 1 A-class cruiser, 5 B-class cruisers, and 4 destroyers; at Colombo, 1 aircraft carrier, 3 A-class cruisers, 4 B-class cruisers, and 4 destroyers; at Bombay, 1 battleship, 3 A-class cruisers, 1 B-class cruiser, and 2 destroyers; at Mombasa, 3–4 battleships, 1 aircraft carrier, 1 A-class cruiser, 5 B-class cruisers, and 5 destroyers; in the Red Sea: 1–2 battleships, 1 destroyer, and 1 submarine.

Because Germany and Italy have become somewhat less active, and particularly because the Italian Navy has become passive, the British Navy has recently acquired reserve power and is gradually adding to its strength in the Orient. At present they are sending the following into the Indian Ocean area: two battleships for certain, and four battleships less certain.

The purpose of this increase is to protect commerce in the Indian Ocean, to prepare for hostilities against Japan, and to protect the ships from German and Italian submarines. Some people say that the increase in the number of battleships, in particular, was brought about by their transfer to this area in order to avoid damage by German planes. As for the strengthening of land forces, it appears certain that 2,000 Canadian troops were landed in Hong Kong.

Thus there has been some strengthening of their forces; but this does not call for changes in the deployment of our forces. It will have no effect on our operations.

HARA: What is the situation with reference to the Army? May I assume that the increase in the number of enemy troops is still within the limits anticipated by the Supreme Command?

SUGIYAMA, ARMY CHIEF OF STAFF: There has been a 2,000-man reinforcement of Hong Kong, as reported by Navy Chief of Staff Nagano. Since our previous Imperial Conference they have landed about 6,000 to 7,000 men in Singapore; and there are reports of additional troops in Burma. But there appears to have been no large-scale buildup.

We have assumed in our planning to date that something like this would occur. It will have no effect on our operations, since we have set up everything in such a way that an increase of this magnitude will be of no consequence.

HARA: Will Thailand ally herself with Japan or with Great Britain? What is the outlook here? What's going to happen if Thailand opposes us? What are you going to do?

TOJO: Concerning Thailand, it is our thought, based on the policy approved by the Imperial Conference of November 5, that we will deal with the situation just prior to our sending in troops. It is uncertain which side Thailand will choose. Thailand herself is in a quandary. It is our hope to bring her in on our side by peaceful means; in order to do this, early [aggressive] action is undesirable, but late action will also have harmful effects. Accordingly, we intend to broach the matter just before we begin the war, and to make her agree to our demands. It is our plan to do everything to prevent her from resisting, even though we may have to use force if worse comes to worst.

HARA: The Minister of Home Affairs has just told us in some detail what effect the war will have on the domestic scene. There is one thing I don't understand, and that is what will happen in the event of air raids. It's admirable that you are providing a good deal of training for emergencies, such as air-raid drills, in order to avoid damage as much as possible. But in the event of a conflagration, can we bring it under control, given the kind of buildings in Tokyo, even though we may try to prevent it from spreading? What are we going to do if a large fire should break out in Tokyo? Do you have a plan to cope with it?

SUZUKI, DIRECTOR OF THE PLANNING BOARD: Let me tell you some of the things we currently have in mind. First, we have enough food stored. Next, we hope that some of the people whose homes are burned can seek refuge elsewhere. As for those who must remain, we are planning to put up simple shelters.

HARA: It is not enough merely to have given some thought to the matter. Your plans are inadequate. I hope that you will be fully prepared. I won't ask any more questions.

Now I will give my views.

In negotiating with the United States, our Empire hoped to maintain peace by making one concession after another. But to our surprise, the American position from beginning to end was to say what

Chiang Kai-shek wanted her to say, and to emphasize those ideals that she had stated in the past. The United States is being utterly conceited, obstinate, and disrespectful. It is regrettable indeed. We simply cannot tolerate such an attitude.

If we were to give in, we would give up in one stroke not only our gains in the Sino-Japanese and Russo-Japanese wars, but also the benefits of the Manchurian Incident. This we cannot do. We are loath to compel our people to suffer even greater hardships, on top of what they have endured during the four years since the China Incident. But it is clear that the existence of our country is being threatened, that the great achievements of the Emperor Meiji would all come to nought, and that there is nothing else we can do. Therefore, I believe that if negotiations with the United States are hopeless, then the commencement of war, in accordance with the decision of the previous Imperial Conference, is inevitable.

I would like to make a final comment: there is no doubt that initial operations will result in victory for us. In a long-term war, however, it is necessary to win victories on the one hand, while, on the other hand, we keep the people in a tranquil state of mind. This is indeed the greatest undertaking since the opening of our country in the 19th century. We cannot avoid a long-term war this time, but I believe that we must somehow get around this and bring about an early settlement. In order to do this, we will need to start thinking now about how to end the war. Our nation, governed by our magnificent national structure [*kokutai*], is, from a spiritual point of view, certainly unsurpassed in all the world. But in the course of a long-term war, there will be some people who will fall into erroneous ways. Moreover, foreign countries will be actively engaged in trying to undermine the morale of the people. It is conceivable that even patriotic individuals will on occasion attempt to do the same. It will be very difficult to deal with these people. I believe that it is particularly important to pay attention to our psychological solidarity. We must be very concerned about this. Be sure you make no mistakes in handling the inner turmoil of the people.

I believe that the proposal before us cannot be avoided in the light of present circumstances, and I put my trust in officers and men whose loyalty is supreme. I urge you to make every effort to keep the people in a tranquil state of mind, in order to carry on a long-term war.

TOJO: The Government is fully aware of the importance of your remarks and views, and is doing everything it can along these lines.

We are fully prepared for a long war. We would also like to do everything we can in the future to bring the war to an early conclusion. We also intend, in the event of a long war, to do our utmost to keep the people tranquil, and particularly to maintain the social order, prevent social disorganization, and block foreign conspiracies.

We have now completed our questions and remarks. I judge that there are no objections to the proposal before us.

I would now like to make one final comment. At the moment our Empire stands at the threshold of glory or oblivion. We tremble with fear in the presence of His Majesty. We subjects are keenly aware of the great responsibility we must assume from this point on. Once His Majesty reaches a decision to commence hostilities, we will all strive to repay our obligations to him, bring the Government and the military ever closer together, resolve that the nation united will go on to victory, make an all-out effort to achieve our war aims, and set His Majesty's mind at ease.

I now adjourn the meeting.

[During today's Conference, His Majesty nodded in agreement with the statements being made, and displayed no signs of uneasiness. He seemed to be in an excellent mood, and we were filled with awe.]

75TH LIAISON CONFERENCE
December 4, 1941

The decision made at this Conference, regarding the note to be sent to the United States, resulted in a long document composed by the Foreign Ministry and delivered by Ambassadors Nomura and Kurusu to Secretary Hull on December 7, after the bombs had fallen on Pearl Harbor. The note showed the bitter frame of mind in which it had been conceived; it charged that although Japan had been conciliatory and patient, "The American Government, always holding fast to unrealistic theories and refusing to yield an inch on its impractical principles, caused undue delay in the negotiations." It accused the United States, in coalition with Britain and others, of seeking to maintain a dominant position in Eastern Asia and to destroy Japan's position. Under such a situation, it said, Japan "cannot but consider that it is impossible to reach an agreement through further negotiations."

As was brought out in this Conference, the timing of the delivery of the long note was important. The decoding and typing of the note were delayed in Washington, apparently because secretaries and typists were not allowed to handle the note due to the need to main-

*tain secrecy. Hence the diplomatic staff, whose forte was certainly not
typing, had to get the note ready for delivery to the State Department.
The Ambassadors handed the note to Secretary Hull about one hour
after the attack on Pearl Harbor. An appalled and angry Secretary of
State called it a statement "crowded with infamous falsehoods and
distortions—infamous falsehoods and distortions on a scale so huge
that I never imagined until today that any government on this planet
was capable of uttering them."*

[Time: 2 P.M. to 4 P.M.

There was a discussion of "What Policy Manchukuo Should Adopt
Following the Outbreak of War," "On Dealing with the Netherlands,"
and "Final Communication to the United States."

["What Policy Manchukuo Should Adopt Following the Outbreak
of War" was approved as drafted. However, [provisions for] the
Netherlands East Indies were added. "On Dealing with the Netherlands" was adopted as drafted.

[The "Final Communication to the United States":]

FOREIGN MINISTER TOGO: I would like to include the following in
the final diplomatic communication we will send to the United States
Government: the American position, Japan's response to this, and the
contents of the Imperial Rescript announcing the declaration of war.
In this way we will bring things to an end and sever diplomatic relations.

SOMEONE: State it in such a way that it will not be the final word,
but that there will be some room for negotiations.

NAVY CHIEF OF STAFF NAGANO: There is no time for that.

TOGO: We have time to send one last statement, but no more. If we
rework this draft communication to sever diplomatic relations, send it
by wire tomorrow afternoon, the 5th, and allow the 6th for translation, it will be delivered on the right day.

SOMEONE: The Foreign Minister can word the text on the basis of
the draft. As for the time when it should be delivered to them: if it
is too early, it will allow them time to get ready; on the other hand,
if it is too late, there will be no point in delivering the note. At any
rate, the most important thing now is to win the war. So the time of
delivery must be coordinated with the requirements of the Supreme
Command.

[In this way it was decided that the text would be left up to the
Foreign Minister; and that the times when the telegram should be

sent and the note delivered would be determined by conferences between the Foreign Minister and the Supreme Command.]

[The texts of the documents "What Policy Manchukuo Should Adopt Following the Outbreak of War" and "On Dealing with the Netherlands" have been omitted in this translation because they do not deal specifically with American-Japanese relations.]

Appendix A

"DRAFT UNDERSTANDING"

Proposal Presented to the Department of State Through the Medium of Private American and Japanese Individuals on April 9, 1941[1]

The Governments of the United States and of Japan accept joint responsibility for the initiation and conclusion of a general agreement disposing the resumption of our traditional friendly relations.

Without reference to specific causes of recent estrangement, it is the sincere desire of both Governments that the incidents which led to the deterioration of amicable sentiment among our peoples should be prevented from recurrence and corrected in their unforeseen and unfortunate consequences.

It is our present hope that, by a joint effort, our nations may establish a just peace in the Pacific; and by the rapid consummation of an *entente cordiale*, arrest, if not dispel, the tragic confusion that now threatens to engulf civilization.

For such decisive action, protracted negotiations would seem ill-suited and weakening. We, therefore, suggest that adequate instrumentalities should be developed for the realization of a general agreement which would bind, meanwhile, both Governments in honor and in act.

It is our belief that such an understanding should comprise only the pivotal issues of urgency and not the accessory concerns which could be deliberated at a Conference and appropriately confirmed by our respective Governments.

We presume to anticipate that our Governments could achieve harmonious relations if certain situations and attitudes were clarified or improved; to wit:

1. The concepts of the United States and of Japan respecting international relations and the character of nations.

2. The attitudes of both governments toward the European War.

---

[1] U.S. State Department, *Papers Relating to the Foreign Relations of the United States: Japan, 1931–1941*, Vol. II (U.S. Government Printing Office, Washington, 1943), pp. 398–402.

3. The relations of both nations toward the China Affair.

4. Naval, aerial, and mercantile marine relations in the Pacific.

5. Commerce between both nations and their financial cooperation.

6. Economic activity of both nations in the Southwestern Pacific area.

7. The policies of both nations affecting political stabilization in the Pacific.

Accordingly, we have come to the following mutual understanding, subject, of course, to modifications by the United States Government and subject to the official and final decision of the Government of Japan.

I. *The concepts of the United States and of Japan respecting international relations and the character of nations.*

The Governments of the United States and of Japan might jointly acknowledge each other as equally sovereign states and contiguous Pacific powers.

Both Governments assert the unanimity of their national policies as directed toward the foundation of a lasting peace and the inauguration of a new era of respectful confidence and cooperation among our peoples.

Both Governments might declare that it is their traditional, and present, concept and conviction that nations and races compose, as members of a family, one household; each equally enjoying rights and admitting responsibilities with a mutuality of interests regulated by peaceful processes and directed to the pursuit of their moral and physical welfare, which they are bound to defend for themselves as they are bound not to destroy for others.

Both Governments are firmly determined that their respective traditional concepts on the character of nations and the underlying moral principles of social order and national life will continue to be preserved and never transformed by foreign ideas or ideologies contrary to those moral principles and concepts.

II. *The attitudes of both Governments toward the European War.*

The Government of Japan maintains that the purpose of its Axis Alliance was, and is, defensive and designed to prevent the extension of military grouping among nations not directly affected by the European War.

The Government of Japan, with no intention of evading its existing treaty obligation, desires to declare that its military obligation under the Axis Alliance comes into force only when one of the parties of the Alliance is aggressively attacked by a power not at present involved in the European War.

The Government of the United States maintains that its attitude toward the European War is, and will continue to be, determined by no aggressive alliance aimed to assist any one nation against another. The United States maintains that it is pledged to the hate of war, and accordingly its attitude toward the European War is, and will continue to be, determined solely and exclusively by considerations of the protective defense of its own national welfare and security.

III. *China affairs.*

The President of the United States, if the following terms are approved by His Excellency and guaranteed by the Government of Japan, might request the Chiang Kai-shek regime to negotiate peace with Japan:

a. Independence of China.

b. Withdrawal of Japanese troops from Chinese territory, in accordance with an agreement to be reached between Japan and China.

c. No acquisition of Chinese territory.

d. No imposition of indemnities.

e. Resumption of the "Open Door"; the interpretation and application of which shall be agreed upon at some future, convenient time between the United States and Japan.

f. Coalescence of the Governments of Chiang Kai-shek and of Wang Ching-wei.

g. No large-scale or concentrated immigration of Japanese into Chinese territory.

h. Recognition of Manchukuo.

With the acceptance by the Chiang Kai-shek regime of the aforementioned Presidential request, the Japanese Government shall commence direct peace negotiations with the newly coalesced Chinese Government, or constituent elements thereof.

The Government of Japan shall submit to the Chinese concrete terms of peace, within the limits of aforesaid general terms and along the line of neighborly friendship, joint defense against communistic activities, and economic cooperation.

Should the Chiang Kai-shek regime reject the request of President Roosevelt, the United States Government shall discontinue assistance to the Chinese.

IV. *Naval, aerial, and mercantile marine relations in the Pacific.*

a. As both the Americans and the Japanese are desirous of maintaining the peace in the Pacific, they shall not resort to such disposition of their naval forces and aerial forces as to menace each other. Detailed, concrete agreement thereof shall be left for determination at the proposed joint Conference.

b. At the conclusion of the projected Conference, each nation might despatch a courtesy naval squadron to visit the country of the other and signalize the new era of Peace in the Pacific.

c. With the first ray of hope for the settlement of China affairs, the Japanese Government will agree, if desired, to use its good offices to release for contract by Americans a certain percentage of their total tonnage of merchant vessels, chiefly for the Pacific service, so soon as they can be released from their present commitments. The amount of such tonnage shall be determined at the Conference.

V. *Commerce between both nations, and their financial cooperation.*

When official approbation to the present understanding has been given by both Governments, the United States and Japan shall assure each other to mutually supply such commodities as are respectively available or required by either of them. Both Governments further consent to take necessary steps to the resumption of normal trade relations as formerly established under the Treaty of Navigation and Commerce between the United States and Japan. If a new commercial treaty is desired by both Governments, it could be elaborated at the proposed Conference and concluded in accordance with usual procedure.

For the advancement of economic cooperation between both nations, it is suggested that the United States extend to Japan a gold credit in amounts sufficient to foster trade and industrial development directed to the betterment of Far Eastern economic conditions and to the sustained economic cooperation of the Governments of the United States and of Japan.

VI. *Economic activity of both nations in the Southwestern Pacific area.*

On the pledged basis of guarantee that Japanese activities in the Southwestern Pacific area shall be carried on by peaceful means, without resorting to arms, American cooperation and support shall be given in the production and procurement of natural resources (such as oil, rubber, tin, nickel) which Japan needs.

VII. *The policies of both nations affecting political stabilization in the Pacific.*

a. The Governments of the United States and of Japan will not acquiesce in the future transfer of territories or the relegation of existing States within the Far East and in the Southwestern Pacific area to any European Power.

b. The Governments of the United States and of Japan jointly guarantee the independence of the Philippine Islands and will consider means to come to their assistance in the event of unprovoked aggression by any third power.

c. The Government of Japan requests the friendly and diplomatic assistance of the Government of the United States for the removal of Hong Kong and Singapore as doorways to further political encroachment by the British in the Far East.

d. Japanese immigration to the United States and to the Southwestern

Pacific area shall receive amicable consideration—on a basis of equality with other nationals and freedom from discrimination.

Conference.

a. It is suggested that a conference between delegates of the United States and of Japan be held at Honolulu and that this Conference be opened for the United States by President Roosevelt and for Japan by Prince Konoye. The delegates could number less than five each, exclusive of experts, clerks, etc.

b. There shall be no foreign observers at the Conference.

c. This Conference could be held as soon as possible (May 1941) after the present understanding has been reached.

d. The agenda of the Conference would not include a reconsideration of the present understanding but would direct its efforts to the specification of the prearranged agenda and drafting of instruments to effectuate the understanding. The precise agenda could be determined upon by mutual agreement between both Governments.

Addendum.

The present understanding shall be kept as a confidential memorandum between the Governments of the United States and of Japan.

The scope, character, and timing of the announcement of this understanding will be agreed upon by both Governments.

Appendix B

ORAL STATEMENT

Oral Statement Handed by the Secretary of State to the Japanese Ambassador (Nomura) on June 21, 1941[1]

The Secretary of State appreciates the earnest efforts which have been made by the Japanese Ambassador and his associates to bring about a better understanding between our two countries and to establish peace in the Pacific area. The Secretary of State appreciates also the frankness which has characterized their attitude throughout the conversations which have been held. This Government is no less desirous than the Japanese Ambassador to bring about better relations between our two countries and a situation of peace in the Pacific area, and in that spirit the Secretary of State has given careful study to every aspect of the Japanese proposal.

The Secretary of State has no reason to doubt that many Japanese leaders share the views of the Japanese Ambassador and his associates as indicated above and would support action toward achieving those high objectives. Unfortunately, accumulating evidence reaches this Government from sources all over the world, including reports from sources which over many years have demonstrated sincere good will toward Japan, that some Japanese leaders in influential official positions are definitely committed to a course which calls for support of Nazi Germany and its policies of conquest and that the only kind of understanding with the United States which they would endorse is one that would envisage Japan's fighting on the side of Hitler should the United States become involved in the European hostilities through carrying out its present policy of self-defense. The tenor of recent public statements gratuitously made by spokesmen of the Japanese Government emphasizing Japan's commitments and intentions under the Tripartite Alliance exemplify an attitude which cannot be ignored. So long as such leaders maintain this attitude in their official positions and apparently seek to influence public opinion in Japan in the direction indicated, is it not illusory to expect that adoption of a proposal such

[1] U.S. State Department, *Japan, 1931–1941*, pp. 485–86.

as the one under consideration offers a basis for achieving substantial results along the desired lines?

Another source of misgiving in the Japanese proposal relates to the desire of the Japanese Government to include in its terms for a peaceful settlement to be offered to the Chinese Government a provision which would permit the stationing of Japanese troops in certain areas in Inner Mongolia and North China as a measure of cooperation with China in resisting communistic activities. While this Government has given careful thought to the considerations which have prompted the Japanese Government to make such a proposal, and while this Government does not desire to enter into the merits of such a proposal, it feels that the liberal policies to which the United States is committed, as explained on numerous occasions to the Japanese Ambassador and his associates, would not permit this Government to associate itself with any course which appears to be inconsistent with these policies. Furthermore, although in matters affecting only this country there might be some latitude of decision as to the qualifying of rights, the matter under discussion affects the sovereign rights of a third country, and accordingly it is felt that this Government must be most scrupulous in dealing with such a matter.

The Secretary of State has therefore reluctantly come to the conclusion that this Government must await some clearer indication than has yet been given that the Japanese Government as a whole desires to pursue courses of peace such as constitute the objectives of the proposed understanding. This Government sincerely hopes that the Japanese Government will manifest such an attitude.

NOTE: In order to bring the current discussions up to date as far as the American attitude is concerned, there is being handed the Japanese Ambassador separately a revision, bearing the date of June 21, of the document marked "Unofficial, Exploratory, and without Commitment," which was handed the Japanese Ambassador on May 31.

Draft Proposal Handed by the Secretary of State to the Japanese Ambassador (Nomura) on June 21, 1941[2]

Unofficial, Exploratory,   [Washington,] June 21, 1941.
and Without Commitment

The Governments of the United States and of Japan accept joint responsibility for the initiation and conclusion of a general agreement of understanding as expressed in a joint declaration for the resumption of traditional friendly relations.

[2] U.S. Department of State, *Japan, 1931–1941*, pp. 486–89.

Without reference to specific causes of recent estrangement, it is the sincere desire of both Governments that the incidents which led to the deterioration of amicable sentiment between their countries should be prevented from recurrence and corrected in their unforeseen and unfortunate consequences.

It is our earnest hope that, by a cooperative effort, the United States and Japan may contribute effectively toward the establishment and preservation of peace in the Pacific area and, by the rapid consummation of an amicable understanding, encourage world peace and arrest, if not dispel, the tragic confusion that now threatens to engulf civilization.

For such decisive action, protracted negotiations would seem ill-suited and weakening. Both Governments, therefore, desire that adequate instrumentalities should be developed for the realization of a general understanding which would bind, meanwhile, both Governments in honor and in act.

It is the belief of the two Governments that such an understanding should comprise only the pivotal issues of urgency and not the accessory concerns which could be deliberated later at a conference.

Both Governments presume to anticipate that they could achieve harmonious relations if certain situations and attitudes were clarified or improved; to wit:

1. The concepts of the United States and of Japan respecting international relations and the character of nations.

2. The attitudes of both Governments toward the European war.

3. Action toward a peaceful settlement between China and Japan.

4. Commerce between both nations.

5. Economic activity of both nations in the Pacific area.

6. The policies of both nations affecting political stabilization in the Pacific area.

7. Neutralization of the Philippine Islands.

Accordingly, the Government of the United States and the Government of Japan have come to the following mutual understanding and declaration of policy.

I. *The concepts of the United States and of Japan respecting international relations and the character of nations.*

Both Governments affirm that their national policies are directed toward the foundation of a lasting peace and the inauguration of a new era of reciprocal confidence and cooperation between our peoples.

Both Governments declare that it is their traditional, and present, concept and conviction that nations and races compose, as members of a family, one household living under the ideal of universal concord through justice and equity; each equally enjoying rights and admitting responsibilities with a mutuality of interests regulated by peaceful processes and directed to the pursuit of their moral and physical welfare, which they are bound to defend for themselves as they are bound not to destroy for others; they further admit their responsibilities to oppose the oppression or exploitation of other peoples.

Both Governments are firmly determined that their respective traditional concepts on the character of nations and the underlying moral principles of social order and national life will continue to be preserved and never transformed by foreign ideas or ideologies contrary to those moral principles and concepts.

II. *The attitudes of both Governments toward the European war.*

The Government of Japan maintains that the purpose of the Tripartite Pact was, and is, defensive and is designed to contribute to the prevention of an unprovoked extension of the European war.

The Government of the United States maintains that its attitude toward the European hostilities is and will continue to be determined solely and exclusively by considerations of protection and self-defense: its national security and the defense thereof.

NOTE (There is appended a suggested draft of an exchange of letters as a substitute for the Annex and Supplement on the Part of the Government of the United States on this subject which constituted a part of the draft of May 31, 1941. For discussion of the fundamental question underlying this whole section, *vide* the Oral Statement handed the Japanese Ambassador on June 21.)

III. *Action toward a peaceful settlement between China and Japan.*

The Japanese Government having communicated to the Government of the United States the general terms within the framework of which the Japanese Government will propose the negotiation of a peaceful settlement with the Chinese Government, which terms are declared by the Japanese Government to be in harmony with the Konoye principles regarding neighborly friendship and mutual respect of sovereignty and territories and with the practical application of those principles, the President of the United States will suggest to the Government of China that the Government of China and the Government of Japan enter into a negotiation on a basis mutually advantageous and acceptable for a termination of hostilities and resumption of peaceful relations.

NOTE (The foregoing draft of Section III is subject to further discussion of the question of cooperative defense against communistic activities, including the stationing of Japanese troops in Chinese territory, and the question of economic cooperation between China and Japan. With regard to suggestions that the language of Section III be changed, it is believed that consideration of any suggested change can most advantageously be given after all the points in the annex relating to this section have been satisfactorily worked out, when the section and its annex can be viewed as a whole.)

IV. *Commerce between both nations.*

When official approbation to the present understanding has been given by both Governments, the United States and Japan shall assure each other mutually to supply such commodities as are, respectively, available and required by either of them. Both Governments further consent to take necessary steps to resume normal trade relations as formerly established under the Treaty of Commerce and Navigation between the United States and Japan. If a new commercial treaty is desired by both Governments, it would be negotiated as soon as possible and be concluded in accordance with usual procedures.

V. *Economic activity of both nations in the Pacific area.*

On the basis of mutual pledges hereby given that Japanese activity and American activity in the Pacific area shall be carried on by peaceful means and in conformity with the principle of non-discrimination in international commercial relations, the Japanese Government and the Government of the United States agree to cooperate each with the other toward obtaining non-discriminatory access by Japan and by the United States to commercial supplies of natural resources (such as oil, rubber, tin, nickel) which each country needs for the safeguarding and development of its own economy.

VI. *The policies of both nations affecting political stabilization in the Pacific area.*

Both Governments declare that the controlling policy underlying this understanding is peace in the Pacific area; that it is their fundamental purpose, through cooperative effort, to contribute to the maintenance and the preservation of peace in the Pacific area; and that neither has territorial designs in the area mentioned.

VII. *Neutralization of the Philippine Islands.*

The Government of Japan declares its willingness to enter at such time as the Government of the United States may desire into negotiation with the Government of the United States with a view to the conclusion of a treaty for the neutralization of the Philippine Islands, when Philippine independence shall have been achieved.

[The Annexes to this document have been omitted.]

The literature in English on American-Japanese negotiations is rather extensive, and only the more important items will be mentioned here. The best source for American diplomatic documents is *Foreign Relations of the United States: Japan, 1931–1941* in two volumes (Washington: U.S. Government Printing Office, 1943), and *Foreign Relations of the United States: The Far East, 1941*, Vol. IV (Washington: U.S. Government Printing Office, 1956). Both of these, of course, were issued by the Department of State. Many of the Japanese messages decoded by American intelligence agencies are available in *Pearl Harbor Attack: Hearings Before the Joint Committee on the Investigation of the Pearl Harbor Attack* (Washington: U.S. Government Printing Office, 1945–1946), 39 volumes. The voluminous records of the International Military Tribunal for the Far East contain texts of various documents, as well as testimony by important Japanese leaders.

Of the secondary works that cover the Japanese scene, Robert J. C. Butow's *Tojo and the Coming of the War* (Princeton, 1961) is the best. It is a careful and detailed account, which emphasizes the role of General Tojo Hideki. Another recent book is David J. Lu's *From the Marco Polo Bridge to Pearl Harbor* (Washington: Public Affairs Press, 1961). Professor Lu has drawn heavily on the archives of the Japanese Foreign Office, and gives, on the whole, a much more sympathetic account of Matsuoka than is found in most books published in the United States. An earlier book, now somewhat outdated but still worth reading, is *The Road to Pearl Harbor* by Herbert Feis. Originally published by Princeton University Press in 1950, it is now available in paperback (New York: Atheneum, 1963). This book makes extensive use of the documents in the International Military Tribunal records. Finally, *Pearl Harbor: Warning and Decision* by Roberta Wohlstetter (Stanford, 1962) is a fascinating study of the inability of American intelligence to predict the attack on Pearl Harbor, even after breaking the Japanese diplomatic code.

By far the best secondary work in Japanese is *Taiheiyo Senso e no Michi* (Road to the Pacific War), produced by a committee of the Japanese International Politics Association under the chairmanship of Dr. Tsunoda Jun. The series, published by the Asahi Newspaper Company in 1962–63, comprises seven volumes, plus a documentary volume from which the documents translated in this book were taken. Volume VII, which deals with Japanese-American relations, was mostly written by Dr. Tsunoda. An earlier work still worth consulting is Hattori Takushiro's *Dai To-A Senso Zenshi* (History of the War in East Asia) (Tokyo, 1953) in four volumes. The first volume covers the negotiations preceding the outbreak of war. The author was a member of the Operations Section of the Army General Staff.

There are, of course, a number of memoirs by Japanese participants in the war decision. One of these by Togo Shigenori, who held the post of Foreign Minister when war was declared, has been translated into English and published under the title *The Cause of Japan* (New York, 1956). *Beikoku ni Tsukai Shite* (My Mission to the United States), by Ambassador Nomura Kichisaburo (Tokyo, 1946), contains useful information, but on the whole it is a disappointing work. Finally, Prince Konoye's *Ushinawareshi Seiji—Konoye Fumimaro Ko no Shuki* (A Losing Political Cause— The Notes of Prince Konoye Fumimaro) (Tokyo, 1946) should be mentioned. Actually, these notes were written by Ushiba Tomohiko, who was Konoye's private secretary.

INDEX

Japan's Decision for War

Records of the
1941 Policy Conferences

*Translated, Edited, and with an
Introduction by Nobutaka Ike*

These invaluable records of 62 conferences held in Tokyo between March and
December of 1941 provide direct access
to the thinking and planning of Japan's
highest leaders as they prepared for war.
It is as if one were looking over the
shoulders of the key decision makers as
they argued and deliberated, weighed the
probable consequences of their actions,
reached conclusions, and made decisions
that were to change the course of world
history.

The documents, which are translated
here for the first time, are of two kinds:
records of 57 Liaison Conferences, which
were held every few days between the
representatives of the Cabinet and the
Army and Navy to decide on questions of
foreign policy; and records of five Imperial Conferences, where the Emperor
ratified key decisions of the Liaison Conferences.

As the editor points out, among the important lessons that can be drawn from
these records is the serious doubt they
cast on the validity of the theory of deterrence, indicating as they do that there
are definite limits to the effectiveness of
threats used by one nation to deter another nation from pursuing a certain
course of action.

*Nobutaka Ike is Professor of Political
Science at Stanford University, and the
author of* The Beginnings of Political Democracy in Japan *and* Japanese Politics.